WHEN THE WORLD BECOMES FEMALE

WHEN THE WORLD BECOMES FEMALE

GUISES OF A SOUTH INDIAN GODDESS

JOYCE BURKHALTER FLUECKIGER

INDIANA UNIVERSITY PRESS
BLOOMINGTON AND INDIANAPOLIS

This book is a publication of

Indiana University Press
Office of Scholarly Publishing
Herman B Wells Library 350
1320 East 10th Street
Bloomington, Indiana 47405 USA

iupress.indiana.edu

Telephone orders 800-842-6796
Fax orders 812-855-7931

♾ The paper used in this publication meets the minimum requirements of the American National Standard for Information Sciences—Permanence of Paper for Printed Library Materials, ANSI Z39.48-1992.

Manufactured in the United States of America

Library of Congress Cataloging-in-Publication Data
Flueckiger, Joyce Burkhalter.
When the world becomes female : guises of a South Indian goddess / Joyce Burkhalter Flueckiger.
pages cm
Includes bibliographical references and index.
ISBN 978-0-253-00952-4 (cloth : alk. paper)
— ISBN 978-0-253-00956-2 (pbk. : alk. paper)
— ISBN 978-0-253-00960-9 (e-book)
1. Gangamma (Hindu deity)—Cult—India—Tirupati. 2. Worship (Hinduism) 3. Tirupati (India)—Religion. I. Title.
BL1225.G362F58 2013
294.5'2114—dc23 2012051547

1 2 3 4 5 18 17 16 15 14 13

For Velcheru Narayana Rao
who introduced me to the imaginative worlds of Telugu
and has been a constant conversation partner in this work

CONTENTS

Preface and Acknowledgments

This is a book about the South Indian goddess Gangamma, whose rituals and narratives offer a range of possibilities and debates about gender at both cosmological and human levels. Gangamma becomes most visible and grows into her fullest power during her annual hot-season festival, during which time, for one week, ultimate reality is imagined and experienced as female.

The relationship between the everyday lives of women and the mythical lives of goddesses—more specifically, whether or how the goddess may be a model or source of empowerment of women—has been debated in scholarly work and has caught the imagination of many others who have not grown up with goddesses (Hiltebeitel and Erndl 2000; Gold 1994; McDermott 2003). My research with Gangamma worshippers suggests that, in this context, the relationship between the goddess and human women is not of one imitation or modeling, but an empowering relationship in which their shared nature as possessors of *shakti* (female power) is asserted and performed. During Gangamma's festival, female celebrants are the "unmarked" gender; they only intensify and multiply what they already do on a daily or weekly basis for the goddess—that is, feed her. Men (and aggressive masculinity), on the other hand, must be transformed (by taking female guises) to be in the presence of an excessive (*ugra*) goddess. These gendered possibilities are characteristic of the south Indian artisan/trader castes that traditionally celebrate Gangamma's festival, possibilities that are being threatened both by processes of brahminization of Gangamma's largest temples and the growth of middle-class aesthetics and gender and sexual mores.

The story of how I first entered the worlds of Gangamma is told in the introduction, first as a curious onlooker and then gradually as an ethnographer who was drawn into the imaginative worlds of Gangamma and the lives of many who share that world. My earlier ethnographic research had been conducted in rural central India (Chhattisgarh) and the city of Hyderabad, during which times my primary research language was Hindi/Urdu and its regional forms. Before I began my long-term research in Tirupati in 1999, I learned the Telugu script and basic grammar in the United States, and then studied Telugu intensively for two months in Hyderabad. Many nouns—such as *ugram, shakti, vesham, gramadevata*—idioms, narratives and narrative motifs, cultural concepts, and practices are shared between Hindi and Telugu, which contributed to my cultural fluency and confidence, if less-than-desired linguistic fluency. On each research trip, I have worked with Telugu native-speaker fieldwork associates and friends, with whom I studiously translated and discussed the voice recordings of conversations and narratives that appear in this book. Because I worked with three fieldwork associates and numerous friends for longer and shorter periods of time over nearly twenty years, in order to avoid confusion to the reader, I refer to them as "fieldwork associates" or friends, rather than by name in the chapters that follow.

I first attended Gangamma's festival (*jatara*) in 1992 and 1993 with V. Narayana Rao, David Shulman, and Don Handelman; and many of the ideas for this book took root through our long discussions over the days and evenings of those *jataras,* for which I offer them my deepest thanks. I returned to Tirupati for the 1996 *jatara* with a friend and fellow folklorist, N. Lakshmi, who is a school teacher in Rajahmundry. That same year, an elder Tamil-speaking friend from Hyderabad, Revati Thangavelu, joined us for the last few days of the *jatara;* she gave invaluable assistance and wisdom in my initial interactions with the Tamil Gangamma devotee who is the focus of chapter 10. Revati and her husband Thanganne always had an open door waiting for me in Hyderabad in my comings and goings to Tirupati, offering encouragement and support on many levels, including endless cups of tea and a listening ear to both the joys and frustrations of fieldwork.

By the time I had attended three *jataras,* I realized that several of the women with whom I hoped to interact more closely, including the Mudaliar-caste matriarch who used to serve Gangamma at her largest Tirupati temple (chapter 8), were Tamil speakers, although most also spoke Telugu. Therefore, it was serendipitous that the Tirupati-born woman who became my fieldwork associate for my year-long research in 1999–2000, Krishna Priya, had attended an English-medium school in Chennai and was fluent in Telugu, Tamil, English, and Hindi. She was, at the time, writing her Ph.D. dissertation on the fiction of John Steinbeck. Krishna Priya and I often spoke Hindi, so that in translating Telugu and Tamil conversations, we were not tacking back and forth between English and an Indian language. Krishna Priya lived at home with her mother at the time, where we usually translated fieldwork voice-recordings; her mother's knowledge of Gangamma-specific vocabulary and rituals were invaluable and her gracious hospitality endless. I offer my deepest thanks to Krishna Priya for putting herself in fieldwork situations that she could have never dreamed of and for her friendship, patience, and perseverance. Finally, a dear friend and linguist from Hyderabad, K. Vimala—with whom I had studied Telugu before moving to Tirupati in 1999—attended the 2000 *jatara* with me and accompanied me to Tirupati for two weeks in 2005, during which time we met the Avilala female storytellers of chapter 4. Vimala's love of language is infectious, and we spent many hours translating voice recordings we had made together and discussing the nuances of significant individual words and idioms. Surya Prakash Gudi, who at the time was a doctoral candidate in anthropology at Sri Venkatesvara University, assisted me on two short trips to Tirupati in 2010 and 2011. Finally, I gratefully acknowledge the tangible and intangible assistance and dependable friendship over these many years of V. Gangadhar, Professor of Anthropology, and Peta Srinivasulu Reddy, Professor of Telugu, both from Sri Venkatesvara University, who first introduced us to the Kaikala family in 1992.

The primary Tirupati families and individuals with whom I worked for this project never questioned why I was there; they understood the attraction of the goddess and assumed I would keep coming back. Perhaps less clear to them was why it seemed to take me so long to "understand" Gangamma and her festival, as indicated by one female householder who exclaimed that she had already answered several years earlier a question I was now asking. I offer here special thanks, for opening their lives to me and their gracious hospitality, to the Kaikala family, CKR and Koteshvaramma, Subbarama Reddy and Dhanalakshmi of Avilala, storytellers Rajeshvaramma and Sumati, *purana pandita* Annapurna, Pujaramma and Veshalamma, the female devotee who is *picci* (mad) for the goddess, and finally the flower sellers and temple attendants at Tatayyagunta Gangamma temple.

My research in 1999–2000 was supported by the American Institute of Indian Studies; Purnima Mehta and other AIIS staff have provided crucial support and wisdom over the years I have been going to Tirupati for this project, even after the year I was an AIIS Research Fellow. Subsequent summer research trips to Tirupati were funded, in part, by the Emory College of Arts and Sciences and the Claus M. Halle Institute for Global Learning, Emory University. I gratefully acknowledge publication subvention funds from Emory College of Arts and Sciences and the Laney Graduate School of Emory University, which enabled inclusion of more photographs than are usually included in a book like this.

My colleagues in the Department of Religion at Emory have been uncommonly generous in their unwavering support of ethnographic approaches to the study of religion since my arrival at Emory in 1992. In particular, I thank Laurie Patton and Paul Courtright for the time they have given to discussing this project with me—its intellectual questions and the practical logistics of balancing fieldwork, writing, and teaching—over many lunches, coffees, and hallway conversations. Laurie and I spent one summer exchanging chapters of our works in progress, which helped to keep up writing momentum and raised important and subtle questions about framing and organization. Ann Gold and David Haberman served as readers of the manuscript of this book for Indiana University Press; I thank them for their keen insights and for their long-term friendships.

Finally, there remain those to whom words of thanks pale in relationship to what the heart holds. Mike, Peter, and Rachel have accepted, if not always fully understood, what one Gangamma devotee called my *picci* ("madness") for this work. They uprooted from their lives in Atlanta to come with to India in 1999–2000, during which time they lived in Kodaikanal and I lived in Tirupati, making numerous trips back and forth; they have never questioned why I need to make so many return visits to India or why our dining room table has been strewn with books and papers for weeks and months at a time.

Velcheru Narayana Rao first introduced me to the imaginative worlds of Telugu. He and I have taken great joy in talking together about the ranges of meaning behind single Telugu words, and at the end of such conversations, I have often thought, "Only Narayana Rao could become so passionate about a single word or phrase." He has been a constant, creative conversation partner throughout the fieldwork upon which this book is based—answering late-night phone calls when I felt I had hit a wall during fieldwork and offering advice as to how to proceed—and has read, reread, and commented on numerous conference papers and drafts of the manuscript for this book. Narayana Rao's voice will be heard in several places in the book, when he remembered a Telugu proverb that was pertinent to the topic at hand or provided unique insights for which he is so well-known in our field of South Asian Studies. This book would not have been possible without him.

Note on Transliteration

I have chosen not to use diacritics in the main text of this book, so that the prose will be accessible to non-specialists. However, I have included a glossary of all Telugu terms at the end of the book with appropriate diacritics. Proper names, except for caste names, do not appear in the glossary. In transliterations in text, I have rendered both *ṣ* and *ś* as "sh." Plural nouns in the main text are indicated by adding an "s" at the end of Telugu words, since Telugu plural forms may confuse a non-Telugu reader. For example the plural of *vesham* is rendered *veshams* rather than *veshalu.*

When English words have been used in a Telugu conversation or narrative performance, I have indicated these words within asterisks (for example, *body*). When Telugu words are also well-known Sanskrit words, I have used the Sanskrit transliteration in order that the words be accessible to a wider South Asian audience. For example, Telugu *santoshamga* is rendered *santosha* (satisfied). Some Telugu words may appear slightly differently than they do in Telugu dictionaries, to reflect the spoken register of the contexts in which they appear; the definitions I have provided for Telugu words also reflect their meanings in Gangamma contexts. There are a few occasions when a word is transliterated differently in its proper-name usage and the transliteration system I have chosen—for example, Sri Venkatesvara University, whereas I have transliterated the name of the god as Venkateshvara; Tattaiahgunta Devasthanam, whereas I have transliterated the name of the temple as Tatayyagunta.

I have retained usage of a few Telugu terms (after translating upon first appearance) whose range of meaning is significant for analyses in this book, such as *ugram, vesham,* and *shakti.* Some other Telugu terms appear regularly whose English translation may evoke something quite different than it does in Telugu. For example, *pasupu* may be quite simply translated as turmeric; however, the English term connotes a spice used in cooking, whereas in Telugu (particularly when paired with *kumkum*), it has a wide range of ritual uses.

WHEN THE WORLD BECOMES FEMALE

INTRODUCTION

The South Indian pilgrimage town of Tirupati is synonymous with the God of the Seven Hills—Sri Venkateshvara, a form of Vishnu. His temple is nestled at the far end of a series of hills that swell from paddy fields and rocky hillocks on the plains to a height of 1,104 meters. God lives on the seventh, interior hill, Venkatagiri. This mountain range anchors and gives identity to Tirupati's physical and imaginative landscapes. From the plains below, the sheer rock face overlooking the town is a striking visual reminder of the god's presence. The rock catches the shifting light throughout the day in a kaleidoscope of color and shadows, changing with the seasons when it becomes a resting stop for monsoon clouds or reflects the sizzling hot-season heat back onto the town.

The God of the Seven Hills draws 50–60,000 pilgrims a day (up to 500,000 on special festival days), and much of Tirupati's economy revolves around serving these pilgrims; the temple is one of the wealthiest religious institutions in the world. Tirupati's train station and large bus stand are filled with groups of pilgrims and families carrying cloth-wrapped bundles, tin trunks, or modern wheeled suitcases. Pilgrims with shaved heads (sometimes covered by a baseball cap or slathered with sandalpaste to protect from the sun) are those who are on their way home, the offering of one's hair being a typical vow to the deity in Tirupati. It was not the god who first called me to Tirupati, however, but rather a rich festival tradition of a village goddess, Gangamma, who lives on the dusty streets and lanes downhill.

In the intense summer heat of May, beginning on the fourth Tuesday after the Tamil New Year, the goddess Gangamma heats, expands, and through multiplying forms becomes ubiquitously present in Tirupati during her week-long annual festival (*jatara*). The most dramatic marker of her presence is the appearance in streets and temple courtyards of men who have taken female guise by wearing women's clothing and jewelry, braided hair, and breasts, and who are thereby transformed into women, even the goddess herself. Men from the Kaikala weaving-caste take a series of Gangamma's guises (*veshams*) and recreate one of her primary narratives, becoming the goddess. Many other men take more generic female guises (*stri veshams*) in fulfillment of vows they (or their mothers on their behalf) have made to Gangamma. The goddess also appears in domestic kitchens as small turmeric mounds created by female householders, who also distribute the goddess to passersby in the form of a cooling yogurt mixture. During the early days of the *jatara,* the courtyard of Gangamma's largest Tirupati temple is filled with women cooking *pongal,* a boiled rice-lentil mixture. As the festival nears its end, family groups offer chicken sacrifices in the temple courtyard. Early on the last morning, Gangamma appears in front of each of her two largest temples in the form of a large clay head. During the week of the *jatara,* the goddess manifests in various forms, substances, and persons—and the world is imagined as female, a world in which the goddess is triumphant, the human female is the unmarked category, and men become women to appear before the goddess.

Gangamma is characterized by Tirupati residents as an *ugra* goddess who is "too much to bear." *Ugram* is often translated into English as "anger, malevolence, ferocity." In the context of Gangamma traditions, however, a better translation may be "excess," or "surplus," in the sense of being simply "too much." This "excessive" goddess requires "excessive" service or ritual, more than most householders have time or resources to offer; and thus she is rarely kept in domestic *puja* shrines. Gangamma's *ugram* is specifically associated with excessive hunger/desire, which has the potential to become dangerous if left unsatisfied, but is not inherently so. This same excess is needed to protect the *uru* (home place) from hot season illnesses such as poxes and fevers and to bring rains to the parched paddy fields. And this is one of the explicit reasons for Gangamma *jatara:* to call the goddess out of her dark stone temple forms and to build up her *ugram.* Gangamma expands and becomes more *ugra* through her multiplication of forms; *jatara* rituals then satisfy this excess so that it does not become destructive. One can compare the potential, but not inherent, destructiveness of *ugram* to life-giving water, which, in excess, may become a destructive flood. Gangamma needs her excessive *ugram* in order to banish illness and drought, but it then must be satisfied so that it does not become destructive.

The narrative of Gangamma as performed by Kaikala men tells the story of a pubescent Gangamma (not yet recognized as the goddess by her adoptive family) who is forced into marriage with a local, aggressive chieftain (Palegadu), known for molesting young women in his domain. As the couple is rounding the sacred fire to solemnize the marriage, Gangamma turns around to show her true self to the Palegadu as a goddess who "stretches from earth to sky." Fearful for his very life, he jumps off the wedding stage and runs to hide. Gangamma chases him, taking a series of disguises so that he will not see her before she sees him. Ultimately, in the disguise of a prince, she beheads him. During her festival, the Kaikala men put on the disguises that Gangamma herself has worn, day by day, and enact the beheading; thereafter, they appear in a series of three guises of the goddess herself, now revealed.

There is evidence that the *ugram* of the goddess may be experienced differently by male and female *jatara* participants. On the last evening of the *jatara,* the large clay heads of the goddess (*ugra mukhis*) built in front of each of her two primary temples are hidden behind a jute curtain until their completion early the next morning. During the first Gangamma *jatara* I attended in 1992, several male celebrants had told us that no one should look directly at the goddess in this *ugra* (excessive, fierce) form except momentarily as the curtain is drawn back and the face is then dismantled into thousands of small clay pieces. However, standing next to us in the large crowd during this final ritual, we overheard a young mother telling the toddler she was holding on her hip, "Look at her. Look right at her." In 1995 I recounted this scene to a female sweeper at the Tirupati guesthouse where I was staying. I asked whether she was afraid of the goddess, as the men had suggested they were. Her answer was immediate and direct: "That's because she [the goddess] is *shakti* [female power], and we [women] have *shakti.* You have *shakti;* I have *shakti.* But men are different. They don't have it, so they're afraid. It's like we're talking now; just like two women can talk together. So women aren't afraid. Men are different, so they're afraid." Her response suggested men may feel overwhelmed by a female quality that they do not possess, but which women share with ease.

Another "contextualization cue" (a term used by Charles Briggs [1988:15]) to the gendered experience of Gangamma was the response of a group of female *jatara* celebrants when I asked them where the goddess went at the end of the festival. I reported that some men had told me that she left Tirupati and crossed the seven seas; I wanted to know where, conceptually, they imagined that far shore to be. One woman responded, "She doesn't go anywhere. We feed her *pongal* every Tuesday and Friday, don't we?" Her response suggested a juxtaposition of women's worship during the festival and throughout the year with male celebrants' interactions with Gangamma that take place primarily during the *jatara.* Another woman suggested, laughing, that the goddess stays "right here"—"If you have a rock in your backyard, it's Gangamma."

The *jatara* world imagines and performs ultimate reality to be female. This female-oriented world is created, in part, through the proliferation of goddess forms throughout Tirupati and the female-guised men who congregate on the last days of the festival in the courtyard of Gangamma's largest temple and the surrounding streets. By adopting female guises through clothing and ornaments, males are transformed to be in the presence of the *ugra* goddess—from male into female, or perhaps from male into a more complete male that admits to a feminine nature as part of masculinity. Women who participate in Gangamma traditions, on the other hand, already share in the nature of the goddess—performed in the ritual application of *pasupu* (turmeric) to the faces of both the goddess and women—and need no transformation; they simply intensify the ritual activities they already perform for the goddess outside the festival, such as cooking.

Analyzing the ritual rationale for the sequence of Kaikala guises that reenact the primary local story of Gangamma, Don Handelman concludes, "As the male is destroyed the cosmos of the Jatra [sic] is feminized, and this female cosmos is one of bounty for all" (1995:284). He continues, "The death of the Palegadu, Gangamma's refusal to let him live as her devotee, turns the ritual-cosmos female and shows the epistemological superficiality of the male who is only that" (302). I propose, however, that Gangamma traditions are quite explicit that this all-female world is not ultimately sustainable, and that the destruction of the male is destruction of a particular *kind* of (aggressive) male. The goddess herself, in her form of Adi Para Shakti, upon having turned the three gods Brahma, Vishnu, and Shiva into women when they refuse to "marry" her, concludes that this all-female world isn't *dharmic* (the natural order of the universe); and she changes the gods back into males. But they are transformed males who now acknowledge her superior *shakti;* and at least one of these gods—Shiva—now carries with/in him a portion of female *shakti* in the form of the third eye that he exacted from the goddess. The female-dominated *jatara* and its *stri veshams* are temporally limited, but nevertheless potentially transformative. They offer a possibility of a gendered world in which aggressive, female-controlling masculinity is destroyed, creating a new kind of masculinity that acknowledges and experiences (even as part of itself) the *shakti* of the female.[1] Through ethnography of ritual and narrative performances and engagement with the families and women in the most intimate relationships with Gangamma, this book analyzes the gendered possibilities—for men and women—created by the "world become female."

Gangamma *jatara,* narratives, and rituals are performed by castes that have been called left-hand caste communities,[2] associated with cash and mobility: traders, herders, artisans, and leatherworkers (Narayana Rao 1986; Beck 1972).[3] Women of these castes have traditionally had more mobility and independence than women of the right-hand castes associated with the land, who are (ideally) protected by males and their mobility restricted, like the land itself. Part 1 of this book analyzes Gangamma ritual and narrative imaginative worlds in which gender is debated and that both reflect and help to create a left-hand gendered world. However, Gangamma traditions in Tirupati are shifting and adapting on several levels to a growing middle-class aesthetics and morality that approximate those of the dominant, right-hand castes. Part 2 focuses on particular families and women who are in close relationship with the *ugra* goddess—who do, in fact, "bear her"—and analyzes both the resources Gangamma ritual and narrative traditions have given them and the personal losses incurred with recent changes in some of these traditions. Like the goddess herself, Gangamma narratives and rituals and their interpretations have long been fluid and multiple; however, it remains to be seen how (or whether) her characteristic *ugra* nature, its ritual demands, and the gender possibilities she creates are sustained under pressures of increasingly dominant middle-class aesthetics and morality, brahminization of her Tirupati temple rituals, and the growing crowds for her festival that include many participants who are not from the left-hand castes.

Gangamma in Networks of Familial and Ritual Relationships

Gangamma lives in networks of familial and ritual relationships that include other village deities (*gramadevatas*), but which also draw in the God of the Seven Hills, Sri Venkateshvara. While the *puranic* god and *gramadevata* goddess have distinct needs and rituals, they also share certain left-hand caste characteristics, and they appear on the same domestic *puja* shelves of the families who directly serve (and thus "bear") Gangamma.

Seven Sisters. Gangamma is one of a set of South Indian Seven Sister goddesses who are guardians of village welfare, protecting humans from disease (particularly poxes, rashes, and fevers associated with the hot season) and ensuring fertility and health of crops and animals.[4] One full set of Seven Sisters in Tirupati was listed by a Kaikala male who regularly takes one of Gangamma's guises as: Matamma, Ankalamma, Cinna Gangamma, Pedda Gangamma, Veshalamma, Mutyalamma, Cintakayalamma.[5] Numerous Gangamma-named goddesses reside in Tirupati, with distinct caste associations, iconography, and narratives;[6] they both are and are not the "same" goddess, depending on the context in which they are spoken about. The set of Seven Sisters is expansive and shifting, and individual names vary from village to village, town to town; sometimes individual sisters are associated with specific illnesses (distinguishing between mumps, measles, chickenpox, and diarrhea, for example), and at other times the sisters are conflated and associated more generally with the entire class of illnesses.[7] However, there is one consistency: the sisters are accompanied iconographically by a single brother whose name is consistently Potu Raju. While his name remains consistent, his character can vary rather dramatically—between Tirupati and Hyderabad, for example—shifts that will be discussed below.

The Seven Sisters protect from illness, but they may also cause illness if left unsatisfied/hungry/heated and their *ugram* overflows its boundaries. This dual character is noticeable when someone contracts a Gangamma illness such as chickenpox or measles. When one of my fieldwork associates contracted chickenpox while working with me, the Tatayyagunta Gangamma temple flower sellers told her that she should have expected the goddess to come to her in this way, since she had been frequenting her temples—that chickenpox was a sign of Gangamma's pleasure with her devotion. In fact, one flower seller added, "If you die with these illnesses, you won't be reborn." Nevertheless, this pleasure of the goddess—even boon—is not something villagers and townspeople seek out and, in fact, make every effort to avoid. The goal of the festivals celebrated annually for the Seven Sisters, including Gangamma *jatara,* is to invigorate them and call for their protection and, at the same time, satisfy the hunger that accompanies their heightened state, so that they will not manifest through illness.

Gangamma and her sisters are characterized in both narrative and ritual as moving/fluid goddesses. In this sense, the *gramadevata* Gangamma shares not only the name but also characteristics of the pan-Indian river goddess Ganga—fluidity and potentially destructive force or *shakti;* and the narrative of Ganga's descent to earth is sometimes told as the story of Gangamma herself. Gangamma rituals and narratives embrace a certain tension between the goddess's restless movement and her stability. The Seven Sisters traditionally reside (in forms of stone heads or iron tridents) in open-air sites under trees or on boundaries between village settlements and adjacent paddy fields; and they are said to actively resist human suggestions for enclosed shrines that may limit their freedom to move. A female ritual specialist in the village of Avilala, on the outskirts of Tirupati, recounted that several years ago, someone tried to "raise up" the Avilala middle-of-the-street tiny Gangamma stone to a larger, enclosed structure; after one baby died and then three others lost their ability to coo and cry—attributed to the anger of the goddess over the suggested enclosure—it was dismantled. The narrator explained that the goddess has a thousand eyes,[8] including some at the top of her head, and this is why she wants no cover, so as to be able to look all around. Nevertheless, as villages and towns extend their habitation to encompass boundary-sister images, many have had cement platforms built around them, and gradually walls and roofs have been added to some of the structures. At one interesting shrine in transition, Gangamma takes the form of three iron tridents that have been dressed in saris and enclosed on three sides by thatch walls and a roof; and the female attendant has plans to make the shrine more permanent with cement walls. This is the process through which the two *jatara*-related Gangamma temples, currently walled-and-roofed, are also reported to have begun their own transformations. Permanent structures tend to stabilize the sisters in a way in which they are not when they dwell at village boundaries, on the edges of paddy fields, and in "jungle" uninhabited spaces, a theme to which we will return.

But the idea that Gangamma and her sisters are moving and do not like to be enclosed, even as their physical stone images may be so confined, is still important. Imaginatively, these goddesses wander outside their stone images and recently enclosed structures. As one Gangamma temple attendant reported: "They don't stay in their temples at night. They wander. For example, the goddess in this temple wanders in our neighborhood like a security *guard*." Because of her inclination to wander, the boundaries of traditional Tirupati (the *uru*) are ritually strengthened (lit., tied) at the beginning of her *jatara* so that Gangamma stays long enough to be enlivened, served, fed, and satisfied.

Two *jatara* sisters. Two sisters of the imaginative set of seven are the focus of Gangamma *jatara:* the elder Pedda Gangamma and the younger Cinna Gangamma. Depending on context, the identity of the two sisters may be distinguished or it may be conflated as, simply, "Gangamma." When distinguished, Cinna Gangamma is characterized as *ugra* and her elder sister Pedda Gangamma as *shanta* (peaceful).[9]

Peddamma is said to be the "first" Gangamma to reside in Tirupati. As one of the Kaikala men, Venkateshvarlu, whose family has the hereditary right and responsibility (*mirasi*) to serve Pedda Gangamma, commented:

Ours [Pedda Gangamma] is older. Cinna Gangamma came in the sixteenth century, but ours was earlier.[10] Somehow she [Cinna Gangamma] became famous with the *jatara;* I don't know why—[pause]—our Gangamma is *shanta.* If people don't serve her, she doesn't care. The other Gangamma, she's not like that. She'll show *ugram* immediately. She makes you swell here [shows throat] and you can't swallow anything. Pilgrims don't go there [Tatayyagunta, Cinna Gangamma's temple] every day, [but] they come here *every* day. They go there [only] on Tuesday/Fridays and *jatara* days, but they come here [Pedda Gangamma temple] *every* day. She [Pedda Gangamma] shows [her power] a little slowly. At Tatayyagunta, she shows it quickly. It was a small temple earlier, now it's become big.

When I asked about the identity of the small rocks on both sides of Cinna Gangamma in her Tatayyagunta temple, I was told a story I was to hear many times thereafter that explains the different natures of the two sisters and how Cinna Gangamma came to be more important during the *jatara.* It is said that one day Pedda Gangamma saw her younger sister coming to visit and, fearing Cinna Gangamma's jealous evil eye (*dishti*)—since the latter did not have children—Peddamma hid her children under a basket. When she turned over the basket after Cinnamma had left, she saw to her dismay that her children had turned to stone (some narrative variants say they turned to chicks). Peddamma ran after her sister, touched her feet, and asked her to forgive her for her duplicity. Cinnamma took away most of the children (twenty of them), leaving only six for her sister. And this is why, Venkateshvarlu told us, most *jatara* offerings are given to Cinna Gangamma. Her elder sister made a vow that this would be the case, so that her (hungry) children would be well taken care of.

The Kaikala matriarch, Venkateshvarlu's mother, emphasized that motherhood accounts for the difference in the nature of the two sisters:

Only our [Pedda] Gangamma has children. That Gangamma doesn't have children. Ours is a mother. She's *shanta.* Others are *ugra.* If you give or don't give, Pedda Gangamma won't care. But, if someone takes a vow to Cinna Gangamma, it must be fulfilled immediately. But Pedda Gangamma is a mother with children, so we can leisurely fulfill a vow to her.

And so, the two sisters are both distinct and the "same" goddess, embodying female qualities of *ugram* and *shantam.* Gangamma is a fanged *ugra* goddess who is also a mother whose priority is to care for her children.

Among the Tirupati Seven Sisters, a third sister unique to Tirupati is also associated with the *jatara:* Veshalamma (lit., "mother of guises"). She has a minimal biography, and her primary purpose would seem to be to enliven the Kaikala *veshams,* transforming them into the goddess herself when they first go to her for *darshan* (taking sight of the deity) before beginning their perambulations around Tirupati. Her presence and name confirm a certain authority to the ritual of *veshams.* The Kaikala matriarch explains that Veshalamma was feeling left out of the *jatara* and complained to her sister Cinna Gangamma, "They perform the *jatara* for you, but what about me?" She was pacified with her sister's promise that "all the *veshams* will first come to you; their first offerings will be yours." And so it is that the Kaikala *veshams* of the goddess are dressed in the Kaikala home, but do not fully become the goddess until they have gone to take *darshan* of Veshalamma in her nearby temple.

Potu Raju, the brother. As the only brother of Seven Sisters, Potu Raju[11] is an ambiguous figure. I describe him at length here, since his transformations give us a cue as to what it may mean for males to become women in the *jatara* world. His name literally means "king of male-ness," which would imply a figure who is the ultimate male. His non-anthropomorphic form, sometimes just a small rounded rock or a conical carved-stone or cement shape, sits facing his sisters outside most of their shrines and temples. In Tirupati and environs, this form is covered with turmeric powder and red vermillion (*kumkum*) dots, looking very much like his similarly decorated sisters. A small yellowed stone identified as Potu Raju is visible at Tallapaka Gangamma temple, outside the temple courtyard wall. But at Tatayyagunta temple, there is no obvious Potu Raju. When I asked Venkateshvarlu where Potu Raju was at this temple, he answered that he was not, in fact, there; there was only one brother to the Seven Sisters, and he resided at Tallapaka temple with his eldest sister, who desired his presence the most.

During Gangamma *jatara,* a brightly painted, red-faced, wooden, two-foot tall anthropomorphic image of Potu Raju (the only such figure I have seen in Tirupati) is brought to the Kaikala home for the duration of the festival; during the rest of the year, this image sits generally untended in the corner of Tallapaka temple. When we first encountered Potu Raju in the Kaikala courtyard during the 1992 *jatara,* we thought he was Gangamma herself; he wore black bangles on his upraised arm and a necklace of lemons, like many of his sisters. He held a raised sword in one hand and a severed head in the other, which we believed to be the head of the chieftain/Palegadu, whom Gangamma beheads in one of her primary narratives.[12] When we returned the next year for the *jatara,* I brought American synthetic saris to gift the goddess and placed one around this image (whom I believed to be Gangamma) and that of Gangamma's metallic head sitting next to it in the Kaikala courtyard. No one stopped me from gifting a sari to a male (or, for that matter, made any comments at all about the gift). When I later learned that this figure was Potu Raju, I admitted my confusion (and chagrin) to Venkateshvarlu, the Kaikala male who organizes the *veshams* taken by his family. He explained:

You know the bride's gifts from Avilala [exchanged between Avilala Reddys and Tirupati Kaikalas as the *jatara* moves from village to town]—they're put in front of Potu Raju first; he's the *chief* god. He's the youngest, after seven elder sisters. He's *shaktisvarupini* [lit., she whose form is *shakti;* female nominal form]. He takes orders from his sisters. They tell him whom to kill, and he goes to kill them. . . . He's the *chief* god.

Perhaps my gifted sari was equated with these bride's gifts, and thus not inappropriate to be given to Potu Raju. But his explanation suggests a new twist: that one form of Potu Raju, the ultimate male, is *shakti*—enlivening power/energy that is imagined as feminine—an appellation and characteristic of the goddess herself. In another conversation, Venkateshvarlu explained that Potu Raju had two forms: the princely Dora whose *vesham* Gangamma took to behead the Palegadu, and Potu Raju, whose form we see outside of shrines. A Cakali (washermen-caste) man, who takes the minister *vesham* that accompanies the Dora, clarified that the Dora who beheaded the Palegadu is actually Gangamma; this explains, he said, why the Potu Raju figure who is brought to the Kaikala home wears bangles. So it would seem Potu Raju both is and is not Gangamma, depending on context; he is both the younger brother (*tammudu*) and the male whose form is *shakti, shaktisvarupini.*

Potu Raju's seemingly gendered ambiguity is performatively visible in the application of *pasupu-kumkum* on his form that faces his sisters, as well as in explanations for his presence there in the company of his sisters. When I once asked directly why he wasn't married (at least there is no visible "wife"), a male ritual specialist from Avilala replied,

> If he had gotten married, he would have gone off with his wife, so the sisters don't let him get married. . . . Ammavaru doesn't want him to get married, so she says, "Her [the bride's] hair shouldn't be long; nor should it be short. The nose shouldn't be long; the nose shouldn't be short; nor should it be sharp. Her feet shouldn't be long; they shouldn't be short." So how would he find such a girl? He says, "I can't find a girl myself. When you find one for me, only then I'll marry her." So he doesn't get married.

The narrator's wife added, "It's because Potu Raju told Gangamma, 'I want to marry a woman as beautiful as you are.' Gangamma got angry. Don't you get angry if someone tells you, 'I want a woman like you' [as if there could be any such match]?" Gangamma told her brother he would never find such a woman—there was no one as beautiful as she—and that he should stay with her, standing guard as (in the words of one narrator, who used the English term) a *gunman* for Gangamma. In some parts of Andhra, David Knipe reports that Potu Raju is said to actually marry the goddess (Knipe 2005b). But here, in the context of Gangamma ritual traditions, I propose something quite different is happening: Potu Raju, "king of male-ness," has been feminized in recognition of the female nature that he embodies and shares with his sisters.[13]

Potu Raju's feminized physical demeanor and appellation *shaktisvarupini* in Tirupati stands in sharp contrast to his appearance and performance in the annual goddess festival Bonalu as celebrated in Hyderabad during the month of Ashadha (July/August).[14] Here, Potu Raju appears in/on the human male body as he leads processions of women carrying *pasupu-kumkum* and neem-leaf-decorated pots of cooked rice on their heads from the shrines of the Seven Sisters to the temple of Mahakali (the goddess who is said to embody them all).[15] Potu Raju appears as hyper-masculine, befitting his name: bare-chested, wearing a tightly wrapped loin cloth, and violently swinging a twisted, braided straw whip, hitting the path in front of him and periodically whipping himself. In this context, Potu Raju is an exaggerated male protector of the Bonalu processions of women as they wind their way from their neighborhood goddess shrines to the Mahakali temple. As is true of the goddess, her brother's nature and ritual roles shift significantly in different ritual contexts and regions. The transformation and identification of Potu Raju as *shaktisvarupini* in Tirupati provides a cue to what happens to the male who takes *stri vesham* during the *jatara,* when the world becomes female.

Gangamma and Sri Venkateshvara

Most of the thousands of pilgrims who go uphill every day to the temple of Sri Venkateshvara, drawn from throughout South India and its diasporas, are unaware of the Gangamma sisters downhill and their *jatara.*[16] But local participants in Gangamma rituals downhill live in an imaginative, performative world that embraces both Venkateshvara and Gangamma—brother and sister inhabiting a left-hand caste Tirupati landscape. Locally, Venkateshvara is known to be a brother of Gangamma who sends bride's gifts to his sister on the first day of her festival.[17] Venkateshvara also appears with his sister in the same domestic shrines of those few families who keep Gangamma at home throughout the year, creating a performative, ritual relationship between the two. Still another level of relationship between the God of the Seven Hills and Tallapaka (Pedda) Gangamma is created through oral narratives about the fifteenth-century poet Annamayya. The same poet who sang to Venkateshvara every day for many years in his uphill temple is also said to have brought Pedda Gangamma with him to Tirupati from his home village Tallapaka, from where she takes her name (Narayana Rao and Shulman 2005a, 115–118). Finally, another ritual association between uphill and down is the *mirasi* of the Kaikala family, whose men take the *veshams* of Gangamma during her *jatara,* to unlock the temple of Venkateshvara's brother, Govindaraja Swamy, every morning. The Kaikalas perform their *mirasi* tasks for both Gangamma and Govindaraja Swamy as integrated, albeit distinct, ritual systems.

Sri Venkateshvara is narratively and ritually associated with a cash economy, a process V. Narayana Rao and David Shulman describe as having begun in the fifteenth century with the rise in power of trading (left-hand) castes, consolidated under the Vijayanagara kings (2005a:118–122). But most local Tirupati residents know little of this history. They associate

Venkateshvara with cash through the story of his need to borrow money for his wedding from his brother Govindaraja Swamy. The god uphill is still paying interest on that loan even today, and pilgrims' gifts placed in his temple *hundi* (cash box) are said to be applied toward interest on that loan. *Hundi* cash contents are conspicuously counted in public at the end of every day, visible to pilgrims on their way out of the temple complex after having taken *darshan* of the indebted god. On his part, Govindaraja Swamy downhill is a reclining image that rests its head on a vessel the god has used to measure the cash interest he has been paid by Venkateshvara; he is tired out from expending so much energy on measuring out the interest.

Venkateshvara's cash/wealth-association is also performatively visible through his *alankara* (ornamentation) with a different set of gemstones every day—rubies, diamonds, emeralds; his image in domestic shrines and portrayed in lithograph prints is similarly glittering with "gems." (Interestingly, a particularly powerful *darshan* is said to be the *nijapada darshan* when the god appears without this heavy ornamentation, wearing only a waistcloth, after his weekly [Friday] *abhishekam* [ritual anointing with a series of liquids]. This is the only time his feet are visible to devotees.) For many pilgrims and devotees, the god's wealth and power to bestow wealth are more important (or at least better known) than his narratives. Another trace of Venkateshvara's left-hand association is visible in the *mirasi* that the Gollas (left-hand caste herders) still retain today to take the first daily *darshan* of the god on the hill.

Telugu scholar and local Tirupati resident P. Srinivasulu Reddy reports that Venkateshvara is sometimes imagined/reported as one whose true form is female (he used the term *shaktisvarupini,* the same term used by the Kaikala brother to identify Gangamma's brother Potu Raju) (oral communication). Reddy reports that some Tirupati residents say Venkateshvara's hair is tied into a woman's bun, hidden from view from pilgrims. Narayana Rao and Shulman similarly report oral traditions that hint at Venkateshvara having been "originally a goddess, converted simultaneously to Srivaishnavism and to maleness by the philosopher Ramanuja . . ." (2005a:117). When I asked a Tirupati devotee more about this tradition, he confirmed that he, too, had heard Venkateshvara was first a woman whom Ramanuja re-carved into a man (Vishnu); however, the story goes, he did not complete the transformation and one of the god's hands is still female and is kept covered with flowers. The attribution of female characteristics to the male extends to both Venkateshvara and Potu Raju in Tirupati—males who are *shaktisvarupini*—and situates the male gods firmly in a left-hand landscape in which masculinity and gendered relationships are imagined quite differently than in right-hand caste rituals and mythologies.

Left-hand caste gendered ethos. The left-hand caste rulers and cash economy that transformed the god and his temple into the wealthy institution that it is today helped to create a broader Tirupati ethos that is resonant with that of left-hand castes. Remember that traditional participants in Gangamma *jatara* are drawn from left-hand castes: Kaikalas (weavers), Acharis (goldsmiths, ironworkers, etc.), Chettis and Balijas (traders), and Madigas (leatherworkers). Most significant for our purposes is the traditional relative independence and mobility of left-hand caste women (like Gangamma herself) when compared to women of right-hand landowning castes whose men "protect" (and thus limit the movement of) their women, like they protect (the fertility of) their land (Narayana Rao 1986).

This characterization of women in left- and right-hand castes is performed in Telugu oral epics associated with these castes. Narayana Rao distinguishes these epics as sacrificial and martial epics, respectively (1986 and 1989). In right-hand caste martial epics, the heroes protect their land from other men of their same families (often cousins, vying for succession and land ownership), and the ideal females are "faithful wives and devoted mothers" (Narayana Rao 1986:148); whereas in left-hand caste sacrificial epics, women take leadership and save the honor of the caste against aggression by a male antagonist of a different caste. Narayana Rao further argues that in the sacrificial epics, not only does the female heroine fill the protective role often associated with males, but the men may take on traditionally female duties such as cooking and raising children and accept female gifts. For example, before the heroine Sanyasamma immolates herself at the end of her epic (and subsequently becomes her caste's goddess), she gives her young brother-in-law the ritual gift of *pasupu-kumkum*, a traditionally female gift (148–159). Gangamma fits this model of the left-hand caste epic heroine, saving the honor of the women of her village from the sexually aggressive Palegadu when men of the *uru* are seemingly unable to do so. However, rather than sacrificing herself to save caste honor (as do sacrificial epic heroines, who then become "virgin goddesses"), Gangamma is already the goddess when she beheads the Palegadu.

The living arrangement of Venkateshvara's wife, Padmavati (also known as Alamelumanga) suggests another trace of a left-hand gender ideology of female independence that is shared with Gangamma and her sisters. Padmavati lives independently of her husband, downhill in Tiruchanoor, five kilometers outside of Tirupati—a living situation that is an extremely rare, if not unique, phenomenon for consort-goddesses.[18] I heard several different explanations for this separate living arrangement, including Padmavati's jealousy over the god letting Lakshmi (a goddess both distinct from and identified with Padmavati) reside on his chest; another story tells of Padmavati's jealousy over Venkateshvara's marriage to a Muslim consort named Bibi Nanchari (said to be a reincarnation of the goddess Bhu Devi), and this is why she refuses to live uphill with her husband. Still another oral tradition recounts Venkateshvara's impatience with his wife after their wedding, when she kept forgetting one thing or another as he waited for her to walk to his residence on top of the mountain. In exasperation, he told her that he was going to spit on the ground and that she should return before the spit dried up. Insulted by this ultimatum, Padmavati told her husband that she was going to stay downhill and that if he wanted to meet her, he would have to come to her (Narayana Rao, oral communication). Whatever the reason for separate residences, it is said to be incumbent on Venkateshvara to come down to visit his wife every night, rather than her going uphill; and all the walking up and down wears out his sandals, which have to be replaced daily.[19]

In the local Tirupati imaginaire, the mountain and the plains below—and the deities that inhabit them—are part of a singular landscape with overlapping relationships, rituals, and traces of a left-hand caste ethos. The presence of the god on the hill and his wealthy institutions, supported by tens of thousands of pilgrims every day, have helped to stabilize the traditionally moving Gangamma sisters on the plain. Their stability, visible in the permanent temples built around them, has created opportunity for more devotional rituals and relationships between them and their devotees than is typical when the sisters reside on village boundaries under open air.

Gangamma in Analytic Schemas

Gangamma traditions provide a fertile context within which to rethink the nature of village goddesses (*gramadevatas*) and human relationships with them. Western academic scholarship has often over-generalized in characterizing *gramadevatas* as uncontrolled (primarily because they are unmarried), dangerous, and even malevolent (Babb 1975; Kinsley 1986). Married/benevolent/*shanta* goddesses are often opposed to unmarried/malevolent/*ugra* goddesses (whom A. K. Ramanujan distinguished as "breast and tooth mothers," respectively [1999]). Although the terms of the dichotomy have been critiqued and modified (see Frederique Apffel-Marglin's work on the goddess Mangala in Orissa [2008]), the marital status, sexuality, and associated "natures" of goddesses continue to be of concern to scholars who study Hindu traditions (See Hawley 1996 for an overview of some of these arguments.)[20]

Tirupati Gangamma belies this analytic dichotomy on several levels. She is potentially both *ugra* and *shanta;* it is the task of her worshippers to calibrate the balance between the two with their ritual service to her. She wears a wedding pendant (*tali*) but has no husband; and the older of the two unmarried Gangamma sisters has children. She is sister both to Potu Raju and Sri Venkateshvara, crossing boundaries often set up in western analytic schemas between village and *puranic* deities. Certain illnesses are a sign of her presence; but she also protects against these same illnesses. Her excessive *ugram* is needed to protect the *uru,* but may become overly excessive and thus dangerous *to* the *uru* if her desires and hunger are not satisfied. She may be demanding ("too much to bear"), but her demands are experienced quite differently by men and women. In urban Tirupati, she is no longer a boundary goddess—the town having grown up around her—but has become what David Knipe calls a "neighborhood goddess," who protects the neighborhood and whose inhabitants have the responsibility to serve her (Knipe 2005a).[21] Gangamma crosses the boundaries of the analytic dichotomy in ways that suggest the importance of regional, caste, ritual, and gender context-specificity to understanding Hindu goddesses. Furthermore, goddesses have the potential to change. As their rituals, service providers, and clientele shift—in the case of Gangamma, incorporating a middle-class aesthetic, Sanskritic rituals, and male Brahman *pujaris* (temple priests)—how goddesses are understood and experienced by their worshippers may also change rather dramatically.

Fieldwork Choices and Relationships

I was first introduced to Gangamma during her *jatara* in May 1992. Three colleagues (V. Narayana Rao, David Shulman, and Don Handelman) were planning to attend the festival; they knew little about the *jatara* except characterizations of it in the press as a festival during which "men became women" and "sang obscene songs." Narayana Rao invited me to join them. I was in Hyderabad at the time teaching at University of Hyderabad's Folklore Centre and thought this would be an opportunity to learn a little more about Hinduism as it is practiced in South India. During that first *jatara,* I took very few notes and was simply an interested observer making mental comparisons with Hindu practices in north and central India with which I was more familiar. That first year, we observed the festival as it moved from the adjacent village of Avilala to Tirupati, and spent the remainder of our time at Gangamma's two largest temples, where female-guised men came to take *darshan,* where women cooked pots of *pongal* over open flames in the temple courtyard, and where, on the penultimate full day of the seven-day festival, hundreds of chickens were offered to the goddess. I happened to be in India the next summer and took the opportunity to attend the festival again with my three companions. This time, we followed the Kaikala-caste men in the guises of the goddess as they walked the streets of old Tirupati, enacting Gangamma's primary local narrative—and I began to take a few notes.

I was reluctant to give up the air-conditioning of my hotel room late one afternoon that second year to accept an invitation by a female professor-friend, D. Padmavati, to come to her home for tea. However, with no excuse other than comfort, I ventured out once more into the heat and was quite unexpectedly introduced to a domestic female festival world about which no one, to date, had spoken to us. In my friend's kitchen were three leaf plates piled with cooked rice and vegetables, sitting in front of three diminutive mounds of turmeric paste atop new pieces of cloth; these were Gangamma. Speaking with the women of the family, I learned of a range of female domestic and temple rituals that performed a world quite different from the public rituals that I had experienced to date—and the seeds for this project were sown. In May of 1995, at the end of a year-long ethnographic project during which I had worked with a Muslim female healer in Hyderabad (Flueckiger 2006), I asked a female schoolteacher and folklorist friend (N. Lakshmi, from Rajahmundry) if she would be willing to accompany me to Tirupati's *jatara.* I explained to her that I wanted to experience the festival with women this time, accompanied by a female fieldwork associate. It was during this festival that I began to develop personal relationships with the families and women who are the key players in part 2 of this book.

After having attended the *jatara* three times, I returned to Tirupati for a full year's fieldwork with the goal of situating the festival within a broader ritual repertoire and getting to know families and individuals who participate in Gangamma traditions. Don Handelman, in his essay on the "causal sequence of ritual action" of Gangamma *jatara,* notes that he takes primarily the "Goddess's point of view" in this analysis (1995:284–285). With this important ritual and structural framework laid out, I was interested in pursuing an analysis of Gangamma traditions from (primarily) the performances and perspectives of their human actors.

I began my long-term fieldwork in 1999–2000 by returning to the families who are key performers in the *jatara* and who serve Gangamma in her two major temples—the Avilala Reddys, Tirupati Kaikalas, and Tatayyagunta-temple Mudaliars. But I also wanted to learn more about lay women's experience of and participation in Gangamma traditions. I began by going to Gangamma's Tatayyagunta temple almost daily, where I sat for many hours with the flower sellers who have set up stalls in the temple courtyard, and from where I observed a wide array of temple-courtyard rituals. Other female temple employees, who keep the precincts clean and "keep order" among worshippers lined up to take *darshan* of the goddess, made sure that I was given space—front and center—at rituals inside the temple, such as the weekly *abhishekam* performed for the goddess in her inner shrine room; and through this access, I came to know some of the Brahman *pujaris* and the Pambala musicians who now serve the goddess at Tatayyagunta temple. My fieldwork network grew as I was introduced to individual female worshippers at the temple; some of these women invited me to their homes and we became friends outside of a research agenda.

However, most of my fieldwork was conducted with individuals and families directly associated with Gangamma in a more formal way, rather than with lay worshippers.

The Kaikala women and flower sellers were, in particular, delighted when I came back to Tirupati with a female fieldwork associate in 1995 and again in 1999–2000. In 1995, when I returned for the *jatara* and walked into the Tatayyagunta temple for the first time on that visit, several flower sellers ran up to me, taking me by the hand and leading me to their stalls, saying, "We were scared of you when you were with those men [my male colleagues]; you were speaking only English, and we ran away from you. But this year you came with a woman, so we ran toward you." The Kaikala matriarch interpreted my return in 1995 as a call from the goddess and correctly predicted that I wouldn't be able to stay away: "My son said you wouldn't come back. But I said, 'The goddess won't stop; she'll bring them. She has the power and she'll make them come.' You'll also be made to come back next time."

This same matriarch, Kamalamma, however, often became impatient with my repeated questions—one disadvantage of long-term fieldwork in a single site. She had a keen memory of what questions she had already answered, a year—or two or three—earlier, and would remind me, "I've already told you everything I know. Every *jatara* is the same." When she tired of our questions, she would forcefully dismiss us, telling us to "go away" ("*po, po!*"). But on other days, Kamalamma was welcoming and hospitable, happy to talk, and insistent on feeding me and my fieldwork associates.

One morning when I was observing her son Venkateshvarlu perform *abhishekam* at Tallapaka temple, Kamalamma chastised me for asking so many questions, which she felt were keeping him from completing his work in a timely fashion. Another early morning, she introduced me to a female worshipper (who comes every morning to the Tallapaka temple to offer the first food cooked in her small restaurant), as "the woman who eats my son's brain with questions." I tried to explain that the first times I attended the *jatara*, I didn't know enough to fully understand what I was seeing; and that, in the interim, I had learned some Telugu and could now understand more directly what she was saying. This explanation sometimes alleviated her frustration and brought laughter. But as the months passed during my year-long research and during follow-up visits, Kamalamma was happiest talking about everyday life outside the *jatara:* her illnesses and arthritic pain, my own family (recommending, for example, a particular style of dangling gold earrings my daughter would surely love), American customs, food, prices of saris, changing marriage customs, etc. And the same held true for my interactions with the flower sellers. Gradually, Kamalamma and other Kaikala-family women, the flower sellers and temple attendants became more than sources of information, and I began to visit them as friends and family; this shift was an important reminder that they lived in a broader world than that of Gangamma and her *jatara.*

On my visit to Tirupati and the Kaikala home in 2010, Kamalamma was lying on her cot in the courtyard, seemingly debilitated by arthritic pain, and spoke very little; and all I could do was offer her some Tylenol and the wool shawl I had brought for her. Her relative silence, so uncharacteristic of earlier years, gave occasion for me to get to know better her daughter-in-law and now-teenage, English-educated grandchildren. Not all of these fieldwork relationships appear directly in the chapters that follow; however, they helped me to build intuitions about the worlds in which participants in Gangamma traditions live and were an invaluable personal gift.

Organization of the Book

Part 1: Imaginative Worlds of Gangamma. In part 1 I analyze the imaginative worlds of Gangamma created through ritual and narrative performance, a world in which ultimate reality is imagined as female, women share the nature of the goddess, and men are transformed to be in her presence. Chapter 1 lays out the performative landscape of the annual Gangamma *jatara* and analyzes what its performance creates through, as I am calling it, an aesthetics of excess. *Jatara* rituals, "excessive" in number and sites of performance, both reflect and help to build up the *ugram* of the goddess in order that she come out of her dark stone forms to protect the *uru.* One rationale of *jatara* rituals is to carefully calibrate this *ugram,* so that its excessiveness will not transform into the illness against which it also protects. Chapter 2 expands on the distinguishing *stri vesham* tradition of Gangamma *jatara,* asking what these guises create for the men who take them on and for those who are witness to them. I suggest that application of turmeric (*pasupu*) on the faces of both the goddess and female worshippers is also a kind of *vesham* that marks their shared nature; whereas male *stri veshams* transform male participants by giving them the experience of female *shakti,* which has the potential to transform the nature of their masculinity.

In chapter 3 I analyze the gendered world of two primary *jatara*-associated narratives, those of the Palegadu and Adi Para Shakti. It is important to hear these narratives in conjunction one with the other and in relationship to *jatara* rituals in order to understand the gendered possibilities they create. The narratives leave certain tensions—particularly that of the world become female and an unbearably *ugra* goddess—unresolved, which the rituals resolve. Chapter 4 centers on a particular storytelling performance by two women in Avilala village that provides an important female commentary on the *ugra* nature of the goddess and the possibilities of a gender-equal relationship with the male. I conclude this section of the book in chapter 5 with analysis of narrative performances of a Brahman *purana pandita* who is an employee of the Tirumala Tirupati Devasthanam (TTD, the trust that manages the temple of Sri Venkateshvara uphill and that oversees numerous educational and charitable institutions downhill). She is sent by the TTD to various temples (including Tatayyagunta Gangamma) to perform *puranic* narratives. As a Brahman, she would not traditionally be involved first-hand in Gangamma rituals, but she has come to know the goddess narratively. She tells the story of the river goddess Ganga as the story of Gangamma herself, thus drawing the *gramadevata* into a pan-Indian goddess-narrative repertoire. Her performances highlight the shared nature between goddesses and women and provide another kind of commentary on the nature of the goddess's *ugram.*

Part 2: Those Who Bear the Goddess. Although I was told many times that Gangamma is too much to bear, her needs too demanding for householders to be able to keep her at home, I learned that many families claim exception to this generalization. They are able to do so, in part, because they are in a kinship relationship with the goddess: she is a daughter of their families, and other select women have entered a kinship relationship by exchanging wedding pendants with her. Part 2 focuses on these families and women who maintain ritual and narrative relationships with Gangamma both in the festival and throughout the year. We begin chapter 6 in the village of

Avilala, on the outskirts of Tirupati, from where the *jatara* moves to Tirupati. Here, Gangamma is both *ugra* goddess and daughter of the family of Reddys whose descendants now organize the festival. The *jatara* moves from Avilala to Tirupati through a ritual exchange of bride's gifts between the Reddy family and the Kaikalas of Tirupati. Chapter 7 takes up the story of this Kaikala family, which also claims Gangamma as a daughter. The males of this extended family take the *veshams* of Gangamma that perambulate the streets of traditional Tirupati as the goddess. The family also has *mirasi* of the smaller of the two Gangamma temples that feature in the *jatara,* where the women of the family are the goddess's primary caretakers. Chapter 8 focuses on the Mudaliar family, whose ancestors built up the largest Gangamma temple in Tirupati—Tatayyagunta Gangamma—from a small shrine into the large temple that it is today. Between 1992 when we first participated in the *jatara* and our return the next year, the Mudaliar family had been evicted by the Tattaiagunta [sic] Devasthanam from the temple as the primary attendants of the goddess, replaced by male Brahman priests. This chapter analyzes this experience of loss from the perspective of the Mudaliar family and the aesthetic and ritual shifts that accompanied this change in personnel, which on some levels have the potential to change the nature of the goddess herself.

The last two chapters shift from ritual families who bear the goddess to individual women who bear her in quite different ways. Chapter 9 introduces a class of women called *matammas* who have formed ritual relationships with the goddess through an exchange of *talis* (wedding pendants) with her. This *tali* exchange with a goddess, rather than in the more common context of marriage to a male, raises new possibilities for what the *tali* signifies and the source of a woman's auspiciousness. The personal narratives of two women who are in a *tali*-relationship with the goddess characterize her as both demanding and protective; and the women's relationship with the goddess has provided them an alternative site of agency to that which may have been available to them as a widow and an abused girl-child and then wife, respectively. Finally, chapter 10 analyzes the personal narratives of a single female devotee who has entered what she suggests is an all-consuming, devotional relationship with the goddess, through which we can begin to understand more fully what it means when the goddess may be, in fact, "too much to bear."

Experience and interpretation of Gangamma's *ugram* and *shakti* are context-specific and highly gendered. Thus, to understand who the goddess is and her relationships to those among whom she moves requires an understanding of a range of actors, narratives, and rituals that contribute to a Gangamma repertoire. This study juxtaposes elements of this repertoire and analyzes the gendered possibilities they create in a Gangamma "world become female."

One

IMAGINATIVE WORLDS OF GANGAMMA

AN AESTHETICS OF EXCESS

1

The most striking aspect of a *jatara* for someone experiencing it for the first time is its dizzying multiplicity of rituals and activities, carried out with a seeming lack of coordinated organization. These festivals are multi-sited, multi-caste celebrations; an elaborate web of castes, ritual families, households, and individuals come together in a flow of activities that sometimes intersect and at other times are relatively independent. No single participant experiences the full range of the ritual repertoire; and so, while the repertoire affects each ritual, its "totality," as described in this book, might appear rather artificially constructed from the perspective of any one participant.[1] And yet there is an organizational, aesthetic force that keeps the *jatara* moving—its rituals performed at the right time in the right place. People seem to know, without being told, what to do, and where and when to show up. In analyzing Draupadi festivals in Tamil Nadu, which share the multiplicity of rituals and sites of Telugu *jataras,* Alf Hiltebeitel writes, "In a sense, we are faced with distilling what is essential from so much variety when variety is its essence" (1991:11). The multiplicity of Gangamma *jatara* helps both to elicit and satisfy the *ugram* of the goddess, the purpose of the festival itself.

Characterizing *Jataras*

Individual *jataras* are local events; most are dedicated to *gramadevatas* for ritual purposes very similar to Gangamma *jatara*, to protect the land and *uru*. The village goddesses at the center of *jataras* are of this place, with local names and narratives of their appearance at a particular place, even as they may attract participants from beyond the local "place." *Jataras* are not transposed to new geographic settings when their celebrants settle in different villages, towns, cities, and countries, as pan-Indian or pan-Telugu festivals may be;[2] for example, *jataras* do not find their way across the seven seas to homes, temples, and high school auditoriums in the United States, as do festivals such as Diwali or Ugadi. *Jataras* are not solely domestic or temple-focused, although they may include both temple and domestic rituals. They are often celebrated at sites at the edge of villages or at their central crossroads; temporary bazaars spring up on open fields and roadsides—stalls selling snacks, low-cost ornaments and bangles, kitchen utensils, and/or toys, sometimes along side small wooden Ferris wheels and other forms of entertainment.

With the multiplicity of *jatara* rituals comes an overload of ritual material: coconuts, *pasupu-kumkum* (turmeric-vermilion), overflowing pots of *pongal,* flowers, fruits, neem leaves, saris, goats and chickens—and, finally, an excess of participating human bodies. The simultaneity and wide repertoire of *jatara* performative genres and materiality contribute to an interpretive frame for any single ritual, creating what I call an aesthetics of excess. By using the term "excess," I draw specifically from the range of meanings of *ugram* in Gangamma contexts.[3] I use the term aesthetics to refer to performative systems that reflect and shape the imaginative worlds—through words, ritual, and action—of their actors (Hobart and Kapferer 2005, 7). Aesthetics implies performativity, creativity, and attention to experience of both performers and audiences.

In the academic study of India, aesthetics has been primarily analyzed in the context of Sanskrit classical aesthetics developed in the Natyashastra, the sage Bharata's classical text (composed between 200 BCE and 200 CE) of dramaturgy, dance, and performance, and the text's commentators such as Abhivanagupta (tenth century). Although some aspects of the aesthetic theory of the Natyashastra are applicable to folk performances—such as assumptions about the creative power of performance—folk traditions perform their own internal systems of creative aesthetics, of which the *jatara* aesthetics of excess is one example. Arguably, Sanskrit *rasa* aesthetics can be characterized as an aesthetics of control and subtlety—a raised eyebrow, sidelong glance, subtle shift of hand position eliciting and/or reflecting particular emotions. In contrast, the aesthetics of Gangamma *jatara* is relatively unrestrained, characterized by excess, over-abundance, multiplicity, and intensity.

A Ritual Rationale of Excess: Creating and Satisfying *Ugram*

Gangamma is rarely kept in household shrines throughout the year because she requires services beyond the temporal and physical means of most householders to be kept happy or satisfied (*santosha*); and a goddess who is not kept *santosha* may become *ugra. Ugram* has often been translated as "anger/wrath" or "ferocity," and when applied to deities whose very nature it is said to be, even "malevolence." While Sanskrit and other Indian language dictionaries certainly include these translations, the term *ugra* has a much wider range of meanings, including huge, strong, powerful, mighty, formidable, terrible, violent, cruel, impetuous, and passionate.

We get several cues in the contexts of Gangamma *jatara* that suggest a similar range of meanings for the term *ugram,* which I have translated as "excess." This translation accounts for the valences of meaning from excessive size, excessive power (*shakti*), to hunger and desire. The term *ugra* is used in the identification of Gangamma's large clay heads, called *ugra mukhis,* built in temple courtyards on the last day of the *jatara.* These heads are literally *ugra*—that is, excessive, over-sized—but they are also the goddess in her fullest form, forms of her *vishvarupam,* whose *darshan* many *jatara* participants assert cannot be sustained by her worshippers for more than a few moments. The goddess has expanded over the week of the *jatara* to an excessive size with excessive demands. One woman said, "By the last day, we can't bear her anymore. We would have to give her piles of food [*kumbham*] every day; we wouldn't be able to bear that. So, saying 'Next year we'll worship you,' we send her off." But during the *jatara,* time and energy are set aside for just this: to create, bear, and satisfy the *ugra* goddess.

In her primary *jatara* narrative, Gangamma is said to become *ugra* when her sexuality is threatened by the aggressive Palegadu; her *ugram* is needed to destroy him, much as her *ugram* is needed to destroy hot-season illness that threatens the *uru.* In another narrative, the goddess Adi Para Shakti, whose story is told as that of Gangamma, is characterized as having too much *shakti,* too much for any male to be able to bear. In this narrative, *ugram/shakti* is associated with excessive desire (the opposite of *santosham,* satisfaction/fulfillment), which has the potential to become dangerous if left unsatisfied.

The excess of *ugram* differs from the abundance that characterizes many other Hindu rituals. While the latter may also utilize wide ranges of material ingredients, their sites of worship or personnel are not as multiple, and their abundance is never potentially threatening. For example, the annual Varalakshmi Vratam (a female, domestic ritual honoring and invoking the goddess of wealth Lakshmi) requires female householders to cook nine types of vegetable curries; and the goddess is covered with an abundance of *pasupu-kumkum* and flowers. And yet, the ritual is confined to domestic space and its abundance does not threaten to overflow its boundaries; there is no threat of danger in the excess of the ritual.

This aesthetic framework helps us to identify the ritual rationale of the *jatara:* to first elicit and build up Gangamma's *ugram* so that she will be present and powerful enough to protect against threatening hot-season illness and drought, and then to satisfy and balance that same *ugram* so that the goddess does not become illness itself. Gangamma's *ugram* is created both through multiplicity of forms (Gangamma herself expands as she inhabits these forms) and particular rituals that both enliven and satisfy the *ugram* of these forms.

Another way to think about *ugram* is its association with heat: the goddess must be ritually heated in order to grow into her full protective power, but if she becomes too hot, she may become the illness or drought. Once sufficiently heated, she is also "brought down," or cooled, through ritual. It is the responsibility of *jatara* participants to finely calibrate the ideal balance between heating and cooling: to heat the goddess enough to call her to be fully present, but at the same time to keep her expanded, multiplied forms cool/satisfied/pacified (*santosha*).[4] An example of this calibration occurs when, on the first days of the *jatara,* young boys beat with neem branches the cement feet of the goddess at the entrance to her Tatayyagunta temple, while singing sexually explicit songs; the physical beating and songs are said to heat the goddess and call her out of her dark stone temple form, while the neem leaves cool her at the same time.

David Knipe observes in possession rituals of coastal Andhra a similar but distinct rhythm of *raudra* (which he translates as rage, anger, fury, ferocity) and *shanti* (repose, gentleness). The *raudra* of the possessing neighborhood goddesses is desired by those who are possessed by her, and it is then converted into *shanti* through the services offered to her:

> Raging powers are invited precisely because their wrath is a necessary conduit of spiritual energy, information, illumination, a channel that hopefully may be employed in reverse with devotion, affection, reassurance so that rage is converted to repose. (2001:345)

Knipe characterizes these goddesses as "fierce (*ugra*) by nature. They do not require explanations for either *raudra* or *santa. They are goddesses*" (Knipe's emphasis; 349). Further, he continues, "Most neighborhood goddesses are illustrations of mobility between poles of the *ugra* (wild) and *saumya* (mild), transformation being their *modus operandi*" (351). In personal communication (2011), Knipe verified that the terms *ugra* and *raudra* are used synonymously by both non-literate possession ritualists and Vedic Brahmans. He quotes a Vedic Brahman saying, "I accept all *danas* [ritual gifts] from benefactors with the exception of a cow. That would be an *ugra dana*!" This is an evocative example of *ugra/raudra* implying excess rather than malevolence; after all, Knipe asks, how could a cow be "malevolent"? But, as Gangamma *jatara*'s aesthetics of excess suggests, there are times when the *uru* needs the goddess's *ugram* to become so excessive as to be destructive, to protect from illness and drought that may threaten the *uru.*

Spatial and Temporal Frames Creating *Ugram*

The intense summer heat, reading over 100 degrees Fahrenheit, during which Gangamma *jatara* is celebrated is itself an important source of the goddess's expansion and growing *ugram.* Summer temperatures reach their maximum in mid-May. One can almost feel the stirring of the goddess as the days heat up and hot winds blow, gathering clouds that should release rains on the final morning of the *jatara* in Tirupati, heralding the approaching monsoons.

Marking the boundaries of ritual space helps to consolidate and concentrate the goddess's *ugram*. The first Tuesday night, as the *jatara* moves from the adjacent village of Avilala to Tirupati, the boundaries of the traditional *uru* of Tirupati are sprinkled with rice mixed with blood of sacrificed animals, in a ritual called *cakrabandhanam* (lit. tying the circle). With this ritual binding, all who reside in that space become, in some sense, actors in the *jatara*. During the *jatara*, no one is supposed to enter or leave the *uru*, a prohibition that is lost these days in the bustling modern pilgrimage town; but just as importantly, the "tied" boundary keeps the expanding, restless goddess herself inside the *uru* (Handelman 1995). Further, the boundaries help to consolidate the *ugram* that is built up through her *jatara* forms and rituals, keeping it from dissipating. And finally, the ritual boundary holds together as a "whole" the myriad of sometimes seemingly unrelated activities that take place within the ritually marked *uru* into a single *jatara* repertoire, in which each ritual site/genre enters into a relationship with the others.

Excess through Multiplicity

Gangamma's *ugram* is created, in part, through the multiplication of her forms on streets, in domestic kitchens, and in temple courtyards. The assumption would seem to be that the goddess in roadside shrine and temple images of dark stone aren't sufficiently present/excessive/*ugra* enough for the task at hand, of protecting the *uru* from hot-season illnesses and drought. Handelman suggests that in these stone, stable forms, Gangamma is not only insufficiently accessible to the *uru*, but perhaps also not present enough to herself (1995); a certain self-consciousness, he argues, is required for the goddess to fulfill her role, a knowledge created, in part, through the multiplying forms of herself that she sees and experiences during her week-long celebration. During the *jatara*, Gangamma's stone images inside her temples become secondary to her temporary, fluid *jatara* forms of human-body guises in the streets, yogurt-millet mixture (*ragi*) and diminutive wet turmeric mounds in domestic kitchens, and the *ugra mukhis* in front of each of her two major temples. But this pervasive presence and the potential intimacy with the goddess that it creates—she is, quite literally, everywhere—is too much to sustain throughout the year; and so clear temporal and spatial frames are established, into which Gangamma is invited and then sent away.

The intensity and excess of the *jatara* is also created by the multi-sited nature of its rituals, and the range of rituals the goddess requires at each site. The primary sites of *jatara* ritual are: 1) the household of the extended family of Kaikalas, whose males take on a series of *veshams* of Gangamma that enact her story; 2) the streets of traditional Tirupati, where the Kaikala *veshams* walk from doorway to doorway and are met and worshipped by female householders, passersby are offered *ambali* (mixture of cooling yogurt, heating raw onions, and cooked millet) by female householders; mothers walk with their children to Tatayyagunta temple, holding "thousand-eyed" clay pots over their heads; on the streets around Gangamma's temples, roving bands of young men sing "abusive" songs (*butulu*) at passersby; and, on the last few days of the *jatara,* lay men in female *vesham* are "displayed" and seen on their way to the temple; 3) the courtyards of the two primary Gangamma temples—Tatayyagunta and Tallapaka—where ritual activity builds in intensity until the last day, when the *ugra mukhis* are built; and 4) domestic kitchens, where the goddess is created in several different forms, fed, and distributed. Each of these sites, each strand in the web of the *jatara* repertoire, is filled with distinct ritual materials and physicality. Performatively and schematically, many of the actors and rituals of these multiple sites come together on the final morning of the *jatara* during the ritual dismantling of the two large clay *ugra mukhis* by a Kaikala *vesham.*

Kaikala *Veshams:* The Goddess in Human, Moving Form

While the Palegadu-Gangamma narrative is being played out on the streets of Tirupati through the Kaikala *veshams*—which bring the expanding goddess to the domestic doorways of the *uru*—no one professionally performs or even informally tells the narrative verbally (unless asked to do so by the anthropologist); that is, there is no indigenously marked ritual site for its verbal performance. But, to give a sense of the rationale and sequence of the Kaikala *veshams,* as they progress from gentle young snake charmer to the goddess in her fullest, most *ugra* Matangi form, I provide a detailed summary of the narrative, which will be analyzed more fully in chapter 3.

As a little girl, Gangamma was abandoned in a dry paddy field, from where she was taken in as a daughter by a Reddy-caste family, in the village of Avilala (on the outskirts of Tirupati). There was a particularly powerful Palegadu (landowner) who used to demand sexual access to (sometimes marriage with) the beautiful virgins living in his domain. When his glance fell on a pubescent Gangamma as she was drying her hair on her rooftop, he desired her and approached her parents with his intention to marry her. Not knowing their daughter was the goddess, they were afraid and tried to resist his overtures. But Gangamma assured them they should assent; she would take care of herself. As the couple (Gangamma and the Palegadu) was circumambulating the sacred fire in the final marriage rite, Gangamma turned around to face the bridegroom and showed him her true self (*vishvarupam*), stretching from earth to sky. Petrified, he ran away. She chased him for six days, taking a series of *veshams* (those of milkmaid, ascetic, snake charmer, shepherd, sweeper, etc.) to disguise herself so that the Palegadu wouldn't see her before she saw him. Finally, hearing the princely (Dora *vesham*) Gangamma being praised in public, the Palegadu came out of hiding to see who was competing with him for such praise; and Gangamma beheaded him. After killing the Palegadu, Gangamma wandered the village (*uru*), showing herself in her true form for the duration of what is now the *jatara*. At the end of the festival (and its narrative), Gangamma departs from Tirupati, "over the seven seas."

The Kaikala *veshams* are dressed in the Kaikala home by the women of the family, who have very clear ideas about what dress and ornaments the goddess desires/requires.[5] The physicality of the ornaments, *pasupu* application to the male faces, and female clothing of the *vesham* itself transforms the males into the goddess. Several aspects of this physicality contribute to the excessive aesthetics of the *jatara*. The *veshams* wear earrings of bright-gold foil paper, which are exaggerated, larger-than-life (in stark contrast to women's everyday more subtle ornaments). The number of flowers worn in their hair and as garlands increases dramatically as the *jatara* progresses, as does the intensity of the *pasupu-kumkum* offered to and distributed by the later *veshams*—which becomes part of their physicality of excess as their arms and sari-fronts become reddened from the exchange of *kumkum* between *veshams* and householders. And then there is, of course, the "over-sized," fully adult male body in the later *veshams* of the guising sequence, a body that would seem to be "excessive" in its portrayal of the female (goddess).

Each *vesham*'s head is covered with a white plain cloth as the now female-guised male runs, quite literally, from the Kaikala home to the nearby Veshalamma temple (the form of Gangamma whose name is, literally, the "goddess/mother of *vesham*"), where the *vesham* performs *harati* (flame offering) to the dark temple form of herself. Only then is the Kaikala *vesham* fully the goddess and worshipped as such. There is one exception; the Dora *vesham* who ultimately beheads the Palegadu does not offer *harati* to Veshalamma; holding an upright sword, Gangamma-in-princely-guise is said to be too *ugra* to enter her own temple.

The clothing of each *vesham* is stylized to depict the various castes and occupational roles in which Gangamma herself guised as she chased the Palegadu: *bairagi,* ascetic; *pamulavadu,* snake charmer; Golla, herder; *banda,* ruffian; Chetti, merchant; Toti, sweeper; and Dora, prince. These first seven of the series of ten Kaikala *veshams* are joined by a male member of the Cakali (washermen, left-hand) caste, who takes male guise of the same caste as that represented by the Kaikala female *veshams.* The paired *veshams* are said to be the two Gangamma sisters, Pedda and Cinna Gangamma. After the Dora beheads the Palegadu, the Cakali *vesham* is dropped, and the two sisters merge in the next Matangi *vesham* (taken by a Kaikala married male). Like the Kaikalas, the Cakali families who participate in the first seven *veshams* consider Gangamma to be a daughter of their caste. However, the Cakali *veshams* are performatively secondary to those taken by the Kaikalas, and there were indications of some tension between the families over ritual status/respect in this context.

After being created in the Kaikala courtyard and rushing to Veshalamma temple for *darshan* of herself, the goddess manifest through *veshams,* accompanied by Pambala (scheduled caste) professional drummers, go from house to house throughout the traditional *uru* of Tirupati. Here at the doorways, they are met by female householders who offer them *harati* and anoint their feet with *kumkum.* The rituals are relatively attenuated for the

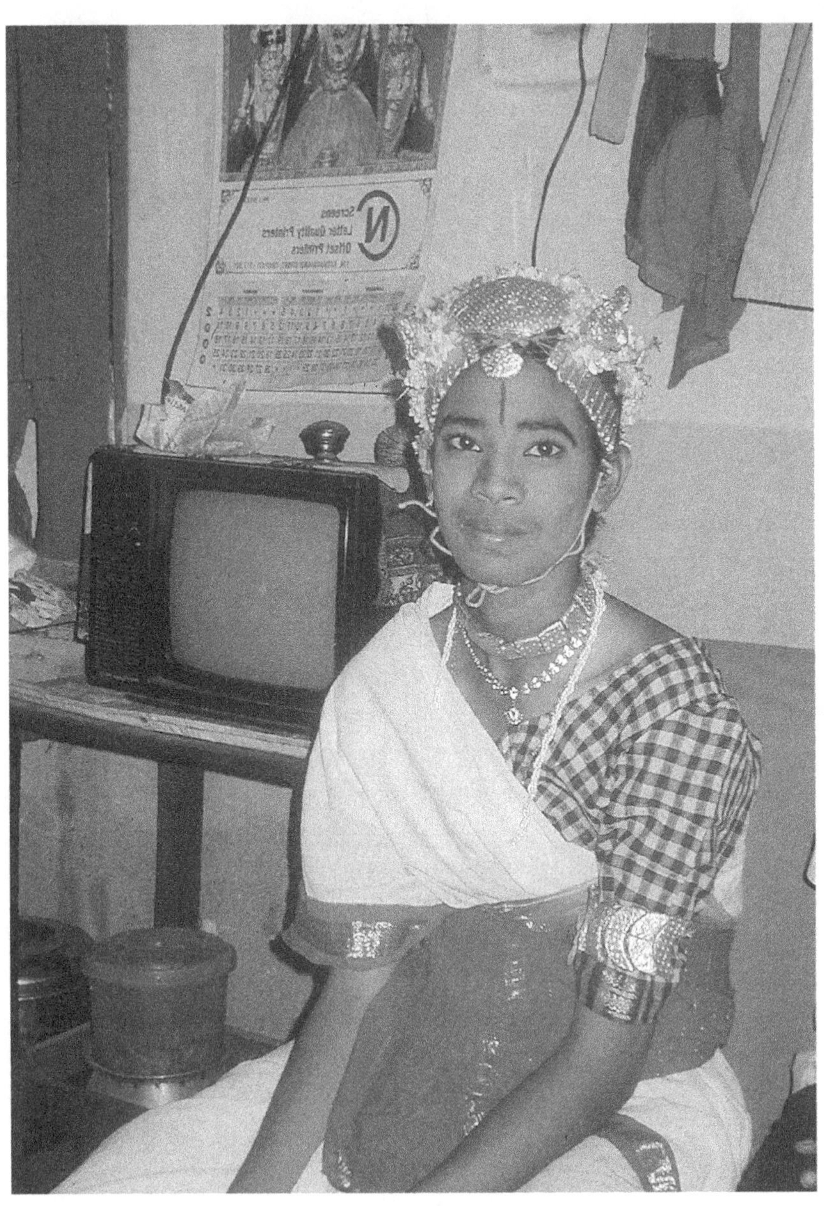

Chetti (merchant) *vesham.*

early *veshams;* but as the goddess grows more fully into herself, becoming more *ugra,* more women in each household come out to greet her, their rituals are more prolonged, and some "big houses" may invite the goddess inside. To the Matangi, in particular, babies may be brought to receive the goddess's blessing. The number of homes visited also increases through the *vesham* sequence, so that the last three Kaikala *veshams*—the Matangi, Sunnapukundalu, and Perantalu—must perambulate the *uru* throughout the night to complete their visits.

Handelman describes the coal-blackened Toti (sweeper) *vesham* as a kind of tipping point in the Gangamma *vesham* sequence, where suddenly the energy around the *vesham* increases dramatically and male and female passersby on the street (rather than only female householders waiting for her at their doorways) stop the Toti for her blessings through a tap on their bodies with her winnowing basket (1995:298–299). He suggests that "Gangamma is now very close to the surface of her disguise and to the world of human beings" (299). She is ready to act; her *ugram* has sufficiently built up that she is ready/able to behead the aggressive Palegadu in her next *vesham* as Dora. I elaborate below on the last four *veshams* of the Kaikala-embodied sequence; for a fuller discussion of the details of the ritual *vesham* sequence, see Handelman's essay "The Guises of the Goddess" (1995).

Dora. The princely *vesham* dresses in a premodern, Islamic-style royal costume: a white, skirted outfit, a royal gold turban, and a large floral garland; on his forehead is a large Vaishnava *namam* marking. He walks with his minister at a dignified pace, holding up his *pasupu*-marked sword with a (cooling) lemon impaled on its end. Venkateshvarlu showed us old pictures of men of his grandfather's generation taking Dora *vesham* in the days when both the Dora and his minister used to ride horses. Householders meeting the Dora would wash the feet of the horses, as well as those of the Dora and his minister. These days, the luxury of horses has been lost; in any case, Venkateshvarlu speculated, the horses would become afraid amid all the traffic and horns.

The *jatara*-enacted beheading of the Palegadu by the Dora *vesham* takes place behind Veshalamma temple in the very early morning hours and is surprisingly undramatic; the only audience is the small group of men accompanying the Dora (and curious anthropologists). The Dora simply

Dora and his minister.

circles the Palegadu (the latter's wooden head held high by a Cakali man) three times and then touches the head with his sword, as the small male audience ululates. The head is quickly covered by a white cloth and the man holding it runs off. Venkateshvarlu explained that, as she kills him, Gangamma asks the Palegadu, "Who do you think a woman is?" She then turns him into ashes and, in an act of defiance and superiority, from these ashes applies a black *bottu* on her forehead.

One might think it would be in this form that the goddess is visually her most *ugra*, but actually the prince is very refined and contained, and the beheading is understated. Gangamma is only fully manifest as her true self (*vishvarupam;* in the narrative, said to "reach from earth to sky"), swollen with her fullest *ugram,* in the next *vesham* of the Matangi, the first form in which she appears without the mediation of narrative guise. Now there is only a single guising (the Kaikala male as goddess), rather than double guising in which men become the goddess, who herself has taken a series of disguising *veshams.* The understated beheading of the aggressive Palegadu suggests that the *jatara* as a whole has a different focus than the narrative that the Kaikalas enact—the *jatara* is focused on the goddess and not her male aggressor. While gender dynamics are, of course, relevant in the daily lives of the *uru*'s inhabitants, during the *jatara,* they are preoccupied with the immediate threat of illness and drought. In this ritual context, the enacted story of the Palegadu's beheading is most important for the *ugram* it creates in the goddess, *ugram* that the *jatara* seeks to create, contain, and calibrate.

Matangi. The Matangi starts her rounds of the *uru* at the same time the beheading of the Palegadu is taking place. To my numerous questions about the identity of the Matangi, I was told over and over again, by Kaikala family members as well as audiences to this *vesham,* simply that she is the *vishvarupam* (true form) of Gangamma.[6] Visually and ritually, the Matangi is certainly the most excessive form of Gangamma in her *jatara vesham* sequence. Her neck is loaded with flower garlands; and by the end of her twenty-four-hour perambulations, her hands, arms, and checked red and white sari are covered with dark red *kumkum* that has been offered to her by householders and from the "lap rice" she has been distributing to them (held in a waist pouch made by her wrapped sari) when she meets them at their doorways.

Midway through her rounds, the Matangi returns to the Kaikala home, exhausted from the heat and the public's demands for her attention. Here, she takes a seat in front of the household metallic head-image of herself and the image of her younger brother Potu Raju, which has been brought from Tallapaka temple by the Kaikalas to bear witness to the *jatara* proceedings in their home. (Venkateshvarlu explained that this is the only time the goddess leaves her temple, and thus she needs her brother as her "guard.") Now, stamping her belled feet, becoming over-heated in the small, crowded courtyard of the house, the Matangi becomes possessed by still another form of herself (along with the forms of the male-bodied *vesham* and her metallic head in front of whom she's sitting). Several female onlookers, too, become possessed by Gangamma, creating still another moment of multiplication, intensity, and excess. At this moment, Gangamma is her fullest *ugra* self—a presence verified by a piercing of her tongue, which is said both to show she is truly present and "to cool her down."

The Matangi's ornaments and flowers are then taken off, and she becomes the Kaikala male. There is no specific ritual marking this transition

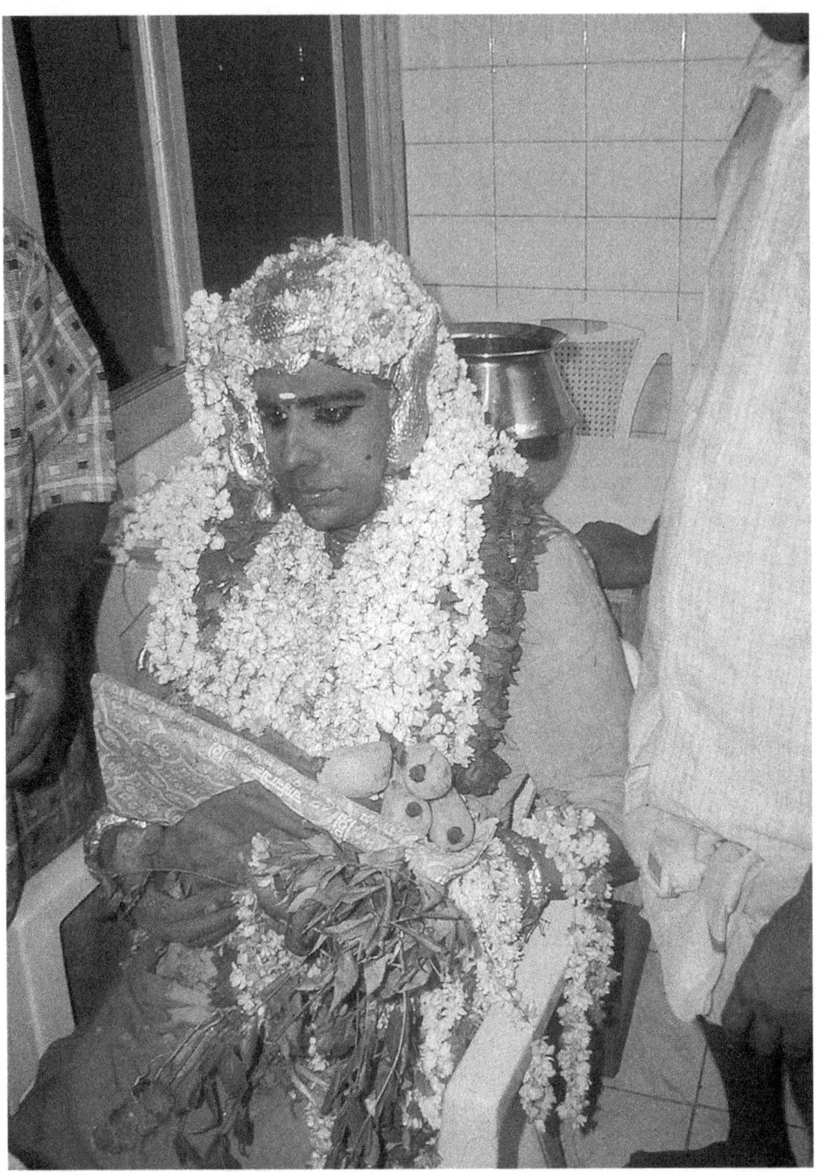

Matangi.

between goddess and the male who becomes her; rather, it occurs simply by taking off parts of the physical guise. The transition is visually dramatic, as the *ugra,* energetic goddess becomes an exhausted human form that cannot even feed itself. The Kaikala male is fed water and cooling yogurt rice by his wife. After a couple hours of rest, the Matangi is readorned and, once again the goddess, she proceeds, with purposeful strides, her perambulations throughout the rest of the afternoon and night.

Gangamma's Matangi presence, her *vishvarupam,* is too much to bear for long, just as many women say Gangamma is too much to bear on a daily basis in their homes. There are numerous other examples of Hindu deities showing their *vishvarupams* to humans who cannot sustain/bear this revelation for long. For example, in the *Bhagavad Gita,* the warrior Arjuna asks Krishna to show him who he truly is; but the *darshan* of that true form that encompasses the entire universe is too much to sustain, and Arjuna begs the god to return to the form he knows as his charioteer (Gita 11:41–46). Wendy Doniger suggests god masquerades as a mortal "to make it possible for us to gaze upon him; he presents us with a shaded lens thru which we can view his solar splendor without being blinded" (1980:69).

Sunnapukundalu. In the *vesham* sequence, the singular Matangi is split in two in the next *vesham* of two twin-looking sister Gangammas who wear lime pots (*sunnapukundalu;* caustic lime is said to be a cooling substance) on their heads. Venkateshvarlu explained that Gangamma has come in this cooled (split, *ugra*-reduced) form to assure the *uru* that she has not, in fact, become so *ugra* as to become *ammavaru* (Gangamma illness). The goddess is now accessible to accept her worshipper's vows (*mokku*), and the Veshalamma temple courtyard is filled to overflowing with women offering such vows and watching the Sunnapukundalus being created. (This is the only *vesham* prepared in the temple courtyard rather than the domestic Kaikala courtyard, and the only one whose preparation is witnessed by an audience beyond the Kaikala family.) The preparation is a particularly time-consuming process during which the lime pots are tied to the heads of the two Kaikala males taking the *vesham;* several strands of hair are pulled through a small hole at the bottom of the limepot, and the hair shank is twisted around and anchored with a small stick that sits at the bottom of the pot. The men taking Sunnapukundalu *vesham* grow their hair a little longer than normal for this purpose. The pot itself is encircled with strands of flower garlands. When the two *veshams* are completed, the women who have patiently observed their creation throng forward to receive the blessings of the Sunnapukundalus. Women seem to find Gangamma's blessings at this moment of *vesham* completion particularly powerful. The goddess has revealed her true *ugra* self in the Matangi, and has now made herself more accessible again, assuring her worshippers that her *ugram* is not ultimately threatening. The Sunnapukundalus then begin their perambulations around the *uru* to receive worship of householders at domestic thresholds. This set of *veshams* completes the widest spatial circuit in the *uru*, taking up to forty-eight hours.

As Gangamma's *ugram* is modulated through splitting into the two Sunnapukundalus, a narrative is performed for her (and she *is* the primary audience) by professional Pambala drummers. This is the only professional narrative performance during the *jatara*, and its timing is interesting. The performance reminds the now-split Gangamma of who she truly is, equating her with the source of all creation—the goddess Adi Para Shakti—while at the same time giving rationale to why she cannot stay in this form if she wants to be in relationship with her creation.

Perantalu. After the split forms of the lime pots, the final *vesham* is once again singular, in the persona of the Perantalu. She wears the same kind of red-and-white checked sari and flowers as the Matangi, but her gait is more graceful and (initially) calmer; she is no longer as *ugra* as the Matangi. Venkateshvarlu describes the Perantalu to be Gangamma returned to the form of an unmarried young girl (he specifies that she is sixteen years old). The term *perantalu* has a range of meanings: lower castes tell stories of women whose husbands die (usually in battle) while they are still virgins; their virginity is then threatened by an aggressive protagonist, but the women sacrifice themselves rather than endure the sexual violence of the aggressive male; in death, they become goddesses, called *perantalus* (Handelman 1995, 314; Narayana Rao 1986, 158–160). This connotation of the term as performed in left-hand caste epics may be lost to contemporary *jatara* participants, or it may never have been present, as I heard no mention of the Perantalu's marital status or self-sacrifice. Contemporary celebrants are more likely to interpret this *vesham* through the common connotations of

Tatayyagunta *ugra mukhi.* Courtesy of K. Rajendran, K. R. Studio, Tirupati.

perantalu in everyday, contemporary Telugu speech—that of an auspicious (usually married) woman who has ritual power to bless other women.

Early in the morning of the *jatara*'s last day, there is one last burst of energy, high energy, as the Perantalu ends her night-long perambulations in front of each of the two dark-blue painted *ugra mukhis* that have been built in front of the Tatayyagunta and Tallapaka temples. She pushes her way through the large, expectant crowds and jumps up to tear out the cheek of each *mukhi,* thus beginning its dismantling. One year when I was able to see her closely at this moment, I observed she was utterly exhausted and looked dazed from her twenty-four-hour rounds of Tirupati. Briefly, at the moment before she jumps up, the Perantalu becomes possessed and then gives *harati* to the *ugra mukhi.* A garland is taken down from the *ugra mukhi* and placed around the Perantalu, and a garland from the Perantalu is placed around the *ugra mukhi.* Venkateshvarlu explained that anyone other than the goddess herself who might attempt to touch the *ugra mukhis* (after the craftsmen creating them have put their silver eyes in place and the goddess is fully "there") would be reduced to ashes; "Only another *shakti* can touch *shakti. Shakti* is *shakti.* No one else can pull her down." The crowds frantically push and shove to try to find a piece of the precious *ugra mukhi* clay, which they keep in their homes to dissolve in water and drink for healing from Gangamma-type illnesses. At this moment of dismantling, it is said that it should rain; and many years it does (including the four times that I have witnessed this ritual). The *ugram* of the goddess has been built up through the duration of the *jatara,* satisfied through ritual, and is now dismantled—by herself—broken up into (quite literally) manageable pieces that can be taken home; the goddess has accomplished her mission to protect from illnesses and bring rains to assure the fertility of the land.

Ritually the Perantalu *vesham* ends her *jatara* tasks—and the *jatara* itself—by taking rest in an open-sided pavilion at a crossroads near the Kaikala home, from where some male celebrants said she leaves to cross the seven seas. However, the rituals taking place in the temple courtyards throughout the year, particularly on the days of the goddess, Tuesdays and Fridays, follow a different rationale, as one woman told me when I asked where this place was where the goddess disappeared to: "She doesn't go anywhere; we feed her every Tuesday and Friday."

Temple Courtyard Rituals

While the Kaikala *veshams* are living out the narrative of Gangamma in Tirupati's streets, the courtyards of Gangamma's two major temples are alive with rituals that would seem to have little to do with this narrative sequence. Many female celebrants I spoke with did not know well the Palegadu narrative and confused the names of the Kaikala *veshams* and their identities; other women confused certain narrative details and sequences and often then suggested that I ask the Kaikalas to tell me the story. Temple rituals in which women are experts are motivated by another rationale—to satisfy the *ugra* goddess through feeding.

Temple courtyard rituals begin with the transformation of a cement pillar (*kodistambham*) into a woman (more specifically, the goddess), through the application of turmeric, adornment of flowers, and wrapping of multiple saris around the top of the pillar. After the pillar-woman is fully dressed and adorned, a cloth holding *vodivalu* (lit., waist/lap rice; a mixture of rice and *kumkum* that is an embodiment of potential fertility) is tied around the pole, atop the saris. *Vodivalu* is similarly tied around the waists of brides of some castes, as well as around the waists of the Matangi and Perantalu *jatara veshams*. At this moment, the crowd watching the transformation of pillar-to-woman salutes the emergence of the goddess through hands held high in *namaskaram* (salutation). The goddess has taken her first step out of the dark form inside the temple. The temple courtyard activity of the first few days flows back and forth between this pillar-woman, to whom piles and piles of food, flowers, and *pasupu-kumkum* are offered, and the goddess's large cement feet.

On the first two days, young children (mostly boys), dressed as *bandas* (lit., ruffians, believed to be strong but unintelligent) with the penal-code number 786 painted on their bare chests, beat the large bare feet of the goddess with neem branches while singing sexually explicit and/or "abusive" songs (*butulu*). Several adult males told us that these songs both rouse and satisfy the sexual desire of the goddess. In the framework of the *jatara* aesthetics of excess, the songs help to create the excess (desire) of the goddess and at the same time fulfill it. One ritual specialist in Avilala elaborated,

> Her *moham* [lust] is fulfilled only through obscene songs. For three days they sing obscene songs; no man can tie and keep her. . . . Her *moham* will be fulfilled through these obscene words; they give her fulfillment/happiness [*santosham*]. Not Lord Shiva, not Brahma, not Vishnu, none of them is able to bear her [referring to the Adi Para Shakti narrative, analyzed in chapter 3].

In 1992, we saw many such *bandas* singing/chanting *butulu;* they were, however, unwilling to sing them for a tape recorder; that year Narayana Rao caught a few phrases such as, "she with a vagina as wide as a winnowing basket."[7] By the time I attended the *jatara* in 2000, very few children seemed to know the words to the songs, but simply mouthed "ahhhhh, ahhhhh" as they beat the feet. But the memory of excessive abuse is still strong among *jatara* celebrants who spoke to me about this ritual (and in the press that seems to revel in reporting about this aspect of the *jatara*). It is significant that the males who sing these abuses to the goddess are boys, not yet men, who may not fully understand the valences of the erotic abuses, and that the abusive chanting is appropriate only during the first days of the *jatara.* Small bands of young *bandas* also accost female passersby in the streets with similar ritual abuse. During the 1992 *jatara,* we were told by several male informants that both the goddess and women on the streets welcomed these insults as a kind of ritual blessing. However, speaking with women themselves in subsequent years, I learned that most of them do not accept this interpretation and, to avoid what they experienced as unwelcomed confrontations with the *bandas,* they were often hesitant to go out onto the main streets of Tirupati on those *jatara* days when they knew these bands of boys would be sharing the streets with them.

During the first several days of the *jatara,* the *ugram* of the goddess is satisfied through profuse feeding of vegetarian items, offered at the base of the *kodistambham* and at her cement feet. Women also build individual small fires along the walls of the temple courtyard, over which they cook *pongal,* which should, according to custom, boil over—overflowing *pongal* reflecting plenty, fullness, abundance.[8] But, *pongal,* flowers, and fruits would seem not to fully satisfy the expanding, increasingly *ugra* goddess; as the week progresses, non-vegetarian offerings of sacrificial chicken and goats begin to take the place of vegetarian offerings. One female participant explained that "nonveg" is more satisfying when someone (in this case, the goddess) is really hungry.

On the final Tuesday, the last full day of the *jatara,* Tatayyagunta Gangamma's courtyard is filled with families (men now accompany the women) performing individual chicken (and a few goat) sacrifices, feathers and blood covering the earth, mixed with ritual leftovers of flowers, neem leaves, and *pasupu-kumkum.* (I was told by several participants that buffalo *bali* (animal sacrifice) used to be offered—and that surely, somewhere in Tirupati, at least one buffalo would be offered under cover of night—but that these days, this was against the law.) Families build small cooking fires right where they've offered the chickens, to prepare the meat for their own consumption. The excess of sacrifice and blood did not feel violent to me as an observer; rather, there's a gentle flow and rhythm of moving bodies as families negotiate among the products of excess—fire, blood, mud and feathers.

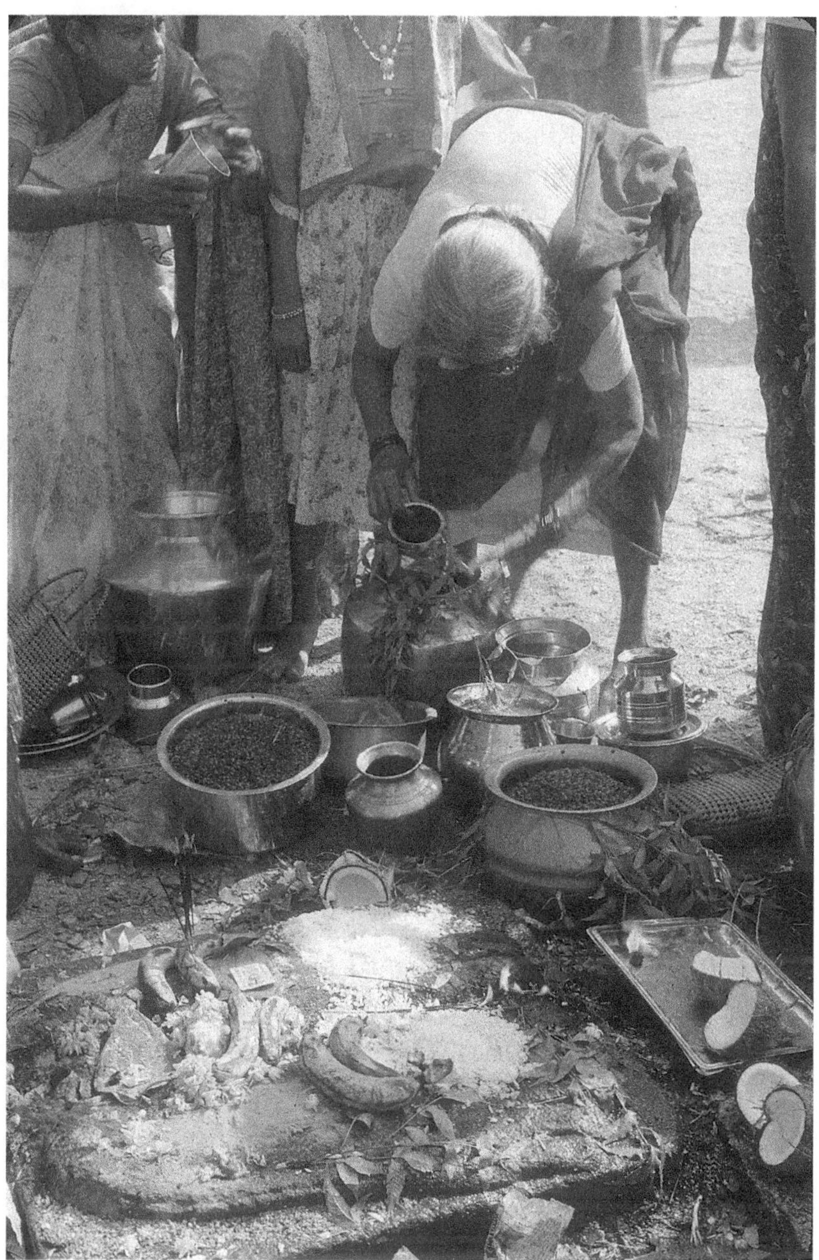

Food offerings at goddess's feet.

Lay *Veshams:* Men Becoming Women

During the last two days of the *jatara,* coinciding with the rituals of temple courtyards and the Kaikala *veshams,* another level of ritual activity unfolds on Tirupati's streets. As the goddess grows in her presence and *ugram,* the presence of aggressive young *bandas* shifts to grown men who take graceful *stri vesham.* By the last Tuesday of the *jatara,* the streets around Tatayyagunta Gangamma temple are filled with men who have become women, wearing saris, braids, breasts, and jewelry. Some sari-ed pubescent boys and grown men specifically take Matangi *vesham,* visualized through application of sandalpaste on their faces and strings of flower garlands wound around their heads. *Stri veshams* are often accompanied by their mothers, wives, and/or sisters, who have chosen their saris and adornments and periodically adjust these as they make their way to temple. Some *veshams* walk confidently, unselfconsciously, and it's difficult to determine from afar that they are men; others reveal their maleness more readily as they climb astride their motorcycles or walk in a fast gait culturally inappropriate for most women. The *stri veshams* make offerings to the goddess out in the courtyard, but the more important ritual seems to be the public display of the *stri veshams.*

Many local *jatara* participants assert that male-to-female ritual guising is unique to Gangamma *jatara* in Tirupati, although I have heard reports of *stri vesham* as part of other *jataras.* I was told several times that Gangamma in Tirupati is more powerful than her sisters in the surrounding villages—her *ugram* greater—and that at the height of this *ugram,* she did not like to see men. For a few days, ultimate reality is female; the male is the marked category, the gender that is transformed, harkening back to the world on the cusp of creation when all that existed was the female, Adi Para Shakti. But this is the ritual, not social, world. And by the last evening of the *jatara,* the streets filled with *stri veshams,* by now no longer accompanied by their female relatives and moving less slowly, feel threatening to many women who are reluctant to go out among them.

Female Domestic Rituals

While the media and male commentary on the *jatara* focus on the drama of male transformation through *stri vesham,* women, too, are (arguably less

Lay *stri vesham.*

visibly) active with an intensification of what they already do every day—cooking—creating and satisfying the goddess through food. When I once asked if Kaikala women take the goddess's *veshams,* knowing that they did not but seeking an indigenous explanation for this, a Kaikala male answered that they did not, both because of menstruation and that they did not have the physical stamina to walk the streets as the *veshams* are required to do. But the elderly Kaikala matriarch who overheard this comment protested that it was not because of menstruation that women don't take *vesham,* but because they are too busy cooking for the goddess. She seemed to equate the two activities as equally necessary to satisfying the *ugra* goddess: *vesham* and cooking. Women first cook *pongal* in the temple courtyards and later participate in non-vegetarian sacrifice/cooking in larger family groups; but they are also active at home.

Many female householders first bring Gangamma into their kitchens or sitting rooms by drawing three simple lines of *pasupu,* with dots of *kumkum* between them, on the wall or a wooden board propped up against the wall. Once here, the goddess needs to be fed. The first ritual feeding is a pot of *ambali,* a mixture of cooling yogurt, heating raw onions, and cooked millet. The stainless steel or clay *ambali*-pot sitting on a bed of cooling neem leaves is marked with *pasupu-kumkum,* and the *ambali* transforms into the goddess herself. She is worshipped with incense; and before they themselves partake of the *ambali* mixture—which is both the goddess and her *prasad* (offerings to a deity, subsequently returned to worshippers)—one of the female householders takes a ladle or pitcher of the mixture to the front door, to distribute to any passerby. And, I was told, there always is someone (always a male), or two or three in a group, waiting. It is a moving sight to walk the small lanes of Tirupati on this day and see women distributing the goddess/*prasad* to the male passersby, who are said to come to these neighborhoods specifically to receive this blessing. Through this ritual, the women are actively multiplying and distributing the goddess, while at the same time feeding and satisfying her (and the *uru*) with a cooling mixture.

On the *jatara* Friday, midway between the two Tuesdays beginning and ending the *jatara,* women create Gangamma in their kitchens, in diminutive mounds of *pasupu.* Each mound/goddess is placed on a piece of new cloth, all atop a fresh green banana leaf, again marked with *pasupu-kumkum.* Large plates of cooked rice and vegetables are placed in front of her; and

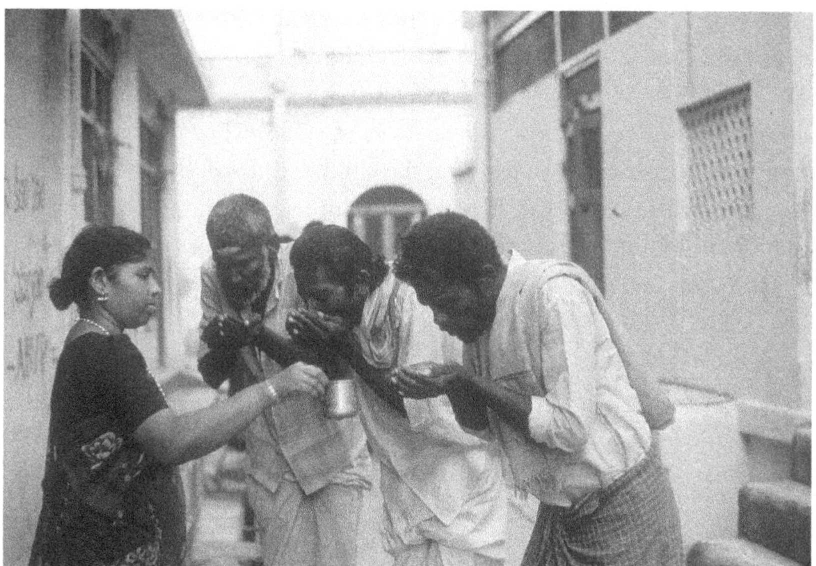

Passersby accepting *ambali* from householder.

the women of the home in which I observed this ritual went into the next room to give her privacy to eat. On this occasion, after photographing the goddess in her diminutive form, I had remained in the kitchen, leaning against the doorsill of the living room, where the rest of the women had moved; they called me to follow them and gently chastised me for (impolitely) continuing to watch the goddess when she was believed to be eating. The *pasupu* forms are then placed on the domestic *puja* shelf; they are now no longer the goddess, but rather her *prasad* that has been infused with her blessings. While on the streets the Kaikala *veshams* are growing in *ugram*, in the home Gangamma is created in a particularly intimate form.

Later this same Friday, mothers accompany their children to the temple, holding small clay pots over their heads as they walk. These pots, called "thousand-eyed pots" (*veyyi kalla duttalu*), have small holes in them and hold a camphor flame, small black bangles, and often a flower and coin. Remembering one name of the goddess to be "the thousand-eyed one," I asked the women with whom I was walking, holding such pots on the heads of their children, if these pots were the goddess. They paused before answering, "Yes, they could be," but they were more assured of the outcome of the ritual, which would protect their children from Gangamma illnesses. The belief that Gangamma is both the protectress from these illnesses and, if not satisfied, may become the illness itself, is embodied in this ritual: she is the protectress as she is held over the child's head walking to the temple. But, after circumambulating the temple, mothers smash the pots violently against the ground behind the temple, a performative destruction of Gangamma illnesses.

Returning to a *Jatara* Aesthetics of Excess

Gangamma *jatara's* aesthetics is a finely calibrated ritual response to and management of her *ugram.* The excess is created and visible on several levels: through multiplicity, distribution, and increased intensity. This fine balance of heating/intensifying/multiplying the goddess and then cooling/satisfying/feeding her creates the primary rhythms of the *jatara.*

The perambulating Kaikala *veshams* connect the multiple sites of the *jatara:* they are met by female householders at the doorways of their homes, walk the streets, and on the final morning of the *jatara,* the Perantalu meets the temple courtyard *ugra mukhis.* Here, the goddess herself breaks the cycle of building and satisfying her *ugram* when she tears out her own clay cheek, beginning the dissembling of the *ugra mukhis.* At this moment, the *ugra/shanta* cycles have reached the limit of their productivity: the illnesses have been defeated (in one ritual, literally smashed) and the rains are surely coming (if not this final morning, then in the coming days). The goddess returns to forms and sites of residence at which she can be more easily sustained on a day-to-day basis or (such as in fields at the edge of the *uru*) almost ignored, where her *ugram* is relatively dormant and her needs more easily managed.

Many *jatara* rituals are prescribed: certain things need to be done to cause certain results. However, in part because of the ritual nature of the *jatara* and the absence of an authoritative textual tradition, interpretation and experience of *jatara* narratives and rituals are not prescribed; and we have seen that this interpretation is often gendered. So, while it is important in the case of Gangamma *jatara* for the goddess's *ugram* to be stimulated, grown, and satisfied, there is no explicit goal to shape or control celebrants' interpretation and experience of that *ugram*. *Jatara* celebrants often gave varying explanations of rituals and narratives in front of someone who had just said something quite different; this multiplicity never seemed to disturb either party. This accepted multiplicity and fluidity of experience and interpretation—including differences based on age, gender, and caste—itself contributes to a *jatara* aesthetics of excess.

GUISING, TRANSFORMATION, RECOGNITION, AND POSSIBILITY

2

While *stri vesham* is the most notorious feature of Tirupati's Gangamma *jatara,* guising also appears in less dramatic forms, including turmeric (*pasupu*) application on the faces of the goddess herself and her female worshippers. When I attempted to confirm with a group of women in Tatayyagunta temple courtyard that women did not take *vesham,* one of them vehemently disagreed, saying, "But we do; we put on *pasupu,* don't we?" This comment led me to understand, analytically, the *pasupu* application on the goddess as *vesham*—that is, as a covering/guise/disguise of the body. In the analysis that follows, I have also included instances of the goddess coming to the human world in forms in which she is not recognized—a context in which the human body itself serves as *vesham,* "taken on" to serve as a disguise. Specialist and lay male *stri veshams,* female *pasupu vesham,* and Gangamma's human form and *pasupu*-covered dark stone heads create a repertoire of guising whose manifestations inform and frame each other; through this repertoire, we can begin to understand the potential creativity of *jatara veshams.*

The term *vesham* (guise) may refer to everyday clothing (any garment that covers the body) or special garments that disguise and/or transform the body (through which the person wearing the clothing takes on a different persona). Studies of guising, masquerade, and masking (see Handelman 1990, Napier 1986, Tseelon 2001) suggest that whatever differences there may be cross-culturally and historically, these acts are moments of reflexivity. They raise questions of the ultimate nature of reality, of identity, of the construction, deconstruction, and/or transformation of self, and of concealment and revelation. Analysis of the broad repertoire of *veshams* suggests guising in Gangamma contexts is primarily a process of recognition: recognition of the nature of the goddess, recognition of masculinity (in this left-hand cultural and ritual context) as including a measure of the female, recognition of women as sharing in the nature of the goddess, and in this *jatara* world, recognition of ultimate reality as female.

Guises of the Goddess: Human Body, *Pasupu*, and *Kavacam*

The guises of the goddess in both narrative and ritual span the widest variations of *vesham*, which inform those taken on by humans; and so we start with Gangamma. Several Gangamma narratives introduce the human body itself as a guise. A female *jatara* participant made this association explicit when she used the word *avatara* (incarnation) when describing *vesham*. Seeing my quizzical look, she explained, "You know, Gangamma takes *avatara* and humans take *vesham*." A favorite story among several of the women with whom I worked suggests that the goddess may take human-body guise in order to make herself accessible. It is said that a wedding party was traveling by foot between bride's and groom's homes when they came upon an old woman walking by herself at the side of the road. The women of the wedding party invited her to join them, saying it wasn't right for an old woman to be traveling by herself. After stopping to camp for the night, one of the younger women offered to groom the old woman by checking for and picking out the lice from her hair (a common everyday ritual during which women converse and relax between household tasks). When the younger woman began to part the elder's hair in sections, to find any hidden lice, she saw on the old woman's scalp the thousand eyes of the goddess, and only then recognized the old woman to be Gangamma.[1] The story suggests that Gangamma's *ugra* nature doesn't inherently prevent intimacy between the goddess and women—although it may be significant that this particular interaction with the goddess occurred outside the village, the kind of space where Gangamma and her sisters traditionally live, rather than in domestic space.

Hindu mythology is filled with stories of gods and goddesses who shape-shift—into human bodies, those of animals, or shapes of other deities—in order to disguise and ultimately reveal themselves. While the reasons for and creative possibilities of these *veshams* are context-specific, they all raise the question of the "realities" of what we see. Shiva, in particular, is known to take guises of human bodies to test the devotion of his devotees. One well-known narrative in South India recounts Shiva appearing as a mendicant to test the strength of his devotee's devotion by demanding the sacrifice of the devotee's own son; he does so by asking for, specifically, human-brain curry (Shulman 1993). An example of gender-shifting through *vesham* in Vaishnava mythology is the story of Vishnu taking on the (disguising) female form of Mohini in the story of the churning of the ocean, a competition between gods and demons to bring up the elixir of immortality (*amrita*) from the ocean. Shiva hears of Vishnu's ability to transform into a woman and asks to witness the transformation with his own eyes. Vishnu tries to dissuade Shiva from his request, knowing that he, too, will fall under Vishnu *maya* (illusion), which he does, falling in love with Mohini.[2]

Gangamma takes a human-body guise when she first enters the village of Avilala as a little girl; the human body disguises her identity as goddess, and she is indistinguishable from any other human little girl. One female narrator observes that "because that child stepped into his house, his [the Reddy ancestor's] household flourished." She isn't identified in this comment as a goddess, but as a girl child, who is a creator of wealth—much like other girls who may be welcomed into South Indian homes as potential wealth-bringers (associated with the goddess of wealth Lakshmi) and brides whose fertility will continue the patriline. The revelation that the girl raised by the Avilala Reddy family is actually the goddess occurs only during the wedding ritual between her and the Palegadu, when she "stretches from earth to sky." Understanding the human body of the goddess as *vesham* raises questions of all human bodies and the identities they carry and perform, both hidden and revealed.

After Gangamma reveals her *vishvarupam* to the Palegadu, she quickly takes on a series of disguising *veshams,* in order to hide/disguise herself from the Palegadu as she searches for him. But these *veshams* are revealing on another level: they are representative of the left-hand castes who are her primary *jatara* worshippers (snake charmer, herders, sweepers, merchants; the Dora prince could be either right- or left-hand caste). Gangamma is a goddess who moves among these castes, and these narrative *veshams* perform that close relationship.

A third site of the goddess's *veshams* is the application of *pasupu* to her dark stone temple/shrine image, which appears as a kind of mask, as it covers her entire face. Gangamma's weekly *abhishekam* (ceremonial anointing with a series of different liquids) on Friday mornings is a powerful ritual to witness, as the turmeric masking runs off and her dark, haunting dark face is revealed.[3] Only at this moment are the goddess's *ugra* fangs visible. The *pasupu vesham* keeps devotees from regularly coming face-to-face with her unguised self; it is as if this fanged form may be too much to bear on a daily basis—just as the Matangi *vishvarupa* form cannot be sustained by her worshippers for prolonged periods of time. *Pasupu* is also considered to be a cooling substance; and so one could also interpret its application that covers her fangs as modulating the goddess's *ugra* nature.

Venkateshvarlu—the Kaikala male who performs Tallapaka Gangamma's weekly *abhishekam,* carefully reapplies her turmeric mask, and dresses and adorns the goddess—gave another explanation, saying that the purpose of the *pasupu* was to make Gangamma *muttaiduva* (auspicious; a term usually applied to married women).[4] Venkateshvarlu's explanation suggests that Gangamma's *pasupu vesham* changes her very nature, not only hides it. However, the *pasupu* mask does not destroy Gangamma's *ugram* when her fangs are covered over with turmeric; they are still present and she is still *ugra.* But she is not only *ugra.*

When I ventured the interpretation of *pasupu* to be cooling, modulating Gangamma's *ugram,* with the flower sellers at Tatayyagunta temple, they disagreed. Rather, they explained, the *pasupu* enabled devotees to see Gangamma's features, so that she could be "known." Other female worshippers likened the *pasupu* to "make-up," which both beautifies and accentuates Gangamma's features. It is true that the features of the dark granite stone images of South India deities are difficult to see from a distance—but not all

Tallapaka Gangamma with *pasupu vesham.*

such dark images are so highlighted. It is only a certain class of *ugra* deities and their associates whose forms are regularly covered with turmeric: the Seven Sister *gramadevatas,* their brother Potu Raju, and anthills and snake stones associated with the Sisters (often found in vicinity of their shrines).[5]

One female temple employee at Tatayyagunta temple elaborated on the performative significance of *pasupu:*

Pasupu gives beauty and radiance [*kala;* brightness] to the face. Look at this stone. If you leave it just like this, it won't look good. Only when we do *alankara* [decoration, ornamentation] does she look like a *muttaiduva.* Married women also wear *pasupu-kumkum* [like the goddess].

The attendant suggests, like Venkateshvara above, that *pasupu* not only makes a goddess beautiful and brings out her *kala,* but also makes her look like a married woman. Interestingly, the attendant then caught herself, after identifying Gangamma as a married woman, saying, "No, no. She's not married." This self-correction suggests that while the dominant characterization of *muttaiduva* is married woman, Gangamma unsettles this usage. Gangamma's *pasupu* masking both reveals and covers; she is simultaneously *muttaiduva* and *ugra,* auspicious and excessive.

Metallic *kavacams* (lit., protective body coverings; armor) are another, more recent form (limited to Gangamma's two largest Tirupati temples) of masking/concealment of the goddess's stone face and fangs. Gangamma's *kavacam* includes a metallic face, hands, and feet that are laid over the stone head that is her original form—in essence, giving her a body. The Mudaliar family that was instrumental in transforming Gangamma's small shrine into a permanent temple made Tatayyagunta Gangamma her first *kavacam;* since then, several other *kavacams* have been gifted by particular wealthy devotees. Much like the *pasupu* masking, the *kavacam* reveals the goddess's features and is said to beautify her.

Potu Raju, Gangamma's brother, traditionally stands outside of his sisters' shrines, much like the *vahanas* (lit., vehicles) of *puranic* deities, such as Garuda for forms of Vishnu and Nandi for Shiva. Here, Potu Raju is covered with solidly applied *pasupu* over which are daubed *kumkum* dots; this *pasupu vesham* performatively feminizes him, identifying him with his similarly adorned, *vesham*-ed sisters, and is likewise transformative and revelatory. He is still called by the male name Potu Raju, but arguably his *pasupu vesham* reveals a different kind of masculinity, one that includes a female quality (an issue to which we will return).

Male Transformative Guising

Like the *veshams* of the goddess that hide, reveal, transform, and identify, male *stri veshams,* too, both disguise and reveal alternative possibilities of identity—in this case, like that of Potu Raju, alternative masculinities. Males taking *stri vesham* is common in many Indian contexts: male actors/dancers take female parts through *vesham* in village dramas and dance genres such as Kuchipudi, in which women did not traditionally perform; baby boys are often dressed in girl-clothing in order to defect the evil eye from the preferred male child or simply for mothers' enjoyment of "beautifying" (as several mothers have told me) their baby or toddler sons. In numerous contexts, as when male priests become the goddess Bhagavati during her annual festival in Kerala (Caldwell 2000), male ritual specialists take *stri vesham* to become the goddess through possession. Because of its prevalence, the occurrence of *stri vesham* in Indian performance and ritual contexts is often not particularly noteworthy for Indian audiences and is, arguably, less "disruptive" to normative gender roles than, for example, drag impersonation is in American contexts (Butler 1999).[6]

Kaikala Gangamma *veshams.* Less significance in public discourse and the media is given to the Kaikala *veshams* that transform men into the goddess—perhaps because of the frequency of this phenomenon in other ritual contexts—than to the lay male *stri veshams.* Venkateshvarlu called the Kaikala *veshams* Gangamma's "festival forms" (*utsava murtis*), similar to the small brass forms of deities taken out in temple festival processions. That is, the Kaikala Gangamma *veshams* make the goddess present and accessible outside of her shrines and temples.

Interestingly, the Kaikala males do not become Gangamma through possession; rather, they do so quite simply through the physical guising itself—taking on the clothing and jewelry of the goddess. At certain key moments the Matangi and Perantalu, who through *vesham* are already the goddess, do become possessed by Gangamma, creating an intensity (doubling) of her presence. Significantly, the transformed Kaikala males are not imitatively female, but ritually so; that is, their gait and gestures remain "male" as they stride purposefully down Tirupati's gullies and periodically sit on folding chairs (brought out for them by householders) with their legs spread wide apart in a posture that is not traditional for females. The Kaikala *veshams* are excessive, and no one would mistake their bodies that carry the *veshams* as female; nonetheless, the *veshams* are accepted as the goddess by those who come to greet her at their doorways. This relatively simple means of gender transformation through *vesham*—but not body language—is in contrast to the transformation of male Kuchipudi classical dancers into the female characters they dance, for which they carefully learn female facial expressions, ways of walking and gesturing, and voice modulation (see Kamath 2012). The distinction between becoming and imitating is also relevant in thinking about the differences between Sanskrit *rasa* aesthetics and *jatara* aesthetics; in Sanskrit drama, the term *anukarana* (imitation) implies a level of distinction between character and actor, a distinction not present in the Kaikala *veshams.*[7]

Venkateshvarlu told us that when he takes the *vesham* of the Dora who beheads the Palegadu, as soon as he holds the sword and puts on the crown, "full *ugram* comes to me. While roaming the streets, I feel like Ammavaru [the goddess] going to war." To be filled with or to experience the *ugram* is not the same as possession; the *veshams* are aware of their surroundings, periodically engaging in "normal" conversation with those around them, and drinking cooling beverages in their stops at domestic doorways. To sustain possession for the long hours during which the *veshams* make their perambulations would, in any case, be difficult, if not impossible.

While on the surface the *veshams* are the goddess, performatively they are also men who have become the goddess. When I tried to elicit from *jatara* participants what this experience might mean—what does it mean for a woman to worship her husband as the goddess or for a toddler to sit on the lap of her father/the goddess—they answered only that "s/he is the goddess." Nevertheless, surely the experience is interiorized by Kaikala wives and daughters at some nonverbal, bodily, sensory level and leaves traces in everyday life of the fluidity of body, gender, and identity.

That the Kaikala *veshams* literally transform the male into the goddess—and this is readily accepted by Tirupati residents—suggests the transformative power of *vesham* in other contexts, such as the lay *veshams* discussed below, where such transformation is less complete. That is, while the Kaikala males in *stri vesham* are identified as the goddess, lay men in *stri vesham* are not identified (or mistaken) as women;[8] rather they would seem to become a different kind of male.

Lay *veshams*. Non-specialist males traditionally take *stri vesham* to fulfill a vow (*mokku*) they—or their mothers on their behalf—have made to the goddess. A mother may make such a vow if her young son has experienced a Gangamma illness—that if he recovers, he will take female *vesham;* a son may make his own vow as he grows older, such as vowing that if he gets into a particular educational institution or receives particular employment, he will take *stri vesham* during the *jatara.* Many men take *stri vesham* only once in their lifetimes; however, some men continue the practice year after year, long after the vow has been fulfilled; and I met several such elderly *stri veshams* at Tatayyagunta temple. On the last days of the *jatara,* Tirupati streets become filled with *stri veshams;* and their visual effect helps to create a temporally bounded *jatara* world become female. Some men are dressed in everyday cotton saris; others are draped in silk or synthetic saris. In earlier days, sari-ed men of left-hand castes may have worn their saris up over their right shoulders, as women of these castes used to do; however, I photographed only one man wearing his sari in this fashion, standing with his elderly mother whose own sari-end is draped over her right shoulder. Most men wore their silk or synthetic saris in what has become the "standard" style, draped over their left shoulders. Part of the ritual fulfillment of this *mokku* is display—not only to put on a sari, but to be seen in *stri vesham,* both by the goddess and, perhaps just as importantly, by other *jatara* participants (which makes it easy and acceptable for journalists and the anthropologist to photograph these *veshams*).

Some men in *stri vesham* come to Gangamma's temples in boisterous groups, for whose members *vesham* seems to take on the role of masquerade and parody (Butler 1999, 188–189), rather than the ritual fulfillment of vows—that is, they seem to be self-consciously and with great fun breaking gendered roles and identities. One year I met two Muslim men in *vesham,* one in a dark green, orange-bordered silk sari and the other in a bright aqua *salwar-chemise* (loose tunic and pants worn by women), riding motorcycles

Lay *stri vesham* with mother.

and stuck in traffic. When I asked whether their mothers had taken *mokku* on their behalf, they laughed and said no, they were Muslims; they were taking *vesham* "for *fun* only."[9] Other sari-ed men seem to use the guise as an excuse for particularly boisterous (and culturally male) behavior, often enhanced by alcohol; their numbers increase by the last day of the *jatara,* when most men who are fulfilling vows have already visited the temple. Many of my middle-class female friends were not willing to go with me to the early morning dismantling of the *ugra mukhis,* saying they were uncomfortable in the mostly male crowds and in the likely encounters with the increasingly aggressive groups of sari-ed men. This parodic performance of *stri vesham* tends to be the dominant representation of the *jatara* in the press, whose members write from urban, middle-class, and dominant-caste perspectives on gender and ritual and who decontextualize the practice from *jatara* narrative and ritual repertoires.

I asked several participants why it is that, for this particular *jatara,* men take vows of *stri vesham,* rather than other kinds of vows. Why, I wondered, does seeing herself replicated through the Kaikala *veshams,* and seeing a feminized space created through lay *stri veshams,* make the goddess content (*santosha*)? One sari-ed man speculated, rather simply, that during the *jatara,* when the goddess is most *ugra,* "We should not appear before her as men." On another occasion, a male who regularly takes *stri vesham* responded, "After all, she's just beheaded a man. But, she's more approachable than other gods and takes care of those who worship her."

Both narratively and ritually (while not always "in fact," on the ground), aggressive masculinity is transformed through the narrative destruction of the Palegadu and the ritual proliferation of *stri veshams* in the *uru* of Tirupati. Within the ritually bound time and space of the *jatara,* masculinity is transformed through a performative identification with the female, much as the "king of male-ness," Potu Raju, is transformed with *pasupu.*

What is male experience of this transformation? The few men I spoke with about their *vesham* experience were (from my perspective) surprisingly unreflective/reflexive about it—perhaps, in part, because I didn't ask the right question, or because of my own gender and/or American identity; but perhaps also because *stri vesham* is an embodied experience about which they have had no need to be verbally articulate. During the *jatara* I interacted primarily with the Kaikala family, temple attendants, and lay women, not these guised men who were subsequently difficult to identify after the *jatara.* In conversations with several acquaintances outside the *jatara,* they remembered taking *vesham* as young boys and pulled out photographs of themselves in *stri vesham* during earlier *jataras;* but they only commented that they had taken *vesham* to fulfill a vow and did not articulate their experience of it.

In 2005, I unexpectedly heard a direct and insightful comment about male experience of *stri vesham.* My fieldwork associate and I had stopped at Hathi Ramji Matham (site of the North Indian religious order of Hathi Ramji, which had earlier administered the Venkateshvara temple uphill) to ask why the Matham was one of the three sites where, during her perambulations, the Matangi's tongue was pierced with a tiny silver trident. Having been directed by a sadhu sitting on the verandah into a large office, at the first desk we were warmly greeted by a Brahman man whom we came to know as Srinivasan, a "superintendent" at the Matham who works with legal affairs and land registration. He answered our questions about the tongue-piercing rather cryptically, and then surprised us by saying (speaking in English): "Madam, you would be interested to know that I've taken *vesham* every year for thirty-five years." For several years prior I had been saying, in talks I had given on Gangamma *jatara,* that Brahmans do not participate except indirectly (perhaps sending *pongal* or *bali* to the goddess through the hands of a non-Brahman servant). But now, here was a Brahman who had participated in the *jatara* by taking *stri vesham* for thirty-five years; and he spoke of this ritual as something quite ordinary, not exceptional for him as a Brahman.

Srinivasan explained that he had been sickly as a child and that his mother had made a *mokku* to Gangamma that if he regained full strength and health, he would take *stri vesham.* At the urging of his grandmother, however, he said he had kept up the tradition for many years following fulfillment of the initial *mokku.* His grandmother had told him (again, reported in English), "Taking *vesham,* just once a year, you can get a corner on women's *shakti.*" The use of the term "corner" is ambiguous, but suggests that *stri vesham* gives men "just a bit" of the experience of being female and/or access to female *shakti.* Or, if we accept that guising not only disguises and creates, but also reveals, then one may speculate that *stri vesham* reveals the full potentiality of the male, which includes a feminine "corner."

Srinivasan.

When I went to Srinivasan's for dinner one night after our initial conversation, he showed me a family photo album that held several professionally taken photographs of himself in *stri vesham.* He explained that he had first taken *stri vesham* at about the age of eight; he first wore "half-saris" (a style worn by young girls—three, instead of six, yards, wrapped around the upper body over a long skirt); as he grew up, the *vesham* changed into a full sari. His mother and, after marriage, his wife had dressed him, carefully choosing his sari, ornaments, and sometimes a fashionable purse. He reported that when he was young, he used to go around in *stri vesham* with his friends: "We would dance. If I didn't dance, they would pinch me. Of course, it's not necessary to dance, but that was for fun only." Srinivasan's two adult sons, who have never taken *stri vesham,* looked on in some amusement.

Srinivasan as a young man in *stri vesham*.

Representing another educational and class level, a tea-stall owner, Venkat (pseudonym), answered my question about whether he had ever taken *vesham* by proudly pulling out from under the counter a photograph, preserved in a dusty plastic sleeve. In the photograph, the tea-stall owner is dressed in an aqua, maroon-bordered silk sari, posing with two male friends (one also in *stri vesham,* likely his brother, as the two *veshams* bear family resemblance, and the other in everyday male clothing). At the time, Venkat added little verbal commentary to that one-time photographed experience except to say he had taken this *vesham* many years ago, in fulfillment of a vow; however, his smile suggested a memory of pleasure and some pride. And it is significant that he kept the photographs of his *stri vesham* close at hand.

Only upon beginning to write this chapter did I realize that I had not asked Venkat his caste. I asked a colleague, V. Gangadhar from the anthropology department at Sri Venkatesvara University in Tirupati, if he would be willing to go back to the tea stall and ask Venkat a little more about his background and his caste.[10] He successfully found the tea stall and heard the following short account of this man's experience of *stri vesham.* Venkat is a thirty-six-year-old Mudaliar-caste migrant from Tamil Nadu. When he was about twelve years old, his father, who was a rice merchant, suffered a devastating loss in his business and migrated to Tirupati in search of a better livelihood. Venkat reported that he had taken *stri vesham* four times and planned on doing so again for the 2011 *jatara.* The first time, in 1998 (he would have been about twenty-three years old), he took *vesham* for *fun,* to join friends who were doing the same. Later, however, when he was experiencing some ill health and difficulties in his business, he decided to take the vow to Gangamma of *stri vesham;* he attributed his return to health and a better economic situation to the resulting intervention of the goddess.

Significantly, to a male interlocutor, Venkat was more forthcoming about his experience of *stri vesham* than he had been with my female fieldwork associate and me several years earlier. Venkat told Gangadhar that when he took on *stri vesham,* he not only wore female garments and jewelry, but tried to enact "the gaze [*kanti cupu*] and seductive gait of a woman." Notably, Venkat tries to approximate a flirtatious woman. He described his male friends' reactions to this *stri vesham:* they "pulled my hand, kissed me, embraced me, fondled my [artificial] breasts, and pinched my buttocks." Finally, Venkat offered the opinion that his wife also "liked" him in *stri vesham;* it's unclear whether she appreciated that he had taken and received the benefits of the vow, or whether she was attracted by the *stri vesham* itself. Venkat's short narrative gives a glimpse into possibilities of male experience of *stri vesham* that include emotional and erotic valences; and that this experience is shared by male friends interacting with Venkat's *vesham.* They took liberties with his *stri vesham* that they would not have likely felt free to do in public with a "real" woman. Venkat started taking *stri vesham* as a kind of masquerade; however, when he was in need, he decided to take the serious vow of *stri vesham* to the goddess. As reported by Gangadhar, Venkat's current narrative seems to embrace both motivations for *vesham*. He has realized the power of the goddess; at the same time, in *stri vesham*, he enjoys a certain freedom and abandonment of traditional, gendered mores of interactions between men and women in public contexts.

Photography and *Vesham*

While male performance of *stri vesham* is only temporary and periodic, its experience (or memory of that experience) is made tangible and continuously accessible through the performance of photography. *Stri veshams* are not iterative performances on the male body that "naturalize" and stabilize gender in a particular way (Butler 1999); but their preservation through photography keeps open the possibilities of transformed gender identities. Many sari-ed men go to photography studios and formally pose (sometimes with a male friend or family member) for a portrait, flowers in their hair and decorated with costume jewelry similar to that worn by classical dancers.[11] These professional photographs depict the *veshams* outside of *jatara*, family, home, or occupational contexts, obscuring distinctions of class and caste. In the studio, the sari-ed men, often holding "modern" purses, stand in front of generic plain or nature-scene backdrops that give few clues of the contexts in which they live their everyday lives.

Christopher Pinney, in *The Coming of Photography in India* (2008), argues that photography is more than simply an index (a "transfer of the real"). Rather, it is an agent that creates, that suggests possibility and impossibility, and that may have "unpredictable consequences" (5). Pinney suggests that, "Photographs become 'image acts' which like J. L. Austin's 'speech acts' are 'performatives': in the act of enunciation they do not simply describe the world: they change it" (145). In the context of *jatara stri vesham* photography, I am particularly interested in Pinney's characterization of the potential of photography to "disturb" and to prophesy (Pinney, chapter 3). That is, in photography,

> . . . faces and subjects that began to adhere to them could be of different kinds: the already achieved and the aspirant. The photograph as index, or chemical trace, and non-discriminating data ratio, was unable to differentiate between existing and subjunctive identities: it merely recorded whatever was placed in front of the camera. (137–138)

Professional photographs of *stri veshams* record in a single image female and middle-class identities—both realized and subjunctive, achieved and aspired to.

The *veshams* that lay men wear in these photographs include silk or polyester saris; their jewelry is pearled or gold-plated (costume jewelry), rather than the silver jewelry typical of lower classes; and in particular the "pocketbook," so frequently present in these portraits, is also a performance of middle-class identity. (It is unlikely that the elder male I photographed dressed in an everyday cotton sari and blouse, with ash smeared on his face and without the adornment of costume jewelry, would choose to pose for a professional photographer.) Looking at our two examples above, both Srinivasan and Venkat borrowed saris from females in their own families, who are likely to wear silk saris to weddings and certain festival celebrations. However, what the silk sari signifies for each family is quite different. Taking into account the backgrounds of the men who took these *stri veshams,* Srinivasan's portrait records an achieved middle-class identity, whereas that of Venkat records middle-class aspiration.

The *stri veshams* externalized in professional photographs similarly create both an actualized and a subjunctive gender identity, a temporary female guise made "permanent" in the photograph. But *stri vesham* is not wholly imitative and the male body is never totally disguised, as it interrupts the female *vesham* through facial features and body stance. Remember Srinivasan's grandmother's injunction that he should experience only a "corner"—not the full measure of—female *shakti.* In contrast to the Kaikala goddess *veshams,* who are experienced by her worshippers as the goddess, lay *stri veshams* do not create fully actualized females. They are seen and experienced, both during their perambulations on Tirupati's streets and in photographs, as *veshams,* not women. But a subjunctive potential is created; while visually this potential may be to become female, imaginatively it may be the potential to become more fully male, or a different kind of male, by accepting as part of his identity a female "corner."

Female Guises and Recognition

Now to return to what women, who already wear sari *vesham* every day, identified as their own ritual *vesham: pasupu.* On Tuesdays and Fridays,

days special to the goddess, many women come to the temple with marks of *pasupu* on their faces, generally a wide swath on each cheek and on their chins; fewer women apply a thin layer of *pasupu* paste all over their faces, similar to the goddess's *pasupu* mask. While the goddess's *pasupu* both hides her fangs and reveals her features, women's *pasupu* application more simply reveals their identification with the goddess and her *shakti.* A female temple attendant explained, "We [women] are equal to Ammavaru [the goddess]; we are equal to Shakti, so we can put it [*pasupu* or sandalpaste[12]] on our faces. We do this to make her *shanta.*" The attendant suggests that it makes the goddess happy/content to see a reflection of her own *shakti* identified in women through their *pasupu* markings—just as it makes her happy to see men-become-female in *stri vesham.* Women are not transformed through their application of *pasupu;* rather, their true nature—the quality of *shakti* that they share with the goddess—is externalized and recognized.

Identification between the goddess and women through *pasupu* is also explicitly performed on several ritual occasions outside the *jatara,* including Varalakshmi Puja. Ritual participants of this all-female vow-ritual tell the story of the benefits that accrue from worship of Lakshmi (goddess of prosperity and auspiciousness), and invite other auspicious married women (*perantalus*) to their homes to bestow blessings of long life, happiness, and health. The visiting women in the *perantam* ritual are recognized and honored as the goddess when the hostess applies turmeric to their feet and turmeric lines on their faces. The householder then gifts her visitors *tambulam,* an offering of "women's things" including betel leaves, *pasupu-kumkum* powder, flowers, and fruit (the more elaborate *tambulam* may include a sari blouse piece and sari, comb, mirror, and bangles). These are the same auspicious female offerings a worshipper can buy outside of many large goddess temples; the comb, mirror, and bangles (packaged together in a cellophane bag) have recently become available at the flower sellers stalls outside of Tatayyagunta temple.

A smaller number of women take the *pasupu vesham* (in various degrees) daily (rather than just Tuesdays and Fridays), along with pronounced, large *bottus* (vermilion forehead markings) and sometimes matted hair. This "excessive" *vesham,* in relationship to the smaller *bottus* and restrained, oiled hair most women wear every day, identifies a greater than "normal" religiosity and service to the goddess. This group of women includes women who ritually exchange *talis* with the goddess, locally known as *matammas.*

Initially, I did not recognize an elderly Tirupati woman, Pujaramma, as a widow because she still wore her *tali* and a large red *bottu* on her forehead, signs I had previously associated exclusively with married women. She told me she had not taken off the *bottu* and *tali* when she became a widow, because the goddess herself, not her husband, had given them to her (see chapter 9 for further details). She also had matted hair that she said she had tried to cut off numerous times because of the problems it caused her by "hiding" lice; but every time she cut off her matted locks, they grew back. Gangamma appeared to her in a dream and asked why she kept trying to cut off the sign of her presence.[13]

Pujaramma specifically identified her matted hair as a kind of *vesham,* a guise that indicates the presence of the goddess on the human female body. She described the shapes in which her matted hair grew back after she shaved it:

> I've shaved my head eight times. It takes the [matted] shape of a three-headed serpent's hood or a Shiva *linga* [a representation of Shiva]. . . .
>
> [Later in the conversation, when describing a dream in which the goddess appeared to her] It's been four months since I had this dream. That night, in my dream, there was a tree this tall [indicates with her hand]. There was a flowering bitter-gourd vine climbing over it. I said, "It's nice to look at the flowers blooming." I was looking at it when she [Amma, the goddess] jumped down from the sky. So my hair took the form of a snake's hood, and all this [the rest of the hair] is smooth. I asked, "Why is it like this? What kind of braid is this?" She said, "This is Venkateshvara's *jada* [lock of hair; braid; matted hair]." She said this and disappeared. As soon as she said this, the bitter gourd vine wound around the tree. The next morning, I found a *jada* climbing over my head.

Pujaramma identifies her matted locks as having taken the shapes of a Shiva *linga,* a three-headed snake's hood, and the god Venkateshvara's *jada;* in a play and disruption of gender, at least two of these shapes are signs of male gods that indicate the presence of the goddess on a female body.[14] Like other *veshams* of the goddess discussed above, her appearance in these shapes of matted hair was generated to make herself known. But they also identify Pujaramma's special relationship with the goddess, by marking her body.

Pujaramma's experience of the goddess through matted locks is similar on several levels to personal narratives of female "ecstatics" in Gananath Obeyesekere's analyses of Sinhalese women's matted hair (1981): the spontaneous appearance of matted locks, the initial resistance against them, their identification with the deity (one woman says she treats her locks as Shiva himself), and the commonly identified form they take, snakes or the hoods of snakes. Several of the women Obeyesekere spoke with directly associated the appearance of the matted locks with their renunciation of sex. One woman describes the god Huniyan telling her that he will give her the locks if she renounces sex and obtains permission to do so from her husband. Obeyesekere's offers this psychoanalytic interpretation: "The god's [they are all male deities] gift for having renounced eros for agape is matted hair. Psychologically . . . the sublated penis emerges through the head " (1981:26). This reading resonates, at least on some level, with the personal narratives he is analyzing. However, the case of Pujaramma's matted locks is indigenously understood quite differently: the commonly understood male forms (Shiva's *linga* and Venkateshvara's *jada*) are invigorated by, and are signs of, the goddess.[15]

Female *veshams* and rituals suggest that women are not transformed into a different identity by the simple turmeric application (and/or matted hair), but rather that they are recognized for what/who they already are—sharing in the nature of the goddess, an identity marked performatively through the shared substance of *pasupu.* In the same way *pasupu* lets us "see" the goddess and her features, its marking on female ritual participants reminds both them and those who see them of who they are, women who share the *shakti* of the goddess.

Jatara veshams perform gendered identities and possibilities that are not as easily or openly recognized outside of the *jatara* context. These possibilities include recognition of an imaginative reality in which women are the unmarked, encompassing category in a world that at its core is female, and men (or aggressive masculinity) are transformed in order to have access to and a place in that world. While *stri vesham* may question what/who is "real," as does all guising, it does not explicitly question the normative duality of gender itself. That is, indigenously understood, while *vesham* may raise questions of the nature of masculinity, it does not question its very existence on some existential level—in contrast to Judith Butler's assertion about the performance of drag that "implicitly reveals the imitative structure of gender itself—as well as its contingency" (1999, 187). *Veshams* have the potential to change the male actor who ritually takes *stri vesham*—not by questioning his gender or fully transforming him into a female—but by transforming the kind of masculinity he performs, one that embraces at least a "corner" of female *shakti.*

NARRATIVES OF EXCESS AND ACCESS

3

Gangamma's narrative repertoire opens up alternative and expanded perspectives on the nature of Gangamma—her excess and access—to those that *jatara* rituals perform. More specifically, the primary narratives of the goddess are a site of debate about gender roles and the nature of the female. Key to this debate is the nature of and relationship between *ugram* and *shakti:* is female *shakti* inherently *ugra*—that is, too much to bear? Taken together, the ritual and narrative repertoires create a cultural imaginaire of gender possibilities that reflect a left-hand caste ethos and provide indigenous commentary on the nature of the goddess, rationales for *jatara* rituals, and its celebrants' gendered experiences of Gangamma.

The two primary stories of Gangamma's narrative repertoire performed during the *jatara* are the localized story of the Gangamma and the Palegadu who tries to marry her or makes sexual demands of her, and the myth of Adi Para Shakti, the primordial goddess who creates the three gods Brahma, Vishnu, and Shiva, hoping for a male to satisfy her desire. I also heard several other Gangamma narrative fragments outside of the *jatara* ritual context as commentary on the nature of the goddess or the *jatara* itself. These include the story of the Asadi (sub-caste of Madigas who are ritual specialists) cart driver who must sacrifice his wife, upon the demand of his passenger Gangamma, in order to get her mud-stuck cart moving again. Women, in particular, often recount the story of the two Gangamma sisters' tension over Pedda Gangamma's children and Cinna Gangamma's lack thereof, which results in the elder hiding her children under a basket, and the younger turning them into rocks.

Other narratives widespread in South India, but not specific to the *jatara,* also adhere to the Gangamma repertoire. These include the narrative of the beheading of Jamadagmi Rishi's wife Renuka (at the hand of her son) when her husband suspected her chastity; when the son attempts to rejoin Renuka's head to her body, her Brahman head is mistakenly mixed up with that of an untouchable. The woman with the Brahman head and untouchable body becomes Mariamma, and the untouchable head and Brahman body becomes Yellamma (Whitehead 1988:116–117), both of whom become one of the Seven Sister *gramadevatas.* Since the sisters are often conflated as "one," the story of these goddesses becomes the story of Gangamma, too. However, the Renuka narrative is an interesting reversal of the local Palegadu story, in which the male rather than the female is beheaded. And in the Renuka story, the beheading is seemingly unjust, and her humiliation at the hands of her husband results in her becoming a goddess; whereas in the second, the Palegadu is justly beheaded when his aggression toward the young women threatens the *uru.* The two narratives also present different views of female sexuality, representing differences in right- and left-hand caste gender ideologies: Renuka's sexuality is subject to her husband's protection/evaluation, whereas Gangamma takes control of her own sexuality (as will become evident in analyses of several variants of this story that follow later in the chapter).

Another story that often adheres to a Gangamma repertoire is of the Brahman woman who inadvertently marries an untouchable, who has taken the disguise of a Brahman. Only when his children see him stitching leather (or, in another variant, when his visiting mother recognizes the smell of cooked meat) is his untouchable identity revealed to his wife. In her righteous anger, she transforms into one of the Seven Sisters and curses her husband to be born as a buffalo that will be offered to her during her *jatara;* her children become the sacrificial chickens and goats. While there is certainly a gendered component to this story, its conclusions would seem to emphasize tensions in caste hierarchies. In contrast, the two primary stories associated with Gangamma *jatara* primarily revolve around and debate gender.

The story of Gangamma and the Palegadu is ritually enacted, but not verbally performed during the *jatara* itself; in contrast, the narrative of Adi Para Shakti is sung by professional performers in Veshalamma's temple courtyard with the goddess as its primary audience. Most *jatara* participants know some variation or segments of the Palegadu story, which is visually present to them through the Kaikala *veshams* who come to their doorways; whereas fewer Tirupati and Avilala residents talk about or seem to know the Adi Para Shakti story. These two stories stand on far ends of a continuum of narrative genres: the first is a uniquely local story that begins with Gangamma as a little baby found in a local cowshed or paddy field in the identifiable village of Avilala and ends with revelation of her true self as a goddess; the second is a cosmological myth that begins with the primordial goddess Adi Para Shakti as the creator of the universe and ends with her fragmentation into thousands of village goddesses (*gramadevatas*), including those residing in Tirupati.

In *Myth as Argument,* Laurie Patton argues for a view of myth as a "sedimentation of debate" that works as "a cultural product that provokes people into an argument or a contentious discourse which then forces people to create alternative versions of the myth" (1996:42–43). The coexistence of these narratives within a Gangamma repertoire suggests such an internal debate about gender, articulated and interpreted variously by male and female narrators in alternative versions. They answer questions about the nature of the female and her *ugram/shakti* and of gender relations quite differently; taken together, performances of these narratives leave the debate unresolved, which means they also leave open possibility.

Gangamma and the Palegadu: Female *Ugram* as Protective Resource

Subbarama Reddy, the chief organizer of the *jatara* as celebrated in the village of Avilala since 1992,[1] has vested interest in the Gangamma–Palegadu story—Gangamma is the daughter of his very family. The following is a translation of one narrative variant of the story he performed many times, with slight variation, over the years:

There were two Reddys—the elder brother, Pedda Reddy, and younger brother, Cinna Reddy. Pedda Reddy had no children.[2] One day, at three in the morning, he came out of his house into the courtyard to milk the cows. She [Gangamma] was lying there in the form of an infant. They heard a baby crying. These days we have electricity; in those days there was no electricity, so they took a lamp. Pedda Reddy came toward this baby and behind him came his wife. They took the baby, went inside, and raised her.

At that time, it was under British rule and the Nawabs were there.[3] These Nawabs, once in a year, once in six months, once in three months, used to come to collect tax revenue from the villagers. There was a very big stone there[4] and the Nawab was sitting on that stone collecting the taxes. It was a Tuesday or Wednesday.

She [Gangamma][5] had washed her hair and was drying it on the rooftop terrace. The Nawab saw the *ammavaru* [goddess] and asked who she was. The Reddy said, "She's my daughter." The Nawab asked, "Would you give your daughter in marriage to me?" and the Reddy said yes.

The Reddy returned home, covered his body with a blanket, and lay on the bed [sick with worry]. She came down from the terrace and, seeing her father, wondered why he was like that. She asked, and he said, "I gave my word to the Nawab to give you in marriage to him. Because of the circumstances [of social hierarchy], I couldn't save myself; I had to give my word." She told him not to worry even if he had given his word, saying, "I'm here to save you. Start the preparations for the wedding." According to her orders, they took all the things needed for a bride and put them in some ox carts, and the carts reached the place where we're going to exchange these things tonight [with the Kaikalas; the ritual exchange initiates movement of the *jatara* from Avilala to Tirupati].

From that side, elephants, horses, camels, were coming with the bridegroom. The Nawab looked at Amma, and saw her stretching from earth to the sky [showing her true form as the goddess].[6] Then he told them, "*She's* not the bride; let me go." They tried to prevent him from fleeing, and he jumped off [the wedding platform]. Seeing him jumping off, she, too, jumped off, and she chased and chased and chased him. She reached

Karnala Street in Tirupati, where the headman lives and where the Kaikala house is. There was a jasmine garden there in which there were three Kaikala houses. There was an old woman outside, and he ran into her hut and hid there. Gangamma ran to the house, ran around the house, but she couldn't find him. She thought, "If I'm in this form [*rupam*], I won't catch him"; so, every week she took a different *vesham*. The last week she took the *veshams* of Sunnapukundalu and Perantalu [the last two of the Kaikala *jatara* sequence of *vesham*]. She went door to door and searched for him.[7]

Where Tatayyagunta temple is now, there was a garden of Nagarazu [lit., king of snakes]; it was a mango garden. The Nawab was running in that garden, and she saw him and chased him. She caught his hair, held him under her feet, and she cut him in half. AHHHHHHH!!! [the narrator's body stiffens and he sticks his arm out straight as if possessed by the goddess; his wife sprinkles water on him to keep him from becoming fully possessed].[8] She then showed her *vishvarupam*. Vivekananda Swami[9] addressed her, "Oh mad [*picci*] woman, if you're in this *rupam*, no one will look at you. Just looking at you, they'll be afraid." She asked him what she should do, then. He told her to divide her whole form into different forms: Veshalamma, Ankalamma, Tatayyagunta Gangamma, Pedda Gangamma, Mulasthanam Elamma, Vankayala Gangamma, and the other Ammas. After changing into nine forms, she almost disappeared into the earth [i.e., became small]. And that's her story [*caritra*].

Gangamma and her sisters (the traditional number is seven, although Subbarama narrates that there are nine) are found in one form or another in every village of Chittoor District; most live on the outskirts of villages and demand ritual only once a year during their own *jataras* or in times of famine and disease crises. Very few of these *gramadevata* goddesses, however, come with unique, localized biographies (*caritras*) as fully elaborate as such as the one above.[10] Tirupati Gangamma thus stands apart from her (relatively) un-storied local sisters. It's difficult to know whether her *caritra* has been elaborated because of her uniquely strong *shakti*, or if her *shakti* is perceived to be stronger than that of her sisters because of its elaboration in her story.

This Palegadu narrative is uniquely local—it identifies Gangamma as a daughter of *this place*, the village/*uru* of Avilala, brought up by ancestors of *this* very narrator. A small group of Avilala women co-performing another variant of the story began with the assertion,

> She came here just as you have come here. Those were the days of our elders. They were going in a cart somewhere. While he was returning, this little girl, she's this little, followed him, crying. You know this really happened in this village. . . . my mother was born then. My grandmother. It happened then; I heard my grandmother talking about this. We heard this when my mother and grandmother were talking each other.

Gangamma is a daughter of one village and, through the ritual exchange of wedding gifts, "marries" into the *uru* of Tirupati.

Interestingly, however, while the Kaikalas are, in this ritual exchange, the "groom's family," they themselves talk about Gangamma as a daughter, not daughter-in-law, of their family; and they have their own story about how a young Gangamma was brought to their home and became a daughter. When I asked a group of men in Avilala who Gangamma's in-laws were, if Avilala was her mother's place, they emphatically answered, "She has no in-laws . . . no man can tie her [tie a *tali*, wedding pendant, around her] and keep her [in one place]. . . . not even the three gods, Shiva, Brahma, Vishnu have the strength to bear her," referring to the story of Adi Para Shakti. Ritually, the *jatara* begins with an exchange of wedding gifts, but in both ritual and narrative, the wedding ritual is not completed. The Palegadu is beheaded; there is no husband. In the context of this narrative, Gangamma is a *daughter*, in an intimate relationship with the families who have the *mirasi* to serve her during the *jatara*, not a daughter-in-law who comes from an "outside" family.[11]

When the Palegadu runs to hide from Gangamma, he runs first through an identifiable local landscape, down the still-existent Tirupati Karnala Street, where the Kaikala family lives, to the gardens that used to be at the edge of Tirupati (where Gangamma's Tatayyagunta temple now stands). One could speculate that such a socially and geographically localized biography is one of the means through which Gangamma in Tirupati is stabilized—more than her un-storied, wandering/moving sisters—thus permitting permanent temple structures to be built over her and becoming more accessible for intimate relationships with this goddess than is typical with many of her local sisters.

The narrative localizes the goddess not only in geographic and social space—in specific places and families of Avilala and Tirupati—but also in time. Subbarama Reddy consistently identified the Palegadu as a Nawab who served under (and collected taxes for) the British. This is not so long ago—a time in living memory of the narrator or his/her ancestors, who orally passed down the story. The more commonly used terms *raja* and *palegadu* are less historically specific; but narrative variants using these terms are still situated in the time "of our ancestors."

While the Palegadu narrative takes place in human, historic time and identifiable contemporary geography, as we know, gods and goddesses are expansive and quite easily cross these time and space worlds, taking multiple forms in both human and mythic worlds. The identity of the goddess in the Palegadu story moves from local village daughter to mythic *vishvarupam* goddess, and then back again to daughter-goddess who, under a series of guises—at this point, we know now that she *is* the goddess—chases and beheads the Palegadu. Where and how Gangamma ultimately resides after beheading the Palegadu differs in different endings to the core narrative and in different interpretations of its enactment through the Kaikala *veshams.*

The Gangamma–Palegadu narrative presents us with two problems to be resolved: first the aggression of the Palegadu, which is resolved through his beheading; and then, at its conclusion, the excessive *ugram* of the goddess that was needed to accomplish the beheading, but which now threatens the *uru.* The verbal narrative leaves the latter problem unresolved; we're left with the *ugra* goddess wandering the *uru* (in a variant discussed below, holding the Palegadu's blood-dripping head in her hand). We will see that this latter crisis is resolved only through *jatara* rituals.

Another variant of the Palegadu story was performed by a high school-educated, married Balija (merchant caste) woman in her mid-twenties whose family used to have the *mirasi* to keep the sword that Gangamma (in her *vesham* as the Dora) uses to behead the Palegadu during the *jatara* ritual itself. We were sitting in the Veshalamma temple courtyard, waiting for the preparation of the Sunnapukundalu *veshams* to be completed. I had asked her to explain who the Sunnapukundalu were, exactly; although her narrative never mentions the Sunnapukundalu and did not directly answer my question,[12] I was happily surprised to hear a particularly female perspective on the Palegadu story:

I'll tell you the story. There were some men, seven of them. They used to go around selling betel leaves. One day they found a small baby girl in the green grass. Among these seven, the eldest had no children. He told the others that he wanted to raise the child. Of course, they agreed. They took her home by cart. From the time she came, she gave them luck. They earned a lot of money. [Another woman interjects: Lakshmi (goddess of wealth) came to them.]

That girl got her *age* [i.e., reached puberty]. Then they [the seven men] said, "Amma,[13] don't come out of the house. Whatever you want, we'll *supply,* but don't come out of the house." But she didn't listen to them. She would sit on the roof, drying her hair. Then you know what happened? *He* saw her; the king saw her. He sent someone to call her seven fathers. He asked them, "There's a girl on your roof. Go and bring her." And then they came back home and started weeping, all these seven, wondering how could they tell this to their daughter.

The daughter came and asked, "Why are you crying?" [They answered], "It's like this; he's asked you to come." She said, "Why should I go to that place? [i.e., why should he expect me to come to him?] I won't go to that place. Ask him to come *here.* But don't come with him; send him here alone." Saying this, she went upstairs.

Then he came wearing lots of scent and things [*scentu-gintu;* the use of the echo word implies scent/perfume and "all those kinds of things"] [the narrator laughs]. They [the fathers] said, "Our daughter has asked you to come upstairs." He went up and she took her *ugra svarupam* [excessive, fullest form]. When he saw the *ugra svarupam,* he was afraid and ran back to his court and locked all the doors.

Then you know what she did? She got very angry [*kopam*]. "I'm not an ordinary woman [*mamulu ammaini*]; I'm Ammavaru. I took this birth only to kill that man. After that, you know what she did? She took the snake charmer *vesham,* then the mendicant *vesham*—next, what happened, do you know? Just like that, she came and scolded that man. She scolded him with abusive language [*butulu*]. But still, he didn't come out. On the second day, they offer *kumbham,* right? [ritual offering of piles of cooked food to the goddess; not part of the story itself, but a comment on *jatara* rituals].

So, all the *veshams* came, right? She came as a Dora the last day. The king wanted to meet the Dora. On Dora day, Gangamma came and said, "I am the only Dora." When s/he spoke like this, the king came out of the palace and said, "I am the Dora; how can *you* be the Dora?" Then Ammavaru beheaded him; she roamed the whole *uru* in her *ugra svarupam.* And everyone was afraid—there was *blood*, and the Palegadu's head was in her hand. Ammavaru told them, "The whole *uru* has become hot [because of her *ugram*]; if you want to cool it, I will come tomorrow in Matamma [Matangi] *vesham.* [At this point, the commotion around the nearly completed Sunnapukundalu *veshams* cut off the narration.]

Gangamma's distraught father feels he has no option but to accept the Palegadu's demand for his daughter. Gangamma tells him to keep his word, assuring him that she will take care of herself. Note that in the Balija female-narrated variant above, marriage is not mentioned; the Palegadu simply demands that the young Gangamma come to his presence. Even in versions that mention marriage, there is the implication that marriage is only a ruse or euphemism for sexual access. The Palegadu has stepped outside of societal bounds in his excessive desire, for which Gangamma punishes him. One narrator added the detail that Gangamma brings the Palegadu back to life after she has beheaded him and he asks for forgiveness; but she doesn't trust his promise of transformation, and kills him again. Having killed the Palegadu, Gangamma protects not only herself from male sexual aggression, but also other young women of the village upon whom the Palegadu has cast his eye (one variant says he desired all the beautiful virgins [*kanyas*] of the village). Further, she protects the honor of her own father, who felt he could not deny the king's demand.

The Palegadu initially does not question his ability to satisfy a woman; nor does he take into account female experience at all, as he forces the young women in his kingdom to satisfy him. He does not know who "a woman" truly is. However, when he sees Gangamma in her full force and size, "stretching from earth to sky," he runs, only now fearing his ability to "bear" the female. Another female-performed variant of this narrative (discussed in the next chapter) emphasizes that the Palegadu had "bad intentions," and that *this* was the reason Gangamma showed her true, full and *ugra* self to him; had he had good intentions, they say, she would have remained pacific (*shanta*). Her *ugram* was activated in the presence of male threat and aggression.

Most variants of the narrative specifically mention that Gangamma was first seen by the Palegadu while drying her hair. The act of a woman drying her unbound hair is an intimate, traditionally domestically situated act; loose hair displayed publicly may suggest a woman's publicly available sexuality, a possession state, or mourning. Note that the rooftop is domestic space, but ambiguously so, since it may be seen from the street or other rooftops by non-familial males. An Avilala female variant of the story describes the Palegadu figure (identified as a merchant rather than king) as first seeing Gangamma as she was pulling a calf out of a well with her beautiful, long, thick braid. In another variant, his desire is aroused simply by the sight of her beauty and braid; and he attempts to grab Gangamma by her braid—an insult of the highest order for a woman, implying sexual violation or a threat thereof.[14]

The Balija female narrator above adds the detail that Gangamma's "fathers" warned her not to go out of the house once she has reached puberty. Gangamma refuses to be sequestered in this way, and defiantly goes to the rooftop to dry her hair, suggesting that a woman's sexuality does not need to be hidden in order for her to be "safe"—and that Gangamma does not need the protection of her father-uncles. This female-performed variant adds still another twist: Gangamma refuses to come into the presence of the king upon his demand—as if she's a second-class person (specifically, a wife or servant) to be ordered around. Rather, she demands that he come to her—and come alone. Surprisingly, he does so. Gangamma's demand and the king's compliance reverse a traditional gendered hierarchy. Only after the king accepts such a submissive role does Gangamma show him (and the audience) her true self as Ammavaru; she declares that she has taken this birth (as a woman) for the sole purpose of destroying this man. She is not an "ordinary" woman, but neither is she an "ordinary" goddess; she is an *ugra* goddess.

While the Gangamma–Palegadu narrative does not have the breadth of social identification characteristic of oral epics (Blackburn and Flueckiger

1989), it follows the basic grammar of left-caste epics that V. Narayana Rao has characterized as "sacrificial epics" (1986): the heroine's honor is threatened by a male/king of another caste; the males of her own caste are unable to intervene; and the heroine saves herself. This is in contrast to right-hand caste "martial epics" in which the hero is a male warrior fighting for control of land with members of his same caste and who dies heroically at the end (140). There are, however, significant differences between the three sacrificial epics Narayana Rao discusses and the Gangamma–Palegadu narrative. In the former, the heroine saves her honor by committing *sati* (self-immolation) and only in death transforms from woman to caste goddess. Gangamma, in contrast, starts out as a goddess—not a caste goddess, but one for the entire *uru*—who has taken guise as a human female; like the epic heroines, her family and community are unaware of her capabilities. However, in the Palegadu narrative, her true nature is not revealed through self-sacrifice but rather during the wedding ritual through which the Palegadu sought to subordinate her.

The Palegadu narrative leaves us with a "world that has become female," in which the female is ascendant and her *ugram* has destroyed the threatening male; however, the excessive *ugram* intensified by the beheading is threatening to the *uru*. It is only through *jatara* ritual that this new "problem" of excessive *ugram* is resolved. And here, it is finally resolved by Gangamma herself when she dismantles her own *ugra mukhis* (or, in the variant performed by Subbarama Reddy, by dividing herself into the Nine Sisters). One might interpret this act as self-sacrifice; however, such sacrifice is not death, neither for the sacrificial epic heroines who become goddesses nor for the *ugra mukhi*-Gangamma. Gangamma wants to be in relationship to the *uru*'s inhabitants and she ritually needs them; so she willingly diminishes her *ugra mukhis,* which are "too much to bear," into multiple forms (small pieces of clay) that are more accessible, easily managed, and taken home by *jatara* celebrants to use medicinally against illness throughout the year.

Adi Para Shakti: *Ugram* as *Shakti*

Ugram in the Tirupati variants of the Adi Para Shakti narrative and its commentaries is equated with both *shakti* (female power) and desire (*korika*). The story itself is not unique to Tirupati's *jatara;* it has a wide geographic and linguistic distribution, with the details and resolution of the story differing in each context. Performances of the story have been reported in at least three other *jataras* from other Telugu regions (Handelman, Krishnayya and Shulman, ms.; Subba Reddy 1992; Surya Prakash, oral communication), and we can assume that there are other Telugu *jatara* performance contexts for the story.

This story is performed by professional Pambala drummers/storytellers at the Veshalamma temple courtyard as the Sunnapukundalu *veshams* are being created. (The name Pambala comes from the drums used in performance, the *pamba.*)[15] The primary audience of the *jatara* Pambala performance is the goddess herself, the words of the narrative barely audible to the human audience amid the commotion of the crowd and the drumming of the singers. My transcriptions of these Pambala performances are patchy, the sound recordings difficult to decipher through the courtyard's din. And so, I provide only a summary of the Pambala variant (based on conversations with them and segments of their performance), and then provide translations of two fuller telling by lay narrators. The Pambalas say their full narrative performance can run fifteen to twenty hours; however, their performance at Veshalamma temple runs only one or two hours.

All narrative variants begin with the primordial goddess Adi Para Shakti alone in the world. When she reaches puberty, she experiences desire (*korika*) and decides to create a male to satisfy that desire. The first male is the god Brahma, but the first word out of his mouth is "Amma" (Mother), precluding him as a sexual partner. The second is Vishnu, and his first word is also "Amma." But when Shiva is created, the first word out of his mouth is "*eme.*" *Eme* is a Telugu word used by a husband to address his wife or another female lower in the social hierarchy; its usage signals that Shiva is a suitable candidate to fulfill the desire of the goddess. From here, fearful of the goddess's superior *shakti,* Shiva negotiates with her to give him some of her power (one Pambala singer explicitly identifies the power as the "power to destroy"). However, once he receives her third eye and trident, Shiva reneges on his "deal" that if he receives her third eye and trident, he will satisfy her. This is where one of my *jatara*-recorded Pambala segments picks up:

She became angry. "Ishwara [Shiva], do you know what you have done? I have satisfied your desire. You didn't satisfy my desire. You neither satisfied my desire nor returned my eye."

Saying this, Ammavaru left with anger. She sprinkled [the three gods with] holy Ganga water [*kashitirtam*], sacred ash [*vibhuti*], and ground turmeric. When she did that, those three men became women. She changed them into women. It is said that those women began to serve her; some were massaging her back, some her feet; some were pressing her hands and forehead. They were all doing the work of maidservants. Then Gangamma looked at them, [thinking] "I myself created them as men. Now if I change them into women, it's not *dharmic* [according to the social order]." So Gangamma recited sacred incantations [*bijaksha*] and *mantras,* and she changed them back into the three male deities [*trimurtilu*].

The world is made female when Adi Para Shakti changes the three gods she has created into women—not just any women, but female servants. However, the goddess realizes that this all-female world is not *dharmic,* and she changes the gods back into males. This is an important cue to a possible indigenous interpretation of the beheading of the Palegadu and what it means for men to take *stri vesham:* the final purpose is not to create an all-female world, but to create a different kind of male, a transformed male.

The Pambala singers direct their *jatara* performance of Adi Para Shakti to Gangamma when she is in a state of transition—from her singular *vishvarupam* Matangi self into the divided/double *vesham* of the Sunnapukundalu. Why this narrative performance at this particular time in the *jatara vesham* sequence, when the goddess—and presumably her *ugram,* too—is being split? Why does she need to hear her own story? And what exactly does she hear? First, even as her *ugram/shakti* is being split, she is reminded of who she ultimately is/was—the ultimate reality and creator of the universe. But she is also reminded of why she needs to be split—that humans (males, in particular) cannot sustain her fullest *shakti;* that if she wants to be in relationship in order to continue the creation and sustenance of the world, her *ugram* must be made *shantam* and cooled. In fact, by the time the Pambalas perform the Adi Para Shakti narrative in the Veshalamma temple courtyard, Gangamma's *ugram* has been satisfied ritually, through offerings of hundreds of chickens and many goats and pots and pots of cooked *pongal;* perhaps the goddess needs to be reminded of this, too.

The following is a more complete variant of the Adi Para Shakti narrative than that I was able to transcribe from the Pambala *jatara* performance. The narrator is a young mid-twenties Mala-caste farmer who is the part-time attendant at a small shrine of Mutyalamma (one of the Seven Sisters) at the edge of the village of Rayalcheruvu (about an hour and a half from Tirupati). We were waiting for village women to come to the shrine precincts to cook the *pongal* to be offered to the goddess, and I asked the Mala attendant if he could tell me the story of Gangamma (without specifying which story). He answered with the story of Adi Para Shakti. He was relatively fluent in English, and I had to persuade him to tell the story in Telugu. He interjected many English phrases or asides into his Telugu narration and also provided his own periodic commentary on the narrative. He began the story by apologizing for not knowing the story of Gangamma as well as the Pambalas do; but, he said, he could give us a summary.

[Narrator begins in Telugu] Before creation, there was nothing. Nothing was there. There were no animals, no life. The sacred sound *omkaram* was heard and from this *omkaram,* Adi Shakti was born. I don't know, but it's according to the Vedas. I haven't read the Vedas, but that's our belief. [English] There's a relationship between Vedas and science; you might have some touch with science. [Telugu resumed] Adi Shakti was born, not Gangamma.

[English] Even if you want electrical current, you should have minus and plus, negative and positive. Only if you have both, the bulb works; only if you have negative and positive, the machine works. [Telugu] That's the secret of the creation, too. Only if male and female are together, there will be creation. That's why Shakti went in search of a suitable man for her. So she went in search of a man who would give her company and would fulfill her desires. During her search, she created Brahma. As soon as he was born, he addressed her as "Amma." When he addresses her as Amma, what will he be to her? Her son. She wanted a husband for herself; but he didn't have the right qualifications. By then she had the third eye, [English] and that is called a *bottu;* that is the third eye. [Telugu] When she looked at him with the third eye, he turned into ashes. Who? The god Brahma.

Again she went and searched. Somehow or the other, she should find a suitable man for herself. Then she created Mahavishnu, and Mahavishnu also called her "Amma" in the same way. Then she created Ishwar. As soon as he was born, he said "*eme.*" There's a difference in the way you call your mother and the way you call your wife, right? [English] Don't think otherwise [i.e., be offended], madam, because here anyhow, we compare the standard of living of our citizens and citizens of other countries—generally they won't have the sentiments of Indians. [Telugu, addressing my Telugu fieldwork associate directly] Like we have *sentiments,* they won't have those, right? She might think otherwise. [My fieldwork associate asks] "Are you referring to your use of *eme?* [Narrator] Yes. They don't have anything like that [distinctions of address]. In India, especially Hindus have such. Our culture is different from theirs; and we are more devoted to god.

When he said "*eme,*" he made [implied] a relationship with her. That means, he accepted her as his wife. That means he loves her. So she concluded that he was the one who suited her; he was a suitable partner. So she showed her desire [*korika*]. He started thinking, "Because women's desires have no limits—first women need saris, then jewels, then they all need comforts; [English] there are no boundaries for the desires of ladies. [Telugu] That's the difference between male and female desires. There are limits for men's desires, but there are no limits for women's desire.

My fieldwork associate and I left to join the procession of women bringing wood for cooking fires and ingredients for *pongal,* and the narrator called out in English, "Don't think otherwise [i.e., don't be offended or misunderstand]." We simply smiled and kept walking. As the women's *pongal* was cooking, we rejoined the male narrator, this time joined by an audience of about fifteen women who had gathered around us, and he picked up the narrative where he had left off. However, he now named and identified Adi Shakti as Ganga Devi.

Ganga Devi showed her desire for him. It's very difficult to bear [*bharincu*] a woman. So he [Shiva] asked for her third eye before he married her. She accepted and removed her third eye and gave it to him. With that third eye, he looked at her from top to bottom. Under the gaze of the third eye, she got flames [*mantalu*] all over her body and blood [*raktam*] started bursting out of her body. Now we call it "going out of house"; people call it *menses*. This took place even before creation. So she asked Ishwar, "I've become like this; what will happen to me in the future?" [He answered,] "No man will be able to fulfill your desire. In the future, in your name, in every village, you will be in different forms [*rupam*] of Shakti: Gangamma, Yellamma, Mulasthanamma, Putalamma, etc." She [the goddess] has other forms, too: Madurai Meenakshi, Kashi Vishalakshi, Kanyakumari. Like that, we keep calling her different names. So we arrange sacrifice [*bali*] in different places for her every form [*rupam*]. [Shiva pronounces,] "In the forthcoming Kali Yuga, every animal, in the name of *bali,* will praise you happily. In this way, you will be cooled; there's no other kind of *mukti* [salvation] for you other than this. So you will have the *jatara;* and your name will be famous all over the world." And he went off. [My associate asks,] "So he doesn't get married to her?" "No."

In this narrative, the goddess's *ugram* is explicitly associated with her desire (*korika*), rather than the destructive anger of the sexually threatened Gangamma in the Palegadu story. The male narrator explains that her desire is equivalent to the limitless desires that women have for saris and jewels, but implicit is that this desire is sexual. And this *korika* is threatening to the male, who realizes her superiority and potentially destructive *shakti.* The Mala male narrator gives a male perspective on female desire; it is more than simple desire, it is a limitless (consuming) desire. As he says, "There are limits for men's desires, but there are no limits for women's desire."

Fearing he will be unable to satisfy her and will be destroyed by her excess, Shiva tries to put off the goddess's demand for sex by asking for the physical manifestations of her *shakti*—her third eye and trident; only then will he will agree to "marry" her. However, even with this additional *shakti,* Shiva does not seem to have confidence in his ability to satisfy and bear the goddess. He's a trickster; once he has her power, he uses it against the goddess, aggressively gazing at her and causing her to burst out in flames all over her body, flames that turn into menstrual blood. In this young farmer's telling, the goddess is seemingly left helpless; at the mercy of Shiva, she asks what she can/should do. Shiva answers that her desire will be fulfilled only through *bali* offered to her during her annual *jatara*—an explicit association in this context between sex and *bali.* The all-powerful Adi Para

Shakti is dismantled and distributed as the *gramadevatas,* and her fame around the world is assured. So what of the male (god)? He seems to be out of the picture altogether in this resolution until we consider *jatara bali* itself—where the buffalo and goats sacrificed are male.

The Pambala variant is not so simply resolved; it keeps narrative and *jatara* agency in the hands of the goddess. Adi Para Shakti, with plenty of *shakti* left after having handed over her eye and trident, is angered by the trickster Shiva and immediately changes the three gods into women. But then, the goddess herself realizes that a "world become female"—in which ultimate reality is singularly female and in which males are, quite literally, turned into women—is not ultimately sustainable; however, the goddess's unsatisfied desire also threatens the very order and future of the universe and is fulfilled through *bali.*

A *purana pandita* (professional reciter of religious narratives), Annapurna, expands upon the *jatara-bali* solution to unfulfilled desire. Before Shiva can burn Adi Para Shakti and turn her into ashes, she admonishes him for thinking that he has taken away all of her power. Adi Para Shakti's superiority over and potential intimacy with the god is indicated when the goddess addresses Shiva as "*ori,*" a term of address for men equivalent to *eme* for women (discussed earlier). Note that in this variant, the goddess commands the gods themselves to offer *bali* to her.

Ammavaru said, "*Ori,* I am more intelligent than you. I am the one who rules this world. With this trident and third eye, you can't do anything." And she expanded into the limitless sky.

Not knowing what to do with [the desire of] her youth, that young *gramadevata*—knowing that she had lost that possibility of *anandam* [bliss; full satisfaction]—that Talli [Mother], that *shaktisvarupini* [she whose form is *shakti*], with all these emotions, went to the ocean, and she made all the seven oceans into one. As soon as they became one, she started wringing the oceans. Why is Ammavaru doing this? Her overflowing emotions—those whom she created [the three gods, who are unable to satisfy her desire] caused her to do this. The seven seas became a storm of destruction [*pralayam*]. There was absolute destruction. Even with that destruction, Ammavaru's emotions did not recede. Ammavaru's desire [*korika*] was not fulfilled. [Narrator herself speaking faster and faster:] Her emotions stirred the water. Seeing those seven seas like this, everyone was afraid, thinking that the whole world would be destroyed, the whole world would collapse in that great destruction. "What can we do?" thought the three gods.

[The gods recite *mantras* to make the goddess peaceful; they offer her turmeric water, flowers, and fruits; they ask what they can do to fulfill her desires. Here, she herself offers the solution of *bali.*]

When they made her peaceful, in that destruction, she came down and started floating on the waves. These Trimurti went to Ammavaru, who was floating on the waves, and prayed to her, "Amma, what do you want? Whatever you desire, we will make happen. "*Ori* Trimurti, you must perform *jatara* for me every year. In that *jatara,* give me *bali.*

The narrator proceeds to explain why the ritual of taking *stri vesham* is part of the *jatara.* Her explanation correlates the sacrifice of animals and the sacrifice of desire. She continues:

With the *veshams*—[pause, narrator explains] That means, whoever has something inside—people think many ways inside their hearts. Some people want to behave like men; some people want to scold/abuse others freely; some people—like various emotions—might want to smear this and that on their skin [such as turmeric, ash, and sandalpaste—a form of *vesham*]. In human beings there are so many hidden desires. They are repressed. Such repressed desires that are inside, those kinds [pause] of physical desires have been tied up, we control them. When must they come out? [The goddess says:] When you come to my into my presence, you must bring that out. In my presence, you must bring them out. In my presence, all desires must be burned. She would burn even the *jiva* [soul] inside—such is the Ammavaru who is the *gramadevata.* That is why you all, happily, delightfully, should take whatever *vesham* you like. You must come into my presence freely. Give me *pongal,* slaughter animals; whatever worship [*puja*] you do, I will accept. It is enough to see me.

In another performance of Adi Para Shakti, Annapurna includes the goddess's multiplication into *gramadevatas* and the gendered experience of their desire (*korika*):

In earlier days, only women did *puja* to *gramadevatas,* not men. Why? Because if a *gramadevata* sees a man, it is believed she'll come onto him [through possession]. That's why only women did *puja* to her. They [women] used to do the *abhishekam,* give clothes, *alankara,* jewelry, with incense, oil lamps, food; they used to satisfy her. Only women used to do *puja*—*ladies, ladies, no gents.* Desire, desire [*kamam, korika*]; that's why men didn't used to do it. Only these days, men have begun to perform it [*puja*]. . . .

Both male- and female-narrated variants of Adi Para Shakti describe the potentially destructive nature of unfulfilled desire. In the Mala farmer's telling, it is Shiva's idea that Adi Shakti's desire can be fulfilled through performance of the *jatara* and *bali.* However, Annapurna attributes the solution to Adi Para Shakti's *korika* to the goddess herself. Not only does she demand *bali,* but she also says that males should take female *vesham* to appear before her during her *jatara;* the *purana pandita* equates the offerings of *bali, stri vesham,* and *pongal* as all satisfying to the goddess. She suggests that (repressed and/or aggressive) male desire itself is potentially destructive and must be externalized (through, primarily, female *vesham*) and burned away.

Non-Telugu variants of Adi Para Shakti

The female-centeredness of the Tirupati variants of Adi Para Shakti is notable when compared to regional versions performed in the Himalayas and Karnataka, which conclude in marriage between the goddess and Shiva, not *bali.* William Sax translates a Himalayan variant of the story as it is performed in the epic song of Nandadevi (1991), which includes significant variations from the Telugu performances. Although satisfied with her creation of earth and sky, the goddess asks, "How can I live without a man? / Without a man, for whom shall I live? / Without a man, there is not wealth. / Without a tree, there can be no shade" (18). Note that the *korika* of the Tirupati variants is not explicitly articulated; other lines of the song imply that the male is needed for creation of the world, not for personal satisfaction of the goddess. In this version, the goddess creates three males from her uterine (or menstrual) blood: Brahma, Jatil Bagyelo, and a mythological ironworker. The first two gods are unwilling to become husbands to the female (mother) who created them. However, the ironworker asks her to give him a task, and she asks him to forge seven knives. Adi Shakti takes the knives on a "tour through the mountains" (28), and then, having worshipped them, she beheads herself with the knives. Her head becomes a form of Shiva on Mount Kailash, and her body that of the goddess Gauradevi in the town of Rishasau. In these newly created forms, the goddess and Shiva become man and wife. While the goddess gives up her head (arguably a site of identity) in order to be in relationship with the god, Shiva is, in fact, created from that very head.

A. K. Ramanujan translates the story of Adi Para Shakti from the Kannada Madeshvara (Shaiva) folk *purana;* it follows the Tirupati variants closely until its conclusion (1993:107–120). When Brahma and Vishnu object to what they perceive would be an incestuous relationship between mother and son, the goddess turns them into ashes. After citing a long list of the possible negative consequences of such an *adharmic* relationship, Shiva realizes that he is the next one to be reduced to ashes. He buys some time by asking the goddess: "Mother, you are the greatest. / You got me so that I could be your husband. / Right? Don't you want to see me grow up / and become bigger than you? / Don't you think / the husband should be stronger than the wife?" (111). Adi Shakti agrees and gives him time to grow taller/bigger. When she asks him again to satisfy her, he again challenges her. "*Shouldn't I, the husband, be stronger than the wife*? [my emphasis]. Teach me all your arts . . . If I have / to be your husband, / I must have at least a feather's worth more / than your powers" (112).

Adi Shakti tells Shiva that her power lies in her ring and the eye of fire in her palm. Without the ring, she'll lose all strength; without the eye of fire, she'll lose life itself. So she offers her ring to Shiva, and he learns all her arts. The text tells us that Shiva knew his mother didn't understand his "tricks." He asks her, "Now who's greater, you or me?" He proposes a dance competition between them to answer the question. He begins the dance and she imitates his every move. Exhausted and sensing defeat, Shiva puts his hand on his head. Adi Shakti imitates him and the eye of fire in the palm of her own hand reduces her to ashes. (This is an interesting reversal of the Tirupati variant in which Adi Shakti reduces the gods to ashes.) As she's dying, she calls to her eye of fire to go to Shiva's forehead and become his third eye; and she curses him: "He refused a woman, so / may his body be stuck / with the very kind of female he refused" (115)—an explanation for the phallic *linga* form of Shiva surrounded by the female *yoni.* But the three gods realize they themselves need wives. So Shiva takes his mother's ring and creates from the heap of ashes that was once Adi Shakti the three consort goddesses, Parvati, Sarasvati, and Lakshmi. The gods seemingly win this gendered competition, in the context of a folk *purana* that sings of Shiva; after all, it is his story, not that of the goddess. Whereas, in the context of the Gangamma narrative repertoire, Adi Para Shakti remains ascendant, if diminished/fragmented so as to enable both gods and humans to bear her.[16]

The Gangamma–Palegadu and Adi Para Shakti narratives have opposing structural movements: the Palegadu story begins with a diminutive little girl and ends with an ascendant, victorious goddess—a world become female in which the threatening male is beheaded/transformed. Adi Para Shakti begins with a world that is only female—the goddess as singular, ultimate reality—and ends with her division into thousands of smaller parts and, significantly, not destruction of but negotiation with the male (the Trimurti/three gods).

The Palegadu story ends with a female-dominated world in which the goddess has fulfilled her mission of destroying the inappropriately aggressive Palegadu. Gangamma is left to wander the *uru* with his blood-dripping head. The blood—the act of destruction—leaves her restless and the inhabitants of the *uru* vulnerable to her excessive *ugram,* which has been aggravated, not dissipated, by the beheading of the Palegadu. In the narrative itself, there is no resolution to this *ugram;* this narrative has solved *another* problem—that of the aggressive male—to which Gangamma's *ugram* is the solution (as her excessive *ugram* is the solution to potential hot-season illnesses). The solution to the new problem created in this narrative—that of unbounded/unmediated *ugram*—is found in the *ritual* world of the *jatara,* particularly *bali.*

The Adi Para Shakti narrative begins where the Palegadu story ends: the goddess as ultimate reality, filled with *shakti/ugram.* However, here the *nature* of her *ugram* is very different. *Ugram* in the Palegadu story is revealed when a woman is in crisis, more specifically, when her chastity is threatened; whereas *ugram* in the Adi Para Shakti story is described as the female's very nature and ever-present. It is not inherently destructive, only *potentially* so if the male with whom she desires a relationship is not her equal and thus not able to "bear" her. Shiva acknowledges the power differential, senses its destructive potential and does not even make an effort to test his own capabilities, even after he asks for—and Adi Para Shakti complies in giving—part of her *shakti* in the form of her third eye and trident. He attempts to use his newly given power not to satisfy the goddess, but to dominate her. The goddess is angered by Shiva's trickery and, in at least one variant, destroys the male deities, turning them into women. But she realizes that this female-only world is *adharmic* and ultimately still leaves her *korika/ugram* unsatisfied. She compromises with the male, then, transforming the now-female gods into males again and dividing herself into the multitude of *gramadevatas* who can be more easily borne and satisfied. The goddess herself suggests the ritual resolution of *jatara bali* to her *gramadevata* forms, rather than through marriage. *Bali,* it would seem, then, is both equivalent to and more satisfying than sex with an inferior.

Analyzing the two stories as part of the same *jatara* repertoire, in relationship to each other and in the context of *jatara* rituals, expands our understanding of Gangamma's *ugram.* The destructive potential and power—*ugram*—of the goddess is crucial to the sustenance and protection of the *uru.* In fact, it must be excessive in order to defeat that which would destroy the *uru*—the Palegadu in narrative and Gangamma-illnesses in everyday life. The Adi Para Shakti narrative confirms that while the goddess's *ugram* is not inherently destructive, it is impossible to sustain, satisfy, and serve day after day. In this narrative, the goddess realizes this and comes up with her own solution—her annual *jatara.* Resolution of desire and *ugram* in the narrative world itself is left in suspension: in the Palegadu narrative, Gangamma does not get married; rather, she destroys her potential husband. Neither does Adi Para Shakti find a male with whom she can be in relationship in her fullest form. In Gangamma's narrative repertoire, the question of the nature of the goddess and her *ugram* and *shakti* is left unresolved and contested; its resolution is found only ritually. A pair of female performers, to whom we now turn, provide us with their own explanations for the goddess's motivations behind her narrative acts.

FEMALE-NARRATED POSSIBILITIES OF RELATIONSHIP

4

When I asked female *jatara* celebrants to tell me the why the *jatara* is celebrated, they almost always answered with descriptions of rituals rather than with a narrative. In contrast, men responded most often to the same question with the story of the Palegadu and Gangamma. When I asked women more specifically about the stories of Gangamma, while they often knew the general narrative outline of the Gangamma–Palegadu story, they reported rather than performed it.[1] Even the flower sellers at the Tatayyagunta temple, who have an intimate relationship with the Gangamma of that temple and are witness to the broad range of *jatara* rituals that take place in its courtyard, were not storytellers; when I asked them for Gangamma narratives, they referred me to the Kaikalas and Pambalas. Until my return to Tirupati in the fall of 2005, I was tentatively concluding that men related to the goddess primarily narratively, whereas women related to her primarily ritually—and that men relate to her primarily during the *jatara* itself, whereas women relate to her throughout the year. While this conclusion may still be relevant, an unexpected, serendipitous meeting with a small group of women in the village of Avilala in 2005 opened up other possibilities.[2]

I had returned to the village of Avilala with my fieldwork associate Vimala to reconnect with and ask some lingering questions of Subbarama Reddy, who organizes the *jatara* exchange of *pasupu-kumkum* with the Kaikalas of Tirupati. He was not home, but sitting on the front stoop of his house were his elderly mother, his wife, and two non-Reddy female friends—Rajeshvaramma and Sumati. They recognized me from my previous visits to the Avilala *jatara* and quickly invited us into their courtyard. After being served tea, we had asked just a few questions about the *jatara* when the two non-Reddy women launched into a Gangamma storytelling session that included both the Gangamma–Palegadu and Adi Para Shakti narratives.

While following the same "grammars" of the narratives I had heard multiple times from male narrators, this female performance, with embedded commentary, provided a different interpretation of desire (*korika*), *ugram,* and *shakti.* The female narrators, both implicitly and explicitly, asserted that fulfillment of desire depends on a full and equal *relationship* (not only sex) between a man and a woman. Further, they identified with Gangamma more as a woman, like themselves, than as an *ugra* goddess. Their performance opened up possibilities of gender equality and expressed their own desires for relationship.

Rajeshvaramma (indicated as R in the narrative translation below) was a fifty-seven-year-old widow of the Balija caste (a trading caste whose members are traditional *jatara* participants); she lived with her son and daughter-in-law, and spoke poignantly of the sudden death of her daughter, whose loss she was still mourning. Rajeshvaramma told us she had studied through fifth class and—to indicate the level of her literacy, an interesting gauge—proudly claimed she could "read *Devi Stotram*" (a praise text to the goddess). Sumati (S in the translation below) was a married forty-year-old of the Karanam caste.[3] Each woman was eager to perform, and they competed for the performance floor, periodically interrupting and disagreeing with each other. Subbarama Reddy's mother and wife looked on with some amusement, but said very little during the performance. I remembered his wife having told me earlier that she didn't like to talk about Gangamma, because she was easily possessed by her, even when she simply spoke the name of the goddess.

Gangamma–Palegadu narrative

Rajeshvaramma began by addressing Vimala and me as her audience: "She came here just like you . . . You know this really happened in this village. . . . I heard my grandmother talking about this. We heard this when my mother and grandmother were talking to each other." She was insistent that we understand that this was a story of the here and now, about *her* village and *her* immediate ancestors. This insistence may have been one way to establish Rajeshvaramma's authority to tell the story—we had come asking questions and she, as an inhabitant of the same *uru* in which Gangamma had been raised, had the authority to answer them. These female narrators also made the characters more familiar than did the male variants discussed in the previous chapter: the male aggressor is a Komati moneylender/merchant, not a *palegadu;* Gangamma takes cattle out for grazing; Gangamma's long, thick braid is described as arousing the merchant's desire; and the local wedding custom of a husband putting his foot on that of the bride is described in detail.

After establishing that we were talking about a story of *this* village, Rajeshvaramma continued:

Because she's Talli [lit., mother; term for goddess], you know, *maha-sadhvi* [great woman of virtue], when that child stepped into his house, the Reddy ancestor's household flourished, like milk boils over—his whole world [*samsara*] flourished: cows, butter, milk, ghee, *junnu* [solidified boiled milk][4]—they became abundant. When she stepped into their house, it was like milk boils over.

Traditionally, brides in South India are called "Lakshmi," the goddess of wealth; a woman's greatest potential wealth—that of bearing sons and continuing the patriline—is ideally achieved only after marriage. Here, however, Gangamma brings wealth as soon as she enters the household as a little girl, so that the house becomes like an auspicious, abundant pot of milk boiling over—a hint that a woman can be a wealth-bringer without marriage.

Rajeshvaramma describes the Komati merchant watching Gangamma as she's saving a calf from drowning in a well, by pulling it up with her long, thick braid; Gangamma knows immediately that he has ill intentions. The narrator uses the word *dishti* (evil eye) for the gaze he casts on Gangamma. Even as he is determined to marry this "shining," beautiful woman, the Komati also recognizes her *shakti* (although he doesn't recognize her as the goddess). He follows Gangamma home and realizes she belongs to the same Reddy farmer with whom he regularly trades chickpeas. He asks the Reddy who this girl is and then asks to marry her.

An engagement ritual is performed, followed by a wedding. The female narrator describes in some detail the local ritual of the groom placing his foot on top of the bride's foot, implying that she is now under his control. But before the Komati can even raise his foot—with the mere attempt to control the bride Gangamma—she shows him (only him, not the rest of the wedding party) her full goddess form:

R: She asked him, "Do you have the *shakti* to marry me?" That's why she had shown him her *shaktisvarupam.*

"How dare you step on my toe?!" But you know, poor man, he had just raised his foot a little bit. He hadn't even put his foot on her, poor man. He hadn't even lifted his foot, and she showed her *shaktirupam.* As soon as she saw his leg, she showed her *shaktirupam.* He fell back like this, and he trembled and trembled and he peed and shit all over himself [i.e., lost control]. *Shaktisvarupam* is not a joke [*tamasha*]. His heart was beating, and the wedding pendant [*tali bottu*] he was holding fell down. He was finished [claps her hands together]. He ran and ran. He started running towards Tirupati—fear, fear.

. . . You know, it's because his intentions were bad; she realized this and showed her true self. If he had had good intentions, she would have acted differently. Going there, did he have the *shakti* to reach her? Did he have that? Where was he and where was she? Do you know the distance between a jackal and the great world of serpents [a Telugu proverb]? If he had worshipped her as a *talli,* he would have definitely have gotten something good. But he had bad intentions; that's why she showed her *nijasvarupam* [true form]. [Vimala asks for clarification]: So his intentions weren't good?

[S responds and briefly takes over the performance floor]: Could he bear [*bharincu*] her *shakti*? Oh Amma, could he bear her? See, if we arrange a marriage between a man and woman, they will have a relationship only if they are compatible. Isn't that right? Say, for example, if you're going to show a bride and groom to each other, even if you show four or five people, only one marriage will be fixed. We will show ten people, but only one will have a relationship, not all. We will show ten boys to a girl, but she will marry whomever she likes. She won't marry someone she doesn't like, right? So she didn't like him. That's why she showed herself without mercy.

[Gangamma said,] "Between you and me, how can this be a suitable match? I am *shaktirupam;* where are you and where am I?" That's why she showed her *shaktisvarupam.* [Gangamma continued, to the merchant] "One could say this is *darshan* [sight of the deity], but you don't have the *shakti* to see the *darshan.*" When she showed her eyes and fangs, he lost everything. If he had had the courage [*dhairyam*] and if he had had *shakti* to stand up, it would have been all right. Because of his ill intention, she showed herself. It wasn't wrong for her to do this. What was wrong was that he [only] *sexually* desired her.

Sumati raises the importance of equality between partners in marriage, even in an arranged marriage (in which, significantly, here the bride has more choice than the males; traditionally many girls are shown to a boy for his choice, rather than the other way around as is narrated here). The criteria of relationship, in this female-performed narrative, are compatibility and equality between the parties. The goddess taunts the Komati for even thinking that a relationship with her would be possible, given their differences and lack of suitability: "Where are you and where am I?" Sumati suggests that Gangamma's *shakti* is not inherently destructive, and would not be so in a relationship with an equal, but is so only with a male not her equal. The goddess shows her true form—*shaktisvarupam*—as a kind of test of the Komati's intentions and character. If a man had *shakti* equal to hers, he would be able to "bear her" and would not be threatened by her power.

When Vimala asked why Gangamma had not shown her *shaktirupam* to her own father, Sumati replied that, actually, she had—Gangamma's *shaktirupam* was manifest when her father's household flourished like "overflowing milk" after she entered the home as a little girl. Presumably, her father had the right character to "bear" her, even if he didn't recognize her as the goddess. However, Sumati continues, the Komati did not have this character or *shakti,* and so Gangamma had to show herself even more dramatically:

Gangamma stretching from earth to sky; Rajeshvaramma.

The merchant didn't have the qualification [*arhata*] to see her like that; he had neither the *shakti* nor *arhata* to get her. If he had those, she wouldn't have shown herself like that. She would have gone as a simple woman to him. As soon as he was going to step on her foot, she showed her *nijasvarupam.* He had no *shakti* to bear her.

Sumati continues with a commentary on the need for equality and respect for a true relationship; and here she equates this relationship with friendship:

A person must have *shakti* to bear another person. Otherwise, there won't be a relationship [*sambandhan*]. A relationship between a woman and a man is possible only if they can bear each other's *shakti.* Otherwise how is it possible? Say, for example, *friendship*—if we are compatible with each other, *friendship* will happen. If there's something wrong either in you or in me, then enmity will be born. Definitely, it will be born! "*Et!* I don't want your companionship. You don't hear my word and I don't hear your word. I don't need you—go away! I don't want it [a relationship]." At that point, we'll separate. That's what *friendship* means. I mean, people might say it's a good *friendship,* but if they're not compatible with each other, they'll separate. . .

Sumati continues to elaborate on the meaning of respect in the context of relationship. The Komati has seen only Gangamma's external form, and not her heart.

The Komati's character [*gunam*] wasn't *correct.* Men are the ones who need to learn about [inner] qualities. Men are the ones who need to learn about the nature of the heart [inner self; *manas*]. "Abba! She's beautiful!" he said. He was attracted only by her beauty, but not by her *manas;* who she was and where she was from—he didn't think about these things. That's why she showed herself, [saying to the Komati] "You have this kind of understanding [*buddhi*], and I have another kind of understanding." . . . He didn't see her inner qualities; he didn't see her *manas;* he saw only her beauty. He never thought of her inner qualities or what she was thinking. It takes someone ten days or a month to get to know these things, but he didn't even think about them. He saw that she was beautiful and he wanted to tie the wedding *tali* right away and arranged for the wedding. Her *manas* also wasn't understood by her father. What happened? When he wept, she consoled him and said, "All right," [she agreed to the marriage that her father had already committed to], but she knew what she had to do. And she did that. . . .

Sumati voices her own (and perhaps other women's) desires for relationship: to be appreciated and understood for who a woman truly is—for her inner qualities, not just for her external beauty.

Vimala asked Sumati for clarification about the relationship between *shakti* and *kopam* (anger)—specifically, in the context of the *ugra mukhi* that is kept curtained off from view until only a brief *darshan* and its dismantling. In her question, Vimala used the word *kopam* rather than *ugram,* which is a broader term; her word choice seems to confirm that *kopam* is directed at the cause of anger; whereas, as I have been arguing, *ugram* is potentially destructive, but not inherently so. Perhaps *kopam* is the better term to describe Gangamma's *ugram* in the Palegadu/Komati narrative, whereas *ugram* is the more appropriate term to describe Adi Para Shakti. Sumati explained that the curtain is hung in front of the *ugra mukhi* because (most) onlookers don't have the *shakti* to bear her. Vimala asked:

[V]: So you mean that her *shakti* is not the same as *kopam*? [S]: No, it's not *kopam.* It is an attraction [*akarshana*]. We have the *shakti* to see her *akarshana.* See, we say, "It's beautiful." But why did he fall down by seeing beauty? [He said to himself,] "Abba! Somehow, if I had the *shakti* to bear her, how wonderful it would be."

Sumati is very explicit here: *shakti* (and note that women seem to equate the goddess's *shakti* with her *ugram*) is an attractive quality (*akarshana*), a quality that draws others to it. But, to recognize Gangamma's *shakti* as attractive, the viewer him/herself must also have *shakti.* Sumati asserts that women have the necessary *shakti* and see the attraction of the *shakti* of the goddess; but the Komati realizes he does not have the requisite *shakti* to be able to bear the *shakti* of Gangamma. This gendered interpretation of *shakti/ugram* mirrors that of the guesthouse female sweeper quoted in the introduction, who asserted that men were afraid of the goddess (specifically, her *ugra mukhi*), because they don't have *shakti.*

Adi Para Shakti

Sumati concluded the Komati narrative: "Because of all this, he faced these troubles; others won't have this kind of disposition. Gangamma asked, "Where do you have the *shakti* to bear me, you bastard!?"[5] Then, perhaps in her effort to retain the performance floor (for which she had been competing with Rajeshvaramma), and as an elaboration on the nature of a woman's *shakti,* Sumati launched into a performance of the Adi Para Shakti narrative:

[S]: She's Adi Shakti. She was born even before this world was created. All these people were born because she created them. We were all born only after her. We were born as the first humans. From there we started our history [*caritra*]. [As Gangamma said to the Komati] "So, who do you think you are?!" For *example*; she showed her *nijasvarupam* to him; that's how it all started. *Ammo!* We don't have the *shakti* to bear her. Whoever has the *shakti* to bear her, it [a relationship] will happen; otherwise it won't happen. It only happens if things are equal. Otherwise, it won't happen.

Bhudevata [lit., earth goddess; here referring to Adi Para Shakti] created Brahma, Vishnu, and Maheshvara [Shiva]. . . . She's *shaktisvarupini,* she's very beautiful.

She came to Vishnu and woke him. He woke up and said, "What, Amma?" He didn't have the right qualification [*arhata*]. In order to be with her, he must have sexual desire [*kama*]. When she herself had *kama* [i.e., had reached puberty], she desired a good man. Then she woke up Brahma. He woke up and said, "What, Amma? Why did you wake me up?" Oh, he's also not equal. Then she woke up Ishwar [Shiva], and he said "*Eme,* why did you wake me?" and then she said, "This man is my husband." As soon as he said "*eme,*" she cooled down. She had sweat on her forehead; she wiped it off and threw it off [narrator imitates wiping one's brow and flicking off sweat from her hand]. It was as if she already felt the storm [*pralayam*] of wife and husband being united. When Ishvar said "*eme,*" she felt as if she had already experienced union with him. In her heart, she was satisfied [*santosha*]. Her *ugram* decreased.

Then there was the sweat, right? From that a female and male were born. That is the sweat of *kama.* It was satisfied as soon as he said "*eme,*" not because of actually meeting [physically]. Her *kama* became satisfied. Then she threw off her sweat and the two came out of it, one girl and one boy. From then on, this Kali Yuga [current age] *started.*

Vishnu's first word upon his creation is "Amma/Mother," disqualifying him from having the right "qualifications" to become a husband. As in variants discussed above, Shiva answers with "*eme,*" and Adi Shakti knows immediately that he has the right qualifications. But Sumati makes an interesting and significant addition: simply hearing the word *eme* cools down the desire (*kama*) and *ugram* of the goddess. It was as if, with the possibility of relationship, she had already been sexually united with Shiva. Sumati uses the word *pralayam* to describe the union of husband and wife, a term generally used to denote the destructive nature of storm or flood, but here may be used as connoting heightened emotion (much like the English phrase, a storm of emotion).

Now Rajeshvaramma interjects and starts the story again, not approving of the way Sumati had ended the story, having left out the important episode of Shiva demanding part of the *shakti* of Adi Para Shakti, in the form of her third eye and trident:

After *shaktisvarupini* was born, she looked around the world. "There's no human form [*rupam*] at all," she thought. She possessed all *shaktis.* That means, she was born as Adi Shakti. After Adi Shakti was born, she created Mahavishnu first. After being born, Mahavishnu said, "Talli [mother]." "*Cha!* He has no *shakti* to bear me." She turned him into ashes. She caused Brahma to be born. He said, "Amma, what, Talli?" "*Ts!* You're of no use. Go away!" and she turned him into ashes, too. She said to herself, "This man has a very good *body,* a very good *body* [she had already created Shiva]. [Everyone laughs.] So she turned that man [Vishnu] into ashes. This other man [Shiva] had a good *body,* a *shakti* *body.*" [She shows strength/muscles in her own upper arm.] If you have this [pointing to upper arm], you have good *shakti.*

She caused him to be born with a lot of *shakti.* Then he said, "What? Why have you called me?" "Oh, he's the suitable person for me. You have to marry me. This is my situation. This is my situation." "I will marry you," he said, "if you pass three conditions that I propose. Then I'll agree to marry you. If I want you or you want me, and we want to be together, after you give those three, I will marry you. Otherwise, you'll stay there and I'll stay here [narrator gestures high and low], so how will it be possible to be together? Tell me. It's true that you caused me to be born, so how is it possible [for us to be married]? Tell me." [She says,] "What I want is your friendship [*sneham*]; so I'll do whatever you ask." She agreed.

Recognizing the power differential between him and the goddess, Shiva proposes three conditions that will equalize this difference; only then will he agree to marry Adi Shakti. It is implied here that the goddess willingly gives up some of her power (in the form of her third eye, trident, and drum[6]) in order that Shiva have the *shakti* to "bear" her.

He took her third eye. You know, he has a third eye? He took that. She started sinking down . . . He took it from her and kept it with him. You know, he needs *shakti* to bear her, right? She's Adi Shakti, Para Shakti; she stretches from earth to sky. We don't have the *shakti* to bear her. [Shiva says,] "If you stand by me in all my troubles and joys, I will marry you. If not, how can I bear you? Without this, it won't be possible to marry you." She said, "For you, I'll do anything." By the time the eye was plucked out, she had sunk halfway down [into the earth]. After that he grabbed—these people play *daba-daba-daba* [sound of a drum], right? The drum and trident—he grabbed these from her. By then, she had sunk down three-quarters of the way.

And then Rajeshvaramma introduces an oblique reference, with a decidedly female twist, to the myth of the brahmincide committed by Indra (Vedic storm god), in which the sin of brahminicide is distributed among women, waters, and trees:

After that—you know, like we women menstruate. The ocean swells, [gives onomatopoetic sound], *busa-busa-busa-busa;* the water swells. The foam of the surf [*nurugu*] sounds *jaba-jaba-jaba.* It rises up, the surf. You know *nurugu,* right? [Sumati laughs]. That *nurugu.* In trees, it's the sap *banka.* In trees, like drumstick trees, *banka* is formed—in any trees. That *banka* is her desire. Her desire. Ishwar plucked out her desire [*korika*] in this form, giving some to women, some to trees, and the rest to the ocean; he plucked it out and threw it down. Then she took on an ordinary form [*mamulu rupam*]. This means, the surf is her desire; our menstruation is her desire; tree sap is her desire. These are all there in her true form [*svarupam*].

After menstruating [lit., going outside], we lose a lot of *shakti.* For those three days, we will just lie down where we are. Why? Because, it goes and goes and goes and we become weak. It's like that. After he takes all these things from her, she became an ordinary woman. . . . He took away her desire. He took three boons from her, right? As soon as she gave those boons to him, she became an ordinary woman. She became a suitable woman for him. . . . If he hadn't taken that desire from her, how would he be able to bear her? [Narrator gets excited.] Does he have the *shakti* to bear this *shakti*? As a common person whom she created, how could he be compatible? He wouldn't be compatible. As soon as he took those three, *she* became an ordinary woman.

According to the Mahabharata version of the story, after Indra kills Vritra (half-demon, half-Brahman) who has captured all the waters of the world, he is left with the unbearable weight of the sin of brahminicide. The god becomes "unrecognizable, and he lived concealed in water like a writhing serpent" (Doniger O'Flaherty 1975:84–85).[7] With Indra hidden, the earth suffers from ruin and drought. The gods, in dismay, go to Vishnu to ask how Indra can be purified from this great sin. Vishnu prescribes a horse sacrifice, which is successfully completed. Indra then "divided brahminicide among trees and rivers and mountains and the earth and women, and having thus dispersed it among beings, the lord of the gods was free of it [brahminicide]" (Doniger O'Flaherty 1975:85).

Rajeshvaramma doesn't tell this story of brahminicide itself, but reinterprets one of its motifs; she identifies the shared qualities of the swelling ocean surf, sap-dripping trees, and menstruating women to be the *shakti* of the goddess (specifically, forms of her desire) rather than the sin of brahminicide. Just as the goddess loses her full *shakti* when she gives Shiva her third eye, drum, and trident (becoming an ordinary woman), human women, too, experience the drain of *shakti* when they menstruate.

Ultimately, as in the other variants of the Adi Para Shakti story, Shiva proceeds to trick the goddess; he doesn't come through with his half of the bargain—at least not in relationship with the primordial form of the goddess as Adi Shakti. He asks the goddess to bring back to life his two fellow gods, Brahma and Vishnu, and to divide herself into the three consort goddesses of the Trimurti. Only in her divided/diminished self is union with her possible; and this union is necessary for the creation of the world.

"Oh, there's one more thing I have to ask you [Ishvar says]. You have to bring these other two back to life. Bring them back to life. You have burned Brahma and Vishnu into ashes; bring them back to life. You have only one form; divide yourself into three parts. If you bring them back to life, I will marry you. I will marry you. Otherwise, the Kali Yuga will end, right? You have taken this incarnation for the Kali Yuga; but in this *yuga,* if you kill them, where will humanity come from then? Who will bless us? So, from you, wives must go to those two, too." Brahma, Vishnu, Ishwar. These three are called the Trimurti [lit., three gods]. They are three; they are called Trimurti. She brought them back to life. Then, from this *rupam,* to him, and to him, and to him, she became three wives to them. That means, they became six people. These three couples, gathering together, got married.

Now Sumati interjects in Rajeshvaramma's performance and provides a final commentary about the nature of female *shakti*—before leaving to take care of her cattle and ending the storytelling session:

[S]: For her, in that *santosham* [the *santosham* she experienced when Shiva said *eme*], she gave them [her eye and trident]. Her *power* decreased. All the *power* decreased. Only then he was able to bear her. Otherwise, he'd be finished. Even Ishwar would be finished. Ours is *shakti rupam, shakti rupam.*

[Vimala asks for clarification: "Ours," meaning "women?"] [S]: Yes, we are *shaktis.* Without us there's nothing. Because of women, the world has come into being. A woman is the one who carries it [the fetus] for ten months and gives birth. A husband is—[pause] he just has sex [*sambhogam*]. *She* has to carry it for ten months. Half an hour? No, he just has two minutes. Creation [*srishti*], creation. Who carries for ten months? The

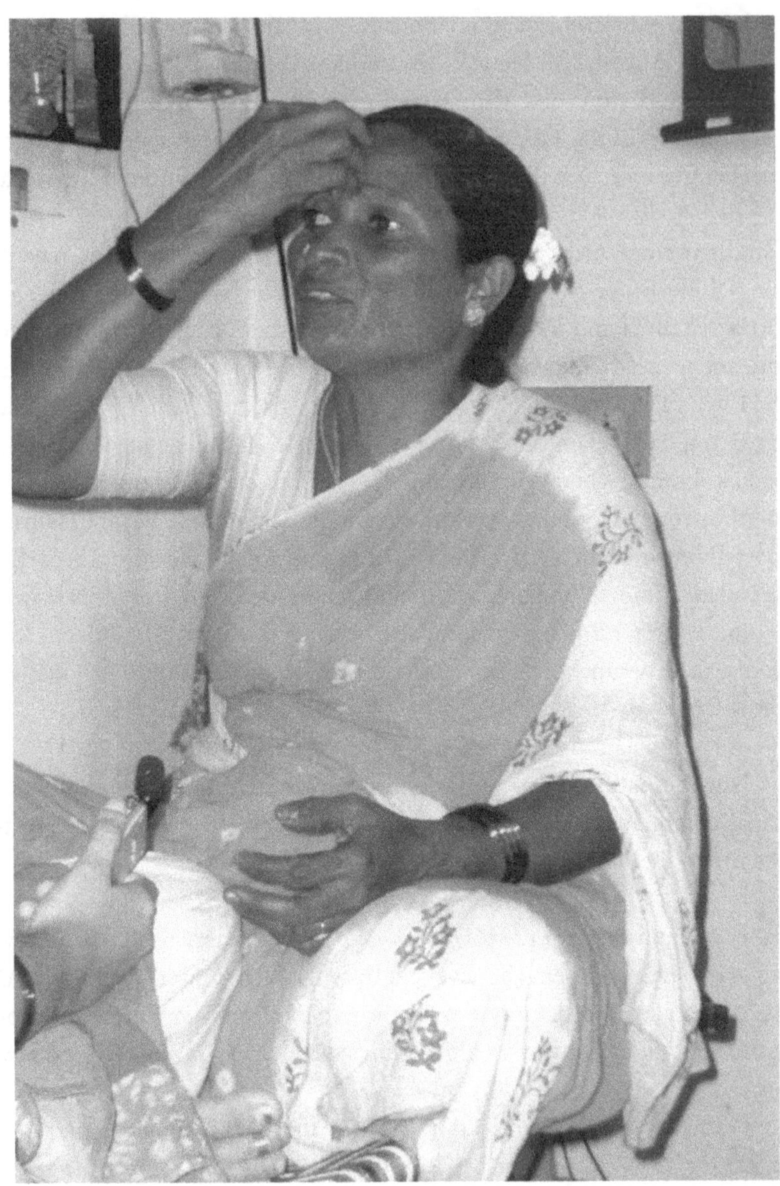

Adi Para Shakti plucking out her third eye; Sumati.

woman. Having carried it for ten months and giving birth and giving milk, raising and making them [children] grow, that is *shaktirupam.*

Sumati seems unconcerned that the goddess gave up some of her *shakti* in order to be in relationship with Shiva. Adi Para Shakti—and human women—would seem to have plenty of *shakti* left. Men, the narrator implies, only provide the (brief) sex needed for reproduction. But it is women who are ultimately responsible for the creation of the world; they are the ones who carry, sustain, and raise children. A. Anand's translation of a segment of the Pambala Adi Para Shakti story makes similar reference to the *shakti* of women's ability to raise a child: "A male could be a great warrior; but however great a warrior a man is, he doesn't have the power (*shakti*) to nurture a child. Only the mother knows how to bring up the family, how to acquire fame (*keerthi*) . . . It's all in the supernatural power (*mahima*) of the females" (2006:68).

Sumati and Rajeshvaramma's interpretations of female *shakti/ugram/korika* and male inability to bear or satisfy these are also reflected elsewhere in Gangamma's narrative repertoire and performances. But these female narrators provide us with a specifically female understanding of *korika* and *shakti.* Remember the male farmer (from the last chapter) who asserted that women's desires have no limits and are ultimately not able to be satisfied. In contrast, these female narrators suggest that, in fact, there *is* the possibility of fulfillment, but that it will occur only in the context of a relationship between equals. We don't have evidence that Sumati's and Rajeshvaramma's perspectives on this ideal are, in their specifics, "representative" of a female perspective; some elements of their performances may be idiosyncratic. However, their performance and commentary point to possibilities that these Gangamma narratives may open up, as a resource within which to imagine relationships of gender equality.

In several conversations I had about the Adi Para Shakti narrative with a male journalist/filmmaker from Hyderabad who has reported on Gangamma *jatara,* he argued that the narrative was simply one more instance of the "triumph" of patriarchy. He focused on the fact that Shiva successfully cheated the goddess and reduced her *shakti,* ultimately causing her to divide into multiple, less-powerful goddesses. However, in Sumati and Rajeshvaramma's performance, we get a different perspective. They suggest that the creation and sustenance of the world depends on relationship; and for this, Sumati concludes, Adi Shakti was willing to give up some of her *shakti*—to be in relationship with the male, who otherwise would not have the *shakti* to bear her. That Shiva ultimately recanted on his promise of marriage seemed of less concern to these female narrators than the possibility the goddess herself imagined—of a relationship between equals.

GANGAMMA AS GANGA RIVER GODDESS

5

As my fieldwork associate and I arrived at Tatayyagunta temple to attend the *alankara* of the goddess during the Navaratri festival in the fall of 1999, I noticed a young woman wrapped in a wool shawl,[1] wearing a large red *bottu,* sitting in the interior temple *mandapam* in front of a microphone. She gestured for us to come and sit down next to her and proceeded to ask who I was. When I told her my research interests in Gangamma, she identified herself as a *purana pandita* (lit., female scholar/reciter of the *puranas*), and said that she knew the stories (using the words *caritra* and *patalu,* history/biography and songs, respectively) of Gangamma. And she immediately launched into the story of the descent of the river goddess Ganga, which proceeded to flow into the narratives of Adi Para Shakti and Yogamaya Devi (the girl child substituted for Krishna when his nemesis, the king whose downfall had been predicted by the birth of this baby, smashed the baby against the ground). Annapurna's performance voice is extraordinarily strong and confident. But in this case, the performance was rushed, and the clattering fan overhead and crowd noise resulted in an unclear recording.

Annapurna was scheduled to perform soon, but she invited us to her home, where she said she could sing for us (and the voice recorder) without interruption. When we arrived at her small two-room rented quarters a few days later, she seated us on her bed, served tea, and then, quickly shutting the door to keep out the noise and enquiries of her close-by neighbors, said she was ready to sing. Again, however, the story she told that day was not of the *gramadevata* Gangamma; rather, she sang the pan-Indian *puranic* story of the descent to earth of the river goddess Ganga. Initially I was disappointed, thinking I had run into another dead-end of fieldwork. However, after multiple conversations and performances, I learned from Annapurna the ways in which the *gramadevata* Gangamma can be—and is—narratively identified with the pan-Indian goddesses Ganga and Yogamaya Devi, particularly through emphasis on their shared *shakti* (and *ugram*). I observed the ways in which Annapurna has come to know Gangamma narratively, and created relationships with Gangamma in ways she, as a Brahman, may not traditionally have had the opportunity to do ritually.

Annapurna experiences Gangamma as one more form of the goddess whom she knows through many forms; and so she easily asserts that she knows stories of Gangamma, proceeding to sing of Ganga Devi, Maya Devi, and Adi Para Shakti. However, not only is Gangamma performatively drawn into pan-Indian traditions, but the river goddess Ganga also becomes Gangamma-ized through the use of local, Gangamma imagery and framing, and by becoming part of a Gangamma narrative repertoire.

In the Service of the Goddess through Story

Annapurna describes her calling into professional storytelling as a calling into the service (*seva*) of god/goddess. She laughingly added, "We need both *bhukti* [food, livelihood] and *mukti* [salvation], right?" That is, she performs both out of devotion and as a way to make her living. She moved to Tirupati from coastal Andhra in 1994 to study for two years at the Tirupati Tirumala Devasthanam (TTD) Music College, from which she earned a certificate as a *purana pandita*. The course culminated in an exam, which she described as "testing in Ramayana, Bharata, and Bhagvatam; then an oral exam on stage, in Annamacarya Project Kalamandaram."[2] She was subsequently hired by the Endowments Department to sing in various temples around Tirupati, and this is her sole source of income. She generally performs for one month at a time at a given temple or series of temples in rotation and may also be called to perform at specific temples for specific festivals and rituals. (Her performances at Tatayyagunta temple are an indication of the shifting middle-class, brahminic nature of the temple.) When required to perform in villages, she leaves the house at six or seven in the morning, sings for two to three hours at a given temple and moves on to the next, returning home only late afternoon (without, she emphasized, eating anything while out all day, likely due to brahminic rules of commensality). She reported that many TTD *purana pandits* and *panditas* were complaining about this rigorous travel schedule and threatening to drop out of the program, but she herself accepted her responsibilities with equanimity.

While Annapurna was enthusiastic to perform for us in her professional role as a *purana pandita,* she was initially less forthcoming about her personal narrative. I eventually heard this rather sad story from her, but she asked me not to record it. At the end of my year-long fieldwork in 1999–2000, however, she opened one of her performances for me (and the voice recorder) with a formal life story that establishes her performative authority; this is the narrative I quote below (one that leaves out the emotional valences of several of her conversational narratives), supplemented by basic facts that are quite public or that Annapurna told me in public contexts.

Annapurna was a single mother of two children, in her early thirties when I met her in 1999. Visiting her home, it was quite obvious that her husband was absent, but she still wore the signs of a married woman—glass bangles, her *tali,* and a large *bottu.* We learned later that she and her husband were separated, but not legally divorced.[3] One of nine children, Annapurna said her father arranged her marriage at a young age to a groom in his late twenties. She had her first baby at fourteen or fifteen and her second child by the time she was seventeen. Soon thereafter, her husband abandoned her. From early on, she took the initiative to study and support herself, earning a B.Ed. and teaching for several years, completing an M.A. in Telugu, and then studying astrology (*jyotish*) and setting up her own business. She joined the Music College after her father died in 1994 (when her children were six and seven years old). After revealing this much personal information in one of our early meetings, Annapurna quickly shifted back to her comfort zone: "Now what do you want? Devi Bhagvatam, Ganga

Caritra [the *purana* of the goddess and story of Ganga, respectively]? How Yogamaya Devi came? What else do you want to hear?"

When I first met her, Annapurna was a temporary employee of the Endowments Department, and she was soon thereafter offered a permanent position. She told us that she had taken great pains to educate her children. In 1999, her teenage daughter was studying in "Intermediate" (tenth grade) and her ten-year-old son was studying at a Veda *pathshala* (school), which he joined at age seven, training to be a *pujari* (he was among a group of young Brahman priests-in-training serving in Tatayyagunta temple one morning when I witnessed a *jatara abhishekam*). Annapurna's dream was to continue her studies for a Ph.D. one day, when her children would be settled and when she might have a little extra money to afford continuing studies.

Like several others whom I met during the course of my fieldwork, Annapurna moved often between rented living quarters in the first years of our acquaintance. When I returned to her quarters several months after Navaratri, I found the door padlocked and her neighbors told us she had moved, but they didn't know where. They suggested going to the Annamacarya Project office, where someone may have seen her; but no one we met in that office knew who she was. However, I met a woman there whose daughter was practicing dance in the Project auditorium; she invited us to a dance recital the next week and we exchanged phone numbers. The next day she called to say that, after having herself made many phone calls and enquiries, she had located Annapurna. She had learned that Annapurna had moved to Tiruchanoor, the temple town in which Sri Venkateshvara's wife, Padmavati, resides, about five kilometers from Tirupati. The dancer's mother had been told we could find Annapurna at Padmavati's temple, where she performed daily between 3:00 and 4:00 in the afternoon. Our new friend accompanied us to the temple the next day, where we spotted Annapurna singing in front of a microphone, wearing her traditional shawl. After her duties were completed, Annapurna took great pride in showing us around the temple; she knew all the *pujaris* and thus was able to take us to the front of the *darshan* queue. As we were leaving the temple, Annapurna suggested we could meet her at the Music College in Tirupati, where she was regularly attending classes from 8:00 to 9:00 AM. However, when we showed up early morning several times over the following weeks, we never found her or even a class in session at that time of day. I hadn't asked her address, since I had assumed we would meet her at the Music College; nor did we find her upon return to the Tiruchanoor temple the next week.

In 2005, when I returned to Tirupati for a few weeks, not having a phone number for Annapurna or the confidence that I could find her at Tiruchanoor, I decided to go first to the Music College on the chance that she would be there. If she wasn't there, I could, in any case, learn more about what kind of training she may have received. I was directed to a room where *purana pandits/panditas* were gathered; and surprisingly she was sitting in the classroom, attending a refresher course. She ran to greet me and interpreted this serendipitous meeting as having been orchestrated by the goddess herself. I sat through the rest of the class with her, and then she insisted we come home with her again; she thought it would be a better place for recording her stories than the cavernous rooms of the Music College. Several days later, I met Annapurna again at the college and took an *auto* with her to Tiruchanoor. I learned that she had purchased a small house in a newly developing neighborhood, where, she said, we would now always be able to find her. We stopped at Padmavati's temple for *darshan* before wending our way to the outskirts of town and Annapurna's newly built little house. She pulled out several printed chapbooks, trying to decide what to perform for us, and settled again on the descent of the Ganga, a segment of the Bhagvatam, and Yogamaya Devi. I realized by this time that these stories were central to her performance repertoire.

I give the house-searching account above to emphasize the fluidity of physical movement that seems to have characterized Annapurna's life before she purchased her home and obtained a permanent position with the Temple Endowments, a fluidity that characterizes several other women from non-ritual specialist families who have unusual, intimate relationships with a Gangamma. Had Annapurna remained in a traditional Brahman marriage, she would likely have been more "settled" and constrained in the opportunities she has followed to study, teach, and perform publicly. Even the permanent position she has obtained as a TTD employee requires that she "move about" in public (from temple to temple, between home and the Music College) more than most traditionally married women of her caste and age would be expected to do.

In April 2000, Annapurna opened a Ram *katha* performance for me with a *shloka* (verse) of invocation and then shifted unexpectedly to the following personal narrative:

I'll first tell about my father and then we'll start the story. My father's name is Vemuru Venkata Subramanyam Garu of Chirala, Paparaju Tota. All of his six daughters have gotten married. Among the three sons, two have gotten married and one is still unmarried. My Pedda Grandfather [grandfather's elder brother] is in Cinna Ganjam and his name is Vemuru Lakshmi Narsimha Murty. He is a devotee of Chamundeshwari [a form of Durga who dwells on top of the Chamundi Hills outside of Mysore]. He's gone all around India teaching *jyotish shastra* [astrology]. Ammavaru used to always appear in his dreams and he became engrossed in her *seva* [service] and died. People belonging to this *vamsha* [lineage], including my father, died in her *seva*.

My father died in 1994 and I took *vairagyam* [lit., renunciation, detachment] after he died. Shanku, Cakram, and Namam [all symbols of Vishnu: conch, wheel, and forehead marking, respectively] appeared to me, and I came to Tirupati. I completed the *purana pandit* course under Dharma Prachar Parishad. I applied for it in 1995 and completed it in 1997. As soon as I started the course, I began reciting *puranas* in Tirupati and surrounding villages, in Chittoor District. Whenever people call me, I go; wherever they call me and whatever *katha* (story) they need, I recite it. I explain it. I was working in Ongole,[4] at Mother Teresa B.Ed. College. I took *vairagyam* after my father died; it's because of this that I came to Tirupati. After coming here, I put my son in Veda Patashala in Dharma Giri [Tirupati neighborhood]. My daughter, too, is learning from me.

My name is Annapurna. My guru's name is Sheshacharlu Garu. He is from Kala Mandiram, Tirupati. He was my first guru in Annamacarya Kala Mandir; he's the one who gave me guru teachings. He taught me everything I know. My second guru is at the Ram temple. He's working as a Vedic *pandit*, a *purana pandit*. He serves Vishnu Murty and he taught us many things which we didn't know. He showed us a golden way to lead our lives. We have our principal, Prabhakar Sharma; he's the principal of

Purana Pandit College. He, too, told us many things that we didn't know. He gave us the opportunity of this course. These three are my gurus.

Bal Subramaniam Shastry [the second guru mentioned above] is a *purana pandit* at the Ram temple, and he teaches *shastras,* too. He's well-versed in all fields. I've been telling all these stories [*kathas*] only because of him. If I'm able to recite well, it's only because of him. Whenever I recite *purana,* I think of him. I have his blessings in my mind and I pray to god with my whole heart. And I know that it's only because of god that I'm able to recite. When I recite *puranas,* I don't recite as if to human beings. I recite *puranas* as if I'm reciting to god. Whatever episode or *katha* I perform, everyone says it's good. Because I'm reciting it to god and I get engrossed in it, I experience devotion [*bhakti*] and joy [*anandam*], and I pass on this experience to other devotees. So I need my gurus' and god's blessings to recite the *kathas.*

So, let's continue. [She turns to the performance narrative at hand.] This is the *caritra* of Rama, who belongs to Surya *vamsha.* This is how Vishnu was born. . .

Annapurna's formal life history framing above leaves out any indication of her painful marriage, the struggles she may have had raising two children as a single mother, and the impact of these experiences on her calling to perform or her performance abilities. Rather, she places herself in an authoritative male family lineage, a lineage she says is characterized by service to the goddess. Significantly, Annapurna never mentioned her mother in our conversations, something I noticed only upon reading my fieldnotes upon return to the United States. Her father and other male teachers presumably gave her confidence and motivation to pursue her public storytelling role. Later, she told me that although her father and uncles were *purohits* (priests), and not professional *purana pandits,* she learned most of her stories from them. Annapurna emphasizes the names of her teachers/gurus, and attributes her skill and positive audience responses to her performances to her devotion to god. Her gurus and devotion sanction and give authority to her public performance, rare for a Brahman woman of her class.[5]

Annapurna's reference to *vairagyam* is a cue to a more personal narrative that is left unspoken in this context. The term *vairagyam* is often

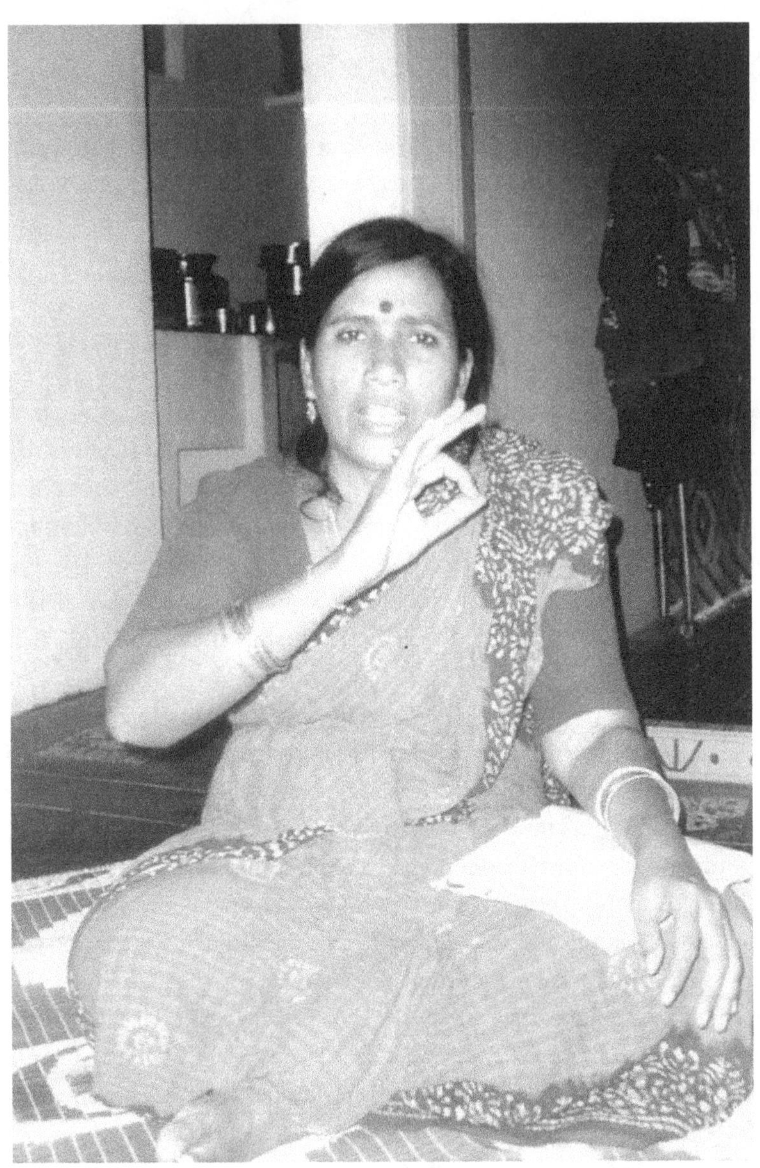

Annapurna performing in her home.

used in the context of persons (predominantly male) who renounce householder roles to become *sadhus*. Annapurna's use of the term suggests she consciously chose (a choice that was likely a necessity when her husband abandoned her) to leave the role of a traditional householder. More specifically, she chose not to not enter another relationship with a male and to dedicate herself to serving the god/goddess through narrative performance. Interestingly, she says she took this "renunciation" only after her father died.[6] Annapurna's religiosity and *vairagya* status is visible in the shawls she wears when performing, her large red *bottu*, and the confidence with which she performs and moves in public. Like many *sadhus*, she teaches through story and is required to keep moving to engage different audiences. Annapurna's self-identification as a *vairagi* also suggests that she herself may sense a conflict between her public performance role as a *pandita* and that of a traditional female householder. However, Annapurna's transition to *vairagyam* is not complete, at least not in a traditional, externally manifest, sense. She is still responsible for raising her children; and, as such, she has not given up making a home for them or the signs of marriage that give her some social status as their mother.[7]

Training, Style, and Commentary

Of seventy to seventy-five students in Annapurna's *purana pandit* certificate class, only a handful were women; interestingly, she never talked explicitly about the gendered nature of this role and/or who chooses to pursue it, although she often commented on gender roles more generally. Nine graduates of her graduating "batch" received positions with TTD as *purana pandits/panditas;* Annapurna explained that most students chose to pursue other kinds of more stable, lucrative, or permanent jobs. Training at the Music College consists of students sitting with renowned *purana pandits,* listening to their recitations and commentary, taking written notes, and replicating in performance what they have heard. However, Annapurna was quick to point out that her most significant education in *puranic* recitation came from listening to her father and other male relatives: "My father taught me all this. Everyone in my house knows Ramayana and Bhagvatam. I know more from my father and grandfather."

While she seems to know most of the stories she tells from memory and her commentary is extemporaneous, in both public and private performances, Annapurna always has an authority-creating book in front of her; at temples, the book is held on a folding wooden book stand. Annapurna described her recitation style as being primarily in Sanskrit, with Telugu translations and commentary. However, in the performances I witnessed in temples and those she sang for me and my voice recorder, she sings only short verses in a Sanskritized Telugu, followed by much longer Telugu spoken narration. She laughed when explaining further, "If we translated every word, who would listen to us? Only to [other] *pandits,* we'll give the literal Sanskrit, but with common people we don't do that." She explained that she often performed for villagers for whom she changes the language, using more Telugu. (She gave the example of changing *vivaham* to *pelli,* the Sanskrit and Telugu words for wedding, respectively).

Annapurna proceeded to illustrate the ways in which translation becomes commentary:

> We have to tell according to the *times.* Sometimes people ask me why we wear the *bottu,* why the *mangalsutra* [wedding necklace], etc., and I explain: Women are tied with *darba* grass [tied around the waist at marriage] for fertility. In marriages they pour milk on their heads to purify their thoughts before marriage, for women. But they don't do this for men. They also keep all these ornaments; they just tie women with all these things: earrings, necklace, ankle bracelet, bracelets. She's tied by customary ritual [*acaram*]. But even if she's "tied," she's *shaktisvarupini.* [My fieldwork associate asked for clarification: why does this happen to women if *bhagvan* (god) is said to look after everyone? Annapurna continues,] Because he's *bhagvan.* . . . When Talli [the goddess] gets angry, she'll kill him and he knows that [laughing] . . . Have you heard any man say he knows a woman fully? Have you? He never can. He knows that if she gets angry, it's a kind of destruction. They say it is catastrophic destruction [*pralayam*]. Men's courage [*dhairyam*] is only on their lips, but women's *dhairyam* is in their hearts.[8] If she [unclear whether the pronoun refers to human women, the goddess, or both] loves someone, she'll give her life; but if she dislikes someone, she'll cause total destruction.

Annapurna's commentary was given (in a heightened, performative mode) as illustration of her recitation style for village audiences, but it goes much beyond commenting on the translation process. It provides insight into Annapurna's views of gender and marriage and the ways in which she characterizes the nature of women. Here, she interprets marriage as binding, an effort, quite literally, to "tie" a woman through certain practices such as purifying rituals and "binding" ornamentation.[9] But, Annapurna asserts, this male attempt is, ultimately, unsuccessful: males cannot truly know the true (unbounded/unbindable) nature of women, which is *shakti.* She ends the commentary with a rather derisive characterization of men—their courage is superficial, while women's is in their hearts—and, finally, warns of the destructive potential of the female if she is displeased with someone.

Annapurna consistently performed a set of three narratives when she responded to my requests to tell the story of Gangamma: the descent of the Ganga river goddess, Yogamaya Devi, and Adi Para Shakti. She usually ended the first two narratives with the story of Adi Para Shakti; they were sometimes fully elaborated and other times presented only as truncated frame stories for Adi Para Shakti. On two occasions, the descent of the Ganga was framed by a concise summary of the Ramayana. The story of Yogamaya Devi, as Annapurna tells it, ends as a relatively straightforward etiological frame for Gangamma as a *gramadevata;* whereas, the Descent of Ganga resonates with and comments on the *ugra* nature of Gangamma. Significantly, the story of Gangamma and the Palegadu is *not* part of Annapurna's repertoire, perhaps because it is not a *purana* according to the standards in which she was taught. However, Gangamma's Tatayyagunta temple is on Annapurna's performance circuit (now that the Devasthanam has brought in Brahman priests and introduced Sanskritic rituals), and she knows the Palegadu narrative in a non-performative mode.

What follows is a translation of the performance Annapurna gave upon our first meeting in Tatayyagunta temple, in which she told all three narratives, the first two performatively and that of Yogamaya Devi in a "reported" rather than performative style due to time constraints. I did not realize she was going to perform right then and there, so turned on my voice recorder a few sentences into the performance. Annapurna did not include in this informal performance the invocatory and periodic internal-to-performance *shlokas* that are typical of her public performances and that help to create her performative authority. One of Annapurna's variants of Adi Para Shakti is found in chapter 3; in this chapter, I provide only narrative variants when significant, to illustrate the ways in which the narrative is framed by Annapurna's own performative repertoire. The *purana pandita* weaves the three narratives together, beginning with Descent of Ganga, then telling Adi Para Shakti to explain how Shiva had the *shakti* to bear Ganga, and finally ending with Yogamaya Devi, who is said to be the *avatara* (incarnation) of Ganga. I have interspersed my own commentary after each narrative, although the three narratives were performed continuously.

Descent of Ganga

Annapurna begins the story of Ganga's descent with the frame story of the sage Bhagiratha calling her down from heaven to purify the souls of his ancestors: There was a King Sagara who had sixty thousand sons. He was performing a horse sacrifice when the horse was stolen by Indra (king of gods). Indra tied the horse up at Kapila Maharishi's hermitage (*ashram*). King Sagara's sixty thousand sons started digging up the earth to find the horse. Their father warned that if they didn't find the horse and complete the *yajna* (sacrifice), their entire lineage would be destroyed. He sent his sons to every *loka* (cosmological realm) to search for the horse. Their digging caused a dreadful sound and the whole earth shook; all the fourteen *lokas,* seven above and seven below, were shaking; each of the four directions was crying; animals, snakes, and all living creatures were being killed. Bhu Devi (goddess of earth) went to Brahma to ask him to put a stop to this destruction. The god assured her that she shouldn't worry; they would soon find the horse at Kapila Maharishi's *ashram.* Annapurna continued:

The sons searched for the horse and found it tied to a tree near Kapila Maharishi's *ashram.* They thought he had stolen it and took a trident to attack him. He opened his eyes and turned them into ashes. When his sons didn't return, their father sent out his grandsons: "Go find where your fathers are; they haven't come back." His five grandsons went in search of their fathers, and they, too, died. One grandson went and found the horse and the king completed the *yajna.* But he wanted to purify all those who had died [by immersing them in Ganga water]. They were struggling in hell [*naraka*]. So that the ancestors could achieve *moksha* [liberation, release], they [the descendants] had to bring Ganga down from heaven. Some of the grandsons performed *tapas* [austerities], but they weren't able to bring her down; and they, too, died.

The last one in their *vamsha* was Bhagiratha. He was newly married. He thought, "All my people are dead and I'm newly married. Somehow or other I need to bring Ganga down." He left his wife and kingdom in the care of his ministers and went to perform *tapas*. He performed *tapas* for many years. He was fifty or sixty years old by then. Then Brahma appeared to him and asked, "What do you want? Ask for any boon."[10] And he replied "I want Ganga Devi to come down to Bhu Loka [earth] and purify my fathers. They are struggling in hell and they need release [*moksha*]. Because of the sins they committed, the people who went to purify them are also in hell. Everyone in our *vamsha* is struggling in hell. All those in our *vamsha* are flowing into hell. So I want Ganga Devi.

Brahma said, "I'll send Ganga. But who has the *shakti* to bear [*bharincu*] her? For that you have to perform *tapas* for Shiva." So he went to perform *tapas* for Shiva. He did *tapas* for many more years, and Shiva appeared to him. Bhagiratha said, "You have to bear Ganga." He accepted and asked Ganga Devi to come down. Bhagiratha went to Brahma and told him, "Shiva has accepted to bear Ganga, so ask Ganga to come down." But Ganga Devi said, "Will Shiva bear me?! Does he have the *shakti* to bear me? I will send him, too, to Patalam [the underworld]. It's not an easy thing to bear me. It's impossible." And she tried to stomp on Shiva, pushing him to Patalam.

Shiva spread out his matted hair, hiding the earth. One could only see his hair, nothing of the earth. Ganga flowed down from above with a big noise, along with fish, whales, trees, snakes and other living things, flowers, trees, animals. The seven *lokas* above and the seven *lokas* below shook from the force. As she fell from above, it was as though there was thunder, as though mountains were crashing down with great speed. All this was to send Shiva to Patalam. He understood her desire [*korika*]. He said, "Are you trying to send *me* to Patala Loka?! Me, Parmashiva?! I'll bring down your pride [*ahankaram*]. He spread his hair and picked up his *trishul.* He bent Adi Shakti [Ganga], along with her third eye. He shouted and stood up.

Some of Annapurna's linguistic choices reflect her literate, brahminic background and training through use of terms such as *moksha* (liberation of soul from cycle of reincarnation; salvation) and *vamsha* (lineage), terms not commonly used in other Gangamma performances. Another example of her *pandita* training is Annapurna's description of an elaborate cosmology that lists all the fourteen *lokas;* folk cosmologies are much simpler, often listing simply the three levels of heaven, hell, and earth. However, one phrase, in particular, is identical to that used to describe Gangamma in everyday speech as "too much to bear [*bharincu*]." In this telling, Shiva identifies Ganga's desire to push him down to the underworld as *korika,* a term used in colloquial Telugu for all kinds of "desire," but which in other Gangamma contexts often implies sexual desire.

Ganga pridefully taunts Shiva, "Will Shiva be able to bear me? Does he have the *shakti* to bear me? I'll send him, too, to Patalam. It's not an easy thing to bear me. It's impossible." Ganga is powerful and independent, and her taunt mirrors what I heard many times in relationship to Gangamma—that no man can bear her, which is why she doesn't have a husband. (While in other *puranic* narratives Ganga is often portrayed as one of the wives of Shiva, in Annapurna's performances, there is no such implication.) This is a test of wills, a test of who is most powerful. In another performance, Annapurna describes the true nature of river Ganga to be like that of women more generally: "Her nature is to be proud, and she has this pride in every part of her. She's naturally *shakti.* With her *shakti,* she can overcome anyone; she's dynamic and moves [*cancal*]; she has the nature of a woman. Ganga Devi has courage [*dhairyam*] and is bold [*sahasa*]."

Cancal is an adjective that literally means "moving"; I have heard the term applied to women—or to minds or eyes, more generally—but not specifically to men. Applied to women, *cancal* usually has connotations of fickle, unstable, or flirtatious. I propose this is a male interpretation of the word; that is, in the dominant gender ideology, a woman who "moves" (unpredictably, or "too much") is so interpreted. But in the context of this sentence, in which the other adjectives have a more positive valence (at least for the narrator), I translate it literally—as a woman who moves, is dynamic. Perhaps it is this "true nature" of woman—courageous, bold, and dynamic—that Annapurna earlier said males attempt to bind through marriage.

Adi Para Shakti

In the Descent of Ganga story, Shiva does, ultimately, have the *shakti* to bear Ganga; but to explain how Shiva procured this *shakti,* Annapurna interjects the story of Adi Para Shakti. In her version, the god's *shakti* is given to him by Adi Para Shakti. She follows the basic narrative grammar of the other variants we have discussed, but in several places she makes explicit the connection between this goddess who is the creator of the world and Gangamma:

Then she created a third person, Parmashiva. He was without form. He didn't say Amma or Talli; he didn't say anything. He came without form and did *namaskaram* [gestural salutation]. [She said] "Fulfill my desire [*kama*]. To reduce my *kama,* enjoy sexual pleasures [*bhogam*] with me. Adi Shakti asked this of Shiva. "I am a *kanya* [virgin]. To satisfy my *kama,* become my husband." Who does all this? Gangamma. Adi Para Shakti.

When Brahma and Vishnu are deemed to be ineligible to become husbands to the goddess because their first words to her were "mother," she doesn't destroy them, as she does in other variants, but gives them a task each: Brahma should become the creator of the world and Vishnu should rule over that creation (their traditional, respective roles in the Trimurti). In the earlier variants we have considered, Adi Para Shakti is not described visually; Shiva simply seems to know her *shakti* and does not "see" its manifestations beyond her third eye and *trishul.* In this performance, however, Annapurna describes the goddess with eighteen arms, holding eighteen weapons—a powerful image that mirrors those of Durga and other pan-Indian deities in their *vishvarupams:*

She had eighteen arms; she held a *trishul* and skulls; in all her eighteen arms she held eighteen weapons. With all this, she looked like Adi Para Shakti. Shiva said, "You're holding all these weapons, and I have no *shakti.*

Just looking at you, I'm terrified. How am I your equal? I have nothing, right? I, too, need *shakti.* If I am to make you happy [*sukha*], I, too, should have *shakti.* For that *shakti,* give me your *trishul;* give me your third eye."

The *vishvarupa* image of the *gramadevata* Gangamma in the Palegadu narrative is quite different: simply stretching from earth to sky. But the power differential is the same in all variants, and Shiva seeks to minimize or reverse it by negotiating for Adi Para Shakti's *trishul* and third eye. But even this isn't enough, and when he grabs the sari of the goddess, it turns red (which may be a reference to her beginning to menstruate, stated more explicitly in some other variants). And a great *pralayam* results. The gods can only make her *shanta* by promising to perform her *jatara* annually (with no specific mention of *bali*).

As soon as he got the *trishul* and the third eye, he caught hold of the end of her sari. As soon as he caught her sari, her clothes became red. That means that even now he didn't have enough *shakti.* She was in her most fearsome [*bhayankar*] form, Ammavaru, Shaktisvarupini. She went with great speed up into the sky. She piled up all the *lokas;* rivers became like seas. She did this because she couldn't suppress her *kama.* She piled everything together. There were terrible waves and she moved through them. There were four waves in the middle, and she slept on them. [Pause.] That means, no one had the *shakti* to "experience" her. Brahma, Vishnu, Shiva; none of them had the *shakti* to experience her. As soon as she fell asleep there, they said, "We should make her *shanta;* we need to reduce her *kama.*"

Brahma, Vishnu, and Maheshvara performed a *yajna* in Bhu Loka. Reciting *mantras,* they took *pasupu-kumkum* [to worship her] and said, "Be peaceful, Talli, be peaceful." They told her, "You're the one who protects villages. Don't let poxes, fevers, and such things come into our village. We will perform *jatara* every year and fulfill vows to you. For every village, you'll be the *gramadevata* and rule over it." They made her peaceful and put her to sleep. That's where the story ends for Adi Para Shakti.

The purpose of the Adi Para Shakti narrative at this junction in Annapurna's performance is to explain how Shiva came to have the *shakti* to bear Ganga's descent—although the *shakti* procured through her *trishul* and third eye was not, significantly, enough for Shiva to bear and satisfy Adi Para Shakti's *kama.*

Back to Descent of Ganga

Annapurna now shifts back to Descent of Ganga at the point where she had left off when she started the story of Adi Para Shakti. She picks up with Shiva's shout of victory:

With all this, he looked at her and shouted out. When he looked at her like that, the mountain peaks fell. He should have gone down to Patala Loka, but he was able to bear her. As soon as Ganga fell [on Shiva's head], he tied his hair up into a knot. When he did that, Bhagirata was unable to see Ganga. So he performed *tapas* to Shiva. He said, "I don't know whether Ganga Devi has come down or not. Shiva answered, "Ganga Devi has a lot of pride and anger [*ahankaram* and *kopam*]. She wanted to send me to Patalam. If this Ganga is let down to Bhu Loka, all the *lokas* will flow along with her [wash away]. She'll send not only me, but all the *lokas* to Patalam. I won't send down all of Ganga. I'll just send down one stream. [Annapurna laughs.] So what we have in the Ganga River today is just that one strand of hair that Shiva sent down. "I'll take out one strand of hair and send her down. You can take her now and go, but be careful."

As soon as he took down that one strand of hair, there was thunder and lightning. As soon as he took down the strand, she flowed with great force. She wanted to drown Bhu Loka. She came down with great force and everything in the way flowed along with her. All the villages flowed away with her. She came to Kapila Maharishi's *ashram* and went to the ascetic Jahnu. He was performing *tapas.* As she came near him, and he drank her up. He drank up all the water because all the villages were flowing away with her. Because of her forceful speed. Then Bhagiratha entreated him, "Swamy, it was with real difficulty that I brought her down, for the sake of my ancestors. They were falling to hell. Somehow or the other, let her go." If he let her out through his mouth, she would become polluted [from his saliva], so he let her out through his ear. He said, "Be careful. At least now, Ganga, reduce your pride." He said this to Gangamma, Ganga Devi, and then let her out through his ear. That's how she got the name Jahnavi [daughter of Jahnu].

Still, she flowed out with great speed. She can't change her nature [*buddhi*], right? Her female nature [*stri svabhavam*] is like that. [Annapurna laughs.] All the auspicious women [*muttaiduvas*] went to her with *pasupu-kumkum,* silk saris, fruits, and offerings. They made her peaceful [*shanta*]. They said, "Talli, don't drown us; don't take our lives away. Take this *pasupu-kumkum.*" And they did *puja.* "Purify us," and they immersed themselves in the water. They immersed in the fast current. To whichever *uru* she goes, people immerse themselves in her.

She flowed to Kapila Maharishi, and as soon as she touched them, all his ancestors went to Punya Loka [heaven]. And Bhagirata performed their last rites. He made offerings in the name of each one.

Brahma then appeared to Bhagiratha and acknowledged that he had suffered great difficulties and lost his kingdom; in the midst of the years of his *tapas,* his youth had passed and he'd become old with no progeny. Bhagiratha asked for only one thing: to have a son to keep his lineage alive. For that to be possible, he would have to be returned to his youth.

That's how Bhagirata brought Ganga to earth. She branched out into different tributaries. . . . Each branch flowed into a different *uru.* If everything flowed together, everything would be swept away. That's why there's the Krishna River; that's the water we drink. Rivers Ganga, Krishna, Godavari, Sarasvati, Narmada [were created].

Shiva identifies the source of Ganga's destructive power to be pride and anger (*ahankaram* and *kopam*). And he intends to bring these down, to put woman in her place, so to speak. (Jahnu, too, implores Ganga to reduce her pride, equating it with her forceful power.) Shiva catches her in his spread-out hair and binds her up in a topknot. He thinks that by letting out a single strand of hair, a single stream of Ganga, the earth will be able to bear her. But even that single stream is so strong as to be destructive: "She came down with great force and everything in the way flowed along with her. All the villages flowed away with her."

While initially Ganga directed her earth-shattering power against Shiva, with the intention of pushing him down to the underworld—responding to his pride, to *think* he could bear her—now, even this single stream of river (like Gangamma's *ugram,* not directed at anyone in particular) is by its very nature excessively forceful and destructive. Annapurna equates this force with female nature more generally: "Still, she flowed out with great speed. She can't change her nature [*buddhi*], right? Her female nature [*stri svabhavam*] is like that."

While Shiva and Jahnu can't control Ganga's destructive speed and force, through their ritual offerings of *pasupu-kumkum, muttaiduva* women can. (Another performance mentions that the women making offerings considered Ganga herself to be a great *muttaiduva,* implying she shares their auspicious female nature.) The women ask Ganga, "Talli, don't drown us; don't take our lives away. Take this *pasupu-kumkum.*" They immerse themselves in her water, and Ganga continues to flow toward the *ashram* of Kapila Maharishi, where the ancestors' ashes are purified.

In another performance of Descent of Ganga, Annapurna gave the following description of Ganga's transition from destructive force into a river goddess whom humans can bear:

She made a sound as though she was going to break the three worlds; with her speed, she wanted to drown Shiva, to push him to Patala Loka, without thinking that he was god; she wanted to escape from the hair of Parmashiva and push him down to Patala Loka; in order to test his *shakti,* she flowed from Deva Loka [the world of gods] to Bhu Loka [the earth] with great speed. [This paragraph is a single momentum-building sentence, without pause].

After falling from the sky, she got entangled in that hair with lots of difficulties; she thought she'd gotten caught in Parmashiva's hands and she was sad. Seeing all those who were drowning, she changed her speed, with great grace, like the elegant curves of the body, even great people performed *puja* to her and fulfilled vows to Ammavaru; they are doing *seva* to her and singing her praises. It is Ammavaru who's coming in the form of the river; they called her *paramapavitra* [lit., supreme, pure one]; they were offering *pasupu-kumkum* to Ammavaru, and were making offerings in the names of the ancestors, and they were bathing in the river. There was catastrophic destruction [*pralayam*]; some people were happy, but other *urus* drowned.

The *pralayam* of Ganga's descent is reminiscent of that caused by Adi Para Shakti in some variants of her story, when she realizes Shiva has tricked her and that her desire will not be satisfied by him. But in this episode,

Ganga initiates her own transformation from *ugra* to *shanta*. She is compassionate when she sees the destruction of villages and people who are in her path: "she changed her speed, with great grace, like elegant curves of the body . . ." The narrative implies that those who worshipped her with *pasupu-kumkum* were saved, even as other *urus* drowned.

Yogamaya Devi

After she had completed the Descent of Ganga narrative in the temple courtyard that first day I met her, I asked Annapurna about the relationship between Ganga and Gangamma. She answered with the story of Yogamaya Devi, the third narrative she consistently performed as part of her Gangamma repertoire. The Yogamaya Devi narrative on this particular occasion was less performative and elaborated than that of Descent of Ganga and Adi Para Shakti. Its narration below implies previous knowledge of the story, so I provide a brief summary first, drawn from other tellings of the story by Annapurna.

Yogamaya Devi is the goddess who came to earth as a newborn girl child to save the life of the infant Krishna, who had been sent to earth as an incarnation of Vishnu to defeat the wicked king Kamsa. Kamsa had been warned that he would be destroyed by the eighth child of his cousin Devaki; he imprisoned Devaki and her husband Vasudeva, so that the child would be born in prison and could be destroyed. However, the night Krishna was born (as the eighth child), his father braved a raging, flooded Yamuna River to take the newborn across to the village of Brindavan, where he was raised by foster parents Yashoda and Nanda. Yashoda and Nanda's own girl-child, born that same night, was substituted for the infant Krishna in prison; that baby was Yogamaya Devi. Hearing of the birth of the baby, the furious Kamsa entered Devaki's prison cell, held up the infant and smashed her against the ground. At that moment, Annapurna relates, Yogamaya Devi took her true powerful form (*shaktisvarupini*) and flew up into the skies. She was reborn at the fourteen *shakti pithas* (pan-Indian goddess sites) and spread across the world as the *gramadevatas.* And then Annapurna made an interesting connection between Ganga and Yogamaya Devi: Ganga river goddess wanted a form through which she could be worshipped, an *avatara,* and that form was Yogamaya Devi.

After Ganga came to Bhu Loka from Deva Loka, she should be worshipped in every temple, right? She told Vishnu, "I've come to Bhu Loka. I need *puja* and everything. I should also have an *avatara*." So he said, "Krishna will come in your *vamsha* [lineage], Chandra *vamsha*. . . . [and Vishnu proceeds to give Yogamaya Devi the task of exchanging the babies, so that Krishna is not murdered by his uncle, a variation of the synopsis above].

Yogamaya Devi took the baby from Devaki in jail and took it to Rohini Devi (Yashoda) and Nanda. . . . The baby had to go to Rohini Devi because otherwise it would be killed by Kamsa. Vishnu asked Yogamaya Devi to take the baby and put it in Rohini. There the baby would be born and these people [Kamsa and all] wouldn't know about it.

Yogamaya said, "I'm doing so much for you, so I should receive a share [of the good outcome], too. What's in this for me, Swamy [Vishnu]?" He said, "Yogamaya Devi, you will be born as Yashoda Devi's daughter. . . . Vishnu said, "Be born from Yashoda Devi as Yogamaya Devi. You'll be born as a girl, and the eighth child will be born as Krishna here. Devaki Devi will give birth to Krishna as the eighth child. As soon as Krishna is born here, you'll be born there to Yashoda at the same time. They'll take Krishna from jail and place him near Yashoda Devi, and you, being Yogamaya, will be brought and placed in Kamsa's hands. When you're given to him, show your *avatara* [implying, true self as goddess].

[Narrator explains as an aside:] She needs an *avatara*. She should be a human. Actually, she's a river. Ganga Devi came to Bhu Loka, but she wasn't in the form of a human. She told Vishnu Murty, "I need some recognition [for doing this]." She comes from Vishnu Murty. She must be worshipped in Bhu Loka in human form. This human form is Yogamaya Devi.

She showed eighteen *avataras*. She had eighteen arms. She was fearsome. She wore skulls around her neck and she had a garland of lemons. At that time, Devaki, Vasudeva, Kamsa and the others present in the jail saw her as *shaktisvarupini*, and she said, "You evil one, the baby who will kill you has been born; Krishna has been born. He was born at the same time as me. Your death is certain; you will die. You didn't even consider that I was a girl, and you tried to kill me like you killed the other seven. Aren't you ashamed? I was a girl baby. You will be destroyed." Yogamaya's eighteen *avataras* are in eighteen forms: Kanaka Durga, Gangamma—each in a different place—Candika, Gaumati in Kashi, and Gaya. Thus she took different *avataras*.

Vishnu Murty said, "You'll be in the form of Candika, Gangamma, Mariamma, Gaumati, Durga, Kali, Mahakali.[11] You'll be called by eighteen different names. Rajarajeshwari, too. You'll receive *puja* in every *uru.* In every *uru,* you should protect them from cholera, smallpox, and diseases like that. And they'll offer you *pongal* and will celebrate *jatara* for you. That's how she came to Krishnapuram, Gangamma. That Gangamma was brought [to Tirupati] by Tattayacharya, and life breath was established in her. There's a *caritra* [story] for that, too. I'll tell that to you some other time.

Another Annapurna performance began with Yogamaya Devi and proceeded into the Adi Shakti narrative, leaving out Descent of Ganga. The transition between the two narratives in this performance hinges on the shared identity between Yogamaya Devi, the *gramadevatas,* and Adi Para Shakti as *shaktisvarupini:*

Having come into the *shakti pithas,* Yogamaya Devi spread across the world. She became a *gramadevata* in each village: Ankalamma, Mariamma, Pochamma, Gangamma, Chinna Gangamma, Pedda Gangamma. Under all these names, she protected the villages and all their inhabitants. She protected them from measles and everything.

The original base of these *gramadevatas* is *shaktisvarupini.* The Ammavaru [goddess] who's called *shaktisvarupini,* the creator. Who did she create? She created the three [gods]. Among those three, whoever was most suitable, she wanted to approach him; she wanted to approach him [for sex]. . . . [narrator continues the Adi Shakti narrative.]

Interestingly, in this variant, Yogamaya Devi is an incarnation of Ganga, which contrasts to the Telugu Katamaraju oral epic, in which Yogamaya, after having been dashed to the ground by Kamsa, is born as Ganga, who plays a central role in the epic (Narayana Rao 1989, 111). The Yogamaya Devi narrative in Annapurna's three-part repertoire provides an etymological rationale for the multiple forms of the goddess, forms taken so she is available for human worship. Yogamaya Devi is the anthropomorphic form of the river Ganga, who needs such a form in order to be worshiped; she is divided and spreads across the world in the forms of *gramadevatas* to protect villages and their inhabitants.

In Annapurna's female-centered performance of Descent of Ganga—which follows her through her incarnation as Yogamaya Devi and then into hundreds of *gramadevatas*—by the end, Shiva drops out of the narrative altogether. This is in rather stark contrast to popular, Shiva-centered contemporary lithographs that picture the Descent of Ganga; in these lithographs, a large Shiva sits in the middle of the scene, with a tiny Ganga flowing into his locks at the top of the picture—Ganga having been subdued, her energetic pride seemingly broken.

Repertoire as Commentary

Each of the three narratives Annapurna performs is a commentary on gender relations—namely, between the gods and goddess, although Annapurna specifically calls the nature of Ganga to be that of *stri* (the female, more generally)—and each contributes unique perspectives on the *shakti* of the goddess. In Descent of Ganga, the goddess is proud and taunts Shiva that he will be unable to bear her: "Will Shiva bear me?! Does he have the *shakti* to bear me? I will send him, too, to Patalam. It's not an easy thing to bear me. It's impossible." However, he catches her in his outspread hair and, in a moment of trickery, ties her up in his head-knot, and then "bends her," and stands up with a shout of victory. But this seemingly victorious conclusion is immediately followed by the story of Adi Para Shakti, in which Shiva's victory would seem to be short-lived. In this story, the god actually does *not* have enough *shakti* to bear her; he tricks her into giving him some of her own power through her eye and trident, but this isn't enough and the god is not willing to even try to satisfy her desire. The goddess's unfulfilled desire creates great destruction and threatens the universe itself.

By performing Descent of Ganga in the same repertoire as Adi Para Shakti, Annapurna equates river goddess Ganga with Adi Para Shakti. Both forms of the goddess are by their very nature "too much to bear." The inherent *shakti* of the goddesses is both life-giving and destructive. Adi Para Shakti creates the gods (and, by implication, the world), but her unfulfilled desire creates threatening *pralayam.* Ganga's waters are needed to purify the ashes of Bhagiratha's forefathers, but the force of even a single stream of Ganga is threatening to the life forms that lie in her path. Ganga then chooses to take a beautiful graceful form that elicits devotion and worship, bringing *anandam* to some *urus* and destruction to others.

The last time I met Annapurna in 2005, after she had performed several narratives and we were getting ready to leave her home, she went to her steel *almira* (cabinet) and pulled out a new starched cotton sari, blouse piece, and turmeric thread for both my fieldwork associate and myself. She told us that the saris had been worn by Gangamma in her *jatara* form of the cement pillar at Tatayyagunta temple courtyard and held her blessings. Annapurna had been given two saris by temple officials, and we were two guests; it was destined, she said. Following an upper-caste tradition, she covered the sari she was gifting with the ends of both her and my own saris and recited, "I give you this *vayanam* [ritual gift]"—to which I should have answered, "I receive the *vayanam.*" But since I didn't know the custom, she answered for me. One last gift indicated Annapurna's entry into the world of Gangamma: a piece of the *ugra mukhi* of Tatayyagunta, recovered by her son in the mad scramble for such pieces as the *mukhi* is dismantled. Annapurna had kept these pieces safely in a glass jar since the last *jatara.* She gave us each a piece of the precious clay and told us dip it in water and drink it if we or our family members were sick.

Over the years of performing in Tatayyagunta temple, Annapurna has developed a personal relationship with Gangamma that is uncommon for a Brahman woman who traditionally would not be an active participant in the *jatara.* Narrative performance itself has helped to give Annapurna entry into and to shape this relationship. Her performative repertoire also creates relationships between goddesses—Gangamma, Ganga, Yoga Maya Devi, and Adi Para Shakti—providing commentary on the phrase "all goddesses are one." Each narrative expands on the shared quality of *shakti* between the goddesses. But Annapurna goes further; she suggests that women, too, share this *shakti:* "She's naturally *shakti.* With her *shakti,* she can overcome anyone; she's dynamic and moves like a woman. Ganga Devi is fearlessness and bold."

THOSE WHO BEAR THE GODDESS

Two

WANDERING GODDESS, VILLAGE DAUGHTER: AVILALA REDDYS

6

Although many Tirupati residents say Gangamma cannot be kept at home because she is too *ugra,* too much to bear, several families and individuals claim exception to this generalization: "While others can't bear her, we can and do." One such family is the Reddy family of Avilala village, only a few kilometers from Tirupati, whose forefathers are said to have found Gangamma as a little baby in the paddy fields outside of the village and who raised her as a daughter. By extension, the village itself considers her to be a daughter of Avilala.

In its movement from village to village in Chittoor District throughout the first month of the Tamil new year, the *jatara* finally completes the migration (with considerable drama) from Avilala to Tirupati. The distance between the boundaries of village and town has shrunk considerably between my first visit to Avilala in 1992 and my last one in 2010; village and town have grown into each other, with only a few fields keeping them apart. In 1992 an auto ride to the village from Tirupati seemed extravagant, but by 2010 there were many autos and jeeps plying the road between. Nevertheless, there is still a distinctly village ethos in the quiet lanes of

Avilala—in which buffaloes and goats wander and rest next to stacks of fodder—and their surrounding paddy fields.

The *jatara* as celebrated in Avilala is known by outsiders primarily for the buffalo sacrifice (*bali*) that is performed for Gangamma in her thousand-eyed clay form. But village residents themselves give equal significance to the exchange of Gangamma's bride's gifts (called *pasupu-kumkum*, shorthand for the entire gifting ritual, which includes a sari, blouse piece, bangles, flower garlands, and *pasupu-kumkum*) between the families of Avilala Reddys and Tirupati Kaikalas. Together, these two rituals—*bali* and *pasupu-kumkum*—identify Gangamma as both as an *ugra* goddess, who fills the *uru* with awe and whose expanding form can be satisfied only with *bali*, and a daughter with whom Avilala residents engage in familial relationship. Gangamma is both a wandering goddess who settles for a short time during the *jatara* and a village daughter who never entirely settles, as she goes back and forth between her natal home and that of her in-laws.

Gangamma as the Thousand-eyed Goddess

In villages, Gangamma and her *gramadevata* sisters traditionally live at the boundaries of the *uru* in the form of simple stone heads or uncarved stones, traces of *kumkum* on them indicating their periodic worship, or as iron tridents stood up in a row, sometimes under a thatched roof covering.[1] Once a year, for her *jatara* (or more often if there is drought or particular Gangamma illness in the village), villagers clear the weeds from around, wash, and apply *pasupu-kumkum* to Gangamma's images and those of her sisters. And then Gangamma is called into the middle of the village, given the form of the thousand-eyed goddess, and offered buffalo and/or goat sacrifice. She becomes Middle-of-the-Street (*nadi vidhi*) Gangamma.

In Avilala, Gangamma's *ugra*, expansive *jatara* form is built over a simple little stone hidden in the niche of a low cement platform on the main street that passes through the middle of the village.[2] During the rest of the year, this middle-of-the-street small form is acknowledged only by a small clay oil lamp that is lit daily.[3] However, as the *jatara* approaches, one can imagine the goddess expanding with the increasingly heated days; she needs a bigger form. On the day before the Avilala *jatara* begins, a three- to four-foot clay mound is built by men of the washmen (Cakali) caste

Thousand-eyed goddess, Avilala.

out at the village tank and then moved to the middle of the *uru.* Here, the mound becomes the thousand-eyed goddess when tens of metallic eyes are embedded in the clay and she is adorned with jewelry given to her by villagers (and, one year, the anthropologist). A thatch-woven "hut" is built over her, with an opening on one side so that the goddess faces east. Women who have made vows to the goddess—asking for fertility, successful childbirth, or general prosperity for the home—offer cotton-print saris and lay them over the hut. (Note that the traditional offering is a cotton, not polyester or silk, sari.) Her primary attendants (accepting offerings and lighting oil lamps) at her new site in the middle of the street are Cakali men and women.

Bali to the Thousand-eyed Goddess

On the last of the two-day Avilala *jatara,* female village celebrants dressed in their finest saris, with their freshly oiled hair adorned with flowers, bring brass or stainless steel plates filled with a coconut, an oil lamp made of flour dough, flowers, fruit, and a piece of new cloth. Only as I was photographing these offerings midday the first year I attended the *jatara* in 1992 did I notice three goat heads among the many offering plates, heads of animals that had been offered earlier in the morning. Soon after the plates have been arranged before the goddess, as the women wait patiently around the back and sides of Gangamma's temporary dwelling, men begin digging a sacrificial pit about fifteen to twenty feet away in front of the goddess for the *dunnapotu* (male buffalo) *bali* which is to follow.

Gangamma's hunger can usually be satisfied during the year with offerings of *pongal* or, on special occasions, mounds of cooked rice (*kumbhạm*); but her expanding hot season hunger is more efficiently and dependably satisfied with chicken, goat, and buffalo sacrifice. And there are severe consequences if her hunger is left unsatisfied. Answering my question of whether or not the *jatara* was performed in her maternal village, five miles from Avilala, the Reddy-family grandmother told the story of a year when the *jatara* was not performed in Avilala and the consequences thereof:

> No, it doesn't happen in my village. Only in this village, we have to perform the *jatara* or Gangamma will destroy everyone. They're afraid. Once when someone objected to the *jatara*, that same night twenty people started vomiting and had diarrhea. . . . After that, they poured *ambali* and performed the *jatara*. They [those struck by illness] went to the hospital and got better.

Animal sacrifice (*bali*) was outlawed by the Government of Andhra Pradesh in 1950, although it is still commonly performed in villages throughout the region. When they heard me talk about it, many urban, middle-class Indians were surprised to hear that ritual *bali* still takes place; while villagers with whom I spoke were equally surprised to hear that anyone would think it could be otherwise, responding, "But it *must* take place. It always takes place." Even in Tirupati, several *jatara* participants asserted that at least one buffalo would be sacrificed *somewhere* in town; it simply had to be, even if not on Gangamma temple grounds. The first year we witnessed *bali* in Avilala (1992), we noticed several policemen on motorcycles arrive at the site before the animals had been brought to the site; presumably they were paid off or otherwise appeased, as they disappeared before the *bali* was performed.

One buffalo is traditionally offered on behalf of the entire *uru*—that is, there should be *at least* one sacrificial animal. But individual village families may also make vows to the goddesses (for health, financial stability, or general familial well-being) that are accompanied by the promise of a *bali* animal. Subbarama Reddy (hereafter, SR), the primary organizer of the Avilala *jatara,* reports that in 2010, eleven buffaloes were offered; and in 2011, nine were offered. The flower-garlanded sacrificial buffaloes (usually young and barely bigger than a large goat) are paraded around the *uru,* accompanied by two or three Pambala drummers, before they are led to the sacrificial pit. Four men hold each sacrificial animal by its limbs, its neck outstretched, and it is beheaded by a Madiga male with a single knife stroke. In striking contrast to the quietly chatting women standing around the thatch hut, on the male side, the energy is heightened and the men seem anxious. Male *jatara* organizers shout out instructions to the Madiga-caste male sacrificers—who themselves wear only cotton undershorts and shout out exclamations. The head is rushed up to the goddess and placed on the ground facing her thousand-eyed form. Each buffalo body is simply thrown to the side of the pit, making room for the next animal. At the end, the animal carcasses are taken back to the Madiga neighborhood for distribution among caste members and the sacrificial pit is quickly filled in with earth.

After they are beheaded, the animals' forelegs are placed in their mouths; a flour oil-lamp is placed on top of each head; and their eyes are covered with intestinal skin or fat.[4] The Asadi narrative discussed below mentions these very ritual details, and its narrator explained their reasons: after an Asadi (ritual specialist) had beheaded his wife at the command of the goddess, Gangamma looked at the head and the eyes stared back at her. She told the Asadi, "She's staring at me, heckling me." She wanted him to cover the eyes, but he had nothing with which to cover them. So he cut open his wife's womb and took out the fat and put it on her eyes and lit an oil lamp (burning from that fat). He cut off the right leg and put it in her mouth to keep her from heckling Gangamma. Then the Asadi cut the fetus in half, mixed it and blood with rice and offered it to the goddess. The narrator closed his explanatory commentary, "This kind of thing is necessary for Gangamma; small things will not satisfy."[5]

Asadi Narrative of Sacrifice

On at least three occasions, I heard SR perform the Asadi narrative, which is an explicit, if not straightforward, commentary on the *bali* that is performed to the thousand-eyed Gangamma. Asadis are a sub-group of Madigas, whose members traditionally serve the Seven Sisters as ritual specialists and who are the actual sacrificers in the Avilala *bali*. The story describes Gangamma riding in an oxcart driven by her brother Potu Raju. The cart gets stuck at the village boundary and Gangamma asks her brother to go call the village Asadi, who has seven wives. She demands of the Asadi the sacrifice of one of his seven wives; and the sacrifice ultimately allows her cart to start moving again.

I first recorded the Asadi narrative in 1995, when I returned to Avilala to observe the village *jatara* for a second time and stopped at SR's home to find out the schedule of events. In 1993, when I had gone with my male colleagues, I had exchanged only a few sentences with him; but now SR was loquacious, enthusiastically orchestrating what I should see and providing lengthy explanations about what was happening. He took me into a back room of his house where he had laid out the bride's gifts he was sending with Gangamma as she moved to Tirupati that night. These were displayed on the floor in front of a clay pot decorated with *pasupu-kumkum* dots and with green neem leaves sticking out of its mouth; the wall behind was marked with three *pasupu* horizontal lines between which were *kumkum* dots. Both the pot and wall-markings are forms of the goddess. Unexpectedly, in the middle of showing off the bride's gifts, SR began to perform the Asadi narrative that follows:

Gangamma's native place is Ayodhya;[6] from there, she started coming toward this side. She reached the outskirts of this village and sat down. When she reached this place, the cart in which she traveled got stuck in the wet mud. Potu Raju was with her and was riding in the cart. She wondered what she should do. She called Potu Raju and told him, "Nearby there is a Harijan[7] neighborhood in which lives a man who is an Asadi. That Asadi man has seven wives; since he had no children with his first six wives, he married the seventh one. The seventh wife is eight months pregnant."

Potu Raju went to the Asadi and told him, "Ammavaru is standing at the outskirts of the village and has told me to call you there."

The man went to his eldest wife and asked her to carry the *pongal* basket [traditional offering to the goddess]; but she refused, saying, "I'm not going to live long anyway. Why should I carry that basket on my head?" All the other wives also refused. The seventh wife, seeing her husband helpless, agreed to carry the *pongal* basket on her head. The two of them went to Ammavaru; and the Asadi told her he'd brought *pongal* for her. The wife cooked the *pongal* and put bananas in it, and she bowed and touched Ammavaru's feet.

Ammavaru asked the Asadi man to cut off his wife's head, which he did immediately. She asked him then to cut off the right leg and right hand, and she asked him to put the hand into her [the beheaded wife's] mouth. She asked him to cut out the womb out of the woman. He took the entrails and wore them around his chest like a sacred thread. *Ahhhhhhhhh*! [SR stares in a frozen manner and puts his arm out straight/stiff, indicating possession by the goddess. SR's wife sprinkles him, and the rest of the people in the room listening to his narrative, with water and tells my fieldwork associate not to be afraid.]

The Asadi circumambulated the goddess three times and did *namaskaram* to her. He told her, "I gave my word; I did whatever you asked me to do. Now what boon will you give me in return?" She asked him to tell her what he wanted. He answered, "Whenever I call you, you must hear and respond to me." She agreed. As soon as she gave her word, the cart in which she had been traveling became unstuck from the mud and started moving—*jala, jala, jala, jala, jala* [onomatopoetic indication of speed].[8] *Ahhhhhhhhh!* [Again, his wife sprinkles water over everyone in the room].

[SR now launches immediately into the story of the Palegadu (see below) and then continues with still a third, more contemporary narrative of how the largest Gangamma temple came to be built in Tirupati, the story of the Mudaliar family that built up the Tatayyagunta temple. He concludes:][9]

This is her story [*caritra*]. Since then, she has been there [in Tirupati].

[Several male audience members clap, thereby closing the frame of "performance."]

This narrative is clearly an etiological narrative of the *jatara* buffalo sacrifice, including the mechanics of *bali:* beheading the buffalo, placing a severed leg in its mouth, the sacrificer wearing the entrails around his neck. But the narrative is also a commentary on *bali,* suggesting that it not only satisfies the hunger of the goddess, but also keeps her moving. When she stays put in one place, as during her *jatara*, her *ugram* consolidates and requires excessive service, which, if not fulfilled, may result in illness in the *uru*. So, it is to the benefit of humans to keep her moving. Furthermore, *bali* puts the goddess under some obligation to humans, generally, and the Asadis, more specifically.

In the Asadi narrative, Gangamma's cart gets stuck at the edge of the village where her physical forms normally reside.[10] She requires human intervention, more specifically the offering of human sacrifice, to keep moving. But not just any human—in fact, she asks for the sacrifice of a female (notice that Gangamma doesn't ask the Asadi to offer himself), and not any female, but a fertile, auspicious female. Initially, it isn't explicit that Gangamma may be asking for human sacrifice; she first simply calls the Asadi to come to her at the edge of the village. He immediately thinks to offer her the traditional offering of *pongal;* and the Asadi himself requests his wives, one by one, to come with him to carry the basket of *pongal* ingredients. One by one, they each refuse. Throughout the year, infertile women often make vows to feed Gangamma *pongal* in her Tirupati temple courtyards or at village shrines for a specified number of weeks. The fact that the Asadi's first six wives refuse to feed the goddess, even upon request, suggests reason for their past and now (presumably) future infertility.

Before the Asadi can ask his youngest, pregnant wife to accompany him to meet Gangamma, she herself offers. She is not, at that moment in the narrative, offering to sacrifice herself, but presumably thinks she is going to the village outskirts to offer *pongal* to the goddess. But when the goddess is stuck, so deeply stuck, *pongal* would seem to be not enough to satisfy her and get her moving again. The goddess asks for human sacrifice—specifically, the sacrifice of a pregnant woman.

In another variant performed by SR, the Asadi is said to be reluctant to ask his pregnant wife to come with him, after each of his six older wives refuse. The seventh wife sees him lying morosely on his cot in the back yard, not eating, and asks him what's wrong. He relates the whole story, and ends by saying, "But it's a sin [*papam*] to ask you to do this." Her response: "If this happens at your hands, I'm very lucky." It's unclear whether or not the Asadi knows he'll be asked to sacrifice his wife; however, this would seem to be the meaning of "It's a sin to ask you to do this," since offering *pongal* certainly would not be a sin. And the wife's response indicates possible knowledge that she will be offered to the goddess, but is happy to submit to this at the hands of her husband. SR's explanation for the need for a *pregnant* woman was that Gangamma really wanted both a mother and a child. "If the two were sacrificed separately, the child would run off, wouldn't he? Because none of the other wives came forward, the pregnant wife had to go." But another *ritual* explanation would be that Gangamma wants an auspicious offering, which an infertile female would not be; and the only way to guarantee a woman is fertile is to see her fetus.

The Asadi puts up no verbal or physical resistance to Gangamma's request, as one might have expected him to do were the sacrifice to imply simply death of his only child and his youngest, most precious (fertile, auspicious) wife. The sacrifice is reported as if it was an ordinary request, although its narrative description is a heightened moment, indicated by the goddess possessing the narrator at this point. The Asadi seems to have faith that Gangamma is asking of him something reasonable, from whom he can expect an equally reasonable return. He asks her, "I gave you my word, now what will you give in return?" She tells him to ask for anything he wants, and he responds, "Whenever I call you, you must hear and respond to me." We can now understand the Asadi story as also being an etiological narrative that establishes the authority and power of the Asadi as ritual specialist. Only when the contract is fulfilled *both* ways—the sacrifice is performed *and* Gangamma responds to the Asadi's request to come whenever he calls—does Gangamma's cart become unstuck and move, which was the explicit reason for the original sacrifice. But a new reason for *bali* is suggested by the contract articulated at the end of the story: not only does *bali* satisfy the goddess and keep her moving, it also obligates the goddess to the Asadi (and, by implication, to the *uru* he ritually serves).

The end of another SR-variant of the Asadi story tells us that Gangamma's cart moved toward the village so that she would be present for her own *jatara:* "The villagers—Reddys, Karanams, Totis, Chettis—all invited her the first week and the next week they performed her *jatara.*" In a reflexive move, the narrative *bali* carries her toward the *jatara bali.* Both narrative and ritual *bali* create a relationship with Gangamma that ultimately serves the Asadi and protects the *uru,* respectively.

But there is a crucial difference between *bali* in the Asadi story and that of the *jatara:* in the narrative, Gangamma demands sacrifice of a female (and her fetus), whereas the *jatara* sacrificial animal (buffalo) is male. Why did Gangamma not ask for the sacrifice of the Asadi himself? Tirupati *jatara* rituals and narratives provide several cues, but no full explanation, to understanding this narrative/ritual discrepancy. In the Adi Para Shakti story, *bali* is very explicitly a substitution for the male: Shiva cannot bear the *shakti* of the goddess and makes no effort to satisfy her desire; rather, the three gods cool down her *ugram* by assuring Adi Para Shakti that she will be offered *bali* during her *jatara,* implying this is the only way her *korika* can be satisfied. Sacrifice of the *male* buffalo during the *jatara* ritual fulfills this explanatory framework; and this *bali* ultimately "saves" the Trimurti.

But what of the sacrifice of the female in the Asadi narrative? One possibility for the sacrificial (pregnant) female is that with this (narrative) sacrifice Gangamma will protect the fertility of all the women of the *uru*—after all, many women make *mokku* to Gangamma for this very promise. The sacrifice of the female ultimately protects and saves the women, just as the sacrifice of the male buffalo protects and saves the male from *korika* he cannot fulfill and *shakti* he cannot bear. *Bali* is, then, not inherently destructive, but also protective. In this sense, the Asadi narrative is thematically similar to the Renuka narrative, sometimes associated with Gangamma, in which the sacrifice of a woman results in her transformation into a goddess who serves to protect the broader community. There are key differences, however; it is the goddess who demands the sacrifice of the Asadi's wife, and the protective goddess is Gangamma; the Asadi's sacrificed wife does not become a goddess. Renuka's sacrifice, in contrast, is demanded by a male who accuses her of sexual transgression, and it is the beheaded wife who becomes the protective goddess.

Or perhaps the sacrifice of female-to-female suggests their shared quality rather than destruction of one to the other. As Venkateshvarlu asserted in explaining the dismantling of the Tirupati *ugra mukhis* by the Perantalu, only *shakti* can dismantle *shakti.* One could interpret this act as self-sacrifice; the goddess sacrifices her *ugra mukhi* (self) in order to be in relationship with the *uru,* so its inhabitants can sustain/bear her. The form, but not the substance of the *ugra mukhi* is destroyed; its tiny bits of clay are distributed among *jatara* celebrants in forms that they can "bear."[11]

Similarly, in the Asadi story, one could interpret the Asadi wife as sacrificing herself/*shakti* so that the goddess/*shakti* can be sustained (in this case by keeping her moving) by the *uru.* But finally, I find none of these cues totally satisfying and remain troubled by the narrative sacrifice of the Asadi female to the goddess, when the *jatara bali* is of a male, not female, buffalo.

Gangamma as Daughter of the *Uru*

Avilala as an *uru* has the confidence that it can satisfy and bear an *ugra* Gangamma with *bali.* However, perhaps the villagers also have confidence to bear her because they know and understand Gangamma as a daughter of their *uru.* Remember the Avilala female narrators of chapter 4 who emphasized this familial relationship between Gangamma and Avilala. Another female villager distinguished the elder and younger Gangamma sisters (a distinction not commonly made in villages, and one that indicates the close relationship between Avilala and Tirupati): "Pedda Gangamma is from the time of our ancestors, when they were alive. She belongs to them. But Cinna Gangamma is kissed like how we kiss a child and was brought up by the village heads. They looked after her with such love that they cried when the Nawab came to ask for her." But even daughters have needs (sometimes strong needs), and a family, rather than the entire *uru,* is responsible for these needs—including bearing the costs of the bride's gifts during her wedding. The Reddy family said to have raised the baby Gangamma through puberty has taken up this responsibility and is sensitive to the subtleties of the demands of their "daughter" throughout the year.

SR, the senior male of this Reddy family, takes pride in being the primary organizer of the *jatara* in Avilala at such a young age, a role that includes organizing the *bali* to the thousand-eyed goddess. He told us that there are nine *kulams* (castes) in the village, including Reddy, Balija Chetti (the majority), Yadav, Karnalu, and Devar. (Significantly, he does not name the Madiga caste whose male members are active in the *bali* itself.) Each caste sends two elders to the village *panchayat* (council), of which SR was in 1999–2000 the head, a position he says he earned through his hard work on behalf of the village: "Whoever is capable of doing the work will get the title of *pedda manshi* [headman]," the elders had told him. In 1999, the other nine members of the *panchayat* were in their fifties or sixties; SR was the youngest at age forty-three. By this time, SR had become known for his religiosity; he had built a temple for Kokalaparmeshwari (one of the *gramadevatas,* whom SR's wife identifies as Pokalamma) at the edge of the village tank, and a Rama temple in the middle of the village. By the time he became *pedda manshi,* he said, he already knew about the *jatara* and how to organize its rituals from having listened to the elders.

I first met SR briefly in 1992, the first year we observed the *jatara* in Avilala. I met him again several times in 1999–2000 for more extended discussions about the *jatara* and his role in it. At the time, he was employed as male nurse orderly (MNO) by a TTD Ayurvedic hospital situated directly behind Tatayyagunta Gangamma's temple in Tirupati. Here, he was known simply as Sitaram, in reference to his loud, vigorous mode of greeting his coworkers in the hospital with "Jai Sitaram!" (lit., Praise to Sita and Ram, goddess and god of the Ramayana). SR's important Avilala association with Gangamma was far overshadowed (perhaps not even known) in his work context by his identity as a devotee of Hanuman, an important actor in the Ramayana. These coexisting identities as both Gangamma *jatara* patron and Hanuman *bhakta* remind us that most Hindus live in multiple ritual, narrative, and imaginative worlds, which too have often been bifurcated in academic discourse as Sanskritic/pan-Indian and non-textual/village Hindu traditions.

SR asserted that more important than his title of *pedda manshi* and involvement with the village-wide *jatara* is his familial relationship with Gangamma as village daughter, a relationship he sustains throughout the year. SR distinguishes the costs of the *jatara* borne through village-wide collections from those of the *pasupu-kumkum* gifts accompanying Gangamma as daughter-bride, for which his family alone bears the costs. In 2005, he said these costs could range between Rs. 1,000 and Rs. 5,000, or even as much as Rs. 10,000. These expenses have, according to his wife, Dhanalakshmi, taken a great financial and emotional toll on the family. She complained that their family had periodically wanted to give up these responsibilities, but that now (2005) things were a little more stable. Between 1992 and 1995, the family had had to sell the larger house in which they were living when we first met them; they moved to a smaller house across the lane from the Rama temple SR had built in the middle of the village. Dhanalakshmi still regretted this move several years later, but understood it as the cost of serving the goddess.

SR says the custom of sending *pasupu-kumkum* to Tirupati was suspended in 1924 after an unmarried woman had died in the house of the Reddy who was patron of the ritual at that time. The family interpreted her death as having been caused by Gangamma's displeasure with the ways in which they had carried out the *pasupu-kumkum* exchange, and they gave up their *mirasi* for this ritual. Other families were afraid to pick up the responsibility, fearing that their own children or cattle would die if the goddess was displeased, and the tradition was suspended for fifty years.

Dhanalakshmi explained that their ancestors (SR and his wife share ancestors, as they are cross-cousins) had been responsible for the *jatara,* her father's grandfather and their grandfathers. "Then, in the middle, there were some problems; you know, this is a village, and there were some disagreements. Others said, 'We should do it; we should do it.' And those families started doing it, but they got some problems and stopped." SR elaborated in another context that his male elders had died off and only women were left. They couldn't sustain the *jatara,* and some other line of Reddys took it over. But no one could sustain the burdens of its requirements, and the responsibilities shifted from one family to another. After all, SR emphasized, "We should have the *shakti* to bear her." Finally, the villagers asked SR to take over the *pasupu-kumkum* exchange at the same time he became *pedda manshi,* realizing his proclivity toward things "religious." SR agreed to take up this responsibility and, in 1992, in consultation and agreement with the Mudaliar caste family that had hereditary rights over Gangamma's Tatayyagunta temple in Tirupati, he reinstated the *pasupu-kumkum* tradition and became the primary organizer of the Avilala *jatara* itself. But the next year the Endowments Department took over the Tatayyagunta temple and, as SR puts it, the Mudaliar family lost their "connection" to the temple. So now the Endowments Department arranges for the *pasupu-kumkum* exchange from the Tirupati side, with the Kaikalas accepting the *pasupu-kumkum* at the actual ritual by the Gangamma rock outside Avilala.

SR says he did not come to his ritual and devotional role by choice, but by the calling of the goddess:

I've been doing this [religious] work since I was five years old. I've been singing *bhajans* [devotional songs] since then. . . . Ammavaru gave me all this. It's only since 1992 that I've been performing the *jatara,* and since

1986 the goddess has come to me [through possession]. I built the Rama temple in 1986 [at age thirty]. That night I got the *darshan* of Ammavaru, and from then on she's been giving me *darshan.* At first it wasn't intense possession, but since 1992 she has stood right in front of me and shown herself. Even if I sit in a corner and think of something else, she comes to me and asks what I'm thinking about.

For the last five years, I've been crazy [*picci*] about this *jatara* work. I also keep singing *bhajans.* From a very young age, I was entrusted by god [*bhagvan*] to do this work. At first, it was childlike, but now I have to do it responsibly. Even the elders feel sad about this, because I got this responsibility at a very young age, when they weren't able to do it. [That is, SR took up the responsibilities at an earlier age than is traditional for the transfer of ritual responsibilities between generations.]

Until 1992, SR's special relationship with the goddess was not known by the public. Then, he says, there was a (unspecified) problem in the village, and they wanted to bring the goddess into the *uru.* However, Gangamma wasn't allowing anyone to lift her (the clay form of thousand-eyed goddess brought from the edge of the village to its interior). SR didn't know about the problem and was sleeping in his house. Gangamma came to him in a dream and told him to go and lift her up—which he was able to do—and this is how his special relationship with her became publicly known. However, even SR had difficulties after the first year of serving Gangamma:

The next year, we weren't able to do anything. It would have cost five or six thousand rupees, so we weren't able to do it. The first year [1992] we had photographs taken; your photo is there. The second year, we asked everyone to donate something. Someone took me to the university. N. Janardhan Reddy [former chief minister of Andhra] had come. He released the book [P. Srinivasalu Reddy's Telugu book on Gangamma *jatara*]. I was introduced to both of them, and they praised me, that at such a young age I had done so much for Gangamma. My younger brother also told me I had become famous and that I should look after Gangamma well. So, I'm responsible to see that all *jatara* rituals are conducted well. In between, we've had problems, but I didn't blame her; I always blamed myself. However much I have to do, I don't stop her work.

SR also serves the goddess throughout the year, beyond the *jatara:* on three consecutive Tuesdays during the month of Kartik (November), he arranges for cooked food (*kumbham*) and *ambali* to be offered to the tiny Middle-of-the-Street Gangamma; for the Sakranti festival one year, he donated new tridents for Ammavaru, which are processed on the third day. Throughout the year, when villagers experience particular difficulties and disease, they come to him for answers to their problems—answers that he himself receives through dreams, visions, or possession by Gangamma. He explained, "Gangamma comes to people not through their own desires, but when she chooses to come. She possesses if there is some problem or particular happiness. When things are going smoothly, she doesn't come." SR describes how he becomes possessed:

I describe her, sing her names, and then she comes. They call the Pambalas [drummers]. Like this, you can cause possession [*punakam*] to happen. I fast for two meals, take a head bath [i.e., full bath] and sit there. I start to worship her—Mutyalamma, Yerallamma, Okalamma, Ankalamma, Siralamma, and Gangamma [note the multiple names of the Seven Sisters being conflated into the singular "Gangamma" who possesses him]. After ten minutes, she comes. Usually when villagers are not feeling well, but are not serious, I give them *vibhuti* [ash] and *kumkum,* and they get better.

On another occasion, SR explained that he learned what I call the "performance of possession" from Govindamma, an elder woman who has exchanged *talis* with the goddess. He had seen her possessed at Tatayyagunta temple and asked her to come to Avilala to help him learn how to call the goddess. SR noted that Govindamma becomes possessed easily, without many cues or stimuli. He, on the other hand, requires more external stimuli for possession, such as Pambala drumming; only with these, he said, does he become possessed. SR's wife also becomes regularly possessed, but without the stimuli SR seems to need, since she can become possessed by simply hearing the name of the goddess. For this reason, she is even reluctant to talk about Gangamma, for fear of becoming possessed outside a ritual context in which such possession can be more easily "managed." Several times when I was in her home, speaking about Gangamma to other women or her husband, she sat uncharacteristically silently until we changed the subject.

Every Tuesday and Friday, SR offers Gangamma a cut lemon and coconut, recites her thousand names (a ritual recitation of names [*sahasranama*] not traditionally associated with *gramadevatas,* but rather with *puranic* deities) and sings *bhajans* to her. Gangamma is kept in his small *puja* room (built onto the courtyard, outside the house per se) as a three-inch clay pot with neem leaves covering its opening. Underneath the pot, on the vertical face of the cement ledge upon which she sits, is the *pasupu-kumkum* representation of her (three *pasupu* lines and dots of *kumkum* between). A small hunk of clay distributed from the *jatara* thousand-eyed goddess lies on a shelf above the small shrine. On the same shelf is a notebook in which SR has recorded the thousand names of the goddess and the *bhajans* he has composed for her and Hanuman, along with a copy of the *Hanuman Chalisa* (a Hanuman devotional text). I asked SR if Gangamma is less *ugra* during the rest of the year than she is during the *jatara* (when she requires *bali*), and thus, is this the reason he can keep her in his house? He answered, "No, she's *ugra* even now [without specifying more or less *ugra* than during the *jatara*]. During Kartik festival, too, she's *ugra* and possesses people." Note the association between *ugram* (excessiveness; here, excessive "presence") and possession.

SR's wife, Dhanalakshmi, described one of the difficulties of "bearing" Gangamma to be her jealousy of other deities who may be brought into the home. She described once seeing in her house a woman they know who used to make and sell *idlis* (steamed rice cakes). Dhanalakshmi asked her why she was making *idlis* "here, not there." The woman complained that she used to make them there—in the *puja* room—but that someone else had come to occupy that space and she wasn't going to stay there any longer. Only then Dhanalakshmi realized that the woman was the goddess herself, complaining about an image of Hanuman that had been placed in the *puja* room. Dhanalakshmi described her vision to SR, and he moved the Hanuman image to another room. So while Gangamma and Hanuman share space in SR's own practices and loyalties, here is an indication that Gangamma demands first loyalty, as a daughter may do when she returns home from her in-laws' place.

SR has felt this competition for his loyalties before, and Gangamma has always been the one to prevail. Although he is known in his workplace primarily as a Hanuman devotee and often characterizes himself as such, he says Amma keeps calling him back closer to her. In 1996 he was transferred to what locals call "uphill," to Tirumala, where the great god Venkateshvara resides. SR continues:

There a *swami-ji* called me for recitation of the name of god [*japam*]. I used to go there every day and stay overnight three or four times a week. He told me that if I would stay awake for four full moons, then I would have *darshan* of the god. So I wrote a few songs about him [Venkateshvara]; I wrote them in a *cinema-style.* I also wrote ten to fifteen songs about Hanuman. But then they transferred me back to Tirupati in November, before the year was up. The village elders told me it was because Gangamma wanted me to be near her; that was why I had been called back.

Gangamma Departs from Avilala

Gangamma departs from Avilala on two levels, just as she lives there on two levels—as thousand-eyed goddess and as daughter. As the thousand-eyed *ugra* goddess, Gangamma should be kept moving, from village to village. Just as she has come into Avilala from one side of the village, at the end of the *jatara* she moves to another village on the other side. SR told us:

From here Pambalas, Totis, Cakalis [caste names of the ritual drummers, sweepers, and washermen, respectively], and all the others, carry the pot [that is the goddess] to a distance of two kilometers. Up to there is our *area,* that of Avilala *panchayat.* From there it goes to Cirtanu, and after that to Davineru. She crosses like that from village to village, up to Kalahasti. Once we drop her there, they take over. When they get vomiting and diarrhea, they take the pot and offer it to the next village. That's how it is.

Note that Tirupati is not named in this sequence of movement from village to village; rather it is through the next ritual that the *jatara* moves to Tirupati. Narratively, Gangamma leaves Avilala village for Tirupati when she chases after the Palegadu and ritually when she is sent off as with bride's gifts to her in-laws' home in Tirupati. In 1995, the daughter-send-off procession consisted of SR and his wife Dhanalakshmi carrying the *pasupu-kumkum,* Pambala drummers and a trumpeter (representing the contemporary "wedding bands" of many urban neighborhoods), several other *panchayat* members, and other mostly male onlookers. The procession periodically stopped to allow time for young male celebrants to dance, much as in any other wedding procession. The Pambalas led the bride's party to the edge of the village, where the Ganga *shila*, a rectangular rock, stands innocuously in a paddy field throughout the year, wearing a simple garland. On this evening the rock was dramatically transformed into a woman/bride, smeared with *pasupu*, dotted with *kumkum*, and heavily garlanded.

At the Ganga *shila*, the bride's party is met by the executive officer (EO) of the Tattaiahgunta Devasthanam and a representative of the Kaikala family. The "big men" of the bride's family and the Tirupati representatives each take turns performing *harati* to the goddess/bride, and then the bride's gifts are exchanged between the two sides. The gifts are taken back to Tirupati, at which time the official announcement (*catimpu*) of the Tirupati *jatara* is made, a goat is slaughtered at the announcement site, and the boundaries of the *uru* are ritually "tied." Significantly, while the Kaikalas accept the bride-gifts as if they are the groom's party, once back in the Kaikala home, they think of Gangamma as a daughter, not a daughter-in-law. In fact, as mentioned earlier, there is no husband in Gangamma traditions, and I was told several times when I asked about a husband, "Who would be her husband? No man can bear her."

Avilala residents participate in Gangamma *jatara* in a manner typical of many Chittoor District villages through offering of *bali*—as does Tirupati itself (although no longer with buffaloes). But it is a unique village in that it is also drawn into the influence of Tirupati's narrative of the Palegadu, which takes tangible form through the exchange of bride-gifts with Tirupati representatives. SR lives in multiple imaginative and religious worlds, as do all *jatara* participants: he's an Ayurvedic orderly and a Hanuman devotee, and he performs *seva* to the god on the mountain, Venkateshvara. But he claims a unique ability to bear the *ugra* goddess and to fulfill her demands—as both thousand-eyed goddess and village daughter.

TEMPLE AND *VESHAM MIRASI*: THE KAIKALAS OF TIRUPATI

7

We first met the Kaikala family whose male members take Gangamma's *veshams* when we entered their domestic courtyard during the 1992 *jatara* to watch preparation of Gangamma's snake charmer *vesham*. A fourteen- or fifteen-year-old boy was being dressed as the goddess by his mother; he sat quietly as his mother applied *pasupu* to his face and his grandmother supervised the preparations with loud orders. The boy was transformed into a particularly beautiful, lithe, gentle Gangamma—seemingly not fully aware of herself either as the male-become-female or the goddess. At the time, my own son was sixteen years old, and I wondered how a teenage boy's concept and experience of gender would be changed through his own transformation through *vesham* into a goddess.[1]

Although only Kaikala men take Gangamma's *veshams*, it was the energy and directives of the Kaikala women that I sensed most powerfully when I first entered their home and over the years that have followed. Venkateshvarlu (hereafter, V), the primary male organizer of the Kaikala families who take Gangamma *vesham* and eldest son of the family matriarch, describes how his family came to be involved with the *jatara* and emphasizes a female lineage of responsibility for the goddess:

We're the only family who can bear her; we're not afraid of her. Only CKR's family [the Mudaliar family that served Gangamma in her Tatayyagunta temple until 1993] and our family can bear her at home. We're not afraid; she won't harm us. Even our great-grandparents and grandparents did this *puja.* My mother's mother and *her* mother. They all did it [kept Gangamma at home]. [And on another occasion:] We're the only ones who can bear her; no one else can take the *vesham.* We have to go around Tirupati in each *vesham;* no one else can do this. . . . Everyone will worship her in one form or another, but no one will keep her in their houses. No one else performs *puja,* keeping her inside. No one has that capacity to bear her. Others fear her. You can see anywhere that no one else keeps *shakti* [Gangamma] inside.

Familial *Shakti* to Bear the Goddess

When V asserts others don't keep Gangamma at home, but his family does, he's referring both to Gangamma *veshams* that Kaikala males take and to the large (about eighteen inches high) metallic Gangamma head that the family keeps in the inner recesses of their home. Until recently, this Gangamma form was kept in a small space set apart by tall cupboards in a bedroom on the ground floor of the home, between which it was difficult to squeeze through to reach the goddess. When I visited the Kaikala home in February 2010, the family Gangamma head had been moved up to a much larger, newly added room on the rooftop. By this time, V and his wife had moved out of the family home into independent quarters in a nearby neighborhood; on their own *puja* shelf sits a much smaller wooden head of the goddess marked with *kumkum* (an image I had not seen earlier in the extended-family home or elsewhere).

V says that his family performs *abhishekam* to their domestic Gangamma head every Friday; even the children take turns pouring the liquids, "without fear." The family feeds her daily whatever they are eating, and on Tuesdays and Sundays they feed her non-vegetarian meals. To feed the goddess food that the family itself is eating and to have her live in their midst creates a relationship of intimacy. Further, as children grow up seeing the *vesham*-transformation of their fathers and uncles into the goddess and interact easily with these *veshams,* the goddess is, at a performative level, "family."

Notice that V articulates the ability to bear the goddess to be a *family,* rather than caste, inheritance. Although technically the descendants who take *vesham* are those of four original Kaikala brothers, V's own *mirasi* has come to him through a matriline that passes through his mother's grandmother, mother's mother, and his own mother. In the 1990s, three women were most actively involved with Gangamma: V's maternal grandmother, his mother, and his maternal aunt: Tulasamma, Kamalamma, and Krishnamma, respectively. V emphasized this matriline when he said:

Our family has many daughters; that's because of our Ammavaru. [Then, pointing to his daughter:] Look, even she's Gangamma [family members present laugh]. We don't have many boys; each family has only one son [he has a son and daughter].

[On another occasion] My grandmother had no sons; that's why we [her two daughters' sons] are her descendents. [Reading from the court decision that gave the Kaikalas the right to stay as priests of Tallapaka temple:] Kaikalas who have *mirasi* here are Kaikala Narsimha Reddy, Kaikala Krishna Reddy, and Tulasamma [the families of two brothers and a sister]. Tulasamma is my grandmother. Kaikala Srinivas Reddy [another brother] is the other one. We descendants rotate the *jatara* between us [taking Gangamma *vesham*]. On behalf of my grandmother, her [two] daughters' children get this [gives names of four cousin-brothers, himself included:] Venkateshvarlu Reddy, Nagabhusan Reddy, Somashiva Reddy, and Subbarama Reddy.

Notice that three brothers and their sister Tulasamma are named. When questioned why his father's name did not appear on the court order anywhere, V replied, "This is my grandmother's property—all *her* property." That is, the inherited *mirasi* was passed equally to three brothers and a sister/Tulasamma; his grandmother had no sons, and the *mirasi* passed on to her daughters, not sons-in-law. While one son-in-law (Krishnamma's husband) was active in Tallapaka temple service, I never met or saw a photograph of V's father. When we met the Kaikalas during that first *jatara* in 1992 and asked about V's father/Kamalamma's husband, a family member told us he was "in the village." But he never returned for the *jataras* in which I participated. A young male cousin of the family was more straightforward about this man: "He left the house and went off. They don't know if he's alive or dead." On another occasion, as V was identifying his grandparents by name while showing us a photograph of them, I again asked about his father; this time he named his father, but there was no picture and no further comment about him. Kamalamma's younger sister, Krishnamma, married her maternal uncle (their mother Tulasamma's younger brother); the two sisters and Krishnamma's husband shared responsibilities serving the goddess of Tallapaka Gangamma temple. In the court case filed by the family to retain *mirasi* of the Tallapaka temple, V filed it in the names of these three (his mother, maternal aunt, and her husband).

Fluidity of Caste

We were first told by Srinivasulu Reddy, who has written a book on Gangamma *jatara* (Reddy 1995) and knows the Kaikala families well, that the Kaikalas were a weavers caste. In 1995, V himself identified a group of men who had woven and brought to the Kaikala home a red-and-white checked sari for one of the Kaikala *veshams* as "from our caste, but a different village"; those men self-identified as Sale (a Tamil caste of weavers). However, in 2000 when I asked one of the in-marrying males about this weaver-caste identity, he responded that the name "Kaikala" was not a caste (*kulam*) name, but that the term comes from the word *kaikalya*, which, he told us, literally means "ritual offering to god." (This is likely a vernacular etymology from the Sanskrit-derived Telugu word *kainkaryam*, ritual service to the deity). The elder explained that this name derived from the family's ritual responsibilities at Govindaraja Swamy temple downhill.[2] The Kaikala family has the *mirasi* (right and responsibility) to open and lock (literally, put a seal on) the temple door every day; they also light the lamps for and take first *darshan* of the god every morning.[3] He continued to explain that in "former days," the family married only within the Kaikalas, but "these days" they can marry others, such as Reddys; and there are also several instances of "love marriages" in the current married generation. Another in-marrying male identified his own family as Reddys and the Kaikala family as Kaikala Reddys, distinguished by the fact that they take *jatara veshams.* More recently (2010), V confirmed, in response to my continuing confusion about their caste, that the family name is Kaikala, a name derived from their Govindaraja Swamy *mirasi,* and that their caste (*kulam*) is Reddy. The different caste identities articulated in different contexts and by various persons in relationship to the Kaikala family suggest a fluidity of caste identities, particularly under the growing influence of middle-class ideologies in relationship to ritual roles, status, and hierarchies.

Kaikala Women's *Shakti*

Even though her husband is absent, Kamalamma (like the *purana pandita* Annapurna) wears a large, dark-red forehead *bottu* and *tali* traditionally associated with marriage. Because the family itself did not talk openly about this male figure—only once referring to him by name and only once stating he was "in the village"—I did not feel free to press them for further details. But what is clear is that Kamalamma is distinguished for her own ritual and familial authority, independent of her relationship with a husband.

On a short visit to Tirupati in the summer of 2011, I was sitting on the rooftop verandah of the Kaikala home talking with Kamalamma and her middle son, Sambhasivaiah, who regularly takes the Matangi *vesham.* When he arrived, V went into the bedroom newly built at that rooftop level and brought out a dusty framed photograph that he thought I would be interested in. It had been taken in a professional studio and pictured his mother wear a Tamil-style, nine-yard silk sari, holding a brass water pot (*kumbham*) against her hip. V said that the photograph had been taken thirty years ago, on the occasion of the last time his mother had performed *kumbham harati* uphill (at the temple of Sri Venkateshvara), and wondered if I even recognized her. Noticing my puzzled expression, he explained that his mother used to perform *kumbham harati* on two kinds of occasions uphill. The first was during the death rituals of the Jeeyangar (chief priest of the temple), when she would pour *pasupu* water on the corpse's head and break 101 coconuts; with this ritual the Jeeyangar was believed to reach heaven (*swargam*). (Of course, this was a relatively rare ritual, perhaps performed only once or twice a generation.) The second occasion was during the annual *brahmotsavam* (week-long festival during which time the deity circumambulates the perimeter of the temple). It was Kamalamma's responsibility to perform *kumbham harati* to

Kamalamma at Tallapaka Gangamma temple.

purify the festival image of the god—remove evil eye (*dishti*)—after it had been exposed to crowds of tens of thousands, before it reentered the temple. For this ritual, an oil lamp is set in the pot and a coconut on its mouth; the *kumbham* is encircled with mango leaves, decorated with *pasupu-kumkum*, and waved in front of the god's festival image, absorbing any *dishti*.

Kamalamma interjected, "I'm no longer doing this now. If I were still healthy—the Jeeyangar offered that I should continue do this." V gave another reason for the suspension of this ritual by a Kaikala woman: "She voluntarily stopped; it's a ritual that is performed only ten days a year, but this Govindaraja Swamy temple [opening and locking the temple] work is all year." (Note that it is Kaikala men, not women, however, who have the responsibility to open and lock the Govindaraja Swamy temple.) He explained that the *mirasi* to perform *kumbham harati* uphill used to be rotated between three Kaikala families, just as the *jatara vesham mirasi* continues to be. But now, the Kaikalas no longer participate in the ritual.

Local Telugu scholar Peta Srinivasulu Reddy confirmed that he had also heard this story from V; but he speculated that the reason the Kaikala women no longer performed this ritual uphill is that TTD no longer *permitted* the *mirasi* for *kumbham harati*—perhaps because of the association between the ritual and *devadasis* (female temple dancers/musicians). *Kumbham harati* was the responsibility of *devadasis* in those brahminic temples with which they were associated (Soneji 2004). While the Tirumala temple has no history of *devadasis* serving in the temple, it would appear that Kaikala women had some similar ritual responsibilities in the temple. Particularly striking is the power of female ritual during the death ceremonies of the Jeeyangar—to assure his immortality in heaven;[4] further, she had the ritual power to remove traces of evil eye from the god himself. This female agency is also visible in the Kaikala home.

The elderly matriarch Tulasamma, Kamalamma's mother, who was authoritatively and loudly directing the dressing of the *vesham* the very first morning we entered the Kaikala courtyard, was most assuredly the primary "stage director" for *vesham* preparations. When she turned her attention to us, she was equally assertive, wanting to know who we were and what we had brought for the goddess. When we admitted to having come empty-handed, not knowing we would meet the goddess, and asked what the appropriate gift would be, Tulasamma requested ornaments for the goddess, specifically stating we should not bring a sari or cash.[5] I last met this elderly matriarch during the *jatara* of 1995, when she was still active; but she died within the next year, a loss her eldest daughter, Kamalamma, felt keenly. In the intervening years, Kamalamma often talked about how much responsibility she now carried—how much she suffered now—having become the matriarch "responsible for everything."

Kamalamma inherited her mother's authority and forceful character, displayed at both home and temple. As her mother had done earlier, she often made direct requests of me to bring certain gifts for the goddess. One year, she specifically asked me to buy a yellow silk sari with green border for Tallapaka Gangamma to wear for the *jatara* (stating with full confidence that this is exactly what kind of sari the goddess wanted). I made the mistake of bringing the sari to the temple itself on the day before the *jatara* began, not knowing that a representative of the Tallapaka Devasthanam would start sitting at the temple from that day and throughout the *jatara*, to keep track, in particular, of all monetary offerings made to the goddess. Kamalamma scolded me openly and loudly for bringing the sari to the temple rather than to her home and told me to go away. I asked the Devasthanam representative if Kamalamma could take the sari home, explaining that I had really brought it for her domestic Gangamma. He readily accepted this request, somewhat bewildered by the commotion caused by the gifting of a sari. Only then did Kamalamma explain to him that I was part of their family and that she had been answering all my questions.

It is open to question whether the Kaikala family will continue to live with this matriarchal, Gangamma-type force in the next generation. V had a "love marriage" (i.e., not an arranged marriage) with a woman of the Balija Naidu caste. While V's wife appears confident, she was demure and stayed in the background when her husband was speaking with us directly; this manner and authority may shift, of course, when she becomes the family matriarch. But for now, as V enters middle age (he was forty years old in 2011, only in his early twenties when we first met him), he has become the primary authoritative voice of his generation—interacting with the press every *jatara,* taking up the court case to keep the family's temple *mirasi* from passing to Tallapaka Devasthanam, and patiently answering questions posed by the journalists, film-makers, and anthropologists. Perhaps because he has been put in a position of responding to this interest by "outsiders" in the *jatara,* V is more reflective and articulate about his family's traditions than are most *jatara* participants.

In 1999–2000, the year I spent in Tirupati, V was officially working as an office attendant for the Endowments Department in a village outside of Tirupati. (One of his brothers worked in public water works, and another at a veterinary hospital as a compounder [pharmacist].) V spent much of that year on leave from his government position, however, since after the death of his maternal aunt's husband, he said, there was "no one" (meaning no adult male) to "look after things" such as the court case over the *mirasi* over the Tallapaka temple, a case that had shifted to the Hyderabad high court and thus involved frequent travel. But such "things" also included the *alankara* of the goddess in the temple, which V said the women in the family didn't know how to perform. Nevertheless, as the Kaikala men work in the "outside" world of steady income, it is the women of the household who serve the goddess on a daily basis, feeding her and keeping her company both at home and at her Tallapaka temple.

Venkateshvarlu performing *harati* at Tallapaka Gangamma temple.

Tallapaka Gangamma Comes to Tirupati

Tallapaka Gangamma temple is the temple of the elder Gangamma sister and, historically, the older of the two primary Gangamma temples connected to the *jatara*—the other being that of the younger sister, Tatayyagunta Gangamma temple. Tallapaka temple stands at a busy crossroads at what used to be the outskirts of traditional Tirupati—one road leading out of town past the RTC bus station and the other leading to the busy train station, both of which serve thousands of pilgrims on their way to take *darshan* of Sri Venkateshvara. The temple itself is on a traffic island, enclosed by a red- and white-striped cement wall typical of South Indian temples, and shaded by a neem tree—a location that filled recorded conversations at the site with loud horns and traffic noise. Several Kaikala family members told me that the reason Tallapaka temple was not as important in the *jatara* as the Tatayyagunta temple was not because of the relative importance of the two Gangamma sisters, but that there simply wasn't space around Tallapaka to expand and to accommodate the large crowds coming to perform individual and communal *jatara* rituals. V asserted that it was Tallapaka (Pedda) Gangamma who "brought this *jatara*" to Tirupati, not Tatayyagunta (Cinna) Gangamma.

Numerous stories circulate about how the two Gangamma sisters came to Tirupati. We've already heard the story of Gangamma being raised as a foundling child in Avilala, chasing the Palegadu to Tirupati, and being taken in by the Kaikala family. The Gangamma in this narrative is not identified with one or the other of the two sisters, Cinna or Pedda Gangamma. But V reports another narrative that distinguishes the sisters: Tallapaka Pedda Gangamma was first brought to Tirupati by the fifteenth-century poet Annamacarya, and only later, in the sixteenth century, did her younger sister follow her. Tatayyagunta Cinna Gangamma initially followed her sister to Tirupati intending to stay for only a few days to observe her elder sister's *jatara,* but she never left.

V recounts that Pedda Gangamma was Annamacarya's *kuladevata* (caste/lineage deity) and that it was he who brought the Tallapaka temple image—a head only—to Tirupati and installed it at the current temple site. It is said that Annamacarya was given a garden and water tank—covering the entire area of the current RTC bus stand—in exchange for his service through song to Sri Venkateshvara uphill. Annamacarya established the Tallapaka Gangamma temple on the banks of that tank, the current site of the crossroads. V explained that Annamacarya established a separate temple for Gangamma because he thought, "We're Brahmans, so this [serving a *gramadevata*] isn't for us." V continued, "It was he who brought and installed her [here]. She's *shakti* and Brahmans shouldn't do *puja* for her."

V's insistence that Brahmans shouldn't perform *puja* to a *shakti/gramadevata* would seem to be at odds with his earlier statement that Gangamma was Annamacarya's *kuladevata* (therefore, a Brahman family's *kuladevata*). However, the seeming contradiction is consistent with the transformation of Annamacarya from serving an *ugra* meat-eating goddess to a devotee of the *satvika* (gentle, *shanta*) Vishnu as depicted in the biography written by his grandson, Cinnanna. Cinnanna's hagiography tells the story of a young Annamacarya running to the back of a *gramadevata* goddess's temple to stick his hand into the anthill, hoping to be bitten and die, thereby saving himself from the humiliation of being beaten by his teacher. The goddess herself tells the boy, "Bow to Lord Vishnu in the village, and he will bestow learning on you." Cinnanna describes the transformation as follows:

> We were engaged in totally dark ritual
> And Annamacarya made us bright.
> What an amazing feat!
> There was no Vaishnava worship in our family
> Before he gave it to us in his kindness.
> (Narayana Rao and Shulman 2005:116)

V. Narayana Rao and David Shulman interpret this verse to be a reference to Annamacarya's family's connection to a goddess whose worship involved animal sacrifice (the dark rituals). The story of why this Brahman family was associated with a meat-eating goddess in the first place is complicated, ending with a curse by the goddess Camundeshvari that the Brahmans serve as priests for the meat-eating Togata weavers caste.[6] The story provides rationale for Brahmans serving a *shakti gramadevata*, but is also a reminder of their *satvika* (gentle, *shanta*) origins, to which Annamacarya returned. The narrative association between the great poet-saint Annamacarya, so closely associated with both Sri Venkateshvara and Tallapaka Gangamma, is another means through which the goddess on the plain and god on the mountain are woven into an inclusive Tirupati religious landscape.

Tallapaka Temple *Mirasi*

V never made explicit reference to how his own family began to serve Tallapaka Gangamma or how they received the *mirasi* of taking her *jatara veshams.* As mentioned earlier, he did, however, tell the story of how his ancestors had moved to Tirupati from Cidambaram and had come to have *mirasi* at Govindaraja Swamy's temple. A Pambala drummer told us (again as we were waiting for the Sunnapukundalu to be prepared in the temple courtyard in 2000—a good opportunity for many conversations, as it turns out) that the *mirasi* of taking Gangamma's *vesham* used to belong to families from the Chetti caste, who used to prepare wedding *pandals*—that is, the Chetti family were also left-hand caste artisans.

According to the Pambala, a man from these Chetti families had relations with a Kaikala woman (unclear whether with or without marriage; literally, he said he "kept" a woman) and then they gave *pasupu-kumkum* to the Kaikalas and the *mirasi* came to the Kaikalas. Later in the conversation, he clarified that the "wedding-making family" didn't have anyone (any descendant) left to perform the *jatara veshams,* and so it came to the Kaikalas. The Palegadu–Gangamma narrative suggests another rationale for the Kaikala authority to take Gangamma's *veshams:* Subbarama Reddy of Avilala narrates that Gangamma chased the Palegadu to Karnal Street in Tirupati, which at the time was filled with a jasmine garden. The Kaikalas were the watchmen for these gardens, and Gangamma gave her first *darshan,* without disguising *vesham,* to this family.

While the Kaikala family has had *mirasi* over the Tallapaka temple for several generations, this right has recently been challenged by the Temple Endowments. Although the Endowments took over formal administration of the temple in 1961, according to V, the family continued to "own the temple" and serve as its caretakers. However, at some point the Endowments Department began to collect the money deposited in the *hundi* (collection box)—the date of which V did not make clear when he was giving me this history. In 1998, the Endowments Department was giving the Kaikalas Rs. 650 per month to purchase the *pasupu-kumkum* used for the goddess's *alankara* (which V made clear was not enough to meet the actual costs), and the family was purchasing all the flowers and food for Gangamma from their own monies.

In 1998, the Endowments wanted to take over all functions of the temple (as they had earlier taken over Tatayyagunta in 1993), but the Kaikalas took the case to court. In 1999 V was confident that they would retain their *mirasi:*

> They told us they would bring Brahmans in [as *pujaris,* replacing the Kaikalas], but we told them we'd take them to court if they did that, and they kept quiet. They wouldn't be able perform the *jatara* properly; we have to do it. It's been eight months since the Trust Board came to ask. They wanted to take it over, but we took it to court. After that, they've kept quiet and haven't said anything. There's the Regional Joint Commissioner; that's where we petitioned. We can't go to any other court; we have to go to the Endowment Department. After that they kept quiet.

Note that V associates the *mirasi* of temple service with that of taking Gangamma's *jatara veshams;* logistically, the two could be separated except for bringing Potu Raju from the temple to the Kaikala home for the duration of the *jatara* and the building of the *ugra mukhi* in front of the temple (over which the Kaikalas have very little authority, even now). It is possible that Gangamma *vesham mirasi* developed into temple *mirasi,* or the other way around. In 2000, during one of my last visits to the Kaikala home after a year of fieldwork in Tirupati, V again raised the issue of his family's rights over the temple and the pending court case. He reported that they were (successfully) using the book written about Gangamma *jatara* by Srinivasulu Reddy to support their case and asked me if I, too, would write a letter of support saying that I had witnessed his family's involvement with the temple since 1992.

When I returned to Tirupati in February 2005, V updated me on further complications regarding the court case, which had been decided in favor of the Kaikalas:

> We filed a case against Endowment orders. One of my uncles used to perform *puja,* but Endowments appointed another person, so we filed a

case. . . . There's a judge in the high court who gave a judgment saying we have all the rights. In 1987 N. T. Rama Rao [chief minister of Andhra Pradesh] passed a resolution abolishing the *mirasi* system altogether. But in 1993 the Supreme Court ruled that family members who are doing the work there, even if they lose the *mirasi,* should retain their positions for their livelihood [as employees of the Endowments Department].

In an earlier conversation, V had been slightly critical of the Mudaliar family who had lost *mirasi* of the Tatayyagunta temple, saying that they could have stayed on as Devasthanam employees—even without *mirasi*—but they had chosen not to. The next chapter tells this story of this family's eviction from Tatayyagunta temple and their replacement by Endowments officers for temple administration and Brahman priests for ritual services, a painful story of loss.

Serving Gangamma at Tallapaka Temple

The boundaries between Kaikala home and Gangamma's Tallapaka temple are fluid. Senior female members of the Kaikala family walk back and forth between their home and temple several times a day during the *jatara;* and at the temple itself, on non-festival days, they are often seen relaxing as if at home, giving the temple a domestic, intimate feel. During the *jatara* itself, as we have described earlier, the Kaikala home becomes a primary site of ritual activity—home becomes, on some levels, "temple."

The "true" form of Pedda Gangamma, the form V says Annamacarya himself brought from Tallapaka village, is a stone head, as are several of her sisters' forms in Tirupati (including Cinna Gangamma at Tatayyagunta) and surrounding villages. This head is covered by a metallic mask-like *kavacam.* However, behind the head, there is a more recently created full-body stone form of the goddess (V says it was added in the 1970s), and this full-body form receives the most attention by worshippers who come to the temple. In one hand, Gangamma holds a *kumkum* container and in another a whip;[7] her other two hands hold a trident and a club. On the right side of Gangamma's full-body stone form are seven small stone heads, and one to her left; these are identified as her children, for whom brass *kavacams* have recently been made.

Kamalamma described Gangamma's diet in the temple to be *idlis* (steamed rice cakes) in the morning, rice and eggs in the afternoon, and a glass of milk and bananas in the evening. Besides feeding the goddess daily, the Kaikalas are also responsible for the weekly *abhishekam* and application of *pasupu* to the face of Pedda Gangamma's full-body form. The *abhishekam* and *pasupu* application is an intimate, time-consuming act, often taking up to two hours. Every Friday, at about 5:30 in the morning, V begins his ritual services by taking off the saris and flowers covering the full-body form of the goddess; significantly, he leaves on her *tali,* which shines visibly against her dark wet surface. He then performs *abhishekam* with milk and water, after which the image is washed with soap nut powder and oiled before V carefully applies the *pasupu* "mask" to Gangamma's face. Towards the end of the nine months I spent in Tirupati in 1999–2000, Kamalamma asked me to sponsor an *abhishekam,* to which I gladly assented. I gave Rs. 500 for the ingredients and thought that this would be a good opportunity to get to the temple at that early morning hour to watch the entire ritual. I was surprised when V handed me the first vessel of milk to pour over the goddess. I hitched up my sari to keep it from getting soaked with the run-off milk and water and poured three times, rather self-consciously, before handing the milk-vessel back to V. The invitation to directly participate in this ritual was a clear reminder of the accessibility of *gramadevatas,* in contrast to *puranic* goddesses whose service in temples is mediated by Brahman male priests.

V is often at the temple by himself in the rare early morning silence—sometimes accompanied by his mother—completing the full *alankara* (decoration) by the time devotees stop by the temple for *darshan* on their way to work. V was proud of the quality (and cost—one-fourth kilogram each application) of the *pasupu* he uses, specifying that it came all the way from Madras (present-day Chennai). First covering the body of the goddess with a cloth, to keep the *pasupu* powder from falling on her body, V flicks small amounts of the powder on Gangamma's dark wet stone face and then smoothes it out evenly with a feather. With the base "mask" in place, he applies *kumkum* to her mouth and carefully draws three dots on the side of the mouth to deflect the evil eye. Having placed little pieces of beeswax to the appropriate places, V reattaches Gangamma's silver eyes, a three-line Shaivite silver forehead marking, and her nose ring. He completes Gangamma's *alankara* by dressing her in a sari and garlanding her with flowers.

The *pasupu* application both covers and reveals certain features of the goddess. Watching the milk flow over the turmeric application, washing the powder off in rivulets around the goddess's facial features, is a poignant moment, as the unadorned body of the goddess is revealed. Even as her *ugra* nature is revealed with the uncovering of her fangs, she seemed to my eye vulnerable, without her layers of clothing and flowers, her dark stone body shining.

V emphasized that the primary reason for the *pasupu* covering is to make the goddess *muttaiduva* (auspicious), to hide her fangs, and make her less fearful (*bhayankar*). He explained, "She is *shakti;* she is *rakshasvarupam* [the form of a threatening *rakshasa* demon]," a form that needs to be covered in order for the goddess to be bearable and accessible to her devotees. The *pasupu* mask also makes her other facial features more visible and is said to beautify her. The alternating rituals of *pasupu* application and the *abhishekam* that washes it off suggest that *ugram* and *muttaiduvam* are not exclusive categories, but both qualities inherent to the goddess. A constructive rationale for the *jatara* is to balance these qualities; here in the temple, they are balanced in a different ritual rhythm.

Bringing Potu Raju Home

Gangamma resides in the Kaikala home throughout the year in her metallic-head form; her *jatara* homecoming is, however, marked by the arrival of her brother Potu Raju. Early that first Tuesday morning of the *jatara,* the Kaikalas bring home the Potu Raju wooden figure from Tallapaka temple, to stand guard and "bear witness" for the duration of the *jatara.* V called Potu Raju the "important person" of the *jatara;* "because Gangamma has no male support and he's the brother, he should be there." In another conversation, when I asked V if the family kept some form of Potu Raju at home with Gangamma's head-form, he clarified that Gangamma particularly needed her brother's protection during the *jatara* since she was moving around; otherwise, she didn't need him. The year I followed the ritual homecoming of Potu Raju, Krishnamma (V's maternal aunt) prepared a large stainless-steel pot, rubbing it with *pasupu,* applying *kumkum* lines and dots on it, placing neem leaves in its mouth, and filling it with curd rice for the goddess. She carried this pot on her head, walking from home to temple, accompanied by

Potu Raju and Gangamma in Kaikala courtyard.

V and a Pambala drummer, a small procession that few passersby and pilgrims on the crowded street seemed notice. Kamalamma was waiting at the temple, where she had been serving throughout the afternoon. The figure of Potu Raju had been brought inside the temple and cleaned up (the day before, he had been leaning against the outside wall, dusty and unattended), and now stood to Gangamma's right side.

V took off his shirt, indicating a shift in persona to ritual specialist, and entered the temple to perform *harati* and offer the curd rice to Gangamma. Kamalamma served the remaining curd rice as *prasad* to the few onlookers. V had told us earlier that when the curd rice loses its savory flavor, "that's how we know that Gangamma has come from beyond the seven seas to attend her own *jatara*." (She is both present in the temple form throughout the year and also absent, across the seven seas.) She is also fed curd rice because she needs cooling, V continued to explain—this time not being hot from *ugram,* but from her long journey, and heated from the physical hot temperatures of Tirupati itself. After Gangamma had been fed and cooled—her presence affirmed both in the change in taste of the curd rice *prasad* and through her possession of Kamalamma—V carried Potu Raju on his head back to the Kaikala courtyard.

In this ritual, more than any other occasion, Potu Raju's identity seems to be subsumed into that of his sister. As mentioned in the introduction, the first year (1992) we saw this figure, holding up a sword with its right (bangled) hand and a head at its feet, we assumed it was Gangamma herself having beheaded the Palegadu. However, several years later I was corrected when I asked again if this figure was Gangamma. No, V asserted, it is Potu Raju, whom he again, however, identified as *shaktisvarupini.* Potu Raju would seem to be a feminized male, subsumed into a *jatara* world become female, as are many other Tirupati males. And it is *his* homecoming to the Kaikala courtyard that signals Gangamma's homecoming from Avilala as daughter, in the early morning after the *pasupu-kumkum* exchange at village edge.

Bearing/Becoming the Goddess through *Vesham*

Perhaps the most intimate Kaikala interaction with Gangamma is that of taking her *jatara veshams.* V explained that these guises are like *utsava vigrahams* (moveable, processional, festival forms), "What's in Cinna Gangamma's temple, that's the *mula vigraham* [original/permanent image]. She is a *shakti*. We can't keep a *shakti murti* on our heads and go around, so instead, *we* become the festival forms. Gangammas have no *utsav vigrahams* in their temples; only *mula vigrahams* are there."[8] Interestingly, while V states that the Kaikalas cannot place a *shakti* goddess image on their heads, they can *become* the *shakti* through *vesham*.

To prepare for becoming the goddess, the Kaikala males who take her *vesham* refrain from sexual relations and sleep on the floor. An oil lamp is lit in front of the Kaikala domestic Gangamma's head-form (now moved to the courtyard), which should stay lit continuously for the duration of the *jatara;* one family member is identified each night to stay awake and refill oil in the lamp so that it never goes out. Further, mutton is cooked every day for the goddess, even on Saturday, a day on which the family usually prepares only vegetarian dishes in honor of Sri Venkateshvara.

When I asked V how he felt becoming the Dora/Gangamma (the *vesham* he has regularly taken since his marriage), he simply responded, "I have her *idi* [a semantically empty Telugu word that takes its meaning by context; one could literally translate it here as "her this, or this thing" referring in this context to Gangamma's power and/or nature]. When we put on the crown [of the Dora prince], great *power* comes. Similarly, while taking the Matangi [*vesham*], there's *power*." His younger sister-in-law tried to join the conversation: "When they take *vesham,* they don't laugh—" and V interjected, "*Kopam, kopam* [anger, anger]." Pushing for further explanation, my fieldwork associate asked, "So when you take *vesham,* you become the goddess, right? How do the people you see everyday appear to you?" Again, the sister-in-law answered, "Everyone looks equal [*samanam*]," and V concurred, "Everyone's *samanam.* Harijan and all—*samanam* [i.e., all castes look equal]. When they say, 'Amma, give us your blessings,' it's the goddess herself who gives the blessing. On Friday [the day of the sweeper *vesham*], we tap people's heads with the winnowing basket." That is, when the Kaikala male body that takes the Toti sweeper *vesham* taps the heads of *jatara* participants crowded around her, it is the blessing of the goddess herself.

Then, sensing the direction of our questions, V continued, "Only after the *jatara,* I come to know all these things: the pains in my legs and pains in my body—only then, I come to know everything . . . only after lifting the Sunnapukundalu and coming back, only then I know these pains." In *vesham,* the Kaikala men seemingly do not experience the physical demands required of them as they walk for hours in the heat of Tirupati summers; at that time, they are not men, but the goddess. But V implies that when they return home, return to their human identities, their bodies carry traces of the grueling physical demands they have endured.

In their ritual perambulations around traditional Tirupati, Kaikala *veshams* also come to their own domestic doorways to be greeted and worshipped by the female householders of their families. Here, a Kaikala woman applies *pasupu-kumkum* to the feet of her son, husband, or brother-in-law who is the goddess. I photographed a particularly evocative image in which V's wife is anointing her husband's feet, which were now the feet of Gangamma in her Dora *vesham.* When I asked what she experienced as she anointed the feet of the goddess, whose *vesham*-ed body was that of her husband, V's wife told me that at this moment of encounter, he is simply the goddess. Reciprocally, V said that the men taking Gangamma *vesham* experience their wives and mothers bowing to them simply as Ammavaru herself—women as goddess. Or, there is the image of one of the Kaikala men's bright-eyed, smiling toddler daughter sitting on his lap as he is resting in the middle of his rounds as the Matangi, and his wife is feeding him cooling curd rice. I assume that such an experience for both mother and daughter becomes embodied and affects their experiences of the possibilities of gender and *shakti;* but, as I've written elsewhere, these images suggest the limits of ethnography and discourse itself (Flueckiger 2010). What neither V nor the wife feeding her Matangi-turned-husband answered, and what they were perhaps unable to answer discursively, is whether or how this experience of husband/father-become-goddess affects marital and family relationships.

Kaikala Women's *Jatara* Participation

Knowing that only men took the Kaikala goddess *veshams,* I nevertheless asked V and his brothers if women could take these *veshams.* Their immediate answer was no, they couldn't, both because of menstruation and the endurance needed to walk the streets for hours and hours in the heat.

Kamalamma, listening in, vehemently objected that it wasn't because of menstruation that women didn't take *vesham;* it was because they were too busy cooking. Her assertion equates the importance of *vesham* and cooking both for the goddess and people who come through the Kaikala home during the *jatara* (for whom, Kamalamma adds, the women make ten different kinds of curries):

> We have to feed the Pambalas, Cakali, Toti [all castes involved in the *vesham* rituals], neighbors, and elders. Men take *vesham* and they go out; women have to see what is there in the house, who comes and who goes, and how many they have to feed each time during the day. Suppose you're here; we have to ask whether you want to eat, drink, etc.; we're the only ones to look after all of these things.

Some readers of this statement may understand Kamalamma's words as a complaint of being relegated to the kitchen while men "become the goddess." However, another reading of Kamalamma's statement, one closer to what I understand her meaning to be in the context of a wider Gangamma repertoire, could be that she is equating the ritual importance of cooking for the goddess (and those who serve her) and taking *vesham:* the goddess needs both. Kamalamma and other women who cook for the goddess both at home and in temple courtyards do not articulate cooking to be a secondary ritual act. Further, in this bounded Gangamma ritual world, females are an unmarked category of *jatara* participants who do not need to change (through *vesham*) who they are to be in the presence of the goddess. They are not striving for a different status in a ritual world in which they are already at the center.

Another Kaikala-women *jatara* responsibility is preparation/dressing of the *veshams*—an intimate act transforming their sons, husbands, and nephews into the goddess. Tulasamma, and later Kamalamma, kept track of the needed supplies for the *veshams*—after a year in storage in tin trunks, were the ornaments in good shape or did new ones need to be made, had the requisite saris been delivered by the other-caste families who had the *mirasi* to do so? The Kaikala women also kept track of *jatara* expenses borne by the family. For example, one year Kamalamma complained that the Pambalas were asking for Rs. 20,000 for their role in accompanying the

Kaikala *veshams;* she argued with them that the family could only afford Rs. 10–15,000: "If we don't perform the *jatara,* some 'big people' will ask why we're not performing. If we don't go to their houses after taking *vesham,* the next day these people will be angry with us. If the *uru* is affected by any disease, then certainly they'll blame the Kaikalas for not taking *vesham* and not performing the *jatara.*"

Kamalamma's elderly mother continued to complain that this year the Endowment Officer of Tallapaka temple had refused to give money to have the temple cleaned and painted for the *jatara.* She said she scolded the EO, asking him, "Has the goddess spoken to you [told you that she doesn't need these things]? Why hasn't she spoken directly to me?" So, that year, the Kaikalas painted the temple at their own expense. As Potu Raju was being carried to the Kaikala home to begin the *jatara* that year, Gangamma herself complained, speaking through a possessed Kamalamma, that certain people weren't paying for *jatara* expenditures for which they were responsible, saying, "Why do I have to beg for my expenditures?"

Vesham in the Next Generation

In 1995, the elderly Kaikala matriarch Tulasamma told us that her own grandchildren—V and his male cousins—didn't want to perform the *jatara* that year, but that she had persuaded them, telling them that this may be the last year she would be alive to witness the *jatara* (it turned out her prediction this year was true). When we reported this to V, he laughed, "Every year, we say that we don't have enough energy to perform the *jatara,* and every year she says that she may not be alive the next year, so that we should perform it. And we do perform every year. We have to do the *jatara* or we'll be dead; no one can take this custom of taking *vesham* from us." While the family may experience some ambivalence in taking *vesham,* Gangamma is *ugra* and not obeying her commands or fulfilling her needs may have dire results. But they also take pride in being able to satisfy her, to bear her. I wondered to myself whether or not V's son and nephews, raised in an increasingly middle-class environment, having attended English-medium schools, would want to continue the tradition of taking the *jatara veshams,* whether or not they would feel some ambivalence in serving a *gramadevata* goddess in this way. In 2000, V seemed to share his grandmother's anxiety that the next generation would not continue the tradition: "Only we [Kaikalas] can do this. Our children are asking, 'Who will do this?' [i.e., they don't want to]. [But] we shouldn't leave behind the inheritance from our elders. Who else will get this kind of respect, having their feet touched and anointed [as Gangamma's *veshams*]? No one will get this. Thinking this, we keep doing this." And the next generation has continued; when I visited the family in February 2010, V's seventeen-year-old son, taller than his father by several inches, spoke confidently of taking *vesham* for the *jatara* in just a few months; and V said he himself would once again take the Dora *vesham.*

THE GODDESS SERVED AND LOST: TATAYYAGUNTA MUDALIARS

8

The first year I participated in Gangamma *jatara* in 1992, a female, middle-aged, gracefully moving attendant was serving Cinna Gangamma in her Tatayyagunta temple. She was assisted by a male in the inner sanctum itself, and several other women were running in and out with various supplies and helping keep the temple precincts clean. A female presence and authority in a *gramadevata* temple was not unexpected, since *gramadevatas* are traditionally served by non-Brahman men or women. With the high energy of *jatara* rituals taking place in the temple courtyard (visiting *veshams*, *pongal* preparations, children beating the cement feet of the goddess in the courtyard, and chicken sacrifices), we paid little attention to the woman serving inside the temple. However, the next year, her absence was immediately palpable.

We learned from the temple flower sellers that, in the intervening year, the Temple Endowments Department had taken over administration of Tatayyagunta temple (presumably because of the increased income generated by the *jatara*) and replaced the primary female attendant with Brahman male priests. The change of personnel had brought with it changes in daily and festival rituals, which now included the recitation of Sanskrit *mantras,* performance of *homam* (fire sacrifice), and the sale of *archana* tickets (a *puja* ritual performed on behalf of an individual worshipper and his/her family and *gotra* lineage). Most of the women who had served the goddess in temple grounds' upkeep and otherwise had helped to maintain some "order" in the temple (including crowd control in the long lines waiting for *darshan* of the goddess during the *jatara*) had been hired as employees of the Tattaiahgunta Devasthanam (spelling of the official name of the temple committee administering this temple) and continued their work in the temple, but they lamented the absence of the matriarch they call Amma. Her given name is Kamakoteshvari; to keep it simple and at the same time be respectful, I will call her Koteshvaramma, employing the familiar and honorific suffix -amma.

I returned to Tirupati in 1995 for the *jatara* and was surprised to see Koteshvaramma back in the temple again, distributing *prasad* of sweet *pongal* to a large throng of women crowded in front of the inner shrine room. Women were touching her feet and taking her blessings. The flower sellers ran up to me as I entered the courtyard, exclaiming that I had returned on a particularly auspicious day, since my return coincided with Koteshvaramma's return. They explained that she had been absent for two years due to a court case over her family's *mirasi* over the temple. But she had, they said, returned to the temple for this year's *jatara*—due to "popular demand"—for the first time since she had been replaced by Brahman male priests. *Jatara* celebrants had complained that the male priests didn't know how to decorate the goddess and had made her look like a Bollywood movie star.[1] One of the female groundskeepers explained the sight we were witnessing: "Women touch Amma's feet because she's had contact with the goddess, and her family has served the goddess for generations. By touching her feet, we, too, can receive some *punyam* [merit] and blessings. We've been touching her feet for the last ten years, morning and evening, and have been blessed with children and other blessings."

Koteshvaramma stayed in the temple over ten hours that first day of her return, performing the auspicious *abhishekam* on the first day of the *jatara*, taking great care in decorating the goddess, and handing out *prasad* to (primarily) female worshippers. On this day, she was assisted by the male assistant whom we had seen in 1992. But one of the female devotees observing the *abhishekam* with us said, "Particularly for this goddess, only *women* should perform *puja*. All these men are only as *support.* Only

Amma should do the *abhishekam*, apply *pasupu*, and dress her in saris. Even if the men actually *do* these duties, she must stand there; at least she has to put a flower on the goddess, as if she was the one performing all this." However, the matriarch's return was temporary; this *jatara* was she last time she entered the temple. She said it was too heart-breaking to enter the temple after that (when she was no longer allowed in the *garbhagriha* [innermost shrine room where deity abides] and the intimate access to the goddess that she had had earlier).

I learned that Koteshvaramma belongs to a Tamilian Mudaliar family that had emigrated to Tirupati from Chennai in the early 1900s. For three generations, this family had held the hereditary right to be caretakers of the goddess at Tatayyagunta temple. While men in this family had held the formal title of *mirasidar*, the women of the family had been the primary caretakers of Gangamma (bathing, dressing, feeding her, etc.). I knew there was a story to be heard about this unusual involvement of a Mudaliar-caste family with Gangamma, since this mid-level caste does not traditionally serve *gramadevatas* as priests/ritual specialists. The eviction of this family by the Endowments Department was in court for several years; however, the family finally dropped the case. The sons said that they simply didn't have the energy to pursue it, given the demands of their professional lives and that, in any case, there was no one in their generation who wanted to take up the *mirasi*.

In *Diaspora of the Gods: Modern Hindu Temples in an Urban Middle-Class World* (2004), Joanne Waghorne has documented similar changes in temples in Chennai to those I witnessed at Tatayyagunta Gangamma temple, from village-goddess temple to middle-class, brahminized/Sanskritized temple. She identifies the processes of transformation as "gentrification." Most relevant are her descriptions of the transformations of the Mylapore (Chennai) temples of Kolavizhi Amman (KA) and Mundakakkanni Amman (MA). She writes that after the KA temple came under the jurisdiction of the Government of Tamil Nadu Hindu Religious and Charitable Endowment (HRCE) and a newly appointed board of trustees, in 1995:

> The goddess was resanctified with Vedic rites and [is now] served by new Brahman priests. . . . this complex project involved not only the physical renovation of the temple but also a controversial removal of people who had encroached on the temple grounds (129).

> . . . MA has, to date, retained its non-Brahman priests, but the village-style shrine has been architecturally and ritually "over-written" by a middle-class aesthetics . . . the continuous renovations move toward propriety . . . I read this process as visual gentrification—everything is maintained but put into a comfortable . . . and tidy environment. (155)

Waghorne characterizes the middle class "not so much as a clearly defined group but rather as style. . . . They speak through the visual impact of valued *things*" (138). She concludes, "As willing as the middle classes are to appropriate the power of the goddess, they do this by cleaning her house and purifying or isolating her coarser elements, including her unrefined devotees" (170). Waghorne's focus is primarily on changes in temple rituals and architecture and on the middle-class patrons who have helped to implement these, rather than on the impact on those who may have been pushed aside to make room for these middle-class and brahminic transformations. However, such transformations of established shrines and temples of *gramadevatas* are often implemented at great personal cost to the non-Brahman women and families who traditionally served these goddesses. This chapter narrates this loss from the perspective of the Mudaliar family that lost its *mirasi* to serve Gangamma at Tatayyagunta temple.

The personal narratives of this Mudaliar family describe the growth of a worship site that was simply a village goddess head situated on the ground under a tree at the edge of the *uru* into a middle-class brahminized temple. However, even as Gangamma's temple is re-visioned by Tattaiahgunta Devasthanam, the goddess has not yet totally lost her *ugra* character; her *jatara* and other *gramadevata* rituals are still part of the ritual repertoire helping to shape worshippers' experiences of the added Sanskritic rituals. For example, I heard several worshippers identify some of the Sanskritic goddesses set up for *darshan* in the Tatayyagunta temple courtyard each evening during Navaratri (a different goddess each evening) to be the same as the series of the Seven Sister *gramadevatas.*

Mudaliar Grandfather Meets the Goddess

I heard the seemingly unlikely story of how a Mudaliar family from Madras came to serve the Tirupati *gramadevata* Gangamma from numerous sources. The Mudaliar matriarch Koteshvaramma, who had served Tatayyagunta Gangamma in her temple for many years, gave the following account of how her family came to be associated with Gangamma (here, translated from Tamil):

Once, Avva [grandmother] and Tata [grandfather] came to visit Tirupati. They took *darshan* of Sri Venkateshvara. On their return, Avva became ill and she was very worried about her health. They happened to see Gangamma, only her stone head. Someone had done *puja,* but her head was thrown on the ground, with no shelter over it. It was all jungle, and Gangamma was only a head, kept on the ground. It had been thrown on the ground. There was an elderly man who used to come on Tuesdays and Fridays [special days for the goddess], and pour water on the stone head and apply *pasupu-kumkum.* That was the only *puja* that was done.

Then Tata went to the man and asked who the goddess was and why he was leaving her like that [on the ground]. The old man answered, "She's *satyamaina talli* [true mother/goddess]."[2] So they asked the goddess to save Avva from her illness. My *peddamma* [aunt][3] was also unwell; so they both took a vow to the goddess. Tata was a drawing teacher and used to play the *vina* [a stringed instrument]. He thought that he should do something for such a great *satyamaina talli.* He told the old man that *he* wanted to do her *puja,* and the latter agreed. Tata should have gone back to Madras, but now he wanted to stay here. They stayed just opposite to Govindaraja Swamy temple, in a house for rent. From then on, Tata used to go to Gangamma morning and evening on Tuesdays and Fridays; he used to do *abhishekam* and decorate her.

He thought that such a *satyamaina talli* shouldn't be left without shelter, and so he built what we now see as the *garbhagriha.* There were then many Reddys here in Tirupati [who may have objected to the building of this temple]. He built the temple and put a neem branch on the goddess's head. He asked the goddess to drop the neem branch down if she wanted to be in the temple that he'd constructed. He waited until noon, and only then did she drop the neem branch.

Tata used to observe ritual purity [*madi*] before worshipping her and offered all the family's cooked food to the goddess first; only then would he offer food even to the smallest child of the family. He did this almost every day. Someone told my grandfather, "Mudaliar, don't offer food to the goddess, because she's a *shakti* [*ugra*] goddess." My *peddamma* was only three months old, and many people told my grandfather not to bring the goddess into the house, because there was a small child in the house. The man said, "If you bring her in, your entire family line will be cut off. The goddess will take your entire family as *bali*." My grandfather said, "I don't care if we're all destroyed; I do this because the goddess agreed that I should bring her inside."

It used to be all jungle; there were no houses around. From then on, Tata and Avva performed all these services to the goddess every Friday and Tuesday. Then Avva had more children. My husband is the seventh child. When she first came here, Avva had only Peddamma; after that she had seven more children.

The *seva* [ritual service] went like this: first Avva-Tata [grandmother and grandfather], then Peddamma-Amma [maternal aunt and mother], then Akka [elder sister] and myself. We never gave this duty to any outsiders. Only recently, two years ago, this happened [that the Devasthanam took over the formal ritual services of the goddess].

[I asked if the goddess *prefers* female attendants, and if that is why her service seemed to have passed between females after the original grandfather-grandmother pair she had listed.[4]] Ours was the only Mudaliar family here [in Tirupati] at that time. So when Tata died, women had to take over. The men of the family were at regular jobs, so the women served. My eldest brother-in-law used to serve the goddess when he was young; but once he graduated and got a job, he had to stop doing this. [She names other males of the family who have moved away.] So only women were left to serve.[5]

In another conversation, Koteshvaramma told us that Gangamma called her through dreams whenever there was "work to be done in the temple." She gave an example:

Once, she appeared in a dream. I had a lot of work at home, since my third daughter had come home for her delivery; I had stopped going to the temple and my mother was going instead. Amma [the goddess] came in my dreams, and I wondered what she needed. But I got involved in my work at home and forgot about it completely. In one corner [in the temple] behind the goddess, there's a *trishul* [iron trident]; I'd wanted to put one in the other corner, but I forgot. After two days, I went to the temple. The second *trishul* was in a space under the *murti,* where all the *trishuls* used to be kept. By the time I went back to the temple, that place where the *trishuls* were kept had been covered permanently [with cement, as part of the process of "upgrading" the temple], and I lost my chance. We need two *trishuls* to hold up the big garlands given to the goddess, right? Especially on the *jatara* day, we get a very big garland from Madras. . . . If I'd been there, I would have taken out that second *trishul;* there are four to five other *trishuls* there under the goddess, too. So now, whenever she comes in my dreams, I now run to the temple immediately.

Amma also has an intimate relationship with the goddess in her domestic *puja* room. Knowing our interest in Gangamma the first time we visited her home, Koteshvaramma invited us into her *puja* room (a little room set aside just for the deities) and identified an eight-inch silver image—protected by a snake hood over her head, holding a trident, and wearing a gold *tali*—as Rajarajeshwari. A small silver head sits at her feet, marked with *pasupu,* who was identified as Gangamma. When I asked if there was a difference between Rajarajeshwari and Gangamma, Koteshvaramma replied:

No, they're all the same. We all used to perform *puja* to Rajarajeshwari at home and outside to Gangamma. As children, we used to call Gangamma "Avva" [Grandmother] because we used to hear my grandfather calling her "Amma, Amma" [Mother]. We used to finish *puja* here at home first and then go to Gangamma's temple. My eldest brother-in-law used to perform Rajarajeshwari *puja* at home and Avva and Tata used to perform Gangamma *puja* at the temple.

Here, Koteshvaramma distinguishes the goddess at the temple as Gangamma and the one at home as Rajarajeshwari, even as she asserts that the two are the "same." The name distinction may support the common belief that Gangamma herself can't be borne at home; or, it may reflect a Sanskritization of the image, as her identity shifts between Gangamma and the more Sanskritic appellation Rajarajeshwari. In either case, Koteshvaramma has an intimate relationship with Gangamma, as a young girl calling her "Grandmother" (since she heard her grandfather calling the goddess "Mother," she assumed Gangamma would be "Grandmother" to her generation), and through daily service both at home and at the temple.

Amma married her mother's youngest brother, according to the common South Indian custom of cross-cousin marriage. Her husband is referred to by his friends and acquaintances as CKR (Chennapatnam Krishnaswamy Ratnavelu). When I first met CKR, he was a retired postal worker who now dedicated his time to serving as a chess tutor and organizing chess tournaments. As the official *mirasidar* of the temple, he gave quite a different account of how his family had come to serve the goddess than that his wife had told us. He framed the family story by opening with their eviction from Tatayyagunta temple by the Devasthanam. Speaking in English, he recounted:

There was a Reddy who ran for some political office. All of the sudden we heard something from him; we didn't know anything; he didn't give notice or anything. He simply said, "You go away." The eviction was given by the MLA [member of legislative assembly] on March 12, 1993. We came out [left the temple] because we are a respectable family; we didn't want a quarrel, so we came out. Then what happened? I immediately wrote a letter to the Endowment Commissioner stating that we have been serving the goddess since 1916.

My father came from Madras in 1913, that is, the First World War. They came from Madras for safety [from the war]. He had worked for some mission school [British-run school] as a drawing master before that. Afraid of the war, he left Madras and settled here. He also knew music. He came here and started to give music tuitions [lessons]—to officers, doctors, advocates. He gave vocal music and *vina* tuitions. He himself made about 100 *vinas.*

In the meantime, my sister had some infection. So he took some *kumkum* to the temple and had faith in the goddess. Also he had no male child. And so he prayed on that day. Then my brother was born. So he had faith in the goddess.

A Reddy was *grama munsif* [headman] of Tirupati at that time. My father was the *dharmakarta* [trustee; temple manager] in those days.[6] That was 1914. Before he was *dharmakarta* of the temple, all those who performed *puja* were Reddys.[7] The There was no temple there, actually; just some stones, idols [*sic*], on the ground. My father, having faith in the goddess, constructed the temple, with the help of the subcollector. He brought stones from Chandragiri [a village on the outskirts of Tirupati]. He constructed the *garbhagriha.* The Reddys had some prejudices against my father. I mean by that [pause]—My father addressed the Commissioner of Endowments of Composite Madras State in 1918. The Commissioner came and saw all the records of the temple.

In the meantime, my father prepared a *kavacam* in 1927, at Kadari [small town in the adjacent Anantapur District]. Because he was a drawing master, he had some idea how to do this. He drew the measurements. The *kavacam* has no faults; it isn't loose; it has perfect measurements. After that, the Endowment Commissioner came to Tirupati and he was satisfied, and he gave orders for my father to perform the *pujas* and to become *dharmakarta;* this was in 1941. My father looked after the temple until 1955. After that, my second brother looked after it. I was away from the family at that time. When my brother died, I took over.

In 1993, a certain Reddy[8] interfered in this affair. We also received orders from the Commissioner. The previous trustees passed a resolution stating that non-Brahmans should not be allowed in the temple; that is, they shouldn't be allowed to perform the *puja.* They passed that resolution. But, without having heard from the commissioner for two years, yesterday we were asked to come back.

In another conversation, CKR included a more personal reflection on his family's relationship to the goddess (this time speaking in Tamil):

Before my father built the *garbhagriha,* there was no temple at all, but there was a *jatara.* From my childhood, my mother used to arrange a cradle there itself [at the temple] and she used to swing me there. Especially on Tuesdays and Fridays, they used to spend the entire day there. . . . I wasn't a healthy child, so I had to discontinue my studies for a while. My parents used to send me to the temple and ask me to attend to the goddess. My father wanted to give me totally to the temple [in service of the goddess], so he asked me to go there and perform the *pujas.* I learned some [Sanskrit] *shlokas;* but I felt that being a *local,* I should learn more about the temple duties. Later, I got a job in the postal department. I have the same *will-power* as my father; but my brothers didn't have this. Because I knew how my father had taken trouble to stay in the temple, how he struggled with the temple people, I took the same trouble to get it back [i.e., registered a court case].

Koteshvaramma and CKR tell very different stories about how their family came to Tirupati and began to serve Gangamma. Koteshvaramma recounts her grandparents (CKR's parents) coming to Tirupati on pilgrimage to Sri Venkateshvara's temple uphill, as do thousands of devotees from Madras. Having taken *darshan* of the god, Avva became ill. They saw a man serving a stone head and asked who she was; he told them she was *satyamaina talli.* So they made a vow to the goddess and stayed on in Tirupati to serve her. Koteshvaramma specifies that the goddess's healing powers and the grandparents' subsequent devotion to her kept the family in Tirupati. Entering a relationship with Gangamma through illness, vows, and healing—as the Mudaliar grandparents did—follows a common narrative grammar among many of her worshippers.

Both Koteshvaramma and CKR emphasize that the Gangamma image that their grandfather/father saw was simply a stone head on the ground, rather than residing in any kind of temple or shrine. Amma's account shows her awareness of the tradition of *gramadevatas* living without shelter and the practice of devotees having to ask their explicit permission to build a temple (numerous oral narratives tell of *gramadevatas* refusing this permission). With Gangamma's permission, Tata built what is now the inner sanctum of the Tatayyagunta temple. Amma's account proceeds to describe Gangamma's reputation for fierce *shakti* that, people told Tata, could threaten to destroy the baby Peddamma and Tata's entire lineage if the goddess was brought inside. But Tata persevered in his service, saying he was willing to be destroyed if this would be the result of obedience to the goddess. Instead, the family was blessed with the birth of seven more children. Koteshvaramma's story establishes her family's (unique) ability to bear such a *shakti* goddess, continuing up to her own generation. She ends with a listing of the familial pairs that have served the goddess: grandmother-grandfather, aunt-mother, sister and herself. Koteshvaramma's narrative focuses primarily on her family and its devotion to the goddess rather than the wider political and social worlds around her.

CKR, in contrast to his wife Koteshvaramma, gives a more "secular" reason for the family's move to Tirupati—to get away from the effects of World War I in Madras. The rest of CKR's narration, too, gives more details of and focuses more on the broader historical and social worlds in which Gangamma's temple was established than does Koteshvaramma's story—although he does mention that Gangamma healed his sister and caused a male heir to be born to his parents. CKR introduces the early tension between his family and the dominant-caste Reddys who had been serving the goddess until his own family began to do so. Koteshvaramma, too, mentions the Reddys' dominance back in those days, but gives no further comment. It should be noted that, like Mudaliars, Reddys are also not traditional caretakers of *gramadevatas;* such goddesses are usually served by lower and former-untouchable castes. Recent Reddy involvement (particularly that of the Reddy MLA) and more direct involvement of the Devasthanam was likely motivated by the significant income (particularly during the *jatara*) the temple had begun to generate. There may well be, however, a Reddy family story that I never heard, about their early involvement when Gangamma was just a head under a tree.

The Mudaliar family's tension with the Reddys continued until the Endowments finally took over daily administration of the temple (when a Reddy was the Devasthanam Executive Officer) and ejected the Mudaliars in 1993. CKR is careful to document exactly what his family did to "improve" the temple and when: they built the *garbhagriha* in between 1914 and 1918; got approval for his family's service from the Commissioner of Endowments in 1918; made the first *kavacam* in 1927; and finally, received permission from the Endowments to perform *pujas* and become *dharmakartas* of the temple in 1941. These details are important in affirming the long service of CKR's family in order to establish his family's rights to the temple *mirasi,* a story which CKR has told many times and produced in court papers. In another conversation, CKR said his family "handed the temple over to the Endowments Department" in 1940; but the family continued to "maintain" it, as they had done from 1916 until 1993 (when they were evicted). Whereas the Endowments now charges monetary fees for *archana, harati,* and other rituals performed on behalf of an individual, CKR said his family did not charge fees for such rituals, because "it is a public temple, and that, too, of a *gramadevata.*"

But CKR's story was not only about business and court cases; after the narrative about the history and politics of the temple *mirasi,* he told another story about those early days, before a permanent structure was built around that goddess (presumably justifying the need for such a structure). This story explains why the Gangamma stone image has a cement addition to her dark stone nose. It's a story that brings pleasure and laughter to its small audiences, even upon frequent repetition:

There was a *rowdy* there.[9] Throughout the day, he worked hard, and in the evening he drank [alcohol]. He used to take something for Amma [Gangamma] everyday—sweets like *jalebi* and Mysore *pak*—and place it there. He used to say, "Amma, I have drunk fully; now you should eat these sweets." After he shouted and went to sleep, the children around the temple used to take and eat the sweets. So he used to think that Amma ate those sweets every day. In the mornings, he used to tell everyone this. One day he thought he should sit and watch her eat, wondering, "How does Amma eat?"—since the children would take the sweets only when he closed his eyes. One day, he didn't close his eyes [and the goddess didn't eat the sweets]. [He yelled at her,] "You've been eating every day. Why didn't you eat today?" He picked up a stone and threw it at her. The nose is broken because of him.

The nose was repaired by the Mudaliar family, and one can still see the scars of this injury during Gangamma's *abhishekam,* which washes away her *pasupu* mask.

On a visit to the Mudaliar home during the *jatara* of 2000, I again asked Koteshvaramma how she (rather than CKR) came to serve the goddess on a daily basis in the temple; more specifically, I asked, was Gangamma's service passed on to daughters or daughters-in-law of their family? She answered by explaining the complicated kinship relationships of (cross-cousin) intermarriage in her family, such that daughters-in-laws were often also daughters of the extended family, but that if daughters-in-law were from "outside," then daughters would serve because they would have learned from working with their mothers. Koteshvaramma's son interjected, "Everyone's interrelated. My father's parents' daughter is my mother's mother. My father's sister is my mother's mother. My mother's brother is married to my sister. Mother's brother's daughter is married to my brother." He added that he himself, however, had married outside the family, and that his own wife had not been directly involved in Gangamma service at Tatayyagunta temple.

Koteshvaramma's and CKR's thirty-eight-year-old daughter told us that, at the urging of both her grandfather and Peddamma, the younger woman had been "given to the goddess" when she was only a girl and was already suffering from heart problems (for which she later had surgery). Her parents felt she was too weak to get married, although the doctor had told her that doing so would have no adverse effects; dedicating her to the service of the goddess implied that she would remain unmarried. She had periodically joined her mother in Tatayyagunta temple, but now (2000) spent her days in serving the goddess in the family *puja* room. Koteshvaramma commented that her daughter now spent more time serving the goddess than she herself did. I asked her whether or not the family had *ritually* offered her daughter to the goddess, thinking of the exchange of *talis* between the goddess and a class of women called *matammas,* who thereafter serve the goddess and traditionally remain unmarried. She answered that no such ritual had been performed; nor does this Mudaliar family belong to the lower castes and class who traditionally participate in these traditions. Although there are parallels between *matammas'* and Koteshvaramma's daughter's dedication and service to the goddess, *matammas* are traditionally free to have sexual relationships with men without marriage, an idea this middle-class, educated family would likely abhor.

When CKR's sons said they had dropped their efforts to get back their family's *mirasi* over the temple administration because there was no one in the family to take it up, I suggested that their sister could have done so. They disagreed: "Our mother says it's not like that; she [the sister] has no support [i.e., is not married]. It's difficult to work at Gangamma temple now because drunks and *rowdies* come there. . . . She's thirty-eight years old, and she's not interested. Even if she were, the *backing* should be there; she's not married. Women should have some *background* [male support]."

The younger generation did not seem to feel the loss over the family's ejection from the temple as deeply as did their parents. Although their daughter expressed sadness for the loss her mother had experienced when she had been ejected from the temple, she seemed satisfied to serve Gangamma at home, without aspirations to serve at the temple.

The Mudaliar Family's Ejection from the Temple

Koteshvaramma and CKR had varying interpretations of why their family had been ejected from the temple by the Devasthanam. In 1995, talking to us in the Tatayyagunta courtyard where she had returned for the first time since her ejection in 1993, Koteshvaramma explained:

For the last eight years, I've been serving in the temple. First Tata, next Avva, Peddamma, Akka—it was all *women* who served the goddess. Then a "big man" interfered in the temple affairs and said that *women shouldn't do this service to the goddess* [my emphasis].

. . . We were told that a male would be appointed and *he* would do the duties. Then we went to court, because we've been doing this *seva* for a long time. They asked for the *kavacam* that we'd taken with us and we said no. [I asked: What happened to that big man who objected to your service?] He lost his seat in the recent elections.

In another conversation, Koteshvaramma described the changes in Gangamma's *alankara* when men began to decorate her (being more specific about what the flower sellers may have observed when they said she was made to look like a Bollywood star):

You saw the goddess when you were here before; could you notice any change between then and this year? When the goddess was covered with our *kavacam,* she was *shanta;* now with this *kavacam,* the goddess looks a little bit *ugra.* The other change is that the *kumkum* on her mouth was longer [than when Koteshvaramma decorated her], and we put dots on either side of her mouth when we did the *alankaram.* They made it shorter like *make-up.* This year it's back to normal [the year Koteshvaramma had returned to the temple]. . . . [Her daughter adds:] Now people are happy with Ammavaru's *alankaram* again, since Amma is doing it perfectly again.

In rather startling contrast to his wife's explanations and reasoning, CKR attributes his family's ejection from the temple to the fact that they were not Brahmans—not because the primary attendant had been a woman (his wife):

In 1993 the Reddy MLA interfered in this affair. We also received orders from the commissioner. The previous trustees passed a resolution stating that *non-Brahmans should not be allowed in the temple* [my emphasis]; that is, they shouldn't be allowed to perform the *puja.* They passed that resolution. Without any communication or orders from the commissioner, yesterday, after two years, we were asked to come back.

In another conversation, remembering the narrative above, I tried to clarify with CKR whether he felt it was primarily because of his family's non-Brahman caste status that they were evicted from the temple when the Endowments took over its daily operations. He paused and then said (in Telugu):

Because she's a Shudra *devata* [low-caste deity], there shouldn't be a Brahman serving her. She's a meat-eater. . . . I told them this—that a Brahman should not be serving her. Do you know Kanchi Kamakoti Peetham *acarya* [spiritual leader of the so-named monastic institution]?[10] Not recently, but in earlier days, he came to the temple and he performed *kumbham abhishekam* and erected the *gopuram* [temple tower] and also some *kalashams* [water-pot ornaments] on top of the *gopuram.* Only Vaishnava temples should have all this—*kalasham, vimanam* [small tower over the *garbhagriha*], and these things. This is a Shudra deity; all these things should not be here. It's a *principle.* Ask anyone and you'll hear the same thing. This is not a Vaishnava temple.

This was the only reference I heard to the *acarya* from Kanchi Kamakoti Peetham coming to Tirupati to perform rituals at Tatayyagunta; and it's not clear when CKR thought he had come. However, CKR is explicit that the *acarya*'s presence had been an inappropriate, *brahminic* intervention in a "*Shudra*-deity" temple. Further, that a Shudra temple has been given attributes of a Vaishnava temple, including the *gopuram, vimanam,* and *kalasham,* is, according to CKR, against *principle* (either customary principle or against Sanskritic *agamic* textual prescriptions for temples). He makes no mention that Gangamma is traditionally served not only by non-Brahmans, but often by women. Another silence in his narrative is that traditionally the non-Brahman attendants to "Shudra deities" are themselves "Shudras," from low or former-untouchable castes—which the Mudaliar caste is not.

In 1999, I asked the Executive Officer (EO) of the Tattaiahgunta Devasthanam what *he* thought the reasons for CKR's family's ejection from the temple were. He responded, "The MLA, a certain Reddy,[11] wanted to install Brahman pandits who recite [Sanskrit] *mantras.* The Trust Board asked Koteshvaramma to stand aside while the *pujaris* performed *mantras,* but she refused. CKR didn't chant *mantras;* they only used to perform *harati.*" Further, he continued, "They used to take the proceeds from the saris and *jackets* [sari blouses] offered to the goddess. After they left, there was a good income from auction of the saris, up to Rs. 50,000 per year. Last *jatara* the saris brought in Rs. 50,600." The EO gave both a ritual and economic explanation for bringing in Brahmans employed by the Trust Board (Endowments Department) to serve the goddess: the Trust Board wanted Sanskrit *mantras* to be recited and wanted to keep temple earnings from accruing to a single family.

In the years since the Mudaliar family was ejected from the temple, for the duration of the *jatara,* they have set up in the foyer of their home the silver *kavacam* their grandfather had crafted so many decades earlier (now set over a form made of saris instead of the dark stone goddess herself).[12] A daughter-in-law of the family proudly showed us the *kavacam* in 1995, saying that no other families could "bear" this in their home. Several friends and neighbors had come to the house to take *darshan* of this form of Gangamma on the two Tuesdays of the *jatara;* and the female university professor who had accompanied me to the Mudaliar home for *darshan* (followed by a lunch of elaborate *prasad*), exclaimed at the size of the *kavacam,* wondering how the family could keep such a large form of Gangamma in the house. She explained that that's why householders make such small turmeric-mound Gangammas in their homes during the *jatara*—because they can't "bear" more; the larger the image, the more service she requires. But the Mudaliars were a family that had intimately served for decades the most powerful of *gramadevata* sisters, Tatayyagunta Gangamma; they could "bear" her.

Although the Kaikala *jatara veshams* visit the Mudaliar family home and the female householders perform *harati* to this form of Gangamma, Koteshvaramma was not fluent with Gangamma's narrative or its embodiment by the Kaikala *veshams.* She frequently confused the names, descriptions, and ritual ordering of the *veshams,* and mixed up elements of the story they embodied. She often deferred our questions about the narrative to her husband, CKR, who, she said, knew better the Palegadu story. But he, too, told us the story in barest outline and conflated elements of other stories with this one.

Koteshvaramma knew the goddess primarily through intimate ritual rather than narrative. Every week, she had anointed Gangamma's temple dark-stone head in the *abhishekam* ritual with a series of liquids: milk, yogurt, turmeric water, fresh water. She then carefully applied *pasupu* to the wet surface of the goddess to create a smooth silky "mask." She marked the goddess's lips with vermilion and placed on her forehead a large red vermillion *bottu* and a brass Shaivite three-line forehead marking. Carefully, she built up with turmeric paste the side of the nose, on which she placed a large nose ring. Before draping the goddess's sari, Koteshvaramma placed a garland of little black bangles around the neck of the freshly anointed goddess, and placed more decorative jewelry and flower garlands over the sari. Finally, she put a large (brass) *tali* and silver eyes on the goddess. Koteshvaramma knew Gangamma's likes and dislikes when it came to ornamentation and saris (preferably cotton, green, yellow, or maroon, or other *pasupu-kumkum* colors—with gold threads).

After watching the *jatara abhishekam* and *alankaram* in 1995, I asked Koteshvaramma about Gangamma's *ugram,* whether she protects or can also cause illness. She answered:

She only protects. Like a mother, like a mother with a child. Whenever we're in trouble, she guards and helps us. We believe that. Whenever we pray to her, she gives strength to us. We pray, "Oh Gangamma, what am I going to do; give me some strength." This morning I prayed like that. I felt very tired and couldn't do any work. I wondered what I would do, how I would cook. I prayed, "Gangamma, help me, give me strength," and now I'm OK. I only felt like that for fifteen minutes. I finished cooking and everything's over—[making] *prasad* is over, *puja* is over.

[My fieldwork associate asked why, then, people say Cinna Gangamma is *ugra.*] Seeing her appearance, they feel like that; she has a knife with her, her face and everything. Seeing her appearance, they think she's like that [*ugra*]. . . . But we see her with a calm face; we can see her like that. Somebody else sees her as *ugra* and fears that she will do something to them. She appears to them like that.

Koteshvaramma seemed resigned to and deflated by her ejection from the temple (without the will to fight it that her husband seemed to have), saying only that she missed the physical contact she had had with Tatayyagunta Gangamma. Meanwhile, CKR's driving concern seemed to be documenting family history of temple service to support the court case lodged in his effort to get back the family *mirasi.*

Koteshvaramma and her daughter moved back to Chennai sometime between 2000 and when I returned to Tirupati in 2007. At that time, I met with CKR, who had moved into rented quarters in another neighborhood and, although looking considerably older, was still active in chess tutoring and competitions. By 2010, he, too, had moved to Chennai and none of my contacts in Tirupati had his contact information.

From Familial Attendants to Temple Employees

When the Mudaliar family was ejected from Tatayyagunta temple, most of the female temple attendants who had served the goddess with Koteshvaramma over many years became permanent Devasthanam employees. And their access to the goddess changed considerably. As one attendant told me in 1995:[13]

We supply water, cut the bananas, etc., for *abhishekam.* We do all other things, but we don't touch the goddess. We only participate in *abhishekam* during the *jatara.* We can only participate in the *abhishekam* of the *kodistambha* [temple pillar]—either five or three *muttaiduvas* climb up to do this—but we're not allowed to perform the inside *abhishekam.*

Koteshvaramma confirmed that the female attendants who had worked with her in the temple had asked her for permission to work for the Devasthanam, which she gave. So, she continued, they went to the "big man" who had objected to women serving the goddess and asked about their work:

When they were working with me, I used to give something [compensation] to them; but now they're appointed like servants [i.e., it's a "job"]. When I was there, I allowed the women to give *harati,* but now they're not allowed. Before, they used to assist me in the service of the goddess; now they only sweep the floor around the goddess's *garbhagriha.* After I left, that older man and other men wouldn't let them enter the *garbhagriha.*

One of the long-term female attendants, herself a Mudaliar who had served in the temple for thirteen years, concurred, telling us:

I've touched Ammavaru many times. Whenever her *decoration* fell off, like her nose ring or eyes, I used to go and put them back on. I've put garlands on her, too. [I asked her: Do you miss the physical touch with Ammavaru?] [The attendant sighed:] Yes. I don't have the chance now except for once a year. During the *jatara,* I can go there, near Ammavaru, and I pour water on her. That is only for us *staff*; no one else can do this.

In 2000, this same attendant explained that she had begun working at the temple at the behest of the Mudaliar family, when her own mother-in-law, who had served with Koteshvaramma at the temple, had died:

I've been working here for thirteen years. I used to come to worship Ammavaru and then I got married. My mother-in-law was working here and because I'm her daughter-in-law, I was given *tambulam* [betel leaf with *pasupu-kumkum;* given to the attendant as a ritual bestowing on her the rights to serve the goddess]. After I'd been married only six months, my mother-in-law died, and they said, because I was her daughter-in-law, "You should serve here." I used to wash all the utensils and clean the whole place. I did this in the evening. In the morning I used to come again and break coconut, give *harati,* and do the *puja* in the *garbhagriha.* I had small children then. It's been seven years since I've worked inside; it's been seven years since I did *harati.* Now I wash the whole place outside and then the *puja* utensils. I keep order in the queue [of persons lined up to take *darshan*]; I've been doing this for the last seven years. . . . Actually, I was first posted inside the temple; I was asked to be a publicist [*pracarak*] and to assist the *pujari.* But then these Brahman *pujaris* said they didn't need women to help them; they say only men should be there.

While economically this temple attendant may be now better-positioned as an employee of the Devasthanam, with a guaranteed income, she misses the intimacy of working with Koteshvaramma and the access that she had then to the goddess herself.

Other "new" temple employees include members of the Pambala family who accompany the Kaikala *veshams* on their perambulations. One of the Pambalas said they had "joined" the temple as drummers in 1993 (when the Devasthanam took over the daily functions), but that they don't sing there: "We only sing [story of Adi Para Shakti] for the Sunnapukundalu in Veshalamma temple." Now, at the temple, they drum briefly during heightened moments of *darshan* and do a lot of waiting in between. In recent years, a Pambala male sometimes sits at the *archana* ticket booth during high-crowd times of the *jatara* and Navaratri.

Aesthetic and Ritual Changes at Tatayyagunta Temple

Ritual innovations at Tatayyagunta temple began long before the Devasthanam took over the full-time administration of the temple in 1993, but they accelerated thereafter. The Mudaliar grandfather himself started the process of creating an evolving permanent structure to protect the goddess—with the goddess's permission. The Devasthanam added other architectural changes after the Mudaliars were evicted; some were for aesthetic purposes, others to control *jatara* crowds, and still others for what were perceived to be matters of practicality.

In 1999 the EO of the Tattaiahgunta Devasthanam told me that the annual income of the temple had grown from Rs. 80, 000 in 1988, to 5 *lakhs* (one *lakh* equals Rs. 100,000) in 1994, and to 10–12 *lakhs* in 1998. In 1990, a "renovation committee" was formed, and the next year the Tirumala Tirupati Devasthanam (the *devasthanam* of the wealthy Sri Venkateshvara temple uphill) contributed 1.15 *lakhs* of rupees to the Tatayyagunta temple, specifically for this renovation. The EO proudly listed the renovations/innovations that had been completed under his leadership to date: building of the *mandapam* (cement-roofed pavilion outside the enclosed temple) and compound walls around the temple courtyard (the latter to prevent encroachment of other building onto temple land), the addition of a brass arch (*makara toranam*) behind the image of Gangamma, the introduction of the *hundi* (locked cash-collection box positioned outside of the *garbhagriha*), and a ticket system for *archana* during the *jatara* and other festival days.

The EO was especially proud of the newly installed ticket system for various rituals sponsored by worshippers, saying, "All these years no one thought to do all this [tickets]; the goddess must have wanted me to serve her." He was about to leave the day after our conversation for Hyderabad to bring back architectural plans for a new gateway arch to be built at the side entrance to the temple compound, which was subsequently built. The Devasthanam also built a large entrance on the eastern side of the temple compound, accompanied by a large sign with the name of the temple, lit up at night by strings of small lights. The EO took pride in eliciting large donations from individuals: "People started coming; you just have to ask and they will donate. In 1991 someone donated a fan; now we have twenty fans, all free of cost." The temple courtyard walls are covered with blackstone engraved plaques naming the big donors to the temple.

In the mid-1990s Devasthanam added cast cement, sculpted images around the top of the temple exterior—brightly painted images of *puranic* deities—that from the outside makes the temple look like many other *puranic* goddess temples. To the side of the temple, in front of the *pipal* tree, a small, independent temple to Ganesha (elephant-headed deity who is the remover of obstacles) has also been built. While some Gangamma worshippers whose families have traditionally been associated with her may complain about some of the aesthetic changes at Tatayyagunta temple, the presence of Ganesha is not included in these complaints. These same worshippers also worship at *puranic*-deity temples, and many have come to expect the presence of Ganesha in temples. The Devasthanam also tiled the *garbhagriha* and enclosed the *mandapam* in front of the *garbhagriha* with metal screening. Later, this open space where worshippers often sat after taking *darshan* was filled with metal guide rails, to help control crowds and keep them in line; now there is little space for worshippers to sit for a few minutes after having taken *darshan,* according to traditional temple etiquette. Nor is there space immediately in front of the goddess for the female ritual of lighting inside-out-lemon oil lamps—a ritual whose popularity has increased since the early 1990s—to remove *naga dosham* (blemish caused by the position of astrological bodies at the time of birth, resulting in late marriage, infertility, and other problems).[14] Women now light these lamps outside of the enclosed antechamber, in front of the cement *kodistambha* pillar and at some distance from the goddess in the *garbhagriha.* The Devasthanam has also removed a line of iron tridents (forms of the goddess herself) that used to stand in front of the *garbhagriha,* replacing them with a single large, low silver-metallic trident head. The EO told me that this was for the "safety of worshippers," to keep them from getting spiked and hurt by the iron tridents; but an elderly devotee told us that Gangamma had appeared to her in a dream and had expressed her anger at this replacement of herself.[15]

The earthen temple courtyard was eventually paved over with large square stones, creating a virtual heating pad during the hot season (especially noted by a female devotee who regularly performs *angapradakshina,* or circumambulation by rolling the body over and over, around the temple). This impermeable surface is also unable to absorb the blood from chicken and goat sacrifices and other liquids used in lay rituals performed in the courtyard; now these ritual "leftovers" are washed away by the temple attendants with buckets of water aimed at the drains at the edges of the courtyard.

Of particular significance to a *gramadevata* goddess such as Gangamma are the changes around the ritual of animal sacrifice (*bali*). Buffalo *bali* was traditionally offered to Tatayyagunta Gangamma during her *jatara* until 1950, when the Andhra Pradesh Animals and Birds Sacrifices [Prohibition] Act was passed. Although in the surrounding villages buffalo *bali* is still performed, today in Tirupati, the offerings are limited to chickens and some goats. However, buffalo *bali* remains in the public imagination.

Koteshvaramma told a story from her grandfather's time when someone challenged the power of the goddess just as *bali* was about to be offered—presumably challenging the need for *bali* itself. A man came up and asked what was going on. Someone told him it was the time of Gangamma *jatara* and soon there would be buffalo *bali.* He asked if the goddess was really such a *satyamaina talli* (*ugra* goddess who would require this kind of *bali*). Yes, they replied. He challenged them, "I'll see; I'll cause her to become a dog and take her with me." He used some *mantras* that prevented them from cutting off the buffalo's head. He taunted, "Have you seen my power? I'll do the same with your goddess." But he had moved only a few feet away from her when he started bleeding from his nose and mouth, and he died on the spot. At that same moment, they were able to cut off the head of the buffalo.

Veshalamma, a woman who has exchanged *talis* with the goddess, reported a similar narrative from more recent times:

> There isn't supposed to be *bali* at Tatayyagunta temple, as ordered by an *officer.* This officer subsequently suffered from vomiting and dysentery, so he permitted chicken and goat sacrifice, but no buffalo. [I asked, "Was Gangamma angry when buffalo *bali* was stopped?"] It's because of that that the officer died. He kept ordering everyone not to perform *bali.* He said, 'Did Gangamma ask for all this? Who told you all this?' For one year, he said there shouldn't be any *jatara,* and they stopped it for one year. There were all kinds of illnesses like dysentery, vomiting, cholera, spreading throughout the *uru.* So they appealed to the government and began celebrating the *jatara* again [with *bali*].

I expected that the presence of Brahman priests at Tatayyagunta temple might preclude any animal sacrifice at the temple at all, even the *bali* of chicken. However, this is not the case—at least not yet. Chicken and goat *bali* is performed outside the temple proper, in the courtyard, out of direct sight of the Brahman priests. They are, of course, aware of the activities in the courtyard, but did not talk to me about the non-vegetarian offerings, nor did they seem to have any intention to try to stop them. They are inwardly focused toward Gangamma's temple image and serve her as if she is a non-*gramadevata* goddess, reciting Sanskrit *mantras* and offering fruits, flowers, and *harati.*

Jatara participants would seemingly know and experience a very different goddess in Gangamma than do the Brahman priests who now serve her. I often wondered how these Brahman priests *know* the goddess, whether and how they distinguish her from *puranic* goddesses. The priests are employees of the Endowments Department and are assigned particular temples, not, they told me, according to their own inclinations or relationships with the deity, but according to the needs of the temples and the Endowments Department. Since 1993, several priests have rotated through (sometimes for only several weeks, or when called upon to serve for a single festival occasion), and most could answer very few questions about Gangamma as a unique deity or about the *jatara.* But one priest has been in the temple since the beginning of Brahman service and has gradually become part of the wider temple community, interacting personally with the female attendants and the Pambala drummers who are often in the temple. He was considerably more jocular and interactive in 2010 than he had been in the late 1990s. Caring for the goddess—including the intimate act of applying her *pasupu* "mask" after *abhishekam*—seems to have created a growing relationship and comfort-level with Gangamma for this Brahman *pujari,* much as ritual performance had created knowledge and experience of the goddess for Koteshvaramma.

Gangamma now sits under a brass arch that characterizes the inner shrine of the temples of many South Indian *puranic* deities. Rather than just on select *jatara* days, she is now always covered with a *kavacam* and piles and piles of flower garlands, with only her *pasupu* face visible. Musicians (playing the reed instrument *nagasvaram* and drumming) have joined the temple staff, singing and playing during *harati;* and many afternoons, one can hear *puranic* recitations broadcast over loudspeakers into the temple courtyard and adjacent streets, performed by *purana pandits/panditas* who are employees of the Endowments Department.

While the basic "grammar" of *jatara* rituals of the streets, homes, and temple courtyards seems to have remained relatively stable—although the crowds have grown exponentially—the *jatara* has been framed by the Devasthanam in new ways. The growing wealth of the temple is exhibited in elaborate decorations of lights strung at the entrances of the temple courtyard; loud music (devotional music in a Bollywood-type musical style, non-specific to Gangamma herself) blares from loudspeakers throughout the nights. On the Wednesday morning after the *ugra mukhi* has been dismantled, a new ritual called *pulangi* (lit., garment of flowers) has been added at Tatayyagunta temple, during which the interior image of Gangamma is buried in flowers. The priests told us the ritual "cooled" the goddess; from their perspective, this ritual now closes the *jatara* ritual sequence, rather than the dismantling of the *ugra mukhi.*

When I returned to Tirupati in the fall of 2005 there were, painted on the courtyard compound walls, explanations for and pictures of each of the Kaikala *vesham,* a separate panel for each—elucidations that presumably would not have been needed by traditional *jatara* participants, but would be for "new" participants. The Devasthanam, aware that many in the growing *jatara* crowds may not know the identities and rationales for the *jatara vesham,* has also printed and distributed pamphlets during the *jatara* that similarly explain the *vesham* sequences and other tidbits of information about the *jatara.* Interestingly, the data for these pamphlets is drawn directly from Peta Srinivasulu Reddy's now-authoritative Telugu-language book about the *jatara* (1995).

New festivals have also been introduced to the annual ritual cycle of the Tatayyagunta temple, festivals that are not directly associated with Gangamma, but are more generically "goddess" festivals. The Devasthanam EO specifically mentioned that Navaratri (the festival of the Nine Nights of the Goddess) is *essential* for Ammavaru, and that the month of Kartik, during which they perform Laksha Kumkum Archana (ritual recitation of the thousand names of the goddess while sprinkling her with *kumkum*) is "especially good for Ammavaru."

Celebration of Navaratri had actually been introduced by the Mudaliars in the 1980s; it was suspended for a few years after the eviction of the Mudaliar family, but the Devasthanam has again taken up its celebration. During Navaratri, various prominent families and politicians sponsor special Gangamma *abhishekams.* The primary visual celebration of Navaratri at Tatayyagunta temple is the placement of a different goddess (in her small metal festival form) each of the nine nights on a swing set up in the inner courtyard; devotees swing the goddess in a ritual called *unjal seva*—a service also offered regularly to Sri Venkateshvara uphill. Many of the women who attended and even participated in the swinging, several of whom I knew from their participation in rituals more specifically associated with Gangamma as *gramadevata,* could not identify the individual goddesses they were serving, when I asked who they were. They often answered with what has now become close to a *mantra:* "they are all the same." For those who know Gangamma, these Sanskritic goddesses are conflated with her; whereas for devotees who do not know her, Gangamma becomes only one more form of the *puranic* goddesses. Attendance at Navaratri rituals in 1999 comprised mostly of the families of the sponsors of each ritual and temple employees (the female attendants and flowersellers, along with a few others); the lack of a wider audience at that time suggests the innovation of including Navaratri celebrations at this *gramadevata* site.

Then there are smaller changes at Tatayyagunta temple that were not initiated by the Devasthanam, such as the variations in what the flower sellers offer at their little stalls set up in the courtyard. When I first started visiting temple in 1992, the stalls were filled with *veyyiduttas* (thousand-eyed clay pots that represent Gangamma), flowers, incense, and camphor. But when I visited in 2010, the flower sellers had added yellow-dyed *tali* strings,[16] gold-spangled red scarves, and red glass bangles to the offerings available to worshippers—standard material offerings found outside many *puranic* goddess temples. A large "modern" jewelry store advertises by providing small plastic bags for worshippers to take home their *prasad,* on which are printed the image of Tatayyagunta Gangamma and the name, address, and phone number of the jewelry store.

Many features of middle-class aesthetics, consumerism, and "modern" efficiencies that are reshaping Gangamma's temple have also affected the god on the hill, Sri Venkateshvara. The same bright lights and signs that have been introduced to Tatayyagunta temple are part of the *brahmotsavams* ("great celebrations") uphill. Most pilgrims no longer walk up the hill on the footpath (which can take three to four hours); rather they take buses and air-conditioned cars. The long waiting line to take *darshan* of the god has been computerized, so that pilgrims who buy entry tickets (rather than standing for hours in the free line) can estimate their entry time and their waiting time is dramatically reduced. To manage the growing numbers of pilgrims inside the temple itself, the TTD has employed "pushers," young men who literally push pilgrims aside after they have taken *darshan* of Sri Venkateshvara for only a few seconds, to keep the *darshan* line moving. Traditionally, pilgrims spent much longer uphill than they do now—visiting various other shrines and temples. It used to be that a visit, including to Varaha Swamy (the boar incarnation of Vishnu), who gave land to Sri Venkateshvara for his temple, was a "requirement" of pilgrimage to Tirumala, as was a visit to Venkateshvara's wife, Padmavati, downhill; many of these traditions are being dropped with the efficiency of travel and the time pressures of middle-class pilgrims.

Whether and in what manner Gangamma will retain her unique *gramadevata*, excessive (*ugra*) persona in the contexts of shifting aesthetics and rituals remains to be seen. But, she seems to be holding her ground, as the following two incidents suggest. One Navaratri evening in 1999, my fieldwork associate and I participated in the swinging of the *utsava murti* of the goddess displayed outside the *garbhagriha*, an auspicious honor, we were told. Several weeks later when my fieldwork associate developed chickenpox, one of the temple flower sellers exclaimed, "It's a blessing from having swung Ammavaru. Gangamma is showing her pleasure." Note that she identified the *puranic* goddess on the swing with Gangamma, not the other way around.

Gangamma's continued *ugra* nature was also the focus of a narrative fragment related by Koteshvaramma as she was showing us the Mudaliar *kavacam* that had been set up during the *jatara* in their home entryway in 1995:

> For the last ten years, we've been performing Navaratri festival for nine days at Cinna Gangamma's [Tatayyagunta temple]. For the last two years, the Endowment Officer has been performing it. We used to decorate the goddess with this *kavacam* for ten days when *we* performed Navaratri. Two years ago, during Navaratri, on the last day, someone killed someone and threw the dead body in front of the temple. People thought that this had happened because Gangamma had not been fed enough meat. This happened the year we quit the temple [when the Devasthanam took over daily temple administration in 1993].

Even outside of the ritually circumscribed week of the *jatara,* Gangamma may become *ugra* and hungry, as she was thought to be during this particular Navaratri. At these times, too, Koteshvaramma's narrative suggests, she needs *bali.* Interestingly, Koteshvaramma doesn't take credit herself for this suggestion, vaguely saying "people thought." When Gangamma is left unsatisfied, things happen and inauspicious signs appear—in this case, a murder—that send a strong message of her needs.

While as scholars some of us may regret the loss incurred with the introduction of middle-class aesthetics to a *gramadevata* temple and the standardization of architecture and ritual according to Sanskritic, *agamic* textual prescriptions, few *jatara* participants and worshippers at Tatayyagunta temple voiced complaints or nostalgia over most of the *aesthetic* changes. In the eyes of the temple attendants and flower sellers, "more" usually seemed only to be "better." Just as their lives were experienced to be "better" and more convenient with the introduction of nylon saris and electricity, running water and TV's in their homes, so, too, many of these new ritual and architectural additions are seen as simply another level of service—beautifying Gangamma's abode, serving her in new ways, and making the goddess happy. The new aesthetics and rituals have not yet, for those who have traditionally interacted with her, performatively obliterated Gangamma's unique persona; however, for worshippers who don't "know her," she has come to be identified as simply "one more" of the many goddesses who consist of Devi, the "great goddess."[17]

Nevertheless, the change in personnel that initiated some of these ritual and architectural changes is accompanied by a deep personal loss for many who traditionally served Tatayyagunta Gangamma. Specifically, lower castes and women have less direct access to the goddess whom they used to serve directly. The contrast is visible by comparing the personnel and service of Tatayyagunta temple with that of Tallapaka Gangamma, the temples of the two sisters Cinna Gangamma and Pedda Gangamma, respectively. While the Endowments Department has also created the Tallapaka Gangamma Devasthanam, it does not have the same investment in this temple as it does in Tatayyagunta, presumably because the smaller temple brings in less income. Tallapaka Gangamma is still served by the Kaikalas, and most often by women of their family. And there are still many such small *gramadevata* shrines and temples elsewhere in Tirupati itself and in surrounding villages. However, with changes in Tatayyagunta Gangamma's adornment and her temple's architecture, the introduction of Brahman male priests and Sanskritic rituals, and the marginalization of women in the service of the goddess, it's difficult to imagine that, eventually, the alternative, unique worldview created and supported by

Gangamma traditions may not itself become marginalized, as she is more and more identified with Sanskritic traditions.

A woman who regularly becomes possessed by the goddess gave poignant commentary in 2000 about some of the changes initiated by the Devasthanam:

I used to go regularly to Gangamma temple, but now it's been handed over to the Devasthanam. So I keep her [the goddess] here at home, and I don't go there. She herself comes here; she said she won't stay there. They [the Devasthanam] just want money and property. They used to cut a neem tree then and there and do the [*jatara*] *puja* for Gangamma. From the days of our elders, they went in the evening, gave *bali* for the neem tree and did *puja,* and cut the neem tree at midnight. They erected it [the *kodistambha* in the temple courtyard that becomes the goddess on the first day of the *jatara*] and performed the *jatara* for her.

But now, for the last ten years [since early 1990s], they've been using a stone [pillar], not a tree. One night they got a stone and kept it there. [Seeing this,] I thought to myself, "What is this?" These people thought they wouldn't always find a tree. They said, "After we die, who will do this [go out and get a tree]? So, we'll get a stone and keep it here [permanently], when we're still alive. A stone like that at Pedda Gangamma temple." That's what they said to each other. I don't know all the details about it.

Just one week before the *jatara,* Gangamma came and knocked at my door. "Who's knocking at my door," I thought, and opened the door. She said, "Follow me." She went to the temple and said, "Since the beginning of time, they've been using a neem tree. Now it's like an *office job.* They brought this without asking me. They brought the stone [pillar] and placed it here. If they bring this stone, then what significance do I and my *shulams* [tridents] have?"

There used to be a lot of *shulams* there [inside the temple, in front of the *garbhagriha*]; they took them away. The brought the stone and erected it there [inside] first; then they brought it outside [where it is now].

Ammavaru took me there [to Tatayyagunta temple] and said, "From the beginning of time, from *yuga* to *yuga* [age to age], they used to satisfy me with a neem tree; but now they've brought a stone and placed it there. What significance do I and my *shulams* have? If I do anything [cause illnesses?], they say, 'Gangamma has no eyes, no ears; she did like this; she did like that.' They revile me."

She told me, "Take all the *shulams* and keep them with you and perform *puja*." I should have taken them then. I told Amma, "But I live in a rented house, a small house. It's not big enough for people to come here. Where will I keep all these *shulams*? If you give me my own house, then I'll keep all these and perform *puja*." [She answered] "Yes, yes. I haven't given you your own house, you're right. Whenever I give one to you, then you can take them and perform *puja*." And she threw the *shulams* away and disappeared.

This narrative gives agency to the goddess herself and reports her own opinions about the changes at Tatayyagunta temple. When Gangamma sees that instead of the temporary neem tree that had traditionally been cut every year and brought to the temple for the *jatara*, a permanent cement/stone pillar had been established, she seems to wonder where/who she is, asking: "What significance do I and my *shulams* have?" The goddess herself equates her *shulams* and the neem tree brought in for her *jatara* as forms of herself. If the neem tree had been so easily replaced by a cement pillar, she questions her own future significance.

Astonishingly, the narrator reports that the goddess said she won't stay in the temple any more and that she has taken away her *shulams*. (Remember that part of the temple renovation of the Devasthanam involved removing the line of *shulams* inside the temple, to prevent worshippers from "hurting themselves.") In another reference to this same episode, she says, "She pouted and went away from the temple," cursing those who brought in the stone, saying, "Let them get unknown illnesses." And the narrator says she herself no longer visits the temple; for her, Gangamma is no longer there. Later, she softens her view a little: "She's there for people who believe in her. The influence of her truth [power] is there at the Gangamma temple. [And then reverts back to her initial position] But she won't stay there. She went off toward the hills; now they're all uphill in the forest [i.e., all the Ammavarus]." While an extreme view, this narrative commentary suggests that the goddess who remains in Tatayyagunta temple may become so changed by middle-class aesthetics and Sanskritic rituals that she may no longer be recognizable as Gangamma.

EXCHANGING *TALIS* WITH THE GODDESS: PROTECTION AND FREEDOM TO MOVE

9

I had attended three *jataras* and lived in Tirupati for several months in the fall of 1999 before I heard of the tradition of *matammas.*[1] A professor at Sri Venkatesvara University invited me to go with him to a school he had started in an adjacent town for children of *matammas.* Seeing my quizzical look, he explained that *matammas* were women who have exchanged *talis* with one of the Seven Sister *gramadevatas.* Many *matammas* are offered to a *gramadevata* as babies or little girls when they or the village are experiencing the physical presence of the goddess in their bodies through poxes and fevers.[2] When they reach puberty, their families celebrate a wedding-like ritual in which the girls and the goddess exchange *talis.* Thereafter, the professor continued, these women are free to enter relationships with men, with or without marriage. He explained that the children born of these alliances, when they are outside marriage, are scorned, socially marginalized, and otherwise at risk; he believed education was one way they could rise above their marginalized status.

I sensed a possible connection to Gangamma traditions, but did not know how to go about meeting *matammas,* thinking it would not be appropriate to attempt to meet them through their children at the school. Soon thereafter, I learned of and visited an NGO that worked with *matammas;*[3] I was also hesitant to ask to interview these particular women, given the prescriptive nature of the goals of the NGO (among others, to get them married to the men with whom they had long-standing relationships). And so I waited for another opportunity. But once aware, I began to see and hear multiple indirect traces of the tradition, began to ask Tirupati residents more direct questions about the *matamma* tradition, and ultimately met the two women whose personal narratives are the basis of this chapter.

Matammas and *Devadasis*

When I asked directly, the Tatayyagunta temple flower sellers and attendants confirmed that the *matamma* tradition was still very much alive, including at this temple itself, and seemed surprised that I hadn't known about it. They reminded me about a woman who had come to the temple a week ago "with the big *bottu*" (whom, quite honestly, I could not identify as distinct from many other women I had seen); she was, they said, a *matamma* who periodically visited the temple. They were quite sure she would come again in the months remaining before I left Tirupati. Several middle-class Tirupati residents whom I asked about the term *matamma* explained, "You know, like *devadasis*," assuming I would know that more linguistically widespread word (lit., servants of god). The term *devadasis* more specifically applies to women who marry the male god and serve him through dance and song, a tradition no longer practiced in the large South Indian temples with which it used to be associated.

Other regionally based classes of women who exchange of *talis* or beads with and serve the goddess are also commonly identified as *devadasis,* such as the *jogatis* of Yellamma in Karnataka (see Assayag 1992, Dalrymple 2010, Ramberg 2009). While these regional traditions have many unique nuances and contexts of practice, the women who perform these rituals are (or were) under obligation to the deity and freed from obligations of human marriage. Further, the women are believed to avert inauspiciousness and create auspiciousness (Kersenboom 1987). Since they are married to or in a *tali*-relationship with the deity, they never become widows (who, in many Indian contexts, are considered to be inauspicious) and are, therefore, considered *nityasumangalis,* ever-auspicious women.[4] Davesh Soneji observes that the elderly *devadasi* performers he worked with in coastal Andhra told him they were not required to observe menstrual- or death-pollution customs, since they were inherently *nityasumangalis* (2004:42).

Nevertheless, today there is a societal ambivalence about these women who do not marry human males, even though the social institutions with which they are or were associated may have once been ritually powerful. This ambivalence may be created, in part, by the perceived threat to the social order posed by a woman not "tied down" by marriage, who *moves* across, and thereby challenges, traditional social, gendered boundaries. The threat of their freedom of movement, unbound by societal norms, can be compared to that posed to colonial power by the wandering *sadhu/faqir,* whose movement, as suggested by Katherine Ewing, "exposed contradictions and challenged the naturalness of the [colonial] order . . ." (1997:63).

Supported by legislation outlawing the practice of dedicating women to temples (particularly the Madras Devadasi Act of 1947) and accompanying reform movements, several NGOs based in Tirupati work with *matammas* in an effort to "rehabilitate" them. The director of one NGO explained that if the parents don't give money for the *tali*-exchange ritual (for the gold and a silk sari), the village headman (or another upper-caste, influential man) will provide the necessary financial support and then take the girl home with him for a few days (implying a sexual relationship). But if the girl's family itself gives the required money, the girls can lead "independent lives" (i.e., independent of a village headman). This director estimated that there were at that time close to 350 *matammas,* ranging in age from a few months to sixty years old, in eastern Chittoor District, one or two living in each village; however, the NGO did not find *matammas* evenly spread throughout the district. A 1998 NGO publication broke down the *matammas* according to caste: 234 Madigas, 73 Malas (both former-untouchable castes), and the rest spread between other low castes. Specifically, the mission of this NGO is to encourage *matammas* to marry the men they may be living with (the persuasion also directed at the men), to provide them with occupational training, to run schools for their children, and more generally to encourage an end to a tradition that the NGO perceives to be exploitative of women. The NGO seems to assume that *matammas* are forced into sexual relationships against their will or otherwise enter these relationships without being given the "protections" of the institution of marriage. These assumptions may be correct for many *matammas* in contemporary Andhra. However, the NGO workers with whom I spoke knew little of potentially empowering Gangamma traditions—for example, the narrative of Gangamma and the Palegadu, who was beheaded by the goddess when he threatened her sexually.[5]

Like many of the women who wear her *talis,* Gangamma herself wears a *tali,* has no husband, and (like Tallapaka Gangamma) may have children. While the *tali* of human marriage may have analytic and indigenous connotations of binding a woman (as suggested by Annapurna, the *purana pandita* of chapter 5), restricting her movement, holding her in both physical and social "place," the life stories of the two women that I discuss in this chapter suggest, in rather dramatic comparison, that the *tali* of the goddess has given them freedom to move across traditional social and spatial boundaries observed by many Hindu women in similar stages of life. This is not to say that contemporary *matammas,* living in a context of an increasingly dominant middle-class morality, may not prefer and choose (if given the choice) the perceived stability and social status of traditional marriage to a male; however, a *matamma* is rarely given such a choice—whether by her family or by the goddess herself.

Tirupati Women in *Tali* Relationships with the Goddess

I spoke at length with two women who have exchanged *talis* with the goddess, but who, unlike most *matammas,* had, in fact, married human males. While the temple flower sellers identified them as *matammas,* neither woman self-identified herself to me as such; and so, I, too, will not do so and will simply identify them as women who have exchanged *talis* with the goddess. Perhaps they themselves used the criterion of marriage to men to exempt themselves from the category *matamma.* The two women, Pujaramma and Veshalamma,[6] have a certain social "respectability" because of their married status, even while they have a *tali* relationship with the goddess. This status may also have freed them to speak more openly to me than they would have were they to have remained unmarried. They are also distinguished from village *matammas* in the fact that they live in the town of Tirupati and are associated with the powerful Tirupati goddess, rather than one of her (arguably) less powerful village sisters. One flower seller told me that the more powerful the goddess, the more protection a *matamma* has—that is, if a woman has exchanged *talis* with Tirupati Gangamma, "no one will dare to touch her," for fear of the wrath of this powerful goddess. The life stories of the two women with whom I spoke share themes of protection by the goddess and the resulting freedom (even compulsion) to move and act in public spheres, although each narrative addresses possible differences of a *tali* relationship with the goddess for women at different life stages and social contexts.

Veshalamma. I first met Veshalamma at Tatayyagunta Gangamma temple during the fall festival days of Navaratri in 1999; at the time I didn't recognize her as a woman who had exchanged *talis* with the goddess, nor did I know about the institution of *matammas.* For each evening of the nine nights, a form of the goddess was installed in the courtyard in front of Gangamma's inner shrine, and each evening Veshalamma swept the courtyard and drew a ritual rice-flour geometric design (*muggu*) in front of the festival form of the goddess before nightly rituals began. Veshalamma was not accompanied to the temple by female relatives or friends (as are most women who come to the temple); sometimes she brought along her young daughter and baby son. She told me she walked about a half-hour to and from the temple every day and, even on non-festival days, spent hours sitting in front of the goddess, sweeping the temple, or sleeping in the shade of the temple *gopuram.*

I met Veshalamma several times thereafter at Tatayyagunta temple. She also invited me to visit her in her home, and she took my fieldwork associate and me on a long walking tour of several Gangamma shrines in the vicinity and then to several forest shrines near the Shiva temple of Kapila Tirtham, on the outskirts of Tirupati (an enactment of what Pujaramma may have meant when she said, "The goddess used to take me from hill to valley [*konda-kona*], village to village"). Veshalamma first identified her caste as Rajulu, a landed high caste in Andhra that claims *kshatriya* (warrior caste) status. Her use of this term is ambiguous; her family over the last few generations may have come across hard times. Or there may also be non-landed castes who use Rajulu as their caste designation.[7]

Pujaramma. I was introduced to Pujaramma through Subbarama Reddy of Avilala as the person from whom he had learned "how to become possessed" (although, he quickly pointed out, she did not need as many external stimuli as he did to call the goddess). She belongs to the Mudaliar Tamil caste, the same caste as CKR's family. Subbarama Reddy arranged for me to meet Pujaramma at her home, and I met her twice at his home in Avilala thereafter. Since I met with her in domestic contexts, although I recognized her strong personality, I did not notice her freedom of physical movement until I heard her extended personal narratives, nor did I initially recognize her as a woman who had exchanged *talis* with the goddess. She wore a large, pronounced dark-red vermillion *bottu,* a *tali,* and had the matted hair that is typical of many Hindu ascetics and marks a heightened religiosity in some women (including the *jogatis* in special relationship with the goddess Yellamma). When I registered surprise upon learning that she was a widow but still wore the *bottu* and *tali* associated with married women, she answered, "One hundred and one Gangammas gave me my *bottus;*[8] why should I take them off when my husband dies?" (One hundred and one is used here as an auspicious number of abundance.) At another point in her conversational narrative, she similarly asserted, "Because a hundred and one Gangammas gave me the *pasupu-kumkum,* I haven't taken it off [upon becoming a widow]."[9]

We do not have evidence from either premodern or contemporary India as to how the institution of *matammas* actually "worked" from the perspective of the women themselves, whether or not they felt sexually exploited or whether the institution provided some women with agency that they may not have otherwise had.[10] However, the personal narratives of Veshalamma and Pujaramma provide traces of the protection, agency, and freedom of movement in public and "jungle" spaces[11] that a tradition of exchanging *talis* with the goddess may have offered *matammas* more generally and these two women specifically, one a widow and the other an orphan and abused wife.

The auspiciousness associated with the *tali* in this context raises questions about the significance of the *tali* more generally. Is the auspiciousness traditionally attributed to a married woman, concretized through her *tali, given* by marriage (i.e., a husband), or is marriage a socially sanctioned context in which pre-existing auspiciousness (fertility) may be performed? I

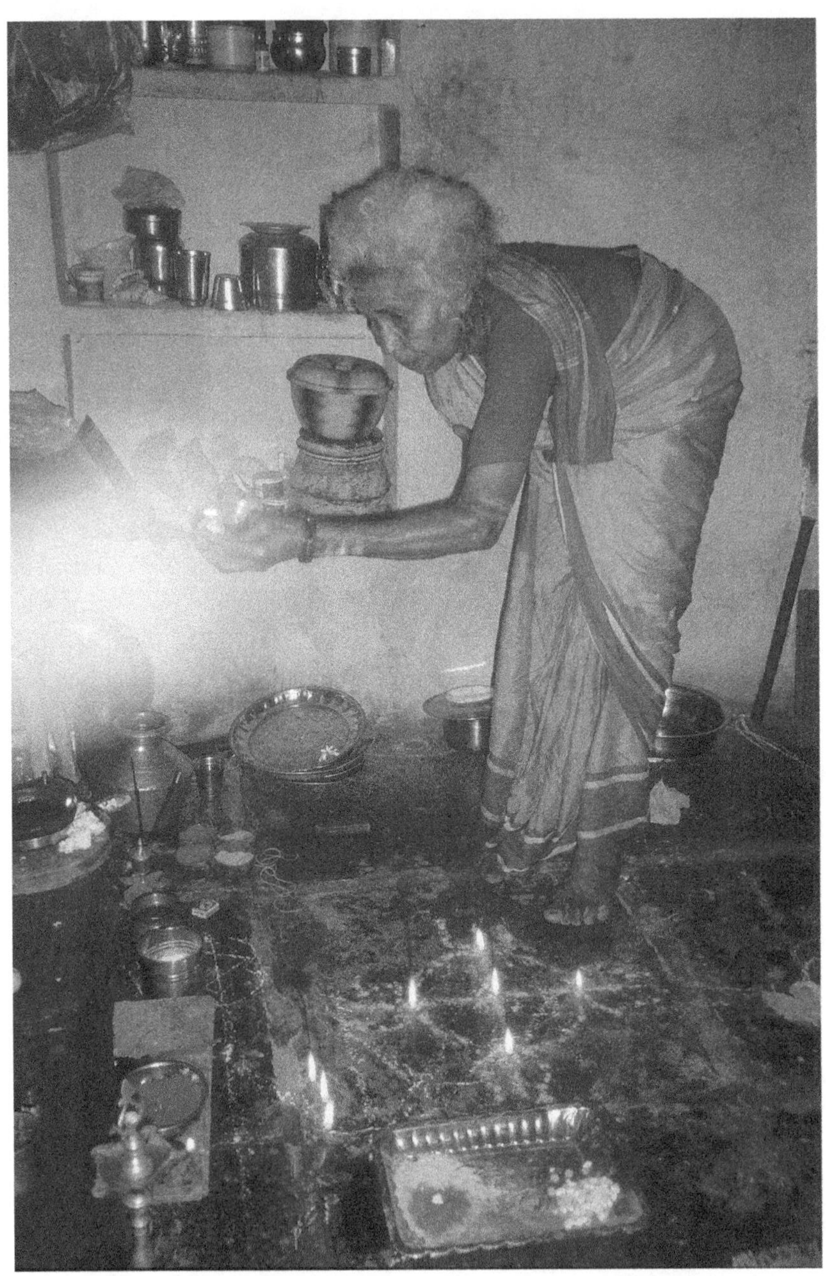

Pujaramma performing *harati* to Gangamma in her home.

first examine several implications of the *tali* for both non-*matamma* women and the goddess, and then look at the implications of the *tali* for *matammas* as suggested through the oral narratives of two women who have exchanged *talis* with the goddess.

Women's *Talis*

Talis in contemporary South India are most commonly associated with human marriage, a woman's *tali* being tied by her husband during the wedding ritual sequence. In an essay in an edited volume titled *The Powers of Tamil Women,* Holly Reynolds interprets the *tali* in contemporary South Indian contexts as follows:

> When a man ties a *tali* around the neck of a woman, he binds her to him with a symbol of all his culturally and socially derived identities, *makes* [my emphasis] that woman a cumankali [auspicious; *sumangali*], and entrusts to her the well-being of himself and his lineage, an act that paradoxically makes the wife the protector of the husband. . . . In owning the *tali,* the husband controls the auspiciousness of his wife: he confers cumankali [*sumangali*] status upon her at marriage and deprives her of it at his death. (1991 [1980]:45–46)

Reynolds argues that in marriage, the *tali* serves as a sign of husband's protection, but also often restricts the movement of the bride/wife, (ideally) confining her to "women's space":

> The *tali* delimits boundaries, sets up barriers, confines woman to a specified domain, that of her husband, a situation captured in one of the words for "wife," *taram,* limit, boundary. It declares that sexual relations are permissible only with the owner of the *tali,* for at issue here is control over and possession of female generative power. (46)

However, the *tali* may have been associated not always with marriage (and its limits) per se, but more specifically with a woman's inherent auspiciousness, her embodied creative power, and potential fertility—that is, marriage did not *give* a woman her auspiciousness/*shakti,* but provided her a context within which to act upon it. In an essay about the goddess in Kerala (among matrilineal castes), M. J. Gentes describes a pre-twentieth century *tali* ceremony that used to be performed for pubescent girls (1992:317). While the girl was joined with a male partner, it was not as "wife," but as "one who has the power to create and withhold life" (318). Gentes suggests that the *tali* ceremony

> may facilitate a young woman's claiming of her *shakti* (power) and role and her control of her own chastity (in the South Indian sense) without expressing it as dissolution of her life into that of a man. . . . As a necessary ceremony it marks and values the young females of the lineage and of society as a whole. . . . From the ceremony onward, the girl was considered a reproducer of the matrilineage. . . . (318)

The young woman was auspicious because she was a potentially fertile woman, marked by the *tali*, rather than because she was a *married* woman. Vasudha Narayanan similarly describes a female puberty ritual among the Pillai community of Tamil Nadu in which a young girl is given the authority to light the oil lamp of the family altar. On this occasion she is also given a gold necklace called *nava tali*, a *tali* strung with nine gold beads and corals. She wears this *tali* until she gets married, at which time it is replaced with that given by her husband (Narayanan, unpublished manuscript, 220). Other South Indian traditional puberty rituals similarly approximate some elements of marriage celebrations, the pubescent girl and her auspiciousness being "displayed" in silks and new ornaments and her community feasted.

Another trace of earlier associations of the *tali* may be found in the custom observed in some Telugu communities in which the bride is given a *tali* by her mother during pre-wedding rituals, before her husband ties another *tali* around her neck during the wedding itself. This "mother's *tali*" is called *puttininti tali* (literally, "*tali* of the house of birth") and should be worn for forty days after the wedding. The bride then often strings the maternal *tali* on the same chain or thread with the *tali* that was tied by her husband during the wedding itself. These rituals suggest the association of the *tali* and a woman's inherent auspiciousness/fertility, independent of marriage, although for most women marriage is the context within which their fertility comes to fruition.

It is important to remember that onset of menarche and marriage used to be much more closely aligned than it is today in contemporary India; that is, girls were often pledged in marriage even before reaching puberty and moved in with their husbands as soon as they reached that stage. The *tali*'s earlier association with female auspiciousness/fertility, which has now been subsumed within the institution of marriage, suggests an alternative interpretation/ideology of the *tali* and marriage: marriage (the husband) does not *give* a woman her power (*shakti*), but *marks* it and gives a context for its expression. The difference is subtle, but important.

Examining the exchange of *talis* between *matammas* and the goddess makes more explicit what is only suggested in the puberty rite and marriage contexts of the *tali.* Receiving a *tali* from the goddess, instead of a man, openly questions the dominant societal need for marriage as a context for the expression of a woman's auspiciousness and *shakti.* More specifically, it highlights the control implied by the marriage *tali* tied by a man on his bride, in contrast to the freedom of movement permitted by the *tali* of the goddess. Pujaramma narrates a very different mandate than that of traditional marriage when she reports the goddess's order that she wander from village to village: "I keep going around every *uru.* I don't know when she'll stop me and where she'll allow me to build [a permanent place]."

The Goddess's *Tali*

The *talis* of the Seven Sisters are usually very visible (including the very large *tali* on the *jatara ugra mukhi*), in contrast to married women's *talis* whose chains or threads are visible at the back of the neck, but whose pendants are modestly tucked under their saris, not to be put on public display. While traditionally women "need" the context of marriage within which to express their auspicious powers (of fertility), Gangamma and her sisters are not bound by this human context; she wears the *tali* and has children without a husband. It occurred to me: if the goddess had children and was wearing a *tali,* who was her husband? When I asked this question during the 1992 *jatara,* the flower sellers and temple attendants were a little puzzled by the question, but then answered that she had no husband. When I returned to Tirupati in 1999, however, these same women answered without any hesitation that Shiva was her husband. The conceptual presence of a husband would seem to be a recent development, a way of bringing Gangamma into a more brahminic and middle-class worldview. There is no mythology of her and Shiva being married—in fact, the local Adi Para Shakti narrative explicitly states the goddess and Shiva do *not* get married, that he does not have the *shakti* to "bear" her. Further, Shiva is iconographically and ritually absent from Gangamma's temples and shrines; the only male present is her brother Potu Raju, who stands facing his sister, usually in an aniconic form that, as I have argued, is itself feminized.

In her description of river goddesses in Maharashtra, Ann Feldhaus describes a similar phenomenon of goddesses who wear auspicious signs of a bride (bangles and the wedding necklace [*mangalsutra*]) but who have no husbands; she calls them "husbandless wives." Feldhaus says that a husband may be implied, but "no one seems particularly bothered about the question of his identity (1995:53, 55). One woman told Feldhaus:

> There is no husband. She's Krsnabai, isn't she? And Krsnabai has no husband. Krsnabai is a river. She's understood to be a river, isn't she? Then, doesn't this river finally join the ocean? So that makes the ocean her husband. That's how you should understand it." And then she added, "If there *has* to be a husband!" (1995:54)

When I asked Veshalamma who tied Gangamma's *tali,* that is, who is her husband, she emphatically declared that there was no husband: "It's actually a vow [*mokku*]; people make a vow that if they get married, have children, or if something good happens to them, they'll give her a *tali.*[12] It doesn't mean that she [the goddess] got married. She's Adi Shakti. Who would be able to bear her by getting married to her? Even my own husband keeps telling me that after getting married to me [as someone in a *tali* relationship with the goddess], he's not able to bear me."

Veshalamma: The *Tali* as Protection of the Goddess

Veshalamma's independence and mobility for a thirty-five-year-old married woman were immediately striking, especially given her advanced state of pregnancy (about seven months) at the time of the Navaratri festival when I first met her. While there were other women who worked on the temple grounds as flower sellers, sweepers, and attendants to the goddess, Veshalamma was a loner and rarely engaged in conversation with them or other worshipers. When I first asked the flower sellers who she was—how she was associated with the temple, since I saw her there so often, looking like an employee—they answered that she simply performed various tasks as service (*seva*) to the goddess. Later, when I had learned of the tradition of *matammas,* I understood the whisperings about her; and when I asked directly, the female temple attendants identified her as a *matamma.*

While others may have only whispered about this identity, Veshalamma herself was not ashamed of her *tali* relationship with the goddess. When I met her to elicit her life story, we were seated in the covered *mandapam* of Tatayyagunta temple and were immediately surrounded by a group of curious onlookers as soon as I pulled out my voice recorder. I suggested that we move out of the *mandapam* to a shaded spot under one of the temple *gopurams,* but she asserted boldly, "Whatever I have to say is by the grace of the goddess. I'll speak here." After only a few minutes, however, when the children around us became too noisy even for Veshalamma, we moved to sit under one of the *gopurams.* Only when we sat down did I notice that this *gopuram* (whose entry was cemented shut) was an unfrequented space that may not have been entirely appropriate for our conversation—there were chicken feathers all around (from previously offered sacrifice); a drunk man sleeping in the corner woke up and moved to sit closer to us, periodically belching and moaning. However, Veshalamma swept the stairs upon which we sat and seemed unconcerned about the additional audience member; she remained fully focused on her story. The story circles around on itself, a format I retain in its presentation below.

The flower sellers had told me that Veshalamma had spent the previous week sleeping at the temple, there under that same *gopuram.* So I began our conversation by asking Veshalamma why she had done so. She answered, "My mind wasn't good, so I slept here. At my place, I felt like I was being crushed, but now I'm feeling energetic again." And then she began her story, which she characterized as one full of "troubles, troubles, and more troubles":

I was born at Manchala Vidhi [Main Street] and matured [reached puberty, while living in the neighborhood] behind Jyoti Theatre. Then they took me to Madras. My parents thought I wouldn't learn any housework, so they took me to Madras and put me in a hostel; but I refused to stay there. Why should I be put in a hostel when I have parents? They themselves took me to the hostel. They called me an adopted child; they called me "sister's daughter." I cried, but they still took me there. . . .

When I was small, I had to face so many troubles, so they brought me to Veshalamma Gangamma [whose name the speaker takes as her own] temple and married me to her. They said, "We're going to give her to you [the goddess]," so they got me married [to her]. They did this in a respectable way [spending sufficient funds to be "respectable"]. After that, I had to sell coconuts and dry fish; I did all the household work. I sold *idlis* [rice cakes] to the hospital. I went to Nagiri, Nagalapuram, Esalapuram to sell pickles. . . . I worked hard and looked after them [my parents], but still they didn't look after me. So I have only her [pointing to the goddess]; I don't have any parents. I've experienced only troubles, troubles, and more troubles.

In another conversation, Veshalamma elaborated further on some of her early "troubles": she was adopted and never knew who her birth parents were; the parents she refers to above were her adoptive parents. It is unlikely that she was "officially" adopted through government bureaucracy, since such adoption is rare among lower classes; more likely, she was taken in by a relative's family when her mother died at birth or otherwise could not take care of her. She says that her parents called her "an adopted child; they called me 'sister's daughter.'"

As a very young girl, Veshalamma contracted measles or some other form of pox (*ammavaru*). Because of this, she said, her parents offered her to the goddess—a ritual of which she has no personal memory, since "I was just little, still playing with dolls." After this, she continued, her adoptive mother never took care of her and cared only for the son to whom she had given birth. Veshalamma regretted that she never found out who her birth parents were: "If I had been told, I would have gone to look for them, to see who they were. When anyone [new] like you comes to the temple, I always hope that they might be my parents. I want to see and talk to them."

At another point in her narrative, in the middle of a description of her mother dressing her up like the goddess when she was a little girl (perhaps during the *jatara* itself), Veshalamma suddenly shifted the narrative:

> They [her parents] actually showed some interest in me before I got mature [reached puberty]; but once I got mature, they began to trouble me. I wanted to jump into a well or fall under a train. At a very young age, I had to face all this; I wanted to give up my life. [Then back to her mother dressing her in *vesham* when she was a girl:] The photographer asked why they were putting me in this *vesham* [with crown and trident]. They said, it's her name [Veshalamma, the goddess to whom she had been offered], so she must put on that *vesham.*

Veshalamma reported that she was "married to" the goddess when she reached puberty at age thirteen: "Just like they do in weddings, like that. They made me sit on a *pitha* [low wooden stool], and the goddess on a *pitha*—opposite to each other. She was Veshalamma from Palli Street. They made us sit opposite to each other. They tied her *mangalasutra* [*tali*] to me and mine to her." Veshalamma said she had attended school through seventh grade; presumably she quit going to school once she underwent this ritual.

While generally women who exchange *talis* with the goddess don't get married to a human, Veshalamma's parents wanted her to get married to an old man (seventy years old) when she was just sixteen. She rebelled, "How could I get married to such an old man! I wouldn't marry him. So I loved and got married to my [current] husband." That is, Veshalamma chose her own husband rather than entering the arranged marriage with the old man. She said that, actually, she shouldn't have married a man at all, but that "you can't trust men [to stay with you without marriage]. We went to the temple to get married." Her parents gave no dowry and her mother-in-law cursed her to have no children, so that her husband would abandon her and get married to another woman—neither of which happened. She had a baby girl within a year of marriage and, after performing the ritual of *angapradakshina* (rolling one's body around the perimeter of a temple) again and again, she "finally" had a son.

In another conversation (when together we visited an NGO working with *matammas*), she again said that she shouldn't have gotten married to a man; that she had gone against the custom, and this is why she was experiencing so many difficulties, presumably caused by the goddess. But, she said, she had gotten married without knowing what the consequences would be. In this same conversation, when the male director of the NGO suggested that *matammas* "go to the village headman" upon reaching puberty and exchanging *talis* with the goddess, Veshalamma quickly stopped him: "No, no, there was no village head in those days [when she reached puberty]; we lived behind Jyoti Theatre in those days." She is trying to clarify here that she did not follow the commonly assumed tradition of "going to the village headman" (for sexual relations) upon reaching puberty.

When I asked Veshalamma how a man feels when he gets married to a woman who has already exchanged *talis* with the goddess—whether he is afraid of her in some way—she answered:

> Yes, he's afraid of me; he doesn't even smoke in front of me. . . . He's afraid because the goddess may come on me [in possession]. Twice, when I was possessed, I beat him; that's why he's afraid of me. [When I'm possessed] he's very respectful of me. But when he's been given trouble outside, he comes home and beats me. He asks me to leave the house and chases the children out.

There is seemingly reason to fear the goddess if someone crosses her will by mistreating the women whom she protects through *tali*-exchange. Veshalamma reported that her adoptive mother took for herself the *tali* and silk sari that had been given to Veshalamma at the time she exchanged *talis* with the goddess. She asserted that, for this transgression, her mother's hand and leg were paralyzed (presumably caused by the goddess).

On another occasion, Veshalamma explained that she didn't stay at the temple during the *jatara* itself, because "once they beat the drums, I become possessed. I don't want to become possessed because it leaves me tired." Further, there's no guarantee that if she becomes possessed outside a ritual context that she controls, there will be someone in those crowds to "serve" her: "Someone should give me *pasupu* water and camphor. Who will do that for me? When she comes into my body, she asks for neem leaves, *pasupu* water, camphor, and whatever else she likes. Who will give all this? No one; everyone will just stand there and look at me." But at home,

> If anyone brings a *kalasham* [clay pot that becomes the goddess] and *pasupu-kumkum,* then I get possessed, and I speak to them. I draw a *muggu* on

the floor and place the *kalasham* there, and if I think on her for five minutes, she comes to me. Whenever I see the burning camphor, she comes to me. So I always have the *kalasham* ready for those who come [to ask the goddess questions].

People coming to Veshalamma to hear the goddess speak through her may bring their own *kalashams,* or Veshalamma may use the *kalasham* sitting on a handful of rice on her *puja* shelf, with a coconut set in its mouth and neem leaves circling it. Behind the *kalasham,* Veshalamma has placed a laminated photograph of Tatayyagunta Gangamma and a tiny brass goddess image (whose features, even body pose are indistinguishable) whom she identifies as Gangamma.

Veshalamma says her husband became physically abusive after she gave birth to their first baby, a girl. He told her that he didn't want any further connection (*sambandham*) with her: "'You can go anywhere you want, and I'll go get married to anyone I want.' He hit me because I gave birth to a daughter and I didn't give birth to a son." She described her husband having left wounds on her and having broken her hand. She remembered that this is when she began to come to the temple regularly, telling the goddess, "You are my mother."

After describing the death of her adoptive mother, the rejection by her brother, and the harassment of her mother-in-law, Veshalamma rather matter-of-factly stated, "I have no one. If I want to go to my native place [i.e., maternal home] and stay for a few days, no one is there for me. I have no one. Whenever I feel sad, I come here [to the temple] and stay. She [the goddess] is my mother and father, and my mother-in-law, too." While the goddess conceptually protects and cares for Veshalamma, her temple is also a literal, physical refuge. Veshalamma often sleeps at the temple, sometimes for days at a time, when she is physically sick, when her husband is abusing her, or when she is simply sad. She says no one at the temple asks why she is there, no one bothers her, and no one from her home comes looking for her. But the goddess continues to look after her here.

Veshalamma told me that the same day that she had first told me her life story, Gangamma herself had come to her in the guise of a Brahman woman (a woman who was possessed by the goddess):[13]

She [Gangamma possessing the Brahman woman] gave me a blouse piece and said, "You don't have to be afraid; I am with you. . . . If you hadn't come to the temple, you would have died. I am protecting you." . . . The goddess came to me earlier, too. I had cooked everything for her, dried fish and eggs, and fed her. Gangamma told me she was satisfied that day, "That day, you filled my stomach, so I'll see to it that your stomach, too, is full. I'll not harm you. Don't cry." She called my husband and warned him, "If you hurt her, I'll kill you." My husband trembled. [The goddess said] "If she as much as cries, I won't allow you to live anymore."

Veshalamma reports that she has always been a hard worker, never just "sitting and eating"; even as a little girl, she worked hard, going from place to place in Tirupati neighborhoods selling pickles. She was resourceful, finding income when and how she could. After marriage she worked at a hospital:

They used to pay me monthly. If anyone gave me food, I used to eat it there. I used to make *laddu* [sweets], *mudugulu,* and *namkin* [both savory snacks] and sell them there at Ruia Hospital, plantains, too. That's how I used to look after my daughter. My husband would ask, "Where are you going? What are you doing?" My father died. And after my daughter was born, I thought I was pregnant again. But it wasn't a baby; it was a growth [tumor]. I had this for thirteen months. I didn't know if it was a baby or what it was. I met a lady at the hospital who gold me, "It's not a baby; it's a growth. Go to the doctor immediately." I worked in the hospital and had some ornaments and took them to the pawnbroker, and had my stomach scanned. The doctor asked if I didn't have anyone with me. I said I was all alone and that my husband had left me. . . . She asked for Rs. 7,000 for the operation. I went to ask my mother for Rs, 2,000, but she didn't give anything, and I fought with her. She gave something then. I gave up my *mangalsutra* and sold it to pay for the operation.

Veshalamma implies that she had moved back to her maternal home after her husband left her, but that her brothers "pushed her out":

My brothers pushed me out of the house, saying, "We don't have any connection with you anymore, so leave. We didn't give birth to you, so leave."

They troubled me a lot. If I think of it now, I feel sad and feel like crying. When my mother was alive, she didn't take care of me; now, too, my stepmother doesn't. My brother, too, doesn't care for me.

. . . After my father died, I went there [to her maternal home] and my brother said, "If this prostitute is here, I won't stay. I won't perform our father's last rites [*kriyalu*]." I got my *jhumka* [dangly earrings—and sold them to pay for the cremation]. I performed the last rites. I lit the funeral pyre. My mother didn't look after me; she only looked after her son. She spent money for him; she built a house for him; she gave him household utensils. Even when my mother was alive, she didn't look after me. There was only trouble, trouble, trouble. When they gave the dead body [of her father, whose corpse her brother refused to cremate if she was present] to me, I had to go at midnight, with four other women, to cremate the body.

Veshalamma's brother's identification of her as a prostitute may refer to the common assumption that *matammas* are sexually available to men outside of marriage, or the term may simply have been used as an abusive term. Note that Veshalamma takes up the traditional male ritual role (of the eldest son) of lighting her father's cremation pyre. Veshalamma didn't narrate how/when she moved back with her husband, but alternated between descriptions of his continued abuse and optimism that he may change (at one point saying that he was paid irregularly in his construction job, but that when he got a more permanent job, he would surely get her ornaments back from the pawnbroker):

After getting married, I haven't been happy. I don't get along with my in-laws. My husband will only talk to me if I work and bring in money. Otherwise, he beats the children and me. Because I can't face these problems, I'm coming to Amma [the goddess]. At least now my husband's mind will change. At least now my husband's mind will change. At least now my husband's mind will change [her repetitions].

Veshalamma is confident that the goddess takes and will continue to take care of her; her repetition of "At least now my husband's mind will change," in a performative declaration, expresses confidence that her husband will change, although to date she's seen little consistent change. Still, her *tali* relationship has given her an identity independent of her status in relationship to her abusive husband. Protection by the goddess does not mean an easy life, but it seems to have given Veshalamma confidence and some peace of mind.

Veshalamma's story of troubles with parents, husband, and in-laws may be shared by many other women as well, women outside of a *tali* relationship with the goddess; I heard several narratives of such women who came to Gangamma for protection from these troubles. But what makes women who have exchanged *talis* with the goddess different than women who have not is that their protection/relationship with the goddess is formalized, and with the protection of the *tali,* they assume the freedom to move, to be independent. It is this freedom of movement that is the dominant motif in Pujaramma's life story. Not only is she free to move, but she feels she *must* move, at the command of the goddess.

Pujaramma: Wandering with the Goddess

As a widowed mother of two grown sons, Pujaramma is at a very different stage of life than is Veshalamma, and they also have different kinds of relationships with the goddess. Unlike Veshalamma, who exchanged *talis* with the goddess at puberty and only later married a man, Pujaramma married a male—a marriage that she says the goddess herself initiated—before ritualizing a relationship with the goddess. Pujaramma's narrative directly addresses her unusual position of wearing the *talis* given by both a man *and* the goddess.

The first time I met Pujaramma, a meeting arranged in her home, she greeted us with a big smile, led us into her two-room house, and immediately began talking—telling us what she thought we had come to hear, her life story. She began by telling us how she had met Subbarama Reddy (SR): someone had told him he should meet her to find out why his sister had committed suicide, telling him that Pujaramma became possessed by the goddess, who would speak the reason through her. She said she first drew a *maila muggu* (literally, "impure" *muggu;* this terminology is ambiguous, but presumably refers to a *muggu* that deflects impurity rather than being characterized by it):

Ammavaru came over me and told the truth. It was because she [SR's elder sister] had taken her exams and failed. She thought, "I've failed my exams; why should I live?" Ammavaru came over her younger brother [SR] and she told the truth. She gave a lemon to the brother because he couldn't speak out. Then he spoke and told the truth [the sister speaking through him]: "I've failed my exams; everyone was mocking me. I couldn't bear this, so I did this." She came over her younger brother and spoke the truth. From then on, he [SR] has come to me, for Ganga *jatara* and all. He comes and offers me milk.

Then Pujaramma began her own story:

I'm not educated. I don't know how to read. I don't know culture [*samskriti*]. No one taught me; I don't have a guru nor do I have a guru's teachings. From my childhood, I used to make Ammavaru [the goddess] out of mud and used to play with her, and she came over me. [I asked at what age she began to get possessed.] When I was young, eleven years old.

She described how she first came to Tirupati:

They were building the Polytechnic College then. I thought I shouldn't work as a prostitute [lit., in prostitution, *lanjarikam*], that I shouldn't go with a man [like that]. I should carry mud and stones; I should work hard and earn. I should work hard and do *puja* for Ammavaru. As long as I have the *shakti* [strength], I should work hard and do *puja* for Ammavaru. If I don't have the *shakti* to do it, I'll beg in a few houses and keep that money for Ammavaru. So I used to do coolie work [construction]; I worked there until they finished the Polytechnic College.

Actually, my husband was in Pune then. He used to do *puja* for a guru there. He used to work as a mason and sculptor. Ammavaru asked him, "Why are you working so hard? Come over to Tirupati. I'll get you married to a very devoted girl. Don't stay there." She brought me to Tirupati, too. Both of us went to work at the Polytechnic College construction. The first time I went there to ask for work, I was wearing a half-sari and two braids, with jasmine flowers in my hair [i.e., dressed as a girl, rather than woman].

Who would give me work if I looked like that? They said, "You look like you're from a good family, a well-educated family, so what work can you do here? We don't have any work for you. Go." I had two earrings. I sold them and bought two saris. I removed all this [clothes and style of a young girl]. I tied my hair in a bun [like a woman, rather than girl's braids]. Then I put ash on my forehead and applied two *bottus*. Then they hired me.

A striking and repeated motif in Pujaramma's life story is that of movement—moving from place to place at the direction of the goddess, a restlessness that does not permit her to "settle down" in any traditional way. In response to the question of where she was born, she said;

In Kolar [Karnataka]. I was there until I was five. My mother's place was Ambur [near Vellore]. From there [Kolar] they brought me to Ambur. When I was twelve [presumably after reaching puberty], the goddess took me all around the world; she didn't allow me to stay in one place. Even now, I keep moving around. Even now, she makes me go to old temples, to powerful goddess *shakti* stones. Wherever people are having problems, she takes me there.

Later in the narrative, she again emphasized movement:

The goddesses keep taking me from hill to hill, valley to valley, village to village. . . . I go wherever she calls me. Even if I go to Hyderabad or Vijayavada, wherever I go, she doesn't allow me to stay more than ten days. She says, "Get up," and she brings me back. . . . I keep going around from village to village. I don't know when she'll stop me and where she'll allow me to build and what she will do.

In another conversation when I asked Pujaramma if she was afraid of the potentially destructive *ugram* of the goddess, Pujaramma implied that wandering/moving had empowered her not to be afraid, "No, no. I'm not. It's because I've been wandering from hill to hill, valley to valley [with the goddess, at her order], since I was young; so I'm not afraid."

Pujaramma did not want to get married to a man, but said that "the goddess married me off. Then the children came." She then shifted her reference for the agent of the marriage from the goddess to the god Vishnu (identified by his position of lying on a serpent on the ocean), who came to her in a vision, giving her reasons why she should get married:

One Friday at twelve o'clock, I sat for *puja.* I thought that I don't need a husband, and so I came [to perform *puja;* where, exactly, is unclear]. That day he [Vishnu] came lying on a five-headed serpent and the wall became a sea. He said, "If you don't get married, you won't achieve release [*moksha*]. You should get married, have children, and experience both suffering and happiness. You can't avoid this. For the good of the world [*loka*], the drama [*natakam*] of marriage cannot be avoided. For twenty-five years, he [her husband] will beat you, cut you, poke you, hit you, and cause you to bleed. You have to experience all of this. This is inevitable. This is the way of the world, and you have to overcome it." He [god] gave me this boon [*varam*] and went off. . . . I sat down at twelve o'clock for the *puja* and he gave me this vision [*darshan*] at three in the afternoon.

I used to perform *puja* at Tatayyagunta Gangamma temple, and I used to sleep there, too, before I was married. But now, after marrying, she [the goddess] asked me to sleep somewhere else: "You're now living in *samsara* [married life], so you should live separately and serve me there." . . . Next to this temple there's Nerelamma's temple. [Pujaramma went there for worship.] She [the goddess] came at one o'clock at night, along with Gudiamma and all the others [Seven Sisters]. I thought to myself, "How should I talk to them?" I came here thinking that I shouldn't get married, but even then, he [god] brought me a match [potential husband]. I said to the goddess, "If you like the match, then get me married." And the flower garland dropped down from the [image of] the goddess. They [others in the temple] asked, "What did you ask Amma, for which she's given you flowers as an answer?" I only answered, "Give me the flowers. Amma knows what I asked for." And I brought the flowers back home. I came back home at one o'clock at night.

It is noteworthy that in this account it is the god Vishnu, and not the goddess, who first tells Pujaramma that marriage (and its accompanying suffering) is necessary for her to achieve liberation. His identity in his "cosmic" form lying on the serpent in the ocean (rather than through one of his incarnations on earth, such as Venkateshvara), represents a textual, Sanskritic tradition and is a tangible manifestation of the multiple discourses (Sanskritic/textual and *gramadevata*/nontextual) that Pujaramma is negotiating through her narrative and vision. The concept of *moksha* (liberation from *samsara*) is itself a Sanskritic concept not commonly articulated in relationship to Gangamma traditions. Pujaramma goes, then, to the temple of Nerelamma, where she meets the goddess and her sisters in a dream or vision. She asks the goddess to give her a sign or permission that she should get married, which she receives through a flower garland falling off the goddess's image.

While Pujaramma had moved about from place to place as a pubescent girl—with and at the order of the goddess—only after she was married and had had children do the goddesses give her the *tali* and *pasupu-kumkum* that mark her special relationship with and obligation to Gangamma. The goddess tells her (presumably in a vision or dream) that she has been with her husband long enough; now she should move about with *her:*

> A hundred and one Ammavarus [goddesses] came to me. They took me to the Gangamma temple. They bathed me, applied *pasupu-kumkum,* and put bangles on me. They told me, "All these days you were with your husband; now you're our own. Wherever we are, you should come there." This was twenty-five years ago, after all the children had been born. This is because I asked Ammavaru to make me like Avvayyar [an old Tamil female devotee who served the god Ganesha], saying, "I don't need my exterior form [*rupam*]; I don't need my beauty; make me Avvayyar." . . . I haven't removed my *bottu* and *kumkum* even though my husband is dead. Because a hundred and one Ammavarus put on my *kumkum-pasupu,* I haven't taken it off.

In a later conversation, Pujaramma said that she was twenty-five years old when the goddesses tied her *tali,* after her three children had been born. "It was to keep me as a *kanya pilla* [virgin girl; i.e., she did not have sex with her husband after receiving the *talis* of the goddesses]. The goddesses tied the *tali.* Now if the goddess comes on me and speaks, everything she says will happen." Pujaramma's narrative expresses some of the tension between ideologies of marriage, gender, and women's auspiciousness that may be present between the tradition of *matammas* and that of landed and upper-caste and middle-class rhetoric and practice.

While for Pujaramma getting married to her husband and receiving a *tali* from the hundred and one goddesses were sequential—first she married a human and then exchanged *talis* with the goddess—in the case of her daughter, there was a clear opposition and struggle between human and goddess marriages. From infancy, Pujaramma's daughter had lived with her two childless maternal aunts. Pujaramma said her aunts thought the girl had brought auspiciousness into their homes, and both women subsequently had their own children. Thereafter, her relatives wanted to marry the ten-year-old girl to Pujaramma's brother (an acceptable marriage partner in conventional South Indian cross-cousin marriage). Pujaramma tried to resist this marriage, however, because of the age difference; and the groom, too, was not interested in marrying someone who would "become possessed just like her mother."

Pujaramma reported this tension with her relatives as one in which the goddess was also an agent. She says the goddess came to her (through a dream or possession) and said, "No, let her remain a *kanya* [virgin]. When her mother becomes old, we'll come to her [i.e., the daughter will take her mother's ritual role]." However, the relatives prevailed and took the girl uphill to Tirumala (site of the temple of Sri Venkateshvara) and dressed both her and the groom in yellow wedding clothes and garlanded them (whether or not this was a formalized wedding is unclear). As they were coming down the hill, a monkey tore the girl's sari, grabbed the flowers, and ran away. When the family returned home, in their domestic *puja* shrine, they found that their picture of Venkateshvara and his wife, Padmavati, had fallen down and broken—an inauspicious sign that they interpreted as the disapproval of the god. Pujaramma's daughter lost her sight at the same time.

The narrative sequence is not entirely clear as Pujaramma did not relate it sequentially. It seems that the girl had some kind of pox at the same time her relatives wanted to get her married. The goddess told Pujaramma that her daughter would live only if Pujaramma went to stay with her (where she was living with her maternal aunts); otherwise her daughter would get not only one kind of pox (*ammavaru*), but seven different poxes. Pujaramma went to her daughter and took her to a Gangamma temple, where she placed her on a banana leaf, without any clothes on, and she sprinkled her with *tirtham* (water that has been offered to a deity) and rubbed her body with *pasupu.* The poxes reduced some. She stayed with her daughter for twenty-five days; but the relatives still insisted on the wedding and took her and the groom uphill. The goddess continued to dramatically fight for the girl. Pujaramma narrates, "The goddess [who is also the pox] peeled off the skin and ate it. The girl's hair came off like a wig comes off. The skin from her hands and legs came off just like that. And the goddess ate it." The girl died after a twenty-five day battle between the poxes (the goddess) and the humans who wanted her to marry her to Pujaramma's brother. The goddess prevailed. This is the powerful goddess who gave Pujaramma her *tali* and who orders her to move with her from village to village, hill to valley.

In her narration, Pujaramma explained her matted hair as a sign of the presence of the goddess:

This happens by itself. However many times I keep braiding my hair, in the night something happens and in the morning the hair has grown [becomes matted]. I keep shaving my head, and it grows again. Amma [the goddess] asks me, "Why are you shaving your hair?" I tell her, "Because I get lice. That's why I shave my hair." Both of us argue, Amma and me.

Once I was getting my head shaved uphill [at Tirumala, where many pilgrims/devotees offer their hair to the god and there is a professional tonsure center run by the Devasthanam]. We kept arguing. She kept asking me [why I was shaving my head] and he [the barber] kept shaving. [I said] "If lice fall out of my hair, I shave it." She says, "Again, I'll cause it to grow." And I say, "If lice fall, again, I, too, will shave it." We keep arguing, Amma and me.

Later in her storytelling that day, she came back to the issue of her matted hair:

I've shaved my head eight times. It takes the [matted] shape of a three-headed serpent's hood or a Shiva *linga* [a representation of Shiva]. I tell Amma, "I shaved it because there were lice in it. I don't shave it without reason. If there are no lice, I don't do anything. If there are lice, only then I shave my head."

It's been four months since I had this dream. That night, in my dream, there was a tree this tall [indicates with her hand]. There was a flowering bitter gourd vine climbing over it. I said, "It's nice to look at the flowers blooming." I was looking at it when she [Amma, the goddess] jumped down from the sky. So my hair took the form of a snake's hood, and all this [the rest of the hair] is smooth. I asked, "Why is it like this? What kind of braid [*jada,* which can also refer to matted hair] is this?" She said, "This is Venkateshvara's *jada.*" She said this and disappeared. As soon as she said this, the bitter-gourd vine wound around the tree. The next morning, I found it climbing over my head.

So [asking us directly], "What do you think of this? This came out like this [showing her hair]. In the morning, this came loose, that came out loose. This lock of hair falls loose; it rubs off my *bottu* like the hood of a snake, so I push it back inside [my bun], saying, "I'll let you grow when you grow. Why do you come now and fall into my face?" It comes down like a snake hood and wipes off the *bottu.* It's the ninth time I'm doing this [letting my hair grow in matted form]. This is a kind of *vesham.*

Pujaramma's description of her arguments back and forth with the goddess about her matted hair reveals an intimate relationship with goddess; but she invariably loses the argument, and her matted hair continues to grow back. Significantly, Pujaramma identifies her matted hair as "kind of *vesham*" that reveals her relationship with the goddess. This *vesham* contributes to her authority to act as a ritual specialist on behalf of the goddess who inhabits these locks.

Pujaramma ended her narration by telling us why she could "bear" the demands of a relationship with such a goddess, when most people are so afraid of her:

You must be born for this in order to bear [*bharincu*] her. Most people can't even bear pictures of her. Ask them to keep these pictures [in their homes] and bear her. Let's see if they can. They'll get scared and take them to a temple. I was born for this and I've faced all these difficulties, without any house, without any stable home place [*uru*]. I wander around from village to village, between tree and snake hole. If it was anyone else, they would have left the goddess and gone off. Because I was born for this, even after having faced all these problems, I'm not worried that I don't have a house, that I don't have this, that I don't have that. Whatever will happen, let it happen. Why should I have what the goddess herself doesn't have? I'm not bothered that I don't have ornaments or property. Let it happen as it should. I was supposed to face difficulties along with the children, and I've experienced all of it. I've faced things with my husband, too. Now I'm serving the public. People tease me, "Ankalamma [one of the Seven Sisters] hasn't given you a house or a plot of land." They've teased me like this, but I don't let it bother me. They say, "This Talli [mother; goddess] is making you roam about like this." But I don't let this bother me. If I'm born like this, this is what should happen.

When she had completed her narration, Pujaramma asked if we wanted to see the goddess come to her (through possession). (She initially identified the goddess who would possess her as Camundeshwari—a goddess who dwells in Mysore, near Pujaramma's birth place—but later named her Gangamma.) She led us into the adjacent kitchen room, where she kept her *puja* shelf. She washed her face, hands, and feet, applied new *kumkum* to her forehead *bottu,* and ash on her forehead and arms. She drew what she called a *maila muggu* on the floor with *kumkum,* lit camphor at its intersecting points, and squeezed a reddened, *kumkum*-ed lemon around its circumference. She then sat in the middle of the *muggu.* (When I asked if the *muggu* was necessary for possession, she said it wasn't; it was her custom to do this, but, she assured us, the goddess would come to her even if she sat under a tree.) Like Veshalamma, Pujaramma keeps the goddess in the form of a *kalasham* on her *puja* shelf. She told us that people come to her with a kilogram of rice, two coconuts—one to break and one to set in the *kalasham*—flowers, fruits, *vibhuti* (ash), and lemons: "They bring all this. . . . Ammavaru's work is with lemons, *pasupu,* and *kumkum.*" (Pujaramma later elaborated that offering lemons to the goddess was the same as offering *bali.*) My fieldwork associate asked what we should do when the goddess came; Pujaramma said, "Just keep the camphor burning; it shouldn't burn out. Amma will come to me and she'll tell everything."

Pujaramma began to sway, swallow air and burp loudly, and call out a litany of names of deities, starting with "*Om namah Shivaya.*" She began to circle her head around, making a hissing snake-like noise. She shouted out, "Govinda, Govinda!" (a name for Venkateshvara), laughed, and then sat quietly before the goddess began to speak through her, directly addressing my fieldwork associate and me. I provide the beginning of the possession speech to give an idea of how the goddess/Pujaramma relates to and teaches those with whom she speaks.

What, Amma? [i.e., what do you want? Then, turning to me]. I'm very fearsome [*bhayankar*]. I'm Adi Shakti, Bhadrakali, Udrakali. Do you understand? Get up and give camphor and *harati.* [Making a hissing sound:] Both of you give. When you've come to me, this is what you should do.

[Looking at and speaking about me:] She has children, right? She has a daughter and son. And she has a husband. She's gone all around the world; to serve humans is to serve god. Only some will get this opportunity. Will everyone get it? No. She has experienced everything: trouble and happiness. . . . Those who have a wife, husband, and children will face troubles; even in small things, there will be troubles. Isn't that right? Even if someone is a millionaire, s/he will face trouble. Every human will have to face troubles. If everyone was happy, this wouldn't be Bhu Lokam [the created world]. Kailash [abode of gods] wouldn't be Kailash, god wouldn't be god, and humans wouldn't be human.

They pray to Jesus, but Jesus won't say, "These people are different and those people are different." He won't say, "This is not milk, this is not water." He won't differentiate; it's humans who've differentiated. Everything is the same. I'm Adi Shakti, Kali. Each place has a different name and each age has a different incarnation. What are the first words a child speaks? Amma or Nanna [mother or father], right? If you give birth to a baby or you have any pain, you won't call out anything other than "Amma."

You're educated, right? You can't tell anyone your problems, but you can't swallow them either. So you're facing a lot of troubles. Are you peaceful at home? Are you happy? You're happy on the outside, but how many troubles do you have? Does anyone know about them? Sometimes you're so sad. While lying down, you keep crying, "Why is god testing me?" Why do you think like that? Why do you think like that? [in a demanding voice.] Because you have troubles, right? Everyone will face troubles. Everyone who comes out of the womb, until his/her death, will face troubles. There's no change in troubles. The ones who are born these days say, "There's no one greater than me." This Kali Yuga is forest, *konda-kona* [hills and valleys], trees, and snake holes. If people get well, they say "I've succeeded [i.e., take credit for getting better]." But if they're asked to bring a person back from the dead, can they do that?

Pujaramma characterizes this age in which we live—Kali Yuga—as inherently trouble-ridden, just as a wilderness area (forest, hills, and valleys) is filled with pitfalls, dangers, and difficulties.

Then the goddess, through Pujaramma, addressed my fieldwork associate and the process and probabilities of her finding a husband. She further described our families, personalities, and life situations, which my fieldwork associate, in particular, found disconcertingly accurate. The goddess then shifted to describing Pujaramma's life without a permanent home and asked what we would give her. Not knowing Pujaramma's possession practices and the ingredients—*pasupu-kumkum* and lemons—that her traditional clients are asked to bring, we had come empty-handed on this visit. As I was leaving her home after the possession ritual and tried to leave some money with Pujaramma for the ingredients, she refused to accept the cash, took my face in her hands, and said with benedictory force, "You are the *pasupu-kumkum.*"

Responsibilities to the Goddess

A *tali* relationship with the goddess does not come freely, nor is it only a private one, but comes with public responsibilities toward the goddess and other humans who seek to interact with her. An NGO pamphlet about *matammas* pictures them (through line-drawings) as wearing neem-leaf skirts and describes their dancing in front of the goddess during *jataras*—a ritual I heard described in other contexts, as well. Several *jatara* participants told me that this custom was a *must* for the *jatara* and, although the tradition was now hidden, somewhere in Tirupati women in neem-leaf skirts would visit Gangamma.[14]

Veshalamma and Pujaramma never spoke about the neem-leaf guise and dancing during the *jatara;* rather, they emphasized their ritual specialty as becoming possessed by the goddess and serving as intermediaries between her and humans who need her help with illness, infertility, and questions about their futures. Further, both women are regularly called upon to aid persons in whom the goddess has manifested as poxes and to discern (through possession) the desires of the goddess. Pujaramma, in particular, narrated several lengthy cases of successful healing of persons who had so called her.

Pujaramma also performs another unique ritual responsibility: to take *garega* (a bamboo temple-shaped structure tied to the top of her head) to various goddess temples in order to bring them prosperity.[15] Pujaramma says that her presence with the *garega* blesses run-down temples, and they "rise up" and become active and prosperous. Note that she speaks here of permanent structures for the goddess, unlike the traditional locales at the edge of villages where the goddess resides under open skies—another sign of shifting village traditions in urban contexts such as Tirupati. Pujaramma started listing the various temples she has visited that then became prosperous:

You know the Neralamma temple, now called Rajarajeshwari. I was the one who made it prosperous. I take *garega* to each temple—Gangamma temple, Ankalamma temple. . . . [Showing a picture of herself with *garega:*] This is me, with Ammavaru's *garega.* These people come and ask me to do *puja.* This is at Ankalamma's temple. I offer *ambali* [a millet/*ragi*/yogurt drink] here every year. When I have offered *ambali, kumbham* [piles of cooked rice], and goat [*bali*], Amma will come over me, and I'll start dancing and singing, along with the Pambalas' drums. Like Veshalamma temple, which was very old [rundown]—Ammavaru came and developed this. She gave life [lit., soul, spirit; *atma*] to all the temples like this.

Whenever I take *garega,* people come and ask Ammavaru, "This temple is like this [i.e., rundown], what should we do?" [She answers,] "In two years, it will develop. I'll cause the money you need to come. Now go." This is what she said for Kalikamma temple. In those days, there was nothing there. For Manchala Gangamma temple, the Gollas asked me in the same way, and they got an answer in the same way. Even Veshalamma temple, the people asked, "The temple is like this, when will it prosper?" [Ammavaru answered,] "In three years, I will repair it and see that *puja* is performed." It happened like this there, and also in Cintakayala Vidhi Gangamma Temple. There was smoking, drinking, and gambling going on there. People complained. And in the same way, I took *garega* there. They put on a flower garland, did *pada puja* [touched my feet], and called Amma. The same pronouncement came from her.

Pujaramma's narrative listing of temples that began to prosper after she visited them with *garega* ended with the declaration, "Wherever I go, they say 'Amma has come; give *harati* to her.' They make me sit inside and everyone gives *harati.* That's how the temples prosper. She [Ammavaru] makes them good, and the *puja* and all are good." When people say, "Amma has come," the distinction between Pujaramma and the goddess is fluid, since both are called "Amma." Carrying the *garega,* Pujaramma becomes or brings Ammavaru, and the goddess speaks through her, giving instructions about the temples. But while her ritual performances bring prosperity to the dwellings of the goddess, Pujaramma herself has no permanent dwelling (she had lived in the rented quarters I visited her in for only four months). She concluded this part of her narrative:

> Now I've come to the end of my life. I don't own a house. Up until now, I haven't asked Amma for this or that. I just keep going around and coming back. I don't go and earn money; I don't cheat and earn money that way. When people come [to the goddess, through Pujaramma's possession], she heals them. People who are childless, she gives them children. Those who are unmarried she gets them married. This is the drama of my life.

The personal narratives that we have been considering were told by two women who have exchanged *talis* with the goddess in a contemporary context that is multi-layered and rapidly shifting. The married (or once-married) status of Veshalamma and Pujaramma itself hints at some of the pressures on the tradition, pressures created, in part, by shifting patronage of *gramadevatas,* early twentieth-century and contemporary reform movements, growing middle-class "sensibilities," and the "upward" mobility of the Gangamma tradition in Tirupati. The two women live in seemingly contradictory worlds of human marriage and a *tali* relationship with the goddess; the advantages and potential social status and security obtained through their human marriages remain unspoken (perhaps assumed), while those of their *tali* relationship are more clearly articulated: identity beyond their marital status (abused wife in one case and widowhood in the other), protection, legitimacy to move (more than most married women), and ritual and social agency. Veshalamma finds refuge in a *tali* relationship when human relationships have left her vulnerable. Pujaramma keeps her social status and identity as an auspicious woman (indicated by her continued wearing of a *tali* and application of a *bottu*), even if she is a widow who would traditionally have lost these.

Each context in which *matamma*- or *devadasi*-kinds of traditions are performed and represented provides a unique interpretive frame for the social/ritual institution; and to address all of these social-historical perspectives is beyond the scope of this chapter. Here, I have focused on the narrative voices of women themselves, voices frequently lost in the dominant discourse about *matammas* in the press, in institutions such as universities and development organizations, and in middle-class conversational discourse. The narratives of Pujaramma and Veshalamma suggest that the *tali* of the goddess marks a woman's agency and auspiciousness in ways similar to the goddess's own *tali*. The *tali*-relationship has provided these women, both of whom in some way occupy a marginal social space, a ritually created space of refuge and agency in the public arena. The relationship also gives them confidence and an identity independent of their husbands. Pujaramma's and Veshalamma's narratives also make clear, however, that their *tali* relationships have not translated into trouble-free lives. But as they negotiate these troubles, their relationships with the goddess have given them freedom (even compulsion) to move beyond their marginal social status and the social and physical constraints often imposed by marriage to husbands.

"CRAZY FOR THE GODDESS": A CONSUMING RELATIONSHIP

10

Veshalamma and Pujaramma articulate some of the benefits of entering a ritual relationship with the goddess; in their narratives, it would seem that these benefits outweigh the troubles they may experience because of this relationship. However, as the narrative fragments of the personal narratives of the female devotee of Gangamma in this chapter will suggest, there may be times when an intimate relationship with Gangamma may, in fact, be "too much to bear."

Gangamma is a restless goddess who traditionally moves too much to accept a permanent dwelling and thus is perhaps not present enough, in one place for long enough, to establish a *devotional* relationship with most worshippers who interact with her. However, in her Tirupati temples, Gangamma is more stable than she is on village boundaries. Here, when female householders have particular needs, throughout the year they make vows to light a specific number of oil lamps (*dipam*) for a specific number of Tuesdays and/or Fridays at her temple or to cook *pongal* for her in her temple courtyards, asking her to fulfill their desires. The relationships between these women and the goddess are primarily ritual/material transactions: Gangamma needs food and other services, and her worshippers need something from her (a husband, fertility, health of or employment for their children). Few householders maintain her at home; her *ugra* nature requires a level of nearly full-time service very few women have time, energy, or even inclination to give.

However, like Veshalamma and Pujaramma, the female householder described below *has* has brought Gangamma into her family spaces and established an intimate, consuming, devotional relationship with her. Through the admittedly fragmental narratives of this devotee, we begin to further understand both the space that Gangamma tradition may give to socially marginal women and the toll such a relationship may take on devotees.

The woman whom I call by her initials MR[1] spends most of her days serving the goddess, both at home and at Gangamma's temples. She describes herself as "*picci* for the goddess," literally, "crazy or mad for the goddess"[2]:

People call me *picci.* I'm *picci* for temples; I like temples. [Pauses.] We all have our *picci* [madness], and this [interest in Gangamma] is yours. People around me berate me [saying], "You go around like a madwoman." There isn't a single person who hasn't scolded me. . . . People don't pay attention to me because they think I'm *picci,* [because] I keep bathing[3] and going to the temple.

The connotation of *picci* here is that MR has "lost her mind" (and perhaps some social graces) in her devotion to the goddess.[4]

I first met MR in 1995 in the hot, crowded courtyard of the Kaikala home while waiting for the Matangi to return midday, from her perambulations, to receive the ritual piercing of her tongue. MR stood out in the jostling, pressing crowd with her large vermilion *bottu* and wide horizontal smear of sandalpaste across her forehead, indications of her heightened religiosity. I later asked her about the significance of her large *bottu,* and she answered, "It's my *paityam* [Tamil equivalent of the Telugu *picci*]." Her teenage son who was sitting with us interjected:

There are the *shastras* [religious texts], right? It's the third eye referred to there. It's the eye of knowledge [*jnana netram*]. It doesn't look at the outside world; it's in our mind. It [the eye] shouldn't been seen [outside], so god will be hidden there. It can be seen; but it will be red in color, like sunlight, bright. Instead of that, they keep the red *bottu.*

Paying little attention to her son's rather philosophical explanation, MR began to narrate an attenuated variant of the story of Adi Para Shakti giving her third eye to Shiva. The resulting empty spot on the goddess's forehead, MR went on to say, was filled with the *bottu*. She then asked her son to leave the room and gave another explanation of the *bottu:* "Another story in the *puranas* says that Ganga Devi is on the head of Shiva, right? She got her period; it flowed down on his head. So they took all that [blood] and made the *bottu*."

Back to our first meeting with MR: her eyes were wide and bright, her large smile looked frozen, and her manic speech was often addressed to no one in particular. As soon as MR noticed my fieldwork associate and me, she came over to introduce herself as a "special devotee of the goddess" who comes every year to witness the Matangi-tongue-piercing ritual; she told us she is also known for her offering to the goddess of *angapradakshinas*. Looking at her painfully thin body, it was difficult to imagine that body sustaining multiple *angapradakshinas* on the stone-slab paving around many temples, particularly during the hot season when the stone absorbs and holds the heat of summer sun. In that first conversation, MR elaborated:

My daughter has written a story about my life. I used to do a hundred and one *angapradakshinas* around Gangamma's temple [Tatayyagunta], even if it was so hot. These days, I'm not feeling well, so I'm not doing it. . . . When I do *pradakshina,* sometimes I can't roll anymore, and the goddess comes to me in the form of a child, and she pushes me all around. Only then I'm able to finish; otherwise I couldn't. This happened three weeks ago. Now and then the goddess calls me to come to the temple to do this. Some people don't believe me. . . . [5]

Because I am Gangamma's devotee [*bhakta*], even my brother scolds me [saying], "You go around these Gangamma temples like a mad [*picci*] woman. I always feel ashamed of saying that you are my sister." My daughter is also like me; she has the same *bhakti* [devotion]. . . .

There is no one who hasn't scolded [insulted] me. "Having so much devotion, why do you live in such poverty?" But, I feel happy in this poverty. One day the goddess will do something for me, I'm sure. . . . Amma is there for those who believe. I don't know what others think or believe, but I have faith [*nammakam*] in her.

MR invited us to come home with her after the Matangi tongue-piercing, where, she said, she would tell us both her own full story and that of the goddess. Her manic speech had shifted quickly from subject to subject and back again, often with no obvious connections, making it difficult to follow. My fieldwork associate was less than enthusiastic about accepting the invitation or prolonging conversation with MR even there in the Kaikala courtyard. She (and many others in the crowd who seemed to be employing tactics of avoidance with MR) had immediately sensed MR's *picci* character, and she was not convinced by the explanation of its devotional origin. She was both greatly annoyed with and a little afraid of MR and insisted that we decline her invitation that day. However, I found my way to MR's one-room home the next day with an older female friend visiting from Hyderabad, who had more patience and life experience within which to contextualize MR's *picci*. And there we began to learn fragments of MR's life story.

In 1995 MR was in her mid-forties; she is from the Achari caste group of artisans who make the *jatara ugra mukhis*. Her husband worked as a carpenter, and her twelve-year-old son was apprenticing with his paternal uncle in a welding shop. The Tamil-speaking abilities of the elder friend who first went with me to meet MR at home (and later those of my fieldwork associate in 2000) were fortuitous, as we learned that MR's family is Tamilian, speaking primarily Tamil at home and a mix of Tamil and Telugu out in public, although her family had lived in Tirupati for several generations. We later learned from MR that she was born in a town called Nindrai, where her father's family served the *gramadevata* goddess named Callamma: "Like we have Gangamma here, Callamma is there. And there, my father used to make that clay face [*ugra mukhi*], like they do here." She had married her cross-cousin and moved to a place near Puttur, a bustling town thirty kilometers from Tirupati, on the road to Chennai.

A Personal, Devotional Relationship with the Goddess

I had expected MR to be as talkative and assertive in her own home as she had been the day before in the Kaikala courtyard. However, she was strangely quiet and initially left most of the talking to her twenty-year old daughter, who, she said, was following in her footsteps as a *bhakta* of Ammavaru (the preferred term both she and her daughter used for Gangamma). She seemed to defer to her daughter because of her literacy (she was educated through sixth grade), particularly her ability to *write* her mother's story and songs to the goddess. The notebooks the daughter had filled with writing seemed to have trumped MR's ritual authority (displayed through *angapradakshina* and her frequent possession by the goddess), as well as the standard age hierarchy of mother-daughter.

When I pressed MR for how she came to be so identified with the goddess, she replied, "From early childhood, I didn't know my mother [she died when MR was seven years old]. I've had it [this fixation on the goddess] from my early childhood. I struggled a lot. In that struggle, my mind got fixed on the goddess. I don't know how it got fixed [like that]." In another conversation several years later, MR elaborated that she seemed to be fated to this relationship with the goddess: "My mother dreamt that a girl would be born and that she'd be devoted to Tatayyagunta Gangamma in Tirupati. My mother, too, was a *bhakta.* My daughter has written all this in the book."

Her daughter, now married and back home visiting her mother for the 1995 *jatara,* explained she had written many songs for Gangamma, as well as her mother's life story. This written life narrative became the focal point of much of our interaction that day, as well as in future interactions; both mother and daughter were obsessed with figuring out ways to get the story published. MR had called us to her home to show us the manuscript of her life story, but when we arrived and she started to pull a notebook out of a tin trunk, she stopped suddenly. MR was conflicted: she had a story, she said, but did not have permission from the goddess to tell or show it. She related another incident when she had shown the written life story without Gangamma's permission:

See that Gangamma photo there [propped up against the wall]. If I put a fruit on it and Amma gives it back [it falls off], that means I can read this story for someone. I always have the desire to read it to others, but we shouldn't do *namaskaram* [respect, salutation] to our own feet. We must do it to someone else's feet. Once I asked a woman to listen to the story and tell me whether she thought it was good or not. I started reading it. As soon as I'd read just a bit, Ammavaru came onto me [in possession]. She asked, "Amma, Amma, what, what? [What do you think you're doing?]" Then we stopped reading and admitted to Ammavaru that what we had done was wrong. We did *gunjilu* [bodily gesture offering respect to a deity] and offered *harati* to the goddess.

MR suggests here that a person shouldn't sing her own praises ("do *namaskaram* to our own feet"), and that the goddess had not given her the permission to do so even now. Later in our conversation, MR and her daughter blamed "the men of their family" for not being able to show us the story. The men, who remained unnamed (but presumably included MR's brother who she had said objected to her *picci* nature, and/or her husband, about whom she said very little), had accused MR and her daughter of trying to gain publicity. Still later, the daughter told us that she and her mother had already given the story to "an actress" whom they had met at Tatayyagunta temple and who had told them she would make MR's story into a film; until the actress herself gave her permission, they now said, they could not let us record the story. With more conversation among themselves, mother and daughter concluded that they could not, in fact, let us hear the story at all, even if I did not record it.[6]

The daughter was, however, willing to sing some of the songs she had composed for Gangamma, which conveyed an *emotional* life story, if not the particulars of its lived events. She began to weep after singing only a few lines and finally had to stop, her chest heaving with sobs. She later showed me the notebook in which she had written the words translated below:

Tatayyagunta Gangamma Talli, Ambala Gunta Gangamma Talli.
I won't forget the promise you gave me,
That you are my mother [*talli*].
My tears are like sweet water for you.
But seeing my troubles, you're silent.
Your heart hasn't melted, even after seeing my tears.
Tatayyagunta Gangamma Talli, Ambala Gunta Gangamma Talli.[7]

Have you forgotten the promise you gave,
That you are my mother?
Believing that you are here, I have lost my sons.[8]
At that time, you told me that faith is foolish.
At that time, you yourself told me to come to you.

I've come to you; speak to me.
Tatayyagunta Gangamma Talli, Ambala Gunta Gangamma Talli

Why, Amma, do I have all these troubles?
Did I ever ask for any status [*antastu*]?
All I'm asking is for my sinful state [*papa rogyam*];
This is all I'm asking of you.
Come to me and pour life breath into my sinful life.
I've come to you because you offer protection [*dikku*].
I'm coming to you for protection [*sharanam*].
Tatayyagunta Gangamma Talli, Ambala Gunta Gangamma Talli

Come to me, come to me.
If I believe in you, you won't let go my hand.
If it's true, come to me.
You pour life breath into my sinful life.
Sharanam, sharanam. Tatayyagunta Gangamma Talli, Ambala Gunta Gangamma.

Sharanam, sharanam, Tatayyagunta Gangamma Talli, Ambala Gunta Gangamma.
Sharanam, sharanam, Tatayyagunta Gangamma Talli, Ambala Gunta Gangamma.
Sharanam, sharanam, Tatayyagunta Gangamma Talli, Ambala Gunta Gangamma.
Sharanam, sharanam, Tatayyagunta Gangamma Talli, Ambala Gunta Gangamma.
Sharanam, sharanam, Tatayyagunta Gangamma Talli, Ambala Gunta Gangamma.

The goddess described in this song could be almost any goddess except for the names, Tatayyagunta Gangamma Talli and Ambala Gunta Gangamma Talli, by which she is addressed. Neither her iconographic distinctions (such as being covered with *pasupu* or having fangs, etc.) nor her narrative characteristics (slaying the Palegadu, for example) are mentioned. Rather, she is characterized in this devotional entreaty simply as a mother who has promised her protection—who has called the devotee to come to her, but who is now silent, seeming to have turned away from the devotee. The singer/devotee is the one who is needy in this relationship; if the goddess has needs to be fulfilled through tangible offerings (as she does during the *jatara*), these are not mentioned. The singer asks the goddess to give her life breath, direction in life, and protection. She entreats the goddess to pour life breath into her "sinful life," an ambiguous reference that would seem to imply simply vulnerability, a life in need of protection. What the singer and her mother need protection *from* became apparent only in the personal narratives they later told. The singer offers the goddess here nothing in return for the protection for which she calls out. She seems to assume that Gangamma will be responsive simply to the heartbreaking entreaties of the song. However, we gradually learned that the goddess *is* demanding something in return—total, all-consuming obedience to her commands.

After the poignant entreaty cited above, the daughter sang part of a litany she had composed of what she identified as the thousand names of Gangamma, which she said she hoped to publish and distribute at Tatayyagunta temple. Here, as the list ends with the names of the series of Gangamma *vesham* the Kaikalas take, the goddess becomes specific to Tirupati, even as she is equated with multiple other forms of the goddess. The singer started the litany with: Neera, Peraga, Yelami, Panchay, Pushpa, Pasupu Alamkara, Shiva Puja, Dhusha, Bushta, Kashta, Sukta, Vedani Cir, Bhakti Kapan, . . . Pedda Mutyalamma, Dakshayani, Durga Devi, Omkar Rupini. She then shifted to the local goddess Gangamma—Tallapaka Gangamma and Tatayyagunta Gangamma—before listing her *veshams* in the order in which they appear during the *jatara:* Bairagi Gangamma, Golla Gangamma, Toti Gangamma, Dora Gangamma, Matangi Gangamma, Sunnapukundalu Gangamma, Perantalu Gangamma. Reciting a thousand-name litany (*sahasranama*) is a traditional form of praise worship to *puranic* deities (the names being drawn from their mythologies or their characteristics—such as, for Krishna: son of mother Devaki, lord of Dwarka, the lotus-eyed one, the mountain-lifter, etc.), but is not a standard ritual in worship of a *gramadevata.* As noted in earlier chapters, I did, however, hear a similar litany of names for Gangamma in two other contexts: sung by the *purana pandita* Annapurna, in the courtyard of Tatayyagunta temple during Navaratri, and by Subbarama Reddy in Avilala. Performatively, the ritual recitation of the thousand names places Gangamma in a Sanskritic ritual register, weaving her into complex patterns of relationship and identity with a wide array of deities who are not *gramadevatas.* But this particular litany brings Gangamma back to her home place, Tirupati, ending with the names of her *jatara veshams.*

The songs MR's daughter composed employ devotional language that has also been borrowed from a different linguistic and ritual register than that in which Gangamma traditionally lives: for example, the images of taking refuge and being given refuge/protection (*sharanam*) at the feet of the goddess, and the language of *pap* (sin). In fact, *gramadevatas* are not traditionally revered through devotional song at all, but rather are worshipped and satisfied primarily through material ritual. MR's daughter draws on *bhakti* vocabulary to express a deeply personal, intense relationship with the goddess; but the language does not fully express what the *ugra* Gangamma has demanded of MR and her daughter.

As her daughter dissolved in tears while singing the song above, MR became more talkative and explained the power of the recitation of names:

I have a book with some songs, stories, and recitation of the goddess's names; if you utter them a thousand times, or if in a hurry, nine times, your desires will be fulfilled. But Amma won't allow you to finish that.

In our street, an evil spirit [*daiyam*] got hold of a girl. I told them to publish this book [of names of Gangamma, composed by MR's daughter], for Rs. 1,000 or Rs. 500. If they were willing to give that amount, I would cure their daughter. And they took that book. I don't want to earn any money from printing this book. I thought of giving that book to Gangamma's temple. If I publish this book, I think I'll get lots of money. This happened to the girl thirteen days before she was supposed to get married. Then they came to my husband and begged him for the book. I'm not greedy. If I get it published and sell copies, I'll get money and can give that to Gangamma temple. My husband convinced me to give that book to them, saying that we might be in need of help some day, so it's our duty to help them. I did *puja* to the pages and gave them to these people; they recited the words and the girl got married. Then one day Ammavaru came on [possessed] that girl; she had fallen, and the girl's husband didn't recognize that this was the result of this [taking the book and not giving it back—as well as not giving money]. Then they sent the girl to her mother's house. This happened six months ago. . . .

There have been many such incidents in my experience. This also happened to my daughter. My daughter married my brother's son. Because I am Gangamma's devotee, my brother scolded me, "You go around these

Gangamma temples like a madwoman. I always feel ashamed of saying that you are my sister." My daughter is also like me; she has *bhakti.* He brought my daughter back after three months [of marriage]. He scolded me, "If you have courage [*dhairyam*], then call Gangamma so that I'll see her." He scolded me a lot. I told him, "I can't tell you whether or not Gangamma is there; she's there for me." Then I went to the temple and wept and wept.

One day, Gangamma came on me and told me, "I'm here; don't worry." Then my daughter recited the book [of names] nine times. Is it wrong to have *bhakti?* I was prepared to die, but not to beg my brother [to take my daughter back]. After nine days, he himself came and took my daughter back to his house. . . .

The devotion of MR and her daughter to the goddess is expressed and experienced primarily through song and ritual that are not directly related to the narrative of Gangamma and her *jatara.* When I asked her to tell me the story of the *jatara,* MR responded hesitantly:

The goddess was like a child, but in order to kill somebody in another village—I don't know the details. In order to kill someone, like Mahishasura, she took these different guises. She kills him on the ninth day. [Note: she is telling the basic story of the goddess Durga, whose triumph over the buffalo demon Mahishasura is celebrated during Navaratri.] This has been done every year for the past five hundred years. It might be older, but I'm saying it's five hundred. I can't tell you this perfectly in Telugu [suggesting she may be able to tell the story more completely in Tamil]. Someone in the village, the village head—[she shakes her head, not able to recall more details]. If you want to know more, read the story in the newspaper.

[The elder woman who had accompanied me:] But her devotees would know the story better than what is in the newspaper, don't you think? That's why we're asking you. [MR] You're right, if you listen to our story, you might understand it better.

This story, presumably the one recorded in the notebooks over which she took such care and which she did not have "permission" to show us, however, is not the story of the *jatara,* but that of MR's experiences serving and being protected by Gangamma and the high costs of that devotion.

To Bear the Goddess

One wall of MR's rented one-room home is covered with an array of god/goddess lithographs, prominent among which are three framed photographs of Tirupati Gangamma temple images.[9] The largest photograph is of Tatayyagunta Cinna Gangamma; the others are Tallapaka Pedda Gangamma and one of her sisters, Mutyalamma. At the base of the wall sit three small clay pots with lids, on top of which a handful of uncooked rice grains has been placed, circled by neem leaves; several costume-jewelry necklaces grace the neck of each pot. These pots, too, are Gangamma, whom MR worships throughout the year. She told us that other women have tried to bring Gangamma home, but that Gangamma's worship is too intense and they're unable to keep it up and have to return the pictures to the temple. But, she emphasized, "I serve her properly; I've had her in my home for years." MR went on to explain that if you keep the goddess at home, then if she calls you to go somewhere or do something, you must obey or suffer severe consequences.

Gangamma seems to have two kinds of demands on MR as her devotee: to keep her ritually satisfied and to make her (publicly) known—but this should be done with humility, without taking pride in being able to sustain her, or there will be severe consequences. The balance is precarious. On our last visit together in 1995, MR told of the death of her infant son many years earlier, the first son to be born after two daughters. She said Gangamma had come to her, patted her on the back (MR demonstrates by patting herself on the shoulders), and told her that the baby had died because MR had been too proud of the fact that Gangamma came to her regularly through possession and dreams. Another time, MR continued, she broke out in big boils all over her face, and Gangamma gave a similar message, that she had been too proud. The consequences of telling her story of relationship with the goddess, then, explain MR's simultaneous impulse and reluctance to share her life story and the importance of waiting for the goddess to give permission before sharing the story.

But the relationship is reciprocal, MR assured us; the devotee who serves the goddess with full obedience can also depend upon her to come to the devotee when she is called:

Whenever I call the goddess, she comes to me. If I'm having any kind of difficulty [*kashtam*], when I weep for her, she comes to me and says, "I'm here. Don't worry; I'll look after everything. . . . I was walking in the rain one day, holding my daughter, who was very young [they were going to the hospital because of the daughter's high fever]. I was afraid. The goddess said, "I'm coming with you; don't be afraid." I could hear her ankle bell sounds behind me [onomatopoetic: *gale, gale, gale*]. I reached the hospital. Usually people like me [i.e., poor] aren't allowed in the hospital. When I remember all this now, I still feel the fear I felt then.

The hospital was closed. The doctor's name was Indira Bai Madam; you may have heard of her. The goddess told me that the doctor was at a certain place and that I should go there. I went there and stood in a corner. The doctor asked me why I had come all this way. She said that I could have gotten an injection where I lived, for only Rs. 2. Why did you bring this child all this way? The goddess made the doctor do all this; she wasn't acting on her own. When I remember all this, I go mad [*picci*] even now. I don't know what the goddess will do with me in the future. Even now, the goddess doesn't leave me alone.

Minimally, Gangamma at home requires daily *puja.* On Tuesdays, one of the days special to goddesses, MR fasts, not eating or drinking anything except for coffee. Further, one Tuesday a month, she observes a vow of silence ("I don't speak even if the goddess asks me to") and doesn't even drink coffee. This ritual rhythm is similar to that offered to many other domestically housed deities. But Gangamma demands more: she calls MR to come to her temples to perform various tasks, including *angapradakshina,* and to bring special ingredients for her temple worship. MR is well known among her neighbors and at temples for her special service to the goddess through *angapradakshina.* A few years after I first met her, I returned to Tirupati and made enquiries from some of the female flower sellers and caretakers of Tatayyagunta temple grounds about MR's whereabouts. One temple attendant immediately recognized who I was talking about:

Oh, she's the one who does *angapradakshina.* Sometimes she goes around only once and sometimes, when she has made a vow, she goes around a hundred and one times; she doesn't even drink water while doing this. Her son-in-law died. She does the *pradakshina* with torn clothes. Seeing her do this, the actress Jayasudha,[10] when she came here, wanted to meet her. We lock the temple and go off while she's still doing *pradakshina.* She begins at 10:30 in the morning and keeps doing it until 4:00 or 5:00 PM. She doesn't ask for water or get up to go to use the latrine. We lock her up [inside] and go [for lunch]. We trust her because she comes daily. She's very thin, so she does *pradakshina* very slowly. She's been doing this for many years, even since before my marriage.

The demanding ritual offering of *angapradakshina* takes not only time (a good part of the day), but also a bodily toll, sapping its actors of energy and strength. MR told us it took eight hours to complete a hundred and one *angapradakshinas,* but sometimes she makes only one round. She asked if we remembered the Tatayyagunta temple inner courtyard before it was enclosed, when its stone-slab floor used to get so hot, where she performed *angapradakshina.* Once, she recalled, a kind-hearted man saw her rolling around on the hot, hot stones (during the hot season) and thought he would cool her off by pouring water over her. The water began to boil, but, MR continued, "I shouldn't get up in the middle [of the rounds], so I got up only after completing the *angapradakshina.* Another time, I rolled over a sharp rod [from construction material left in the courtyard]. But when I got up at the end, it left no mark."

For the *jatara,* if her health is good and she has energy to sustain the worship of an enlarged, enlivened Gangamma, MR creates an elaborate worship site (which she calls a *pandal,* pavilion) to house the *jatara*-form of the goddess and feeds her *ambali.* To create Gangamma in this form is not a decision made lightly, since, MR said, "It's difficult to control her." This special *jatara* Gangamma is a coconut head seated atop one of the clay pots that are her form throughout the year in MR's small *puja* corner. The coconut is covered with *pasupu,* into which silver eyes (outlined with kohl) are embedded. Flowers and neem leaves crown her head, and (the year I observed the ritual) a new red, light-weight cotton sari with dark green border was pleated and spread out around her. Next to her, leaning against the wall, is the goddess's large iron sword, covered with *pasupu* and large *kumkum* dots. MR lights several oil lamps in front of the image. And at the very front of the altar space are the three tiny *pasupu* forms of Gangamma that most householders who participate in the *jatara* create in their kitchens. Five little mounds of rice sitting on neem leaves are served to the tiny *pasupu* Gangammas, and MR offers a neem-covered pot of *ambali* to all the Gangammas in the display. The high level of service required by this *jatara* creation of Gangamma corresponds to its size and elaboration, which is why most householders only make the three diminutive *pasupu* forms.

Gangamma is not alone in MR's ritual display. She sits in front of a busy array of framed and unframed god posters, including several of Venkateshvara and his wife Padmavati, and one each of Krishna, Hanuman ripping open his heart to show Ram and Sita enthroned there, Lakshmi, and Shiridi Sai Baba. The altar itself draws Gangamma, the *gramadevata,* into the Venkateshvara world—in much the same way the litany of a thousand names does—another reminder that both *gramadevatas* and *puranic* deities inhabit the religious imagination of Tirupati Gangamma worshippers. But this array of deities raised a different question for me. Why had MR chosen Gangamma over other possibilities, displayed in her *puja* corner, as the deity to whom she poured out her sufferings and with whom she was most

MR's domestic *jatara* shrine.

intimately tied? MR's narratives suggest the goddess chose her rather than the other way around.

During the *jatara* of 2000, MR invited me to watch her create this elaborately decorated Gangamma, and watching this ritual installation, I understood more fully the time (the ritual preparation of the goddess and site itself took nearly four hours), energy, and financial requirements of the *jatara* temporary image. As she fed Gangamma *ambali,* MR became possessed by her, swaying in the alcove she had curtained off for the temporary altar, until her son called her daughter to do *harati* to "dismiss" the possessing form of the goddess. MR told us that she didn't know anyone else who made such elaborate domestic displays of Gangamma during the *jatara* or who regularly bore the goddess through possession in her home, except for her husband's family:

My husband's house makes it. They had *talapatralu* [palm-leaf manuscripts] in their house; they were *bhaktas* of Shiva. Their devotion was so great that they even lit an oil lamp with water. . . . Even now, we have the *talapatralu* somewhere; they're in my husband's brother's house. It's in our lineage. They've written many things there; but now it's all lost. The brothers separated, so we don't know what happened to them.

Ownership of the palm-leaf manuscripts seemingly gave her husband's family, and perhaps MR herself, authority or *shakti* to bear the goddess at home. She added that her husband's maternal uncle had also kept Gangamma in the form of a silver head in their house and had performed goat *bali* to her there in the home itself, rather than at a temple.

Losing a Daughter to the Goddess

After not seeing MR for a couple of months, in February 2000 I went looking for her and learned she had moved residence once again. MR has never been a homeowner and lived in a different rented room each of the times I returned to Tirupati and tried to find her. In September 1999, I had found her living in a different rental room than the one she had been living in during the *jatara* of 1995; and she had moved again when I looked for her six weeks later. MR shares this quality with the goddess, moving and restless. But moving from rental room to rental room is also common for other members of the working classes to which MR belongs, and looking for acquaintances who had moved was a common (and frustrating) occurrence in my fieldwork (as mentioned in relationship to Annapurna, the *purana pandita* of chapter 5, as well).

Fortunately, when I looked for her that February 2000, MR had moved to a room just down the road from her earlier residence, and her neighbors were able to forewarn me that her daughter, the Gangamma devotee, had died only days earlier. The young woman, in her mid-twenties, had not died of any identifiable physical problem or illness. Rather, MR explained, she had simply started eating less and less after the death of her husband seven months earlier; finally, forty days ago, she had stopped eating altogether—literally starving herself to death. MR saw this as an act of courage and devotion, telling us proudly, "Even while we were taking her [to the cremation ground] everyone fell at her feet, saying that she had so much wisdom even at such a young age." The wall where Gangamma photographs would normally have been kept was cleared off and a small shrine had been built around a photograph of the daughter. MR explained: "In our caste, we keep the dead body in a seated posture, so we had to remove the photos from this wall [where Gangamma and god posters were last time]. You saw this last time. We'll keep it like this until the thirteenth day [after death]."

Slowly, with many starts and stops, MR told us of both the broader context and immediate circumstances of her daughter's death. Because they had had little money for dowry, MR had married her daughter to her brother's son (cross-cousin marriage being a common custom in many South Indian castes). She had assumed the beneficence of her brother, as brothers are traditionally obligated to take care of their sisters and particularly their sisters' daughters. But, from the beginning, the marriage had not been smooth. Contrary to his word, her brother had asked MR's family for more and more money as dowry, even after the wedding itself. MR's brother was abusive not only to his daughter-in-law, but also to others in the family. MR told of an episode when her sister's son had gone to his uncle's house, and they had "pushed him inside a tub of water," trying to drown him. He had then slept in a car, but they dragged him out and threw him into some nearby thorn bushes. MR continued:

> It was like a *cinema* story. Everyone says that our family story is a big story [*caritra*]. Everyone asks me to go and complain to the police, but these family matters shouldn't go to a police station. Is a family that goes to the police station a family? That's what I thought. The son [her daughter's husband] could have at least come for his wife, couldn't he? He's his mother's son. He did come to take her back. But when he went back home, his father left the house and said, "If she's there, I won't stay there." [When my fieldwork associate asked for some clarification of the sequence of events, MR answered:] I myself don't know how to explain this—that's why you can't understand.

The primary reason MR's brother didn't want her daughter (his daughter-in-law and niece) in his house was, he told MR, that his *tantric* (ritual, magical) powers had diminished since the new bride had come to his home. This is why he sent her back to her maternal home. The implication is that MR's daughter's *bhakti* to Gangamma interfered with the father-in-law's negatively employed ritual powers. MR identified her brother as a *mantrakaran* (one who manipulates/performs *mantras*); she never made it clear what exactly he *did* with the power of his *mantras,* whether or not he used them on behalf of other clients or just personally. Her younger daughter told us, "The main reason she was sent back to our house was that when she was there, her father-in-law's power from the *dushta shakti* [evil *shakti*], to whom he does *puja,* was not effective. They say that's why they pushed her out, but we don't know the real reason."

Several weeks after he first sent her home, MR's brother took back his daughter-in-law, but then again sent her back. The young husband had resisted his parents' suggestion that he marry someone else and had come to visit his wife every so often at her mother's place, but then he died. First, MR told us that they weren't informed of his death and had learned of it only from other mutual acquaintances. Perhaps, these acquaintances suggested, he had died of TB or maybe someone killed him; no one knew for sure (the implication being that someone may have cast *jadu* [magic] on him, a common explanation for unexplained, sudden death). Later in the conversation, she said they learned from others that the young husband was dying, but when they went to the home to see him, they were pushed out and not allowed to see him. We asked for clarification: did MR think her brother had killed his own son? She replied, "Not only his son; he would kill us, too. He's challenged us, saying, 'Just see what I will do to your family.'"

Before her husband's death, MR's daughter could not bear the shame of being sent back to her mother's home, nor could MR bear the shame of asking her brother to take back his daughter-in-law. Now, after his death, MR reported her daughter lost all will to live and had told her, "I can't live without my husband. Whatever happens, I should die. Don't go to Amma [Gangamma] and ask her to save me. I won't live without my husband." On her deathbed, she had asked that her *tali* be melted down and sold, and the money be used to engrave Gangamma's thousand names on a stone slab and placed in her temple. MR described her daughter's last moments: she was sleeping and simply "went away."

The small room became oppressive as the story unfolded. MR simply shooed away, with a flip of her hand, several mice scurrying from behind a pile of tin trunks on top of which the family's bedding had been folded. My fieldwork associate became visibly distraught and kept questioning MR why she wasn't able to keep her daughter alive, why she didn't force-feed her. MR replied, "Of course, I tried. Am I not her mother? But she was very stubborn. She didn't eat for more than forty days." With a lull in MR's narration, and feeling bad for our intrusion on her grief, we got up to leave and told her we would come back in a few days. But she gestured for us to stay, saying:

I'm feeling so *picci*. [Pause.] I know what's going to happen before it happens. I knew my son-in-law would die. I knew this even before they got married. But if we married her somewhere else [into a different family], we would not have been able to meet the dowry demands. No one can change what is written on the forehead [fate]. I told my husband that if we gave our daughter there, this would happen, but he wouldn't listen to me.

MR shifted back to her daughter's death again, describing how the young woman had taken glowing embers into her hand (a signal of her spiritual power and veracity) the day before she died and pronounced that something was going to happen tomorrow.

MR then asked her teenage son to sing for us, from the daughter's handwritten notebook, the song she had written down the day before her young husband died—interpreted as an indication that her daughter had had a premonition of her death, and a sign of the goddess's presence:

> I've put on a *mala* [rosary of *rudraksha* beads] and come to you, Tirupati Ganga,
> To show my anguish [*avedana*], Tirupati Ganga.
> I've taken a vow, Tirupati Ganga.
> I've come to beg for my life, Tirupati Ganga.
> I've put on a *mala,* Tirupati Ganga,
> To show my anguish, Tirupati Ganga.
> What sins have made me guilty [*doshi*]?
> Tell me, Tirupati Ganga; tell me, Tirupati Ganga.
>
> I've put on a *mala,* Tirupati Ganga,
> To show my distress, Tirupati Ganga.
> I don't know what curse and sin [*shrap* and *pap*] I've committed, Tirupati Ganga.
> I don't know what curse and sin I've committed, Tirupati Ganga.
> I've lost the sweetness of life.
> I've lost the sweetness of life.
> My life has become only ridicule.
> There's no limit to your testing, Tirupati Ganga.
>
> I've put on a *mala,* Tirupati Ganga,
> To show my anguish, Tirupati Ganga.
> You've tied the knot [of my marriage] with a foolish man.
> You've tied the knot with a foolish man.
> You're set on ridiculing me, Tirupati Ganga.
> You're set on ridiculing me, Tirupati Ganga.
> For which crime am I being ridiculed?
> I've come to you saying, "Your feet are my protection."
> Let me reach your feet.
>
> I've put on a *mala* and come to you, Tirupati Ganga.
> I've put on a *mala* and come to you, Tirupati Ganga.

Through song, the daughter had cried out to Tirupati Gangamma. Implicit to the song is the story of having been sent back from her marital home to her mother's home. She interprets the tragedy of her life and the ridicule she suffers as being sent to her by the goddess as a test (accusing the goddess herself of causing her to get married to a "foolish man" and ridiculing her). She's come to the feet of Tirupati Ganga for protection, as her last refuge—which, ultimately, was death.

When MR told us that after her daughter's death, she, too, would not eat for thirteen days, my fieldwork associate pushed her for the rationale for not eating, saying "I, too, have difficulties [*kashtam*]—my father and my sister died—but I eat."[11] She later told me she felt like she was being smothered in that small room, "like something was holding my hand tightly; I couldn't breathe; I couldn't think." MR countered:

> You have difficulties, but if you listen to mine, you'll burst into tears. Everything is a test for me. It's not simply a matter of difficulties, it's a test for me. I was seven years old when my mother died. From then, my difficulties started. . . .
>
> Even if I put rice on a plate, I don't eat it. Someone is asking me not to eat. ["Who?" I ask.] I don't know. Someone. It may be Ammavaru. Ever since my children were small, sometimes early in the morning, someone asks me not to talk, and all of the sudden I don't talk. I look at my children and don't speak. Someone asks me not to talk. In the month of Purattasi [Tamil month of mid-August to mid-September], I don't talk on Saturdays. I don't eat and I don't talk on these five Saturdays.
>
> I miscarried after the birth of my last son. Something happened to the cloth [used to absorb the blood], and for six months, I didn't talk. They were all small children. I was the only one [in the family] who could do the *puja,* so I decided not to talk and I slept. My daughter went to sleep at my sister's house. She [the goddess] said, "As long as you give camphor and *harati* [in worship of me], your body will be in good health, but you shouldn't talk." [My fieldwork associate asks, "You don't talk for an entire day?!"] Yes, the first week of the *jatara* I don't talk; the second week I don't talk; the third week; I don't talk; the fourth week of *jatara* I don't talk. [I ask, "Does your husband not say anything?"] I've been like this since the children were small. No one can scold me or do anything to me when I'm like this [not talking].

MR's personal narratives suggest a tension between too-much speech and silence. She both wants to tell the story of her relationship to the goddess and is prohibited from doing so (either the goddess doesn't give her permission to do so, or she quite literally silences MR). MR's *picci* character is identified by others, in part, through her incessant speech; and yet she is unable to speak the full truth of her experience. When she found my fieldwork associate and me as an audience, she wanted to tell her story; but it had many gaps, as she knew what the consequences of fully speaking may be.

Costs and Benefits of Bearing the Goddess through Devotion

What happens to the *ugra gramadevata* Gangamma when she participates in a personal, devotional relationship, when she is brought into a home rather than dwelling on village boundaries or in temples? And at what cost and benefit does a devotee bring the goddess home?

We know less in MR's narratives about what happens to the goddess than we do about what she herself has experienced. But through the songs MR's daughter has composed, we can conclude that in a *bhakti* relationship, Gangamma loses some of her "Gangamma specificity"—her unique Tirupati biography and some *gramadevata* characteristics (such as mobility)—if not her demanding *ugra* nature. She enters a *bhakti* ritual and verbal repertoire that situates her, in part, in a *puranic* family of deities. She becomes one of the manifestations of the pan-Indian more generic Devi, rather than primarily one of the *gramadevata* Seven Sisters. A similar move can be observed in the changes the goddess has undergone in her Tatayyagunta temple, where since 1992 she has been served by Brahman priests who don't know her as Gangamma, in her specifics, as much as one of many forms of the *puranic* Devi. But, as we have seen, she hasn't changed so much so as become easy to sustain at home. She remains *ugra* and demanding in her relationship with MR. As MR says, "She doesn't leave me alone."

It is unclear whether MR was in some way *picci* to begin with, and the nature of this "madness" was transformed through relationship with the goddess; or whether she was drawn into a relationship with the goddess because of her unique circumstances and difficulties and, once in that relationship, she became (more) *picci.* We cannot know what MR's life would have been without the goddess, whether or not she (and her life circumstances) would have been more or less stable, more or less "socially acceptable."

But it is clear that MR's relationship with Gangamma gives a cultural context within which her *picci* nature is understandable to those who interact with her. Even if they deride her, they accept her. There's an explanation for her *picci,* and those around her (including her husband) do not "bother her," even when she doesn't speak for days at a time. She finds an identity (albeit an ambivalent one) through her relationship with the goddess—one that she struggles to make public and keep hidden at the same time. She says she finds "life breath," refuge and solace "at the feet of the goddess," even if she remains poor and doesn't still understand why certain things happen, even if the goddess is sometimes silent when she calls out to her. After her daughter's death, she told us she was resigned to the wishes of the goddess, even if she did not understand them, saying:

Even the day before my daughter died, I went to Gangamma temple at 8 o'clock at night. But I shouldn't go to the temple now [as she still carries death pollution], so I'm not going. I can't understand anything; I can't understand my own family. . . .

I don't know what will happen now and what Ammavaru will do. It's her wish; let her do what she wants. What will she do? Whatever she wants. She's keeping quiet. [Usually] she comes and tells me everything, but now she's quiet. What will I do? She [daughter] has written so many *picci, picci* books. She was *picci akka* [elder sister].

The emotional and social protection/refuge of the *ugra* goddess has come at a cost to MR. The goddess is demanding, and serving her has become all-consuming, both figuratively and literally. Not only did MR offer herself to the goddess, but her children also suffered the consequences of this relationship. The last time I spoke with her in 2000, she told us that her eldest son had health problems and was weak. So she had decided she would not arrange a marriage for him, but rather, offer him to the goddess. If he wanted to get married and arrange his own marriage, he could; but she would not arrange it for him. But she did not think he would do so, since he was constantly threatening to become a *sannyasi* (ascetic). But this life, too, she did not want for him, and she was "keeping him under control" to prevent him from taking this path.

And, of course, MR's eldest daughter was drawn into the web of MR's personal relationship with Gangamma. She became *picci* herself, as MR characterized the process, through her compulsion to write and publish her mother's story. The power of the daughter's own devotion (and perhaps *picci* nature) affected her father-in-law's ritual powers, which resulted in her being sent back to her maternal home. But finally, according to MR's own interpretation, her daughter developed a consuming relationship with Gangamma that ultimately resulted in the daughter's death. We're left with a troubling story, with no easy answer as to whether or not a personal relationship with the *ugra* goddess is empowering, or is, in fact, "too much to bear," its costs too high. My fieldwork associate and I returned to my flat late in the afternoon after hearing this fragmented narrative, feeling helpless, vulnerable, and agitated—having experienced, to use Ruth Behar's phrase, "anthropology that breaks your heart" (1966).

When I returned to Tirupati in 2007 and tried to locate MR, I learned she had moved once again, and no one in the neighborhood in which she had lived in 2000 could tell me where she was. The flower sellers and other employees at Tatayyagunta temple seemed to have no memory of her, not even the same woman who had recognized immediately who I was talking about several years earlier as the "woman who does *angapradakshina.*" Or, they may simply have dismissed her—a *picci* woman who threatened the social order. After creating an identity and persona as "she who is a *picci* for the goddess" and becoming a regular fixture at Gangamma's two major temples, MR seemed to have disappeared from Tirupati's Gangamma landscape. However, her troubled story lingers on these pages. Perhaps because of its *picci,* fragmented form and content, MR's story helps us to begin to understand on an experiential level how or why the *ugra* goddess Gangamma is, finally, "too much to bear" and what it means to be *picci* for the goddess.

CONCLUSION: POSSIBILITIES OF A WORLD BECOME FEMALE

This ethnographic study of the goddess Gangamma and those who live her traditions has raised several questions that are woven throughout the book. First, what is the gendered nature of the *gramadevata* goddess who is characterized as *ugra,* as "too much to bear"? How does understanding this *ugra* goddess who wears a *tali* and has children, but no husband, reconfigure our analytic understandings of Hindu goddesses? How do her ritual and kinship relationships with the god on the hill, Sri Venkateshvara, cause us to reimagine analytic distinctions often made between *gramadevatas* and Sanskritic *puranic* traditions, as if they were hermeneutically sealed worlds? Second, what are the possibilities of gender created through Gangamma's narratives and celebration of her week-long *jatara,* during which ultimate reality is imagined (for at least this week) as female, and males become women (or their masculinity is transformed) to be in her presence? Third, what is the experience of individuals who are in close relationship with this *ugra* goddess; what kinds of resources do Gangamma traditions offer them, and how are these shifting under pressures of increasingly dominant middle-class aesthetics and morality and the introduction of Sanskritic rituals and Brahman male priests at her Tatayyagunta temple? And finally, is the goddess herself changing with recent ritual, aesthetic, and personnel changes in her Tirupati temples? We get answers (or sometimes only cues) to these questions through analyses of a rich repertoire of Gangamma traditions in relationship one to the other: *jatara,* rituals, myths and legends, and the personal narratives and experiences of those who worship or "bear" the goddess.

Ritual and Narrative

We often assume that to know a deity is to know the story of a deity; and many ethnographers begin their work with goddesses (or gods) by asking participants in their rituals to tell the story of the deity. However, we have seen that many women, in particular, know the Gangamma primarily ritually, rather than through her narratives.[1] Women offer *pongal* or thousand-eyed clay pots to the goddess because they have heard about or experienced the *shakti* of the goddess and the efficacy of her rituals in protecting their families from illness. The Tatayyagunta temple female attendant Koteshvaramma came to know Gangamma through the intimate rituals of feeding her, performing *abhishekam,* gently applying her *pasupu* mask, and dressing and ornamenting her. Her ancestors, too, had first come to know this Gangamma ritually. When they had asked a man standing nearby who the *pasupu-kumkum* decorated stone head was, sitting under a tree on the outskirts of Tirupati, he identified her as a *satyamaina talli* who had powerful healing powers; he did not tell them her story. Experiencing some ill health in the family, the travelers from Madras offered her *puja,* were healed, and decided not to return to home, but to stay on in Tirupati to serve Gangamma. Significantly, Potu Raju is also known in Tirupati through his ritual role as guardian of his Seven Sisters, rather than as an actor in either of Gangamma's two primary narratives.

On the other hand, we have the example of the *purana pandita* Annapurna, who as a Brahman had not traditionally participated in Gangamma rituals; she came to know the goddess primarily through narrative when she was hired by the Devasthanam to perform as a *purana pandita* at Tatayyagunta temple. She integrated Gangamma in her narrative repertoire by identifying Gangamma with the *puranic* goddesses whose stories she already performed and with whom Gangamma shares qualities of *shakti,* movement, boldness, and courage. Annapurna was only gradually then drawn into some aspects of Gangamma's ritual world.

However, rituals and narratives together create a repertoire that helps us to understand the possibilities and some of the internal debates of Gangamma's *jatara* "world become female." Many *jatara* rituals—creating and feeding multiple forms of the goddess—stand independently from Gangamma's Tirupati-specific narratives and are also performed in many surrounding villages in which these narratives are not known. Which rituals should be performed, by whom, in what order, is clearly articulated by *jatara* participants. And their success or efficacy is gauged by whether or not the *uru* is protected by the goddess from hot-season illnesses and drought. However, the rationale for and interpretations of some ritual elements—the thousand-eyed pot and beating the cement feet of the goddess, for example—are multiple and open for debate. We get cues for understanding some of these rationales and debates in Gangamma's narratives.

The Tirupati-specific perambulations of Kaikala *veshams* are a unique way to bring the goddess to the *uru* through both (embodied) narrative and ritual. For those pilgrim-passersby or *jatara* participants who have come from afar and who don't know the Palegadu narrative, these *veshams* may be seen as simply as multiple forms the goddess has taken to make herself present. But for those who do know the basic narrative, the Kaikala series of *veshams* enacting that narrative bring to mind both the access and excess of the goddess—who was raised as a village daughter and subsequently revealed her *vishvarupam* stretching from earth to sky. While the last three of the Kaikala series of *veshams* and the *ugra mukhis* are not narratively based, they ritually resolve the potential narrative crisis of Gangamma's excessive *ugram* left over after she has beheaded the Palegadu—as one narrator ended the story: she wandered the *uru* full of *ugram,* holding the Palegadu's blood-dripping head. Narrative and ritual worlds come together, when on the final early morning of the *jatara* the goddess (in her Perantalu form) dismantles her own *ugra mukhi* in order that inhabitants of the *uru* be able to bear her and that she be able to enter relationship with them.

Ritual and narrative are similarly interdependent in Tirupati's second Gangamma narrative, that of Adi Para Shakti. At the end of the narrative, the goddess is left both with unfulfilled *korika* (desire) and *ugram.*

The world itself is threatened by the *pralayam* (destruction) created by the infuriated, betrayed Adi Para Shakti. The ritual solution to this *ugram* is articulated in most variants of the narrative itself: the goddess proclaims (or the gods tell her) that her *korika* can be satisfied only through *bali*, which will be offered during her annual *jatara*. Ritual promises to balance the precarious world that the narrative has created.

Female *Ugram* and *Shakti*

We have learned that experience and interpretation of Gangamma's *ugram* and *shakti* are gendered and context-specific. Householders who characterize Gangamma as "too much to bear" would seem to acknowledge both the protective and destructive potential of the goddess's *ugram*—knowledge they have come to through personal and communal experiences. They realize that to ritually satisfy Gangamma's *ugram* requires more time and resources than most householders have; hence most do not bring her home to stay throughout the year. Translating *ugram* as "excess" is an attempt to express the ambivalence inherent in their experience. But Gangamma's narratives extend the connotations of *ugram* to include anger, desire, and *shakti*—and their performances provide gendered commentaries on the same.

In the Palegadu narrative, *ugram* is first and foremost the goddess's righteous, destructive anger against sexual aggression. In this context, it is similar to the female powers of *sat* (lit., truthfulness), acquired through faithfulness in marriage, that is articulated in numerous oral narratives throughout India. Both *ugram* and the powers of *sat* may be elicited when a woman is sexually threatened by an aggressive male or, in other narratives such as that of the beheading of Renuka, when she is falsely accused of unfaithfulness. In *The Powers of Tamil Women* (Wadley, ed., 1991 [1980]), Susan Wadley and other authors offer a model that bridges the apparent contradiction between women's *shakti* and their subordination in marriage, suggesting that women's subordination (suffering) itself is what creates their *shakti*. In contrast, Gangamma's power of *ugram/shakti* is not created through marital fidelity or sexual purity, but is inherent to who she truly is—an identity revealed only when the Palegadu threatens her and she shows him her *ugra vishvarupam* and is self-evident to Shiva in the Adi Para Shakti story.

Putting the Gangamma-Palegadu and Adi Para Shakti narratives in relationship to each other, as part of a single repertoire, suggests a gendered experience of *ugram* and *shakti.* Remember the woman who answered my question about *ugram* (whether she was afraid of Gangamma's *ugra mukhi*) with an answer about *shakti:* "No, we're not afraid, because she has *shakti* and we have *shakti.* But men, they don't have *shakti,* so they're afraid." Her answer suggests that what is identified as *shakti* by a woman may be interpreted as *ugram* by a male, who doesn't share this *shakti* and thus fears it, sensing its excess and destructive potential. The Adi Para Shakti narrative expands on male fear of being unable to bear female *shakti.* In this myth, *shakti* is the power that activates/creates the world and is associated with desire (*korika*). The goddess, upon reaching puberty, experiences *korika* and creates the three gods in an effort to find someone to satisfy this desire. When Shiva addresses her as "*eme,*" a pronominal term of address that may be used by husbands toward their wives, he is technically eligible to satisfy the goddess's *korika;* but he fears he will not be able to bear the fullness of her *shakti.* He asks the goddess to give him her third eye and *trishul* in a tangible transfer of *shakti;* but even with these, he seems to doubt his capability to bear the goddess and reneges on his offer. Interpretations of this story varied significantly according to the gender of the narrator. The basic story is told primarily from a male perspective: the goddess's (female) *shakti* is portrayed as excessive and overpowering, and the male god tricks her into giving up some of her *shakti.* One young male narrator made explicit the association of Adi Para Shakti's *shakti* and human female desire that has no limits and thus is incapable of being satisfied. But the two female Avilala narrators articulated quite a different perspective when they claimed the goddess's *shakti* to be superior to Shiva's, but asserted that she was willing to give some of her *shakti* to Shiva, so that their relationship would be one of equals, the only kind of relationship that can move forward smoothly (like an oxcart with two wheels the same size, the narrators specified). That Shiva ended up going back on his part of the deal, to "marry" Adi Para Shakti, did not seem to concern the female narrators as much as the *potential* or possibility for an satisfying relationship between equals.

When *shakti* is associated with sexual desire (and fertility), in the human realm, marriage is traditionally needed for it to find full expression.

However, Gangamma traditions suggest that marriage does not give women (like the goddess) their *shakti* and auspiciousness; rather, the quality is inherent to who they are. Gangamma and the *matammas* who exchange *talis* with her (rather than a husband) do not need marriage to display their *shakti* or satisfy their *korika.* However, the legitimacy of this display outside of marriage is coming under pressure with an expanding middle-class morality, which approximates the dominant right-hand caste ideology of the male-protected woman.

Possibilities of Gender

In the *jatara* "world become female," women are ritually the unmarked category. They do not change who they are, but intensify what they do already: cook *pongal* in greater quantities, apply more *pasupu* to their faces, and come to the temple more often with their children. Men, in contrast, are transformed through the *jatara* ritual of *stri vesham.*

Gangamma's narratives give us some cues toward the rationales of *stri vesham* and possibilities for what this ritual transformation creates, questions to which very few men gave verbal responses. In the Palegadu narrative, the aggressive male is beheaded; there is no marriage, and men would seem to be superfluous. However, the Adi Para Shakti narrative offers a different resolution—and reminds us of the importance of full repertoire to understanding any single ritual or story. Remember that Adi Para Shakti changes the three gods who have betrayed her into women. But then she herself realizes such a "world become female" is unsustainable—is not *dharmic*—and changes them back into males. However, the gods are presumably transformed by this experience of having been changed into women, now realizing the full *shakti* of the goddess. On her part, the goddess realizes that her fullness cannot, in fact, be borne by either gods or humans; and she divides herself into four parts, three parts to become the consort of each of the three gods. The last fourth of her *shakti* becomes the hundreds of *gramadevatas* who, significantly, don't need husbands, but are satisfied through their *jataras.* While the narrative gives us a cue of the transformative possibilities of *stri vesham,* so, too, does the wider repertoire of other rituals of guising. For example, the *pasupu* guise applied to the goddess herself suggests that—according to the Kaikala brother whose task it is to apply the *pasupu—veshams* do more than mask; they also reveal and transform those who take *vesham.*

The exhortation of his grandmother to the Brahman male who took *stri vesham* for thirty-five years gives us another cue of the transformative possibilities of *vesham.* She encouraged him to keep taking *stri vesham* year after year, telling him that by so doing, at least once a year, he would get a "corner on women's *shakti.*" Her exhortation implies that *stri vesham* gives men the possibility of experiencing female *shakti,* which has the potential to transform men into different *kinds* of men, who have experienced (and perhaps now accept) female *shakti* as part of themselves. This possibility is also suggested in the transformation of Potu Raju, Gangamma's younger brother, who is feminized in the presence of his Seven Sisters through the *pasupu-kumkum* application to his stone forms. In Tirupati, while Potu Raju is still identified both by his male name ("king of male-ness") and kinship role as younger brother, he is also known as the feminized *shaktisvarupini* (lit., whose form is *shakti*)—a different kind of male.

In everyday life, this transformation of the male is not assured, but remains a potential. Among left-hand castes who are the traditional participants in the *jatara,* we see traces of the possibility of a gendered world that is not male-dominated: in their oral epics in which the caste is saved by a heroine rather than male warrior; in the matriarchally oriented family of the Kaikalas; in the female temple attendants who traditionally serve the Seven Sisters; in the *matamma* tradition in which women are free (even compelled by the goddess) to move and wander, and are not constrained by marriage to a male; and in the social space the world of Gangamma gives to women (such as the *picci* devotee, and the widow and abused wife who exchanged *talis* with the goddess) who may be marginalized by dominant gender ideologies.

Contemporary Changes in the Worlds of Gangamma

Under increasingly dominant middle-class gender ideologies and morality and the brahminization of Gangamma's largest temple, some of the gender possibilities described above are being closed off. Many, perhaps even the majority, who are joining the growing numbers of *jatara* spectators and participants—attendance at the 2012 *jatara* was estimated to be 5 *lakhs*—do not belong to the local, left-hand castes who traditionally celebrated the *jatara*. They know little of the narrative and ritual possibilities of this Gangamma world (as evidenced in the necessity of the signs painted on the walls of Tatayyagunta temple courtyard that explain each of the Kaikala *veshams*). Many outsiders to the traditional *uru* attend the *jatara* because of its reputation for *stri vesham;* they come as spectators whose gaze has, at the same time, both popularized the *jatara* and marginalized, in the public imagination, its unique transformative possibilities. Viewing internet news clips of the 2011 *jatara,* I noticed that the visual images focused exclusively on the crowds around Tatayyagunta temple and a range of different kinds of *veshams* (particularly *stri veshams*) that wandered around its courtyard and neighboring streets. There were no images of the Kaikala *veshams,* very few of the ritual *pongal* offerings, and none of temple-courtyard *bali* or domestic rituals. The increasing numbers of *jatara* participants who don't know the goddess as the unique *ugra* Gangamma—that is, who participate in what we might call the "exterior" of the *jatara*—are likely to create and reflect quite different possibilities than those imagined by traditional celebrants who belong to Tirupati *uru.* The subtleties of the necessity to carefully calibrate Gangamma's *ugram* and *shantam,* as well as the gender debate internal to her narratives, are likely to be lost. The future of the *jatara* itself is not in question: crowds are growing, substantial income is being generated, and the Devasthanam has taken over its administration and publicity. However, *what* exactly is being continued is open for question. With rapidly shifting aesthetics, rituals, and clientele, will (or for how long will) Gangamma remain who she is—an *ugra gramadevata* who is "too much to bear" and whose narratives and rituals offer a range of alternative gender possibilities?

Glossary

abhishekam (*abhiṣekam*) ritual anointing of image of deity with series of various liquids
Acari (*ācāri*) artisan caste; goldsmiths, blacksmiths, carpenters
acarya (*ācārya*) spiritual leader or guide
adiparashakti (*ādiparaśakti*) first, supreme power; as proper noun, Adi Para Shakti, name of goddess
agama (*āgama*) texts on religious rites
ahankaram (*ahaṅkāram*) pride
akarshana (*ākarṣaṇa*) attraction
akka elder sister
alankara (*alaṅkāram*) ornament, decoration
ambali mixture of cooling yogurt, heating raw onions, and cooked millet
amma mother; suffix to female name
ammavaru (*ammavāru*) goddess; also poxes and rashes associated with Seven Sister goddesses
ananda (*ānandam*) joy; delight; bliss
angapradakshina (*aṅgapradakṣiṇam*) circumambulation by rolling the body over and over
antastu position, status, social rank
archana temple ritual; *puja* offering made by priest on behalf of worshipper
Asadi (*āsādi*) a subcaste of ritual specialists/priests from Madiga caste; particularly, professional singer of goddess's narrative
atma (*ātma*) soul, life
avatara (*avatāram*) incarnation
avedana (*āvedana*) anguish

bairagi (*bairāgi*) mendicant
bali animal sacrifice
Balija trader caste
banda (*baṇḍa*) ruffian
banka (*baṅka*) sap of tree; gooey substance

bhakta devotee
bhakti devotion
bharincu to bear
bhayankar fearful, dreadful
bhogam pleasure
bijaksharam (*bījākṣaram*) lit., seed syllable; sacred incantation
bottu (*bŏṭṭu*) auspicious forehead marking
brahmotsavam seven-day temple festival
buddhi intelligence; disposition
butulu (*būtulu*) obscenities

Cakali (*cākali*) washermen caste
cakrabandhanam lit., binding circle; ritual marking of boundaries of *uru* by sprinkling blood-rice to start *jatara*
cancal moving; quick; active; unstable; fickle
caritra account; long story; biography
catimpu (*cāṭimpu*) announcement made by village drummer by beating his drum
cinna small; young

darshan (*darśanam*) sight; taking sight of a deity
devasthanam (*devasthānam*) temple trust board
devata goddess
deyyam evil spirit
dhairyam courage
dharmakarta trustee; temple manager
dharma (*dharmam*) code of conduct; social order
dikku direction; protection; refuge
dipam (*dīpam*) lamp; oil lamp
dishti (*diṣṭi*) evil eye
dora (*dŏra*) ruler; lord; prince
doshi (*doṣi*) guilty
dunnapotu male buffalo
dupatta (*dupaṭṭā*) woman's scarf
droham betrayal, treachery

eme informal vocative addressed to women

garbhagriha (*garbhagṛham*) inner part of the temple where main deity is located (lit., womb room)
garega bamboo temple-shaped structure, tied atop a devotee's head
gopuram temple tower/gate

grama munsif (*grāma munsif*) village headman
gramadevata (*grāmadevata*) village goddess
gunam (*guṇam*) quality, character
gunta (*guṇṭa*) pond; low-lying area
gunjilu (*gunjīlu*) deep knee-bend, with arms crossed in front of chest and holding ears; gesture offering respect to or asking forgiveness of a deity

harati (*hārati*) flame offering to deity
homam fire sacrifice
hundi (*huṇḍī*) money box at temple

idli (*iḍlī*) steamed rice cake

jadu (*jādū*) magic; spell
jatara (*jātara*) village festival
jiva (*jīvanam*) life, existence
jyotish (*jyotiṣkuḍu*) astrologer

Kaikala (*kaikāla*) caste of weavers
kalasham (*kalaśam*) water pot
Kali Yuga (*kali yugam*) last of the four ages of the world; the age in which we live
kama (*kāmam*) desire
kanya girl; virgin
kashi tirtham (*kāśī tīrtham*) holy water from the Ganga River
kashtam (*kaṣṭam*) difficulty
kanti cupu (*kaṇṭi cūpu*) glance; gaze
katha story
kavacam metallic covering for the stone image of a deity (lit., armor)
kodistambha (*koḍistambham*) temple pillar that becomes goddess during *jatara*
kopam anger
korika desire
kshatriya (*kṣatriya*) warrior caste level (*varṇa*)
kulam caste
kumbhabhishekam (*kumbhābhiṣekam*) consecration by ritually pouring pots of water over object
kumbham water pot; heap of cooked rice
kumkum vermillion

lanjarikam (*lañjarikam*) prostitution
linga (*liṅgam*) form of Shiva
loka (*lokam*) world; realm

madi (*maḍi*) state of ritual purity
mala (*māla*) rosary; garland
manas (*mānasam*) mind, heart
mandapam (*maṇḍapam*) pillared pavilion outside temple
mangalsutra (*maṅgalsūtra*) wedding necklace
mantra (*mantram*) incantation; sacred verse
mantrakaran (*mantrakāran*, Tamil) one who manipulates or performs *mantras*
marhai (*maṛhai*) fair (Chhattisgarhi)
matamma (*mātamma*) woman who has exchanged a *tali* with the goddess
mirasi (*mirāsī*) hereditary right for service
mirasidar (*mirāsīdār*) one who holds *mirasi*
mokku (*mŏkku*) vow
moksha (*mokṣam*) salvation; liberation of soul
Mudaliar caste name
muggu; maila muggu auspicious geometric or floral design made of rice flour; *muggu* to deflect inauspiciousness
mukti release; salvation
muttaiduva auspicious woman

nadi vidhi (*naḍi vīdhi*) middle-of-street
naga dosham (*nāga doṣam*) snake blemish, caused by position of astrological bodies
nagasvaram (*nāgasvaram*) reed instrument
namaskaram (*namaskāram*) salutation
nammakam trust; faith; confidence
naraka hell
natakam (*nāṭakam*) play
Natyashastra (*nātyaśāstra*) sage Bharata's classical text of dramaturgy and dance
nawab (*navābu*) local Muslim ruler; ruler
navagrahas (*navagrahālu*) nine planets
Navaratri (*navarātri*) festival of Nine Nights of the Goddess
neem (*nīm*) margosa tree
nityasumangali (*nityasumaṅgali*) ever-auspicious woman
nurugu foam; ocean surf

ori informal vocative for males

palegadu (*pālĕgāḍu*) local chieftain
Pambala professional, scheduled-caste Mala drummer/storyteller
pancamritam (*pancāmṛtam*) lit., five nectars; mixture of milk, yogurt, clarified butter, sugar, and honey
panchayat (*pancāyati*) village council

pandal (*paṇḍāl*) pavilion
panduga (*paṇḍuga*) festival
pap (*pāpam*) sin
parihasam (*parihāsam*) ridicule, derision
pariksha (*parīkṣa*) test
pasupu turmeric
peddamma (*pĕddamma*) mother's elder sister or father's elder brother's wife
pelli (*pĕḷḷi*) marriage
perantalu (*peranṭālu*) auspicious (married) woman
perantam (*peranṭam*) visit of *perantalu* to another woman's house on auspicious occasion
picci mad; crazy (Tamil: *paityam;* Hindi: *pāgal*)
pitham (*pīṭham*) seat; low stool
pongal (*pŏṅgal*) cooked rice and lentils
pracarak (*pracārak*) publicist; temple employee
pralayam (*praḷayam*) storm; destruction; calamity
prasad (*prasādam*) food offered to deity and redistributed to worshippers
puja (*pūjā*) worship; specifically, through offerings to deity
pujari (*pūjāri*) temple priest
pulangi (*pūlaṅgi*) lit., garment of flowers; ritual of flower offering to deity
punakam (*pūnakam*) possession by deity or spirit
punyam (*puṇyam*) virtue; merit
purana (*purāṇam*) lit., old story; legend; myth
purana pandit/pandita (*purāṇa paṇḍit/paṇḍita*) male/female scholar of *puranas*
purohit family priest

ragi (*rāgi*) millet; yogurt-millet mixture
raja (*rājā*) king
rangoli (*raṅgoli*) auspicious geometric or floral design made of rice flour
rasa aesthetic emotion
rudraksha (*rudrākṣa*) seed of *rudraksha* tree, used as rosary bead
rupam (*rūpam*) shape; form

sahasa (*sāhasa*) bold; courageous
sahasam (*sāhasam*) boldness; courage
sahasranama (*sahasranāmālu*) the thousand names of a deity
sambandham connection
samanam (*samānam*) equal
sambhogam sexual union
samsara (*samsāram*) worldly life
samskriti (*samskṛti*) culture

santosha (*santoṣa*) happy; satisfied
santosham (*santoṣam*) joy; happiness; satisfaction
sati chaste woman
satvika (*sātvika*) gentle; peaceful
satyamaina talli goddess who shows truth
seva service; worship
shakti (*śakti*) power; female power
shaktisvarupini (*śaktisvarūpini*) she whose form is *shakti*
shanta (*śānta*) tranquil; pacified
shastra (*śāstram*) sacred text
shrap (*śrāp; śāp*) curse
sharanam (*śaraṇam; śaraṇyam*) protection; shelter; surrender
shloka (*ślokam*) verse; stanza in Sanskrit
shringar (*śṛṅgāram*) ornament; decoration
Shudra (*śudra*) low caste
shulam (*śūlam*) trident
shila (*śila*) stone
sristi (*sṛṣṭi*) creation
stri (*strī*) woman
sukha happy; joyful
sunnapukundalu (*sunnapukuṇḍalu*) lime pots
svabhavam (*svabhāvam*) personal nature; personal quality
svarupam (*svarūpam*) shape; form

talapatralu (*tāḷapatrālu*) palm-leaf manuscripts
tali (*tāḷi*) marriage pendant
talli mother
tambulam (*tāmbūlam*) betel leaf and areca nut; ritual gift
tapas (*tapassu*) austerity; penance
toranam; makara toranam (*toraṇam*) brass arch behind temple deity
tipi (*tīpi*) sweetness; fondness
Trimurti (*trimūrtulu*) trinity of three gods: Brahma, Vishnu, and Shiva
trishul (*triśūlam*) trident

ugra excessive; ferocious
ugra mukhi goddess with fierce face
ugram excessiveness; ferocity
unjal seva (*uñjal seva*) ritual of swinging the deity
uru (*ūru*) village; town; city; home place
utsava murti (*utsava mūrti*) festival (processional) image of deity

vairagyam (*vairāgyam*) detachment; renunciation
vamsha (*vamśam*) lineage
vayanam (*vāyanam*) female ritual gift
vesham (*veṣam*) guise
veyyi kalla dutta (*vĕyyi kaḷḷa dutta*) "thousand-eyed" clay pot
vibhuti (*vibhūti*) sacred ash
vimanam (*vimānam*) tower over inner sanctum of temple
vishvarupam (*viśvarūpam*) true form; cosmic form
vodivalu (vo*ḍivālu*) lit., lap-rice, tied to waist of bride

yajna (*yajña*) ritual sacrifice

Notes

Introduction

1. A comparative vision of masculinity embracing a female component can be seen in the iconography of Shiva as Ardhanarishvara (lit., the lord who is half woman). For further discussion of Ardhanarishvara, see Goldberg 2002.

2. Left- and right-hand castes are not indigenously identified as such in Telugu, as they are in Tamil; however, Telugu caste groups share attributes of the Tamil-identified left- and right-hand castes, distinguishing between those castes associated with land and those associated with trade, cash, and mobility (Narayana Rao 1986, 142).

3. Women of left-hand castes traditionally used to wear their sari over their right shoulders, rather than over their left shoulders, as women of right-hand castes do and which has now become the standard style. V. Narayana Rao remembers a proverb that identifies the shift when left-hand-caste women began to wear their saris on their left shoulders: "For the caste, right shoulder; for the public, left shoulder" (oral communication). The proverb suggests that left-hand-caste women wear their saris on the right for ritual, caste purposes; but when they go out into the public, they wear it on the left. Even Gangamma seems to have made the shift, and at least her two Tirupati temple images wear the sari on the left shoulder.

4. These Seven Sisters are not coterminous with the Sanskritic *saptamatrikas* (lit. seven mothers) who are often identified as wives of the seven *rishis* and the Pleiades constellation; however, the *saptamatrikas* share some of the qualities of the *gramadevata* Seven Sisters, such as "afflicting a fetus or child with disease or death" (Knipe 2005a, 322). Charles Nuckolls reports a reversed configuration of siblings in an Andhra coastal fishing village, where the *gramadevata* Ramanamma is the only sister of seven brothers (1993). The motif of many brothers and a single sister is common in Indian folklore, more generally (see, for example, "The Song of Subanbali" in Flueckiger 1996).

5. In a nearby village, the names listed by a Gangamma ritual specialist shifted slightly: Gangamma, Mutyalamma, Ankalamma, Yerallamma, Okalamma, Pokalamma, and Matamma. A Golla priest at the Tirupati Dhanakonda Gangamma temple distinguished the Sisters by the geographic range of their protection: "Tirupati is protected

by four: The first is Pedda Gangamma. No, actually, it's Ankalamma, that *mahatalli* [lit., great mother] is our village *gramadevata.* Second is Pedda Gangamma. She's just behind her. Then there's Veshalamma. Mutyalamma is in Giripuram. And then this one [Dhanakonda Gangamma]. For Ankalamma the railway station is the boundary [*hadu*]. For Veshalamma it's from there to Balaji Nagar—you know, that's on university road. From there to near the hill where we go up to Swamy [Venkateshvara], that's Mutyalamma *hadu.* For this goddess [Dhanakonda Gangamma], from here to municipal office is her *hadu.* These four protect us." Note that the goddesses are both boundary *and* neighborhood goddesses.

6. For example, the Gangamma who is the caste deity of the Gollas (whose "true" form is coiled jute ropes housed in a trunk) here in Tirupati is considered to be both independent of *and* one of the Gangamma sisters.

7. In Tamil Nadu, the most well-known of the sisters is Mariamma, who has eclipsed her lesser-known sisters; similarly, in Karnataka, Yellamma is the most important of the sisters.

8. Rigveda 10.90 similarly describes Purusha, the primordial man, with a thousand eyes—as well as a thousand heads and feet—imagery that imagines Purusha as pervading the universe before being sacrificed for the creation of the physical and social worlds.

9. This distinction is visible in the difference between the *jatara ugra mukhis* built in front of each sister's temple: Cinna Gangamma's *ugra mukhi* bares its teeth, whereas Pedda Gangamma's open mouth shows no teeth. Their distinction also provides an explanation for why Cinnamma's temple is the primary site of the *jatara;* she is the sister whose *ugram* must be most carefully calibrated and managed.

10. Venkateshvarlu explained in another conversation that Pedda Gangamma was brought to Tirupati in the fifteenth century by the poet Annamacarya from his village of Tallapaka. Cinna Gangamma came in the sixteenth century to observe Pedda Gangamma's *jatara;* she had intended to stay for just four days, but ended up never leaving.

11. Various spellings of Potu Raju are Pota Raju and (Tamil) Pottu Raja. I thank Don Handelman for our conversations over the years about the identity and nature of Potu Raju.

12. Hiltebeitel describes a similar, red-faced, sword- and head-holding wooden Potu Raju image in Tamil Draupadi festivals, where he leads the festival procession and is described as Draupadi's chief guardian and army leader (1991:48 and 82). The head he holds in this Tamil context is said to be that of his father, whom he has beheaded (107). In Tamil contexts, Potu Raju has a narrative, whereas in Tirupati, while he is integrated into Gangamma *ritual,* he is not a part of any of her narratives. This is not true of all Telugu Potu Rajus, however; for example, he is a narrative player in the Telugu Golla oral epic of Katamaraju, in which he is a brother to the goddess Ganga and a guardian of her territory (Narayana Rao 1989).

13. In reading a draft of this introduction, Paul Courtright insightfully observed, "Only a male secure in his male-ness can do a proper job of becoming a woman."

14. Several media accounts (including local newspapers and websites such as Nrityanjali Academy, www.nrityanjali.org/fd_mbonalu.asp [accessed January 21, 2011]) report that the festival was inaugurated in 1869 when an epidemic of plague broke out in Hyderabad. Bonalu thus shares many characteristics of other Seven Sister *jataras* elsewhere in Andhra.

15. Like the movement of Gangamma *jatara* from village to village, Bonalu, too, moves from neighborhood to neighborhood in Hyderabad, starting at Golconda, progressing through various neighborhoods to the Mahakali temple in Secunderabad.

16. Venkateshvarlu, whose family has the *mirasi* of Tallapaka temple, told us that it used to be a "requirement" of all pilgrims that they should first visit Gangamma, and then go uphill. However, this is a custom long lost.

17. This relationship is outside of the system of Seven Sisters and Potu Raju; that is, I have never heard Venkateshvara being called a brother to Potu Raju.

18. Narratively, Parvati often lived separately from her husband Shiva when he left home for long periods of time to practice asceticism. The exceptional case of Padmavati and Venkateshvara is their separation in their temple residences.

19. At the bottom of the footpath going uphill is a temple whose main image is the feet of the god. Pilgrims here place a pair of brass sandals on their heads as they circumambulate the god's feet, showing humility toward the god as well as performing an embodiment and reminder of this distance covered nightly by the god, as he visits his wife.

20. In *Fierce* Gods: *Inequality, Ritual and the Politics of Dignity in a South Indian Village* (2005), Diane Mines distinguishes three levels of deities in the Tamil village in which she worked: brahminical gods, village goddesses, and fierce gods. She characterizes the fierce gods as sharing features of mixed ancestry, a violent death, and their place as village guardians (185). This ferocity would seem to be distinct from the *ugram* that characterizes Gangamma, although both powers are excessive.

21. See Amy Allocco 2009 for descriptions of similar *gramadevatas* become neighborhood goddesses in Chennai.

1. An Aesthetics of Excess

1. This sense of artificiality of the "whole" is similar to that of Indian oral epics, which are traditionally performed episodically, not from beginning to end. The whole appears only in the text created by scholars who have asked singers to sing from "beginning to end," and, in a more general sense, in the imaginations of audiences and performers—but not in performance (Flueckiger and Sears 1991).

2. Telugu distinguishes between locally performed *jataras* and pan-Telugu/pan-Indian *pandugas,* such as Ugadi or Navaratri. Chhattisgarhi has similar distinctions

between the uniquely Chhattisgarhi *marhais* and *melas* and pan-Indian festivals, such as Divali, called *tyohars*.

3. After I had settled on the phrase "aesthetics of excess" to think about the ways in which the multiplicity of *jatara* rituals created and satisfied the *ugram* of the goddess, I came across two books with similar or identical titles: Rohan Bastin's *The Domain of Constant Excess: Plural Worship at the Munnesvaram Temples in Sri Lanka* (2002) and *The Aesthetics of Excess* by Allen Weiss (1989). Bastin uses the term "excess" to characterize the plurality of rituals and clientele at the temple complex of Munnesvaram. Here, excess produces power and possibility, but not specifically power that threatens to overflow its boundaries if left untended, as does *ugram*. Weiss's collection of essays examines the relationship between language, speech, silence, and passion/desire within the context of western literary and aesthetic traditions. "The risk in speaking," Weiss asserts, "is due to the fact that the linguistic system far surpasses the limits of our expression: language is the *space of excess* of our speech" (my italics; x). While there are some resonances between the ways in which Bastin and Weiss employ the term "excess" and *ugram*, I use the term specifically as it is performed in Gangamma traditions.

4. See Dennis McGilvray's photo essay *Symbolic Heat: Gender, Health and Worship Among the Tamils of South India and Sri Lanka* (1998) for a discussion of the range of material culture and rituals through which this balance between heating and cooling is performed in Tamil Hindu culture.

5. In fact, the preferences of the goddess seem to be widely known. I wanted to gift the goddess a sari the first year I attended the *jatara* in 1992. When I told the shopkeeper for whom I was buying a sari, he knew just what I needed and pulled out a range of maroon, green, and gold colored cotton saris with gold threads.

6. Handelman notes (citing Elmore 1984, 22–26) that the Matangi has been said to be the incarnation of the goddess Ellamma, who ritually absorbs the impurities of the *uru* (1995:305 and 308). However, this meaning is seemingly lost or has never been present to most contemporary *jatara* participants, as I never heard this identification to my questions about the Matangi.

7. The verses of several such *butulu* are found in Srinivasalu Reddy's book (in Telugu) on Gangamma *jatara* (1995); and while my fieldwork associate K. Vimala and I translated several of them, I've chosen not to reproduce them here, since, quite honestly, I do not have sufficient linguistic skills to interpret how these verses may be received or experienced today or what they may have "meant" in earlier times before the middle-class lens through which they are interpreted today became so dominant. Since I am most interested in contemporary experience, more important than their specifics are the reputation these songs have, especially since knowledge of the words seems to be fading among *jatara* participants themselves.

8. Overflowing *pongal* pots of the festival of the same name "perform" the abundance of the winter harvest that the festival celebrates.

2. Guising, Transformation, Recognition, and Possibility

1. David Knipe quotes a Telugu female ritual specialist identifying lice with the goddess herself, when she comes to her in this form exclusively during the Navaratri festival: "All the goddesses are there . . . dancing violently in my hair. . . . They drop continuously from my hair. They should never be crushed!" (Knipe 2001, 351).

2. For quite a different purpose, Vishnu takes on animal and human *veshams* in his ten *avataras,* through which he (literally) "descends" in order to be active in the world and restore *dharma.*

3. The term and ritual of *abhishekam* is not traditionally associated with the Seven Sisters and is an indication of the introduction of Sanskritic rituals to the two Gangamma temples in Tirupati. However, Gangamma's village sisters, too, wear the *pasupu* mask.

4. *Pasupu* is applied to the bodies of South Indian brides as part of the ritual sequence that is called "making a bride," which (grammatically) implies that, quite literally, the identity of the unmarried "girl" is transformed into a bride through *pasupu.* Grooms also often have *pasupu* applied to them prior to the wedding, one of the rare occasions when *pasupu* is applied to men.

5. There are, of course, exceptions to this generalization. For example, the goddess Sri Parvathavardhini in the Shiva temple of the Hindu Temple of Atlanta is periodically given a sandal-powder (often a substitute for *pasupu*) "mask." A priest explained that while *pasupu* is "required" for *gramadevatas,* it is optional for goddesses whose service is regulated by Sanskrit textual proscriptions; he said sandal powder is, on occasion, smoothed over Sri Parvathavardhini's face "only to make her look beautiful."

6. See Kamath 2012 for a comparison of *stri vesham* in Kuchipudi dance and western drag performance contexts and the implications of these performances on concepts of gender in their respective cultural contexts.

7. I thank V. Narayana Rao for this observation.

8. This is in contrast to *hijras* (transvestites) who dress and identify as female and practice a range of sexualities (see Reddy 2005). In the *jatara* context, lay *stri veshams* provide performative commentary on gender, not sexual practice, following Judith Butler's observation that, "the performance of gender subversion can indicate nothing about sexuality or sexual practice" (1999, xiv).

9. Some *jatara* participants also take animal (particularly tiger) and mythological *veshams.* Participants whom I asked about these kinds of *veshams* explained that they were only for *fun*, rather than the culmination of a vow, as are *stri veshams.*

10. I thank Gangadhar for taking the time to find the tea stall and its owner.

11. I went to several photography studios to ask if they had old pictures of *stri veshams,* hoping to observe changes in sari styles and poses; however, none of them had such old photographs nor could their proprietors speculate when this custom of taking formal portraits of *veshams* had begun.

12. Sandalpaste (*candan*) and *pasupu* are interchangeable in these ritual contexts, sandalpaste being the more expensive substance.

13. Patrick Olivelle characterizes matted hair in South Asia as symbolizing an individual's withdrawal from "social living but not necessarily from social geography" (1998:23).

14. It is noteworthy that some Tirupati residents say that Venkateshvara's *jada* (which is not visible to pilgrims taking his *darshan*) is actually a woman's braid/bun, a trace of his original female identity (Peta Srinivasulu Reddy, oral communication).

15. Lucinda Ramberg has analyzed the "medicalization" by reformists of the matted locks of women dedicated to Yellamma (2009). In this context, as in that of Gangamma, the matted hair is understood to be a manifestation of the goddess. Ramberg suggests that the reformists' efforts to cut the matted locks are an "effort to remake the body as a fit site and sign of modernity" (501), remaking the bodies of the *devadasis* into subjects of the modern nation and undermining their ritual/religious identities.

3. Narratives of Excess and Access

1. Specifically, Subbarama Reddy organizes and participates in the exchange of bride's gifts (*pasupu-kumkum*) with the Kaikala family of Tirupati when the *jatara* moves from Avilala to Tirupati (the Kaikala family at that point represents the groom's family, although, importantly, it's not entirely clear who the groom is). See chapter 6 for a fuller description and analysis of Subbarama's ritual relationships with the goddess.

2. This pairing is an interesting reversal of elder and younger siblings as compared to the Gangamma sisters. In the case of the sisters, the elder has children and the younger does not.

3. *Nawab* is one term for local ruler; other versions of this story identify the local ruler as the Palegadu, or simply the king/*raja*.

4. Mention of this stone is also found in the Avilala lay women's variant of the narrative; it is a specific localization of the narrative, as the stone is still visible today.

5. Note that the narrator rarely calls the goddess by her name, Gangamma, in this narrative, but simply refers to her as "she." SR's wife once told me that she herself doesn't say the name of Gangamma out loud because of her experience of becoming possessed by the goddess when she does so; and she doesn't want to become possessed just "any time."

6. Other versions narrate that her *vishvarupam* is displayed specifically as the couple rounds the sacred wedding fire, but before the ritual is completed, which would have fully solemnized the marriage.

7. This reference to the Sunnapukundalu and Perantalu does not comply with the ritual enactment of the narrative, since these *veshams follow* that of the Dora, Gangamma's *vesham* form in which she finds and beheads the Palegadu. In the ritual *jatara vesham* sequence, the Sunnapukundalu and Perantalu are Gangamma unguised, as she appears after she finds and kills the Palegadu.

8. This narration itself seems to call the goddess to be present—through possession—much as Subbarama's wife told me simply saying her name does so. Aftab Jassal (Emory University) is writing a dissertation on the Garhwali tradition of *jagar*, in which he argues that the narratives performed during *jagar* bring the deity "here" and the audience members into narrative time—a juncture that results in the deity possessing ritual participants.

9. While Vivekananda, a Hindu reformist who traveled widely—including speaking at the World Parliament of Religions in Chicago, 1893—was born and based in Bengal (1863–1902), he has recently become more popular in Andhra. The reference here is likely not Vivekananda-specific, but rather stands as a reference for a well-known spiritual authority. The narrator, Subbarama, is literate and familiar with both local and pan-Indian religious traditions; his reference to Vivekananda may be a (conscious or unconscious) "display" of that knowledge.

10. *Jataras* in other regions, involving other local configurations of sisters, may also have uniquely local *caritras* of the primary goddess, such as the Paiditalli festival analyzed by Handelman, Krishnayya, and Shulman (ms.).

11. In fact, more generally, most folksongs and folk narratives take the position of the daughter, rather than daughter-in-law; they may sing in third-person *about* the daughter-in-law, but first-person experience is that of the daughter (even as she may be describing her mistreatment as a daughter-in-law). See Flueckiger 1996, "Land of Wealth, Land of Famine: the 'Parrot Dance' in Ritual and Narrative" (chapter 4) and "*Pandvani* Heroines, Chhattisgarhi Daughters" (chapter 7) for discussion of oral traditions that take the position of daughters.

12. Answering such specific questions with a story was typical of many of my interactions with *jatara* participants.

13. "Amma" literally means "mother"; however, all females may be addressed in Telugu as "Amma," even little girls.

14. Another well-known narrative episode depicting the insult of a male grabbing hold of a woman's hair, with which the narrators of the Palegadu–Gangamma story would be familiar, is the Mahabharata incident in which the Pandava brother Yudhishthira has lost his kingdom and his brothers' and his own freedom in dicing against his Kaurava cousin-brothers. He is prodded on to stake the only thing he has left, his wife, Draupadi. The Kaurava brother Dushasana, at the command of his elder brother Duryodhana, goes to the women's quarters and grabs Draupadi by the hair and drags her to the court where her husband has staked her—and loses her—in dicing. After further humiliation, when Duryodhana taunts and attempts to disrobe Draupadi, she takes a vow that she will not wash or oil her hair until she can wash it in Dushasana's blood.

15. Pambalas are identified as a Backward Caste according to the Government of India schedule of castes. K. Jayaram, a Pambala drummer currently working as an employee of Tattaiahgunta Devasthanam recalled how his family came to have the *mirasi* to perform at Gangamma *jatara:* seventy years ago, in the time of Jayaram's

great-great-grandfather, the Tirupati Municipal Chairman held a competition among various families of Pambalas to determine who would be granted the *mirasi*. The test was to see who could make the goddess speak. When Jayaram's ancestor called to the goddess, she answered, "What do you want, grandchild?" Since then, this Pambala family has had the *jatara mirasi*, which includes the right to both drum and claim a portion of the income generated during the *jatara*.

16. Ann Gold relates a Rajasthani variant of the Adi Para Shakti story in which Shiva asks for the goddess's third eye (unstated, but implied as a portion of her power) and that she revive Brahma and Vishnu, whom she has beheaded for their refusal to marry her. Even then, as in the Tirupati variant, Shiva refuses to have sex with her. However, this attenuated version does not give motivation to his refusal; he's simply "annoyed" at her repeated demands for sex. Finally, he cuts off his penis and throws it up in the air; and the goddess spreads out her vagina to catch it as it falls to earth. The conclusion connotes "marriage," as other childless couples worship the now-united *linga* and *yoni* (Shiva and Parvati) and are granted fertility (Gold 1994, 32–33). The implicit superiority of the goddess's *shakti* is seemingly resolved without the lingering tension of unequal partners that necessitates *bali* or fragmentation of the goddess in Tirupati variants.

4. Female-Narrated Possibilities of Relationship

1. See Dell Hymes's distinction between performed and reported rhetoric in "Breakthrough Into Performance" (1975).

2. See Flueckiger 2010 for a short essay, "Limits of Ethnography," in which I identify the serendipitous nature of fieldwork as both a joy and potential limitation of ethnography.

3. Karanams are traditionally Brahman village accountants; however, here, it must be a reference to another caste, since Sumati is not a Brahman.

4. *Junnu* is made from a cow's milk produced in the first three days after she gives birth.

5. The word of abuse here is *vedava*, a variation of the Sanskrit *vidhava* (widow). In Telugu, it is a term of abuse when addressed to a male.

6. This is the only narrative variant I heard that mentions the drum that is (subsequently) associated with Shiva.

7. See Wendy Doniger's translation of the entire episode in *Hindu Myths* (1975:77–85), as well as other variants of the myth from the Rig Veda and elsewhere in the Mahabharata.

5. Gangamma as Ganga River Goddess

1. I later observed that her shawl was a marker of her role and status, part of her *purana pandita vesham*, so to speak.

2. The Annamacarya Project seeks to preserve, propagate, and teach performance of the songs of the fifteenth-century poet Annamacarya; the organization sponsors musician training, Annamacarya festivals, and research into the life and works of the poet. The project is housed in a building in Tirupati that has a large performance hall, where Annapurna was tested.

3. It is typical for a woman to continue to wear her *tali,* even if separated from her husband, until either divorce or his death. The *tali* is (traditionally) a sign of a woman's auspicious married status, not the quality her relationship with her husband.

4. Ongole is a coastal Andhra town.

5. While public performance is relatively rare for a Brahman woman, Telugu women of other castes do perform publicly in genres such as *hari katha.*

6. It's unclear whether or not she was living at her father's place at that time; if so, perhaps at his death, she no longer felt welcome in the home, to be dependent on her brothers. Again, there is no mention of her mother at this point and it's unclear whether or not she was living.

7. See DeNapoli (2013) for a study of Hindu female *sadhus* in Rajasthan, some of whom also lead, on some levels, a householder's life, with home and children.

8. In a celebration of the female vow ritual of Varalakshmi Puja in an Andhra village, after listing the names of the eight Lakshmis (goddess of wealth and prosperity), a woman identified Dhairya Lakshmi, Lakshmi of courage, to be the most important for women.

9. While several scholars of India have interpreted female jewelry as binding (myself included; Flueckiger 1996, 72–79), this is the first time I have heard a Hindu woman articulate this concept so directly. More frequently, the women I have worked with over the years have expressed their experience of ornamentation to be protective and a marking of their auspiciousness.

10. The performance of *tapas* and the power it generates creates instability in the world and is potentially dangerous, so the god asks what Bhagiratha wants that will cause him to stop his ascetic practices.

11. Candika, Gaumati, Durga, Kali, and Mahakali are not traditional *gramadevata* goddesses, whereas Gangamma and Mariamma are.

6. Wandering Goddess, Village Daughter

1. Four sisters of the Seven Sisters on the boundaries of Avilala are identified as Pedda Gangamma, Ankalamma, and Mutyalamma, and Pokalamma—one sister on each of the four directions of the *uru.* Mutyalamma and Pokalamma live in small permanent stone temples.

2. Gangamma takes other kinds of "middle-of-the-street" forms in other villages, some of which are a large rectangular stone with a rounded smaller stone in front (her brother Potu Raju), or simply an empty platform to which a wooden image of Gangamma is brought from a village-edge temple.

3. During Kartik Purnima (festival of Kartik-month full moon), while Gangamma is not the center of ritual activity, the village women who walk to the tank at the edge of the village to set oil lamps in the water stop at the small Gangamma stone on their way.

4. Elmore (1913) and Whitehead (1921) record details of the *bali* strikingly similar to what I witnessed in Avilala: the fat from entrails spread over buffalo eyes; the foreleg in the mouth, the lamp placed on the head.

5. Subba Reddy (1993:92–93) writes that the villagers he observed offering *jatara bali* to the *gramadevata* Poleramma, in Nelore District, told him that the buffalo head becomes too powerful, threatening to devour the village or scorch it with its gaze. Hence, the foreleg is put in its mouth and a layer of fat is placed over the eyes.

6. SR is the only narrator or commentator of Gangamma traditions who mentions Ayodhya as Gangamma's place of origin. In his narration of the Asadi story found in Peta Srinivasulu Reddy's book (Reddy 2007:26), he says the reason Gangamma came to Andhra was that temples were being destroyed by the *nawabs* in Ayodhya; this detail is not in the story he told me.

7. Harijan is a relatively new word for those castes that were formerly known by upper castes as untouchables. In most traditional Telugu contexts, the specific caste names Madigas and Malas are used rather than Harijans. The use of the term Harijan may indicate SR's socialization in more upper-caste, literate contexts, such as those in which he works and his connections with the Tirumala Tirupati Devasthanam (TTD). I have never heard the more politicized word "Dalit" in Gangamma-related conversations.

8. *Jala-jala-jala* is an onomatopoetic phrase most often used to describe moving water; it may not be coincidental that this phrase is used for a moving Gangamma, who is associated with the river goddess Ganga (Narayana Rao, oral communication).

9. These three narratives are the primary narratives of Gangamma in Avilala; I did not hear the Asadi narrative performed in Tirupati. Interestingly, SR did not perform in this sequence any segment of the other significant narrative performed in Gangamma contexts: that of Adi Para Shakti.

10. SR told us that the wheel engraved on the Gangamma *shila* (stone) in the fields between Avilala and Tirupati, at which the bride's gifts are exchanged, is the wheel of Gangamma's cart that got stuck.

11. One might interpret the sacrifice of the pregnant female as a kind of *purusha sukta* (hymn to the cosmic man, Rig Veda 10.90), in which sacrifice of *purusha* is a creative, not destructive act, one that creates the physical and social worlds themselves (David Shulman, oral communication).

7. Temple and *Vesham Mirasi*

1. Several years later, another pubescent Kaikala boy proudly pulled out a photograph of himself on the occasion of his first *vesham* (as the snake charmer) at the age

of ten. I asked him what he had felt that first time becoming Gangamma. He answered only that to take *vesham* was an honor, and that he had, quite simply, become Gangamma; he offered no emotional descriptors.

2. I subsequently heard this explanation from others in the family, as well as from the Pambala drummers.

3. In 2010, V related the story of how their family came to have the *mirasi* at Govindaraja Swamy temple. Several generations ago (later he specified twelfth century), a matriarch named Thilla Govindamma had had a dream that the god wanted to be moved from Cidambaram (in current Tamil Nadu) to Tirupati, where he could be worshipped more openly. At the time, Cidambaram was under the rule of a Shaivite king who had destroyed many Vaishnava images. She put Govindaraja's small image in a cart and took him to Tirupati. V said that the large image of the god that worshippers can see today was built out of "mud" *over* the small image, the mud being dark shining black from application of oil. The family was given a land grant for their services, land that has since dissipated into the hands of others. While the *mirasi* system has been abolished by the courts, the Kaikalas continue these duties as employees of the Endowments Department.

4. *Devadasis* were known as *nityasumangalis*—ever-auspicious women, since they are married to the god and thus never become "inauspicious" widows. This *nityasumangali* characterization would seem to be shared with the Kaikala female who has the ritual power to send the soul of the Jeeyangar to heaven.

5. That year we ended up buying a sari for the Kaikala-home Gangamma, however, since this was a more traditional gift than the more expensive ornaments Tulasamma had requested.

6. As Narayana Rao and David Shulman report the story (2005:114–115), there was a king Nanda of Nandavaram (today's Kurnool District) who wanted to go north to Banaras everyday to bathe in the Ganga River. A certain *siddha* (*yogi*) gave him magical sandals that transported him there and back every morning. When the king's wife discovered where he went every morning, she wanted to accompany him and they went together. But on their return, the queen's *mantras* that were to have transported her home failed and she got stuck in Banaras. The couple was able to return only with the help of some Banaras Brahmans. In return, the king, in the presence of the goddess Camundeshvari as witness, promised that he would come to their aid whenever needed. However, when the time came that the Brahmans needed the king's help during a famine, he denied that he had made such a promise. The Brahmans called on the goddess Camundeshwari to follow them south from Banaras to bear witness to their claim on the king, and she stayed on there in Nandapuram. A certain Brahman had followed the group of Brahmans going south to make their claim on the king; he subsequently wanted to marry his daughter to one of their sons, a proposal they refused due to their different sub-castes. This rejection caused the Brahman to kill himself and his family. "At this point the goddess—now called Caudesvari—also cursed the Brahmans, who

had caused the death of another Brahman, to live by worldly jobs and to serve as priests for the meat-eating Togata weavers. These Brahmans are the Nandavarikas, from whom the Tallapaka people came" (115).

7. V explained that this whip was made of the same kind of braided hemp that Yadavas/Gollas (whose caste deity is Gangamma) use on festival days to hit themselves with while possessed by Gangamma.

8. Recently, a devotee donated a brass *utsava vigraham* to Tatayyagunta temple; it sits in front of her stone image. But I never saw this form taken in procession or out of the temple for any other ritual.

8. The Goddess Served and Lost

1. I was unsure what was meant by this comparison between the goddess and a movie star; a garish look, I assumed, but exactly how this was understood by local worshippers is unclear to me.

2. *Satya* literally means "truth," but it has deeper connotations of "that which exists."

3. *Peddamma* may refer to a mother's elder sister or father's elder brother's wife. In this context, the reference is to Koteshvaramma's husband's mother's elder sister.

4. I asked this question after having heard from the female temple attendant that only women should serve this *shakti* goddess.

5. See Laurie Patton's work on contemporary women Sanskritists, in which she describes their access to Sanskrit learning (traditionally limited to upper-caste men) to be the result, in part, of men moving into other (more lucrative) professions (2007).

6. The term *dharmakarta* is a term generally used to describe bureaucratic structures of brahminic temples, not those of the more loosely organized temples of *gramadevatas*.

7. Srinivasulu Reddy reports in his book on Gangamma *jatara* that CKR's family took over the responsibilities of Gangamma *puja* at this site from a Kamasali (goldsmith) attendant (1995).

8. CKR names this Reddy (as well as the man whose father was *grama munsif* [village headman]), but since I was not able to interview these Reddy families to hear their side of the story, I have chosen to leave them unnamed.

9. *Rowdy* is a commonly used English word in Telugu everyday speech, used to refer to a troublemaker. In his book on Gangamma *jatara*, P. Srinivasulu Reddy identifies this "rowdy" as his own maternal uncle (1995:30).

10. The philosopher Shankara Acarya (b. 788 CE) is said to have retired to Kanchi and founded the Kanchi Kamakoti Peetham there. Kancipuram is about seventy-five kilometers southwest of Chennai.

11. The Executive Officer named the MLA, but I have chosen not to, since I was unable to speak directly with him.

12. The Devasthanam asked the Mudaliars to leave this silver *kavacam* at the temple when they were evicted, but they did not comply. Koteshvaramma exclaimed,

"When they eject us from the temple, there's no question of giving back the ornaments!" Since then, the Devasthanam has had several different kinds of *kavacams* made for Gangamma, including one of silver, one of brass, and a "jeweled" one.

13. Since these attendants are still serving in the temple, I have not used their names.

14. See Amy Allocco's 2009 dissertation, "Snakes, Goddesses, and Anthills: Modern Challenges and Women's Ritual Responses in Contemporary South India," for a full description of the growing phenomenon of *naga dosham* and its mitigating rituals.

15. A row of tridents does remain, however, under an adjacent *pipal* tree in the back of the temple, where there are also several *naga* snake stones.

16. *Tali* strings are traditionally rubbed with *pasupu* paste to make them yellow; but these are pre-dyed a yellow color.

17. See Tracy Pintchman, ed., *Seeking Mahadevi: Constructing the Identities of the Hindu Great Goddess* (2001) for a collection of essays that addresses the relationship between the "one and the many" goddesses.

9. Exchanging *Talis* with the Goddess

1. An earlier version of this chapter was published as "Wandering from Hills to Valleys with the Goddess: Protection and Freedom in the *Matamma* Tradition of Andhra," in *Women's Lives, Women's Rituals in the Hindu Tradition,* edited by Tracy Pintchman (2007).

2. That an offering of a girl-child is satisfying to her, rather than a male child, reflects the comment made by several men who took female *vesham* during the *jatara,* that men shouldn't appear as men before Gangamma, that she wanted to see women only. A 1998 pamphlet published by an NGO that works with Chittoor District *matammas* lists the following conditions under which they had been offered to the goddess: "fits," failure to open eyes at birth, dehydration, smallpox and chicken pox, infertility of parents, inability to breastfeed, wounds, polio, illness of family members, among others.

3. I am not naming this NGO, and thus also not giving a bibliographic citation for the pamphlet published by them, mentioned in this discussion, so as to preserve its anonymity.

4. See Davesh Soneji's work with living *devadasi* performers/dancers of coastal Andhra (2012, 2004). He is particularly concerned with the ways in which these women, after losing their public performance roles in temples, courts, and the salons of large landowners, sustain their identities through acts of memory and private performance.

5. In 1999–2000, I did not see evidence of the intense governmental or NGO intervention in *matammas* "reform" that Lucinda Ramberg describes among Yellamma's *jogatis* in 2001–2002, when "a thousand such [matted] locks were cut from the heads of Yellamma women. . . ." Ramberg analyzes the "medicalization of matted locks," a process that framed them "as vectors of disease and embodiments of superstition. . . ." (Ramberg 2009:502–503).

6. Pujaramma (lit., the Amma who performs *puja*) was the name this woman frequently used for herself. Veshalamma exchanged talis with Veshalamma Gangamma and took on the name of the goddess. Because of the personal nature of the narratives analyzed in this chapter and the status of *matammas* in contemporary Andhra, I would have chosen pseudonyms except that these names, Pujaramma and Veshalamma, are themselves attributive names, not personal given names, and thus serve as pseudonyms.

7. The fluidity of caste identification is typical of several Gangamma-associated persons I spoke with throughout my fieldwork. For example, another woman who serves Gangamma at a roadside shrine on the outskirts of Tirupati, where the goddess takes the form of sari-ed tridents, first identified herself as a Madiga, and later in the conversation identified as a Vanna Reddy.

8. *Bottus* is plural here, referring both to the forehead marking and the marriage pendant, which is often called a *tali bottu.*

9. A coastal Andhra *devadasi* told Davesh Soneji something almost identical: "We are always in possession of turmeric and kumkum. We do not remove it when our man dies" (2004:42).

10. See Davesh Soneji's *Unfinished Gestures: Devadasis, Memory, and Modernity in South India* (2012) for an excellent discussion of the social and cultural history of a particular community of Andhra coastal courtesans (*devadasis*) as constructed and performed by living women of this tradition.

11. In Indian languages, "jungle" (*jangal*) connotes uninhabited "wild" space, not necessarily forested space. The phrase *konda-kona* (lit., hills and valleys) used by Pujaramma, in describing the spaces in which the goddess compelled her to wander, connotes this kind of *jangli,* uninhabited space.

12. Note the difference between offering the goddess a *tali* as an act of devotion or fulfillment of a vow and offering a *tali* as a *matamma,* when the *matamma* also receives a *tali* from the goddess.

13. In South India, it is very unusual for a Brahman woman to become possessed by the goddess.

14. During the first few days of the *jatara,* young children (boys and girls) also take on this *vesham* of neem-leaf skirts.

15. Some *jatara* participants also put on *garegas* as fulfillment of vows they have made to Gangamma, visiting her temples with this guise on the last day of the *jatara.*

10. "Crazy for the Goddess"

1. I am using the initials of her name as a pseudonym for this devotee. Although she gave permission to tape our conversations, her precarious situation and the ambivalence she expressed about showing me her biography (written by her daughter), as well as her reputation as being "crazy," suggest a pseudonym is appropriate.

2. *Picci* in this context has a similar range of connotations to the Hindi word *pagal.*

3. Traditionally, worshippers bathe before they go to the temple.

4. See Ramanujan (1981:117–121) for a discussion of possession, madness, and devotion in Tamil devotional poetry. He translates a *bhakti* poem by Nammalvar that could be a partial description of MR herself: "Mumbling and prattling / the many names / of our lord of the hill / with cool waterfalls, / long strands of water, / while onlookers say, / "They're crazy . . ." (119).

5. I have inserted many ellipses in MR's conversation, in part, due to her manic speech in which she often shifts from subject to subject and back again, or inserts a random sentence in the middle of a discussion, which makes it difficult to follow her train of thought. Another kind of research project, focusing on an ethnography of speaking, would leave in these seemingly random sentences and analyze their performance. However, for our purposes, their primary effect on those listening to her was to intensify MR's *picci* nature.

6. In 2000, just a few days after MR's eldest daughter's death, when MR was still deeply grieving, she asked her younger daughter to read only two lines of the life story the eldest had written. The younger daughter refused even to come upstairs. MR commented, "They're refusing to read it. Now I'm talking like a mad [Tamil, *paityam*] woman."

7. Ambala Gunta Gangamma identifies a Gangamma who resides at Ambala Gunta (water tank), a tank I have not been able to identify.

8. This line may refer to the devotee having severed family ties in order to be in relationship with the goddess.

9. As of 2011, there were no stylized lithographs of Gangamma available in the bazaars, only photographs of her temple images.

10. This is likely the same actress MR had told us about earlier, who purportedly wanted to portray MR's story through film.

11. This day's entire conversation and interaction with MR was extremely difficult for my fieldwork associate, causing her, she said, to think of her own losses—particularly that of her sister, over whose untimely death (reported as suicide, but suspected by the family to have been murder) the family had had no control. She characterized the feeling she had in that small room as that of being smothered; "I couldn't think." She was unwilling to go back with me to visit MR in her home after this interaction, although she agreed to meet her somewhere else, for example at the temple.

Conclusion

1. I first started thinking about this possibility several years ago, when I read Wynne Maggi's description of the goddess Dezalik, who presides over Kalasha menstrual huts in northwest Pakistan, protecting women and infants residing there. Maggi reports, "I could find no woman who claimed to know myths or stories about Dezalik, and she appears not to have a characterizable personality" (2001:139–149). Women relate to her *only* ritually and only in the menstrual huts.

References

Abu-Lughod, Lila. 1993. *Writing Women's Worlds: Bedouin Stories.* Berkeley: University of California Press.

———. 1990. Can There Be a Feminist Ethnography? *Women and Performance* 5 (1): 7–27.

Akundy, Anand. 2006. Bards and Goddess Festivals: The Pombalas and the Gangamma Jatra of Tirupati. In *Performers and Their Arts: Folk, Popular and Classical Genres in a Changing India,* ed. Simon Charsley and Laxmi Narayan Kadekar, 59–81. New Delhi: Routledge.

Allocco, Amy. 2009. Snakes, Goddesses, and Anthills: Modern Challenges and Women's Ritual Responses in Contemporary South India. Ph.D. diss., Emory University, Atlanta.

Apffel-Marglin, Frederique. 2008. *Rhythms of Life: Enacting the World with the Goddesses of Orissa.* New Delhi: Oxford University Press.

Assayag, Jackie. 1992. *La Colère de la Déesse Decapitée: Traditions, Cultes et Pouvoir dans le Sud de l'Inde.* Paris: CNRS Editions.

Babb, Lawrence. 1975. *The Divine Hierarchy: Popular Hinduism in Central India.* New York: Columbia University Press.

Bastin, Rohan. 2002. *The Domain of Constant Excess: Plural Worship in the Munnesvaram Temples in Sri Lanka.* New York: Berghahn Books.

Beck, Brenda E. F. 1972. *Peasant Society in Konku: A Study of Right and Left Subcastes in South India.* Vancouver: University of British Columbia Press.

Behar, Ruth. 1996. *The Vulnerable Observer: Anthropology That Breaks Your Heart.* Boston: Beacon Press.

Blackburn, Stuart, and Joyce Flueckiger. 1989. Introduction. In *Oral Epics in India,* ed. Stuart Blackburn, Peter Claus, Joyce Flueckiger, and Susan Wadley, 1–14. Berkeley: University of California Press.

Bradford, Nicholas J. 1997. Transgenderism and the Cult of Yellamma: Heat, Sex and Sickness in South Indian Ritual. In *Que(e)rying Religion: A Critical Anthology,* ed. Gary David Comstock and Susan E. Henking, 294–310. New York: Continuum.

Briggs, Charles L. 1988. *Competence in Performance: The Creativity of Tradition in Mexicano Verbal Art.* Philadelphia: University of Pennsylvania Press.

Brubaker, Richard L. 1978. The Ambivalent Mistress: A Study of South Indian Village Goddesses and Their Religious Meaning. Ph.D. diss., University of Chicago, Chicago.

Butler, Judith. 1999 [1990]. *Gender Trouble: Feminism and the Subversion of Identity.* New York: Routledge.

Bynum, Caroline Walker. 1986. " . . . And Woman His Humanity": Female Imagery in the Religious Writing of the Later Middle Ages. In *Gender and Religion: On the Complexity of Symbols,* ed. Caroline Walker Bynum, Stevan Harrell, and Paula Richman, 257–289. Boston: Beacon Press.

Caldwell, Sarah. 2000. *Oh, Terrifying Mother: Sexuality, Violence and Worship of the Goddess Kali.* New Delhi: Oxford University Press.

———. 1996. Bhagavati: Ball of Fire. In *Devi: Goddesses of India,* ed. John S. Hawley and Donna M. Wulff, 195–226. Berkeley: University of California Press.

Carman, John B., and Frederique Apffel Marglin, eds. 1985. *Purity and Auspiciousness in Indian Society.* Leiden: E. J. Brill.

Chitgopekar, Nilima, ed. 2002. *Invoking Goddesses: Gender Politics in Indian Religion.* India: Shakti Books.

Clark, Mary Ann. 2005. *Where Men are Wives and Mothers Rule: Santeria Ritual Practices and Their Gender Implications.* Gainesville: University Press of Florida.

Coleman, Eli, Philip Colgan, and Louis Gooren. 1997. Male Cross-Gender Behavior in Myanmar (Burma): A Description of the Acault. In *Que(e)rying Religion: A Critical Anthology,* ed. Gary David Comstock and Susan E. Henking, 287–293. New York: Continuum Press.

Courtright, Paul B. 2001 [1985]. *Ganesa: Lord of Obstacles, Lord of Beginnings.* Delhi: Motilal Banarsidas Publishers.

Dalrymple, William. 2010. Daughters of Yellama. *Nine Lives: In Search of the Sacred in Modern India,* 56–77. New York: Alfred A. Knopf.

DeNapoli, Antoinette. 2013. *"Real Sadhus Sing to God": Gender, Asceticism, and Vernacular Religion in Rajasthan.* New York: Oxford University Press.

Dimock, Edward. 1986 [1982]. A Theology of the Repulsive: The Myth of the Goddess Sitala. In *The Divine Consort: Radha and the Goddesses of India,* ed. John Stratton Hawley and Donna Wulff, 184–203. Boston: Beacon Press.

Doniger, Wendy. 1999. *Splitting the Difference: Gender and Myth in Ancient Greece and India.* Chicago: University of Chicago Press.

Doniger O'Flaherty, Wendy. 1980. *Women, Androgynes, and Other Mythical Beasts.* Chicago: University of Chicago Press.

———. 1975. *Hindu Myths.* Baltimore: Penguin Books.

Egnor, Margaret. 1991. On the Meaning of Sakti to Women in Tamil Nadu. In *The Powers of Tamil Women,* ed. Susan S. Wadley, 1–34. Syracuse: Maxwell School of Citizenship and Public Affairs, Syracuse University.

———. 1984. The Changed Mother or What the Smallpox Goddess Did When There Was No More Smallpox. *Contributions to Asian Studies* 18: 24–45.

Elmore, Wilbur Theodore. 1984 [1913]. *Dravidian Gods in Modern Hinduism: A Study of the Local and Village Deities of Southern India.* New Delhi: Asian Educational Services.

Erndl, Kathleen. 2001. Goddesses and the Goddess in Hinduism: Constructing the Goddess Through Religious Experience. In *Seeking Mahadevi: Constructing the Identities of the Hindu Great Goddess,* ed. Tracy Pintchman, 199–212. Albany: State University of New York Press.

———. 1993. *Victory to the Mother: The Hindu Goddess of Northwest India in Myth, Ritual, and Symbol.* New York: Oxford University Press.

Ewing, Katherine. 1997. *Arguing Sainthood: Modernity, Psychoanalysis, and Islam.* Durham: Duke University Press.

Feldhaus, Ann. 1995. *Water and Womanhood: Religious Meanings of Rivers in Maharastra.* New York: Oxford University Press.

Flueckiger, Joyce Burkhalter. 2010. Limits of Ethnography: Notes from the Field, in "Ethnography and Theology: A Roundtable Discussion." *Practical Matters: A Transdisciplinary Multimedia Journal of Religious Practices and Practical Theology,* 3: 2–4.

———. 2006. *In Amma's Healing Room: Gender and Vernacular Islam in South India.* Bloomington: Indiana University Press.

———. 2005. Guises, Turmeric, and Recognition in the Gangamma Tradition of Tirupati. In *Incompatible Visions: South Asian Religions in History and Culture. Essays in Honor of David M. Knipe,* ed. James Blumenthal, 35–49. Madison, WI: Center for South Asia, University of Wisconsin–Madison.

Flueckiger, Joyce, and Laurie J. Sears. 1991. Introduction. In *Boundaries of the Text: Performing the Epics in South and Southeast Asia,* ed. Joyce Flueckiger and Laurie Sears, 1–15. South and Southeast Asian Center Publications, University of Michigan.

Foulston, Lynn. 2002. *At the Feet of the Goddess: The Divine Feminine in Local Hindu Religion.* Brighton: Sussex Academic Press.

Gatwood, Lynn E. 1985. *Devi and the Spouse Goddess: Women, Sexuality, and Marriages in India.* Riverdale, CO: Riverdale Co.

Gentes, M. J. 1992. Scandalizing the Goddess at Kodungallur. *Asian Folklore Studies* 51: 295–322.

Gold, Ann Grodzins. 1994. Gender, Violence and Power: Rajasthani Stories of Shakti. In *Women as Subjects: South Asian Histories,* ed. Nita Kumar, 26–48. Charlottesville: University of Virginia Press.

Gold, Ann Grodzins, and Bhoju Ram Gujar. 1992. *In the Time of Trees and Sorrows: Nature, Power, and Memory in Rajasthan.* Durham: Duke University Press.

Goldberg, Ellen. 2002. *The Lord Who is Half Woman: Ardhanarisvara in Indian and Feminist Perspective.* Albany: State University of New York Press.

Hancock, Mary. 1999. *Womanhood in the Making: Domestic Ritual and Public Culture in Urban South India.* Boulder, CO: Westview Press.

Handelman, Don. 1995. The Guises of the Goddess and the Transformation of the Male: Gangamma's Visit to Tirupati and the Continuum of Gender. In *Syllables of Sky,* ed. David Shulman, 283–337. New Delhi: Oxford University Press.

———. 1990. Christmas Mumming in Newfoundland. *Models and Mirrors: Towards An Anthropology of Public Events.* New York: Cambridge University Press.

Handelman, Don, M. V. Krishnayya, and David Shulman. Unpublished manuscript. Growing Kingdom: The Goddess of Depth in Vizianagaram.

Hawley, John Stratton. 1996. Prologue. In *Devi: Goddesses of India,* ed. John Stratton Hawley and Donna Marie Wulff, 1–28. Berkeley: University of California Press.

Hawley, John Stratton, and Donna Marie Wulff, eds. 1986 [1982]. *The Divine Consort: Radha and the Goddesses of India.* Boston: Beacon Press.

Hiltebeitel, Alf. 1998. Hair Like Snakes and Mustached Brides: Crossed Gender in an Indian Folk Cult. In *Hair: Its Power and Meaning in Asia Cultures,* ed. Alf Hiltebeitel and Barbara D. Miller, 143–176. Albany: State University of New York Press.

———. 1991. *The Cult of Draupadi.* Vol. 2. *On Hindu Ritual and the Goddess.* Chicago: University of Chicago Press.

Hiltebeitel, Alf, and Kathleen M. Erndl, eds. 2000. *Is the Goddess a Feminist? The Politics of South Asian Goddesses.* New York: New York University Press.

Hobart, Angela, and Bruce Kapferer. 2005. Introduction: The Aesthetics of Symbolic Construction and Experience. In *Aesthetics in Performance: Formations of Symbolic Construction and Experience,* ed. Angela Hobart and Bruce Kapferer, 1–22. New York: Berghahn Books.

Hymes, Dell. 1975. Breakthrough into Performance. In *Folklore: Performance and Communication,* ed. Dan Ben-Amos and Kenneth S. Goldstein, 11–74. The Hague: Mouton.

Jenett, Dianne. 2005. "Shaktis" Rising: Pongala, a Women's Festival in Kerala, India. *Journal of Feminist Studies in Religion* 21 (1): 35–55.

Jordan, Kay K. 2003. *From Sacred Servant to Profane Prostitute: A History of the Changing Legal Status of the Devadasis of India, 1857–1947.* New Delhi: Manohar.

Kamath, Harshita Mruthini. 2012. Gender Impersonation, Gender Illusion: Aesthetics, Performativity, and Discursivity in South Indian Poetry and Dance Performance. Ph.D. diss., Emory University, Atlanta.

Kapferer, Bruce. 2005. Sorcery and the Beautiful: A Discourse on the Aesthetics of Ritual. In *Aesthetics in Performance: Formations of Symbolic Construction and Experience,* ed. Angela Hobart and Bruce Kapferer, 129–160. New York: Berghahn Books.

———. 1991 [1983]. *A Celebration of Demons: Exorcism and the Aesthetics of Healing in Sri Lanka.* Bloomington: Indiana University Press.

Kersenboom, Saskia C. 1997 [1987]. *Nityasumangali: Devadasi Tradition in South India.* Delhi: Motilal Banarsidass Publishers.

Kinsley, David. 1986. *Hindu Goddesses: Visions of the Divine Feminine in the Hindu Religious Tradition.* Berkeley: University of California Press.

Knipe, David. 2005a. Rivalries Inside Out: Personal History and Possession Ritualism in Coastal Andhra. *Indian Folklore Research Journal* 5: 1–33.

———. 2005b. Devi. *Encyclopedia of India,* Vol. 1, ed. Stanley Wolpert, 319–324. New York: Macmillan.

———. 2001. Balancing Raudra and Santi: Rage and Repose in States of Possession. In *Vidyaanavavandanam: Essays in Honour of Asko Parpola,* ed. K. Karttunen and P. Koskikallio, 343–357. Helsinki: Finnish Oriental Society.

MacDougall, David, and Judith MacDougall, producers. 1991. *Photo Wallahs: An Encounter with Photography in Mussoorie, a North Indian Hill Station.* Berkeley: Berkeley Media.

Maggi, Wynne. 2001. *Our Women Are Free: Gender and Ethnicity in the Hindukush.* Ann Arbor: University of Michigan Press.

Marglin, Frederique Apfell. 1985. *Wives of the God King: The Rituals of the Devadasis of Puri.* New Delhi: Oxford University Press.

McDaniel, June. 2004. *Offering Flowers, Feeding Skulls: Popular Goddess Worship in West Bengal.* New York: Oxford University Press.

McDermott, Rachel Fell. 2003. *Encountering Kali: In the Margins, At the Center, In the West.* Berkeley: University of California Press.

———. 2001. *Singing to the Goddess: Poems to Kali and Uma from Bengal.* New York: Oxford University Press.

McGilvray, Dennis B. 1998. *Symbolic Heat: Gender, Health and Worship Among the Tamils of South India and Sri Lanka.* Middletown, NJ: Grantha Corporation.

Menon, Usha. 1991. Mahadevi as Mother: The Oriya Hindu Vision of Reality. In *Seeking Mahadevi: Constructing the Identities of the Hindu Great Goddess,* ed. Tracy Pintchman, 37–54. Albany: State University of New York Press.

Michaels, Axel. 2004. *Hinduism: Past and Present.* Princeton, NJ: Princeton University Press.

Mines, Diane. 2005. *Fierce Gods: Inequality, Ritual and the Politics of Dignity in a South Indian Village.* Bloomington: Indiana University Press.

Naidu, Subramanyam. 1993. *The Sacred Complex of Tirumala Tirupati: The Structure and Change.* Chennai: Institute of South Indian Studies.

Napier, David. 1986. *Masks, Transformation and Paradox.* Berkeley: University of California Press.

Narayan, Kirin. 1997. *Mondays on the Dark Night of the Moon: Himalayan Foothill Folktales.* New York: Oxford University Press.

Narayana Rao, Velcheru. 1989. Tricking the Goddess: Cowherd Katamaraju and Goddess Ganga in the Telugu Folk Epic. In *Criminal Gods and Demon Devotees: Essays on the Guardians of Popular Hinduism,* ed. Alf Hiltebeitel, 105–121. Albany: State University of New York Press.

———. 1986. Epics and Ideologies: Six Telugu Folk Epics. In *Another Harmony: New Essays on the Folklore of India,* 131–164. Berkeley: University of California Press.

Narayana Rao, Velcheru, and David Shulman. 2005a. *God on the Hill: Temple Poems from Tirupati.* New Delhi: Oxford University Press.

———. 2005b. A Family that Sang for the God: Annamayya at Tirupati. In *Incompatible Visions: South Asian Religions in History and Culture. Essays in Honor of David M. Knipe,* ed. James Blumenthal, 21–34. Madison: Center for South Asia, University of Wisconsin–Madison.

Narayanan, Vasudha. Unpublished manuscript. A Hundred Autumns to Live: An Introduction to the Hindu Traditions.

Nuckolls, Charles. 1993. *Siblings in South Asia: Brothers and Sisters in Cultural Context.* New York: Guilford Press.

Obeyesekere, Gananath. 1981. *Medusa's Hair: An Essay on Personal Symbols and Religious Experience.* Chicago: University of Chicago Press.

Okely, Judith. 1991. Defiant Moments: Gender, Resistance and Individuals. *Man* 26 (1): 3–22.

Olivelle, Patrick. 1998. Hair and Society: Social Significance of Hair in South Asian Traditions. In *Hair: Its Power and Meaning in Asian Cultures,* ed. Alf Hiltebeitel and Barbara D. Miller, 11–49. Albany: State University of New York Press.

Patton, Laurie, ed. and transl. 2008. *The Bhagavad Gita.* New York: Penguin Classics.

———. 2007. Cat in the Courtyard: The Performance of Sanskrit and the Religious Experience of Women. In *Women's Lives, Women's Rituals in the Hindu Tradition,* ed. Tracy Pintchman, 19–35. New York: Oxford University Press.

———. 1996. *Myth as Argument: The Brhaddevata as Canonical Commentary.* New York: Walter de Gruyter.

Pearson, Anne MacKenzie. 1996. *"Because it Gives Me Peace of Mind": Ritual Fasts in The Religious Lives of Hindu Women.* Albany: State University of New York Press.

Pinney, Christopher. 2008. *The Coming of Photography in India.* London: British Library.

Pintchman, Tracy, ed. 2001. *Seeking Mahadevi: Constructing the Identities of the Hindu Great Goddess.* Albany: State University of New York Press.

Raheja, Gloria Goodwin, and Ann Grodzins Gold. 1994. *Listen to the Heron's Words: Reimagining Gender and Kinship in North India.* Berkeley: University of California Press.

Ramachandran, C. N., and Padma Sharma, transl. 2007. *Strings and Cymbals: Selections from Kannada Oral Epics.* Hospet, Karnataka: Kannada University-Hampi.

Ramanujan, A. K. 1999. Two Realms of Kannada Folklore. In *The Collected Essays of A. K. Ramnujan,* ed. Vinay Dharwadker, 485–512. New Delhi: Oxford University Press.

———. 1993. On Folk Mythologies and Folk Puranas. In *Purana Perennis: Reciprocity and Transformation in Hindu and Jaina Texts,* ed. Wendy Doniger, 101–120. Albany: State University of New York Press.

———. 1981. *Hymns for the Drowning: Poems for Visnu by Nammalvar.* Princeton, NJ: Princeton University Press.

Ramberg, Lucinda. 2009. Magical Hair as Dirt: Ecstatic Bodies and Postcolonial Reform in South India. *Cultural and Medical Psychiatry* 33: 501–522.

Reddy, Gayatri. 2005. *With Respect to Sex: Negotiating Hijra Identity in South India.* Chicago: University of Chicago Press.

Reddy, Peta Srinivasulu. 2007. *Tirupati Ganga Jatara* (English). Tirupati: Published by author.

———. 1995. *Tirupati Ganga Jatara* (Telugu). Tirupati: Published by author.

Reynolds, Holly Baker. 1991 [1980]. The Auspicious Married Woman. In *Powers of Tamil Women,* ed. Susan S. Wadley, 35–60. Syracuse: Maxwell School of Citizenship and Public Affairs, Syracuse University.

Sax, William S. 1991. *Mountain Goddess: Gender and Politics in a Himalayan Pilgrimage.* New York: Oxford University Press.

Shulman, David. 1993. *The Hungry God: Hindu Tales of Filicide and Devotion.* Chicago: University of Chicago Press.

———.1980. *Tamil Temple Myths: Sacrifice and Divine Marriage in the South Indian Saiva Tradition.* Princeton, NJ: Princeton University Press.

Soneji, Davesh. 2012. *Unfinished Gestures: Devadasis, Memory, and Modernity in South India.* Chicago: University of Chicago Press.

———. 2004. Living History, Performing Memory: *Devadasi* Women in Telugu-Speaking South India. *Dance Research Journal,* 36 (2): 30–63.

Sree Padma. 2001. From Village to City: Transforming Goddesses in Urban Andhra Pradesh. In *Seeking Mahadevi: Constructing the Identities of the Hindu Great Goddesses,* ed. Tracy Pintchman, 115–144. Albany: State University of New York Press.

Subba Reddy, N. 1992. The Village Deities and Cosmic Forces: Differential Conception of the Supernatural in Changing Environments. In *Contemporary Indian Society: Essays in Honour of Professor Sachchidananda,* ed. Vijay S. Upadhyay, 81–97. Delhi: Anmol Publications.

Tseelon, Efrat. 2001. Introduction: Masquerade and Identities. In *Masquerade and Identities: Essays on Gender, Sexuality and Marginality,* ed. Efrat Tseelson, 1–17. New York: Routledge.

Turner, Victor. 1974. *Dramas, Fields, and Metaphors: Symbolic Action in Human Society.* Ithaca, NY: Cornell University Press.

Venkatesvara Ravu, Katuri. Circa 1962. *Paulastya Hrdayamu Gudigantalu.* Machilipatnam: Triveni Publishers.

Vijaisri, Priyadarshini. 2010. In Pursuit of the Virgin Whore: Writing Caste/Outcaste Histories. *Economic & Political Weekly* 35 (4): 63–72.

———. 2005a. Contending Identities: Sacred Prostitution and Reform in Colonial South India. *South Asia: Journal of South Asian Studies* 28 (3): 387–411.

———. 2005b. In Search of the Outcaste Sacred Prostitute in Colonial India. *Women's History Magazine* 51: 4–13.

Wadley, Susan. 1980. Sitala: The Cool One. *Asian Folklore Studies* 39: 33–62.

Wadley, Susan, ed. 1991 [1980]. *The Powers of Tamil Women.* Syracuse: Maxwell School of Citizenship and Public Affairs, Syracuse University.

Waghorne, Joanne Punzo. 2004. *Diaspora of the Gods: Modern Hindu Temples in an Urban Middle-Class World.* New York: Oxford University Press.

Weiss, Allen S. 1989. *The Aesthetics of Excess.* Albany: State University of New York Press.

Whitehead, Henry. 1988 [1921]. *The Village Gods of South India.* New Delhi: Asian Educational Services.

Index

Page references in italics indicate illustrations.

abhishekam (ritual anointing of deity's image), 14, 57, 171–172, 196, 197, 273, 285n3
Abhivanagupta, 28
acarya (spiritual leader or guide), 194, 273
Achari caste (artisan caste), 15, 245, 273
adiparashakti (first, supreme power), 273. *See also* Palegadu and Adi Para Shakti, narratives of
aesthetics of excess, 27–53; definition of, 28, 284n3; in female domestic rituals, 48, 50–52, *51;* of *jataras,* 28–29, 52–53; by Kaikala *veshams,* 33–35, *36,* 37–44, *38, 40;* via multiplicity, 32–33, 52–53; overview of, 21, 27; by *stri veshams,* 48, *49;* in temple courtyard rituals, 44–46, *47,* 284n8; totality of a *jatara,* 27; *ugram,* spatial/temporal frames creating, 31–32; *ugram* created/satisfied via excess, 29–31, 52; variety in *jataras,* 27, 52–53
agama (texts on religious rites), 194–195, 273
ahankaram (pride), 126, 129, 130, 273
akarshana (attraction), 104, 273
alankara (ornament; decoration), 113, 165, 196, 273; auspiciousness via, 59; of the goddess, 168–169, 171, 193; of Venkateshvara, 14; by women vs. men, 93, 193
Ambala Gunta Gangamma, 247, 295n7
ambali (dish made from yogurt, onions, and millet), 50, *51,* 273
Amma (mother; females), 82, 287n13
amma (mother; suffix to female name), 273
ammavaru (goddess; poxes and rashes), 273. *See also* Gangamma
Anand, A., 111
anandam (*ananda;* joy; delight; bliss), 91, 119, 136, 273
Andhra Pradesh Animals and Birds Sacrifices Act (1950), 201
angapradakshina (circumambulation by rolling), 201, 244, 253–254, 273
animal sacrifice. See *bali*
Ankalamma, 6, 79, 134, 153, 236, 239, 289n1
Annamacarya, 166–168, 170, 282n10, 289n2
Annamacarya Project, 114, 116, 289n2 (chap5)
Annapurna, *120;* Adi Para Shakti story performed by, 91–93, 123, 127–129, 134, 135; commentary by, 122–123, 136; cosmology described by, 126; Descent of Ganga story performed by, 123–127, 129–132, 134–136; life story and family of, 115–119, 121; linguistic choices of, 126–127; as a *purana pandita,* 113, 114–115, 118, 266–267, 289n2 (chap5); recitation style of, 122–124; relationship with Gangamma, 136; religiosity and *vairagya* status of, 119, 121; repertoire as commentary, 135–136; saris gifted by, 136; as serving the goddess through storytelling, 114–121, *120;* shawls worn by, 113, 121, 288n1 (chap5); training of, 121, 126; *ugra mukhi* pieces gifted by, 136; Yogamaya Devi story told by, 123, 132–135
archana (temple ritual; *puja* offering), 180–181, 273
Ardhanarishvara, 281n1
Arjuna, 41
Asadi (subcaste of ritual specialists), 273
Asadi narrative, 76, 143–149, 290n6, 290nn10–11
Austin, J. L., 69
avataras (incarnations), 55, 132, 133, 273, 285n2
Avilala. *See* Reddys of Avilala

bairagi (mendicant), 35, 273
bali (animal sacrifice), 46, 90–93, 95–96, 142, 201–202, 273, 290nn4–5. *See also under* Reddys of Avilala
Balija (trader caste), 15, 81, 83, 84, 98, 149, 164, 273
bandas (ruffians), 45–46, 273
Bastin, Rohan, 284n3
Behar, Ruth, 264
Bhagavad Gita, 41
Bhagavati, 60
Bhagiratha, 124–125, 129–130, 135, 289n10
bhakta (devotee), 245–246, 274
bhakti (devotion), 251, 258, 262, 274. *See also* consuming relationship with Gangamma
Bharata: Natyashastra, 28–29, 276
bharincu (to bear), 89, 100, 125, 126, 235, 274
bhayankar (fearful; dreadful), 128, 172, 237, 274
bhogam (pleasure), 127, 274
Bibi Nanchari, 16
Bonalu festival, 12–13, 284nn14–15
bottu (auspicious forehead marking), 274; on Gangamma, 38; large vs. small, on women, 71–72; as marriage pendant, 122, 294n8; as the third eye, 88, 243–244; on the widow Pujaramma, 72, 215, 232, 241
Brahma: and Adi Para Shakti, 127; brought back to life, 109; changed into a woman, 5, 87, 91; creation of, 75, 86, 88, 93–94, 105, 106; and Ganga, 124–125, 130
Brahman caste: curse on/origins of, 167, 291n6; women's possession by Gangamma, 225–226, 294n13; women's public performance, 119, 289n5 (*see also* Annapurna)
Brahman male priests' role in the Tatayyagunta temple, 181, 199, 202–203, 262
brahmincide, 107–108
brahminization of temples, ix, 6, 271
brahmotsavam (seven-day temple festival), 161, 163, 274
Briggs, Charles, 4
buddhi (intelligence; disposition), 103, 130, 131, 274
buffalo sacrifice. See *bali*
Butler, Judith, 74, 285n8
butulu (obscenities), 45–46, 274

Cakali (washermen caste), 140–141, 274
Cakali *veshams,* 35
cakrabandhanam (binding circle; ritual marking of boundaries), 32, 274
Camundeshwari/Caudesvari, 236, 291n6
cancal (moving; quick; active; unstable; fickle), 126–127, 274
Candika, 134, 289n11
caritra (account; long story; biography), 79, 113, 274
castes, 294n7; left-hand, 5–6, 14–16, 42, 57, 75–76, 271–272, 281nn2–3; right-hand, 15, 85, 270, 281n2. *See also specific castes*
catimpu (announcement made by drumming), 156, 274
Chennai, 182
Chetti caste, 168
Chetti *veshams,* 35, *36*
Chhattisgarhi, 283n2
chickenpox, 7
Chittoor District, 212
Cidambaram, 291n3
Cinna Gangamma, 8–10, 149, 166, 282nn9–10
Cinnanna, 167
CKR (Chennapatnam Krishnaswamy Ratnavelu), 187–197, 292nn7–8 (chap7)
consuming relationship with Gangamma, 242–264, 295n8; MR's bearing of the goddess, 252–256, *255;* MR's life story, 245–247, 295n6; MR loses a baby son, 252; MR loses a daughter to the goddess, 256–262; MR on costs/benefits of bearing the goddess through devotion, 262–264; MR's personal, devotional relationship with the goddess, 245–251; overview of, 23, 242–245; songs for Gangamma, 247–250, 259–261; thousand-name litany, 249–250
contextualization cues, 4
Courtright, Paul, 283n13

darshan (sight; taking sight of a deity), 14, 205, 274
desires, 85–86, 89, 90, 98, 111–112
devadasis (female temple dancers/musicians), 163, 291n4, 294n9. See also *tali* exchange with Gangamma
Devaki, 132–133
devasthanam (temple trust board), 274. *See also* Tattaiahgunta (Tataiahgunta) Devasthanam
Dhairya Lakshmi, 289n8
dhairyam (courage), 122, 274
Dhanalakshmi, 150–151, 153, 154, 155–156
dharma (code of conduct; social order), 274
dharmakarta (trustee; temple manager), 187–188, 274, 292n6
dishti (evil eye), 100, 161, 163, 274

Mutyalamma, 289n1
myth as argument, 77

nadi vidhi (middle-of-street), 140, 276
naga dosham (snake blemish), 201, 276
namaskaram (salutation), 45, 246–247, 276
Nammalvar, 295n4
Nanda, 132–133
Nandadevi, 93–94
Nandavarikas, 291n6
naraka (hell), 125, 276
Narayana Rao, V., x, xii–xiii, 18; on Annamacarya, 167; on the Brahmans, 291n6; on sacrificial and martial epics, 15, 84–85; on sari styles associated with castes, 281n3; on Sri Venkateshvara, 13–14
Narayanan, Vasudha, 218
narrative vs. ritual knowledge of deities, 266–268, 295n1
Natyashastra (Bharata), 28–29, 276
Navaratri (festival of Nine Nights of the Goddess), 183, 204–205, 206, 251, 276
Nawab (*navab;* local Muslim ruler; ruler), 78–79, 81, 149, 276, 286n3, 290n6
neem (margosa tree), 14, 29, 45, 184, 208–209, 238, 276, 294n14
nijapada darshan, 14
nityasumangali (ever-auspicious woman), 211–212, 276, 291n4
Nuckolls, Charles, 281n4

Obeyesekere, Gananath, 73
Olivelle, Patrick, 286n13
oral epics, 283n1
ori (informal vocative for males), 91–92, 276

Padmavati, 16, 116, 283n18
palegadu (local chieftain), 276
Palegadu and Adi Para Shakti, narratives of, 75–96; Adi Para Shakti narrative, 30, 85–93, 267–270 (*see also under* Shiva); Adi Para Shakti's third eye/eye of fire and trident, 88–91, 94–96, 106–108, *110,* 244 (*see also under* Shiva); Annapurna variants of Adi Para Shakti, 91–93, 123, 127–129, 134, 135; Avilala variants of Palegadu, 79–81, 84; Balija female-narrated variant of Palegadu, 81–83, 84; beheading of Palegadu, 33, 34, 38–39, 76, 81, 95 (*see also* Dora *vesham*); female *ugram* as protective resource in, 77–85; Gangamma as daughter vs. daughter-in-law in, 80, 287n11; Gangamma's drying her hair, 84; Gangamma's location after the beheading, 81; Gangamma saving a calf from a well, 99–100; gendered hierarchy reversed in, 84; marriage/sexual aggression/*bali* in, 83–84, 90–93, 95–96, 100–101, 213, 270; narrative genres of, 77; non-Telugu variants of Adi Para Shakti, 93–96; overview of, 3, 22, 33, 75–77; Palegadu's aggression, 15–16, 30, 76, 81, 83–84; Pambala variants of Adi Para Shakti, 86–91; performances of, 77, 86; Rajasthani variant of Adi Para Shakti, 288n16; Rajeshvaramma's variant of Palegadu, 98–100, *102,* 106–109, 111–112; sacrificial epic vs. Palegadu narrative, 84–85; vs. *stri vesham* tradition, gender in, 270–271; structural movements of, 95–96; Subbarama Reddy variant of Palegadu, 78–79, 286nn2–7, 287nn8–9; Sumati's variant of Adi Para Shakti, 105–112, *110;* Sumati's variant of Palegadu, 98, 101–105; *ugra* of the goddess after Palegadu's beheading, 81, 85; *ugram* as *kopam* in, 104; *ugram* as *korika* in, 86, 95–96, 267–268; *ugram* as *shakti* in, 85–93, 95–96, 104, 268–270
Pambalas (professional, scheduled-caste Mala drummers/storytellers), 276; Adi Para Shakti story by, 86–91; as a Backward Caste, 287n15; *jatara mirasi* held by, 287n15
panchayat (village council), 149, 156, 276
panduga (festival), 277, 283n2
pan-Indian religious traditions, 28, 283n2, 287n9. *See also* Ganga/Ganga Devi
Parvati, 95, 283n18
pasupu (turmeric), 50–51, 171–172, 254–255, 277, 285n4. See also under *stri vesham* tradition
pasupu-kumkum (turmeric-vermillion; ritual gift): by Brahma, Vishnu, and Maheshvara, 128; to Gangamma, 128, 130, 131, 140; during *jataras,* 34–35, 45, 98, 140, 155; and the Kaikalas' *mirasi,* 168; to male as goddess, 176; on married women, 59; Potu Raju's gendered ambiguity shown via, 11–12, 271; to Pujaramma, 215, 232, 238; by Sanyasamma, 15; suspension/reinstatement of, 151
Patton, Laurie, 77, 292n5
Pedda Gangamma, 8–9, 13, 149, 166–167, 170, 282nn9–10, 289n1

JOYCE BURKHALTER FLUECKIGER

is Professor of Religion at Emory University. She is author of *In Amma's Healing Room: Gender and Vernacular Islam in Southh India* (IUP, 2009) and *Gender and Genre in the Folklore of Middle India.*

CPSIA information can be obtained
at www.ICGtesting.com
Printed in the USA
JSHW040258150721
16909JS00002B/79

9 780253 009562